The *Cambridge Companion to German Idealism* offers a comprehensive, penetrating, and informative guide to what is regarded as the classical period of German philosophy. Kant, Fichte, Hegel, and Schelling are all discussed in detail, together with a number of their contemporaries, such as Hölderlin and Schleiermacher, whose influence was considerable but whose work is less well known in the English-speaking world. The essays in the volume trace and explore the unifying themes of German Idealism, and discuss its relationship to romanticism, the Enlightenment, and the culture of seventeenth- and eighteenth-century Europe. The result is an illuminating overview of a rich and complex philosophical movement, and will appeal to a wide range of readers in philosophy, German studies, theology, literature, and the history of ideas.

THE CAMBRIDGE
COMPANION TO

GERMAN IDEALISM

OTHER VOLUMES IN THE SERIES OF
CAMBRIDGE COMPANIONS

THE CAMBRIDGE
COMPANION TO
GERMAN IDEALISM

EDITED BY
KARL AMERIKS
University of Notre Dame

CAMBRIDGE
UNIVERSITY PRESS

PUBLISHED BY THE PRESS SYNDICATE OF THE UNIVERSITY OF CAMBRIDGE
The Pitt Building, Trumpington Street, Cambridge, United Kingdom

CAMBRIDGE UNIVERSITY PRESS
The Edinburgh Building, Cambridge CB2 2RU, UK   www.cup.cam.ac.uk
40 West 20th Street, New York, NY 10011–4211, USA   www.cup.org
10 Stamford Road, Oakleigh, Melbourne 3166, Australia
Ruiz de Alarcón 13, 28014 Madrid, Spain

© Cambridge University Press 2000

First published 2000

Printed in the United Kingdom at the University Press, Cambridge

Typeface Monotype Sabon 10/13 pt.   *System* QuarkXPress™ [SE]

A catalogue record for this book is available from the British Library

Library of Congress Cataloguing in Publication data
The Cambridge companion to German idealism / edited by Karl Ameriks.
p.   cm.
Includes bibliographical references (p.) and index.
ISBN 0 521 65178 6 – ISBN 0 521 65695 8 (pbk.)
1. Idealism, German.   2. Philosophy, German – 18th century.   3. Philosophy,
German – 19th century.   I. Ameriks, Karl, 1947–
B2745.C36   2000
193–dc21   00–020469

ISBN 0 521 65178 6 hardback
ISBN 0 521 65695 8 paperback

CONTENTS

CONTRIBUTORS

KARL AMERIKS is McMahon-Hank Professor of Philosophy at the University
of Notre Dame. He is co-editor of the series Cambridge Texts in the History
of Philosophy. He has written *Kant's Theory of Mind* (2nd edn., 2000) and
*Kant and the Fate of Autonomy: Problems in the Appropriation of the
Critical Philosophy* (2000). He has co-edited *The Modern Subject:
Conceptions of the Self in Classical German Philosophy* (1995), and co-
translated *Immanuel Kant/Lectures on Metaphysics* (1997) and Edmund
Husserl, *Experience and Judgment* (1973).

FREDERICK BEISER is Professor of Philosophy at Indiana University. He has
written *The Fate of Reason: German Philosophy from Kant to Fichte* (1987),
*Enlightenment, Revolution, and Romanticism: The Genesis of Modern
German Political Thought 1790–1800* (1992) and *The Sovereignty of Reason:
The Defense of Rationality in the Early English Enlightenment* (1996). He has
edited *The Cambridge Companion to Hegel* (1993), and *The Early Political
Writings of the German Romantics* (1996).

ANDREW BOWIE is Chair of German at Royal Holloway College, University of
London. He has written *Aesthetics and Subjectivity from Kant to Nietzsche*
(2nd edn., 2000), *Schelling and Modern European Philosophy: An
Introduction* (1993), and *From Romanticism to Critical Theory: the
Philosophy of German Literary Theory* (1997). He has edited Manfred Frank,
The Subject and the Text: Essays on Literary Theory and Philosophy (1997),
and edited and translated Schelling, *On the History of Modern Philosophy*
(1994), and Schleiermacher, *Hermeneutics and Criticism and Other Writings*
(1998).

DANIEL O. DAHLSTROM is Professor of Philosophy at Boston University.
He has co-edited *The Emergence of German Idealism* (1999). He has co-
edited and translated *Schiller: Essays* (1993) and edited and translated

Mendelssohn: Philosophical Writings (1997). He has written *Das logische Vorurteil: Untersuchungen zur Wahrheitstheorie des frühen Heidegger* (1994) as well as numerous articles on aesthetics and topics in classical and contemporary German philosophy.

PAUL FRANKS is Assistant Professor of Philosophy at Indiana University. He is a contributor to *The Cambridge Companion to Fichte* (forthcoming). He has written several articles on Kant, Fichte, Hegel, transcendental arguments, and skepticism. He is completing a book on the transcendental methods of Kant and some post-Kantians. With Michael L. Morgan, he edited and translated *Franz Rosenzweig: Theological and Philosophical Writings* (2000).

PAUL GUYER is Florence R. C. Murray Professor in the Humanities at the University of Pennsylvania. His books include *Kant and the Claims of Taste* (2nd edn., 1997), *Kant and the Claims of Knowledge* (1987), *Kant and the Experience of Freedom* (1993), and *Kant on Freedom, Law, and Happiness* (2000). He has edited *The Cambridge Companion to Kant* (1992) and other anthologies. He is general co-editor of the Cambridge Edition of the works of Immanuel Kant, in which he has co-translated the *Critique of Pure Reason* (1998) with Allen Wood. He has also co-translated (with Eric Matthews) Kant's *Critique of the Power of Judgment* (2000).

ROLF-PETER HORSTMANN is Professor of Philosophy at the Humboldt University in Berlin. He is author of *Ontologie und Relationen: Hegel, Bradley, Russell und die Kontroverse über interne und externe Beziehungen* (1984), *Die Grenzen der Vernunft: eine Untersuchung zu Zielen und Motiven des Deutschen Idealismus* (3rd edn., 2000), and *Bausteine Kritischer Philosophie* (1997). He has co-edited Hegel, *Jenaer Systementwürfe*. He has also co-edited collections of works on Kant, transcendental arguments, Rousseau, aesthetics, Hegel, and German Idealism. He is currently serving as editor for a new translation of Nietzsche's *Beyond Good and Evil*.

CHARLES LARMORE is Professor of Philosophy in the Department of Philosophy at the University of Chicago. He has written *Patterns of Moral Complexity* (1987), *Modernité et morale* (1993), *The Morals of Modernity* (1996), and *The Romantic Legacy* (1996).

TERRY PINKARD is Professor of Philosophy at Georgetown University. He has written *Democratic Liberalism and Social Union* (1987), *Hegel's Dialectic: The Explanation of Possibility* (1988), *Hegel's Phenomenology: The Sociality of Reason* (1994), and *Hegel: A Biography* (2000).

ROBERT P. PIPPIN is Raymond W. and Martha Hilpert Gruner Distinguished Service Professor of Philosophy and Chair of the Committee on Social Thought at the University of Chicago. He is editor of the Cambridge series Modern European Philosophy. His books include *Kant's Theory of Form* (1982), *Hegel's Idealism: The Satisfactions of Self-Consciousness* (1989), *Modernity as a Philosophical Problem* (2nd edn., 1999), *Idealism as Modernism: Hegelian Variations* (1997), and *Henry James and Modern Moral Life* (2000).

DIETER STURMA is Professor of Philosophy at Essen University. He is the author of *Kant über Selbstbewusstsein: zum Zusammenhang von Erkenntniskritik und Theorie des Selbstbewusstseins* (1985), *Philosophie der Person: die Selbstverhältnisse von Subjektivität und Moralität* (1997), and *Rousseau* (2000). He has co-edited *The Modern Subject: Conceptions of the Self in Classical German Philosophy* (1995). He has written numerous essays on German Idealism and also on topics in contemporary systematic philosophy.

ALLEN WOOD is Professor of Philosophy at Stanford University. His books include *Kant's Moral Religion* (1970), *Kant's Rational Theology* (1978), *Karl Marx* (1981), *Hegel's Ethical Thought* (1990), and *Kant's Ethical Thought* (1999). He is general co-editor of the Cambridge Edition of the works of Immanuel Kant, in which he has co-translated the *Critique of Pure Reason* (1998) with Paul Guyer. He has also edited and translated other works by Kant on ethics, anthropology, philosophy of religion, and philosophy of history.

GÜNTER ZÖLLER is Professor of Philosophy at the University of Munich. He is the author of *Theoretische Gegenstandsbeziehung bei Kant* (1984) and *Fichte's Transcendental Philosophy* (1998) and has edited or co-edited *Minds, Ideas, and Objects: Essays on the Theory of Representation in Modern Philosophy* (1993), *Figuring the Self: Subject, Individual, and Others in Classical German Philosophy* (1997), and Arthur Schopenhauer, *Prize Essay On the Freedom of the Will* (1999). Currently he is editing *The Cambridge Companion to Fichte*, the volume of Kant's writings on anthropology, history, and education in the Cambridge Edition of the works of Immanuel Kant, and Fichte's *System of Ethics*. He is a general editor of the Bavarian Academy Edition of Fichte's Complete Works.

CHRONOLOGY OF GERMAN IDEALISM

Titles of main works are given in English only where a translation has been generally available

1724–1804 Immanuel Kant, *Critique of Pure Reason*, 1781
1729–1781 Gotthold Ephraim Lessing, *Nathan the Wise*, 1779
1729–1786 Moses Mendelssohn, *Jerusalem*, 1783
1730–1788 Johann Georg Hamann, *Aesthetica in nuce*, 1762
1733–1813 Christoph Martin Wieland, *Teutscher Merkur* (ed.), 1773f.
1741–1801 Johann Caspar Lavater, *Physiognomie*, 1775–8
1743–1819 Friedrich Heinrich Jacobi, *On the Doctrine of Spinoza*, 1785
1744–1803 Johann Gottfried von Herder, *On the Origin of Language*, 1772
1749–1832 Johann Wolfgang von Goethe, *Wilhelm Meister's Apprenticeship*, 1795–6
1753–1800 Salomon Maimon, *Versuch über die Transzendentalphilosophie*, 1790
1757–1823 Karl Leonhard Reinhold, *Briefe über die Kantische Philosophie*, 1786–7
1759–1805 Friedrich von Schiller, *On the Aesthetic Education of Humanity*, 1795–8
1762–1814 Johann Gottlieb Fichte, *Science of Knowledge (Wissenschaftslehre)*, 1794
1763–1809 Caroline Schlegel(-Schelling), *Briefe der Frühromantik* (edn., 1871)
1763–1825 Jean Paul Richter, *Vorschule der Ästhetik*, 1804
1764–1839 Dorothea Veit(-Schlegel), nee Mendelssohn, *Florentin*, 1801
1767–1845 August Wilhelm von Schlegel, *On Dramatic Art and Literature*, 1808
1767–1835 Wilhelm von Humboldt, *On Language*, 1820
1768–1834 Friedrich Schleiermacher, *On Religion*, 1799
1769–1859 Alexander von Humboldt, *Kosmos*, 1845
1770–1831 Georg Wilhelm Friedrich Hegel, *Phenomenology of Spirit*, 1807

1770–1843   Friedrich Hölderlin, *Hyperion*, 1797–9
1772–1801   Friedrich von Hardenberg (Novalis), *Christianity or Europe*, 1799
1772–1829   Friedrich von Schlegel, *Athenaeum* (ed.), 1798–1800
1773–1853   Ludwig Tieck, *Phantasus*, 1812
1773–1798   Wilhelm Heinrich Wackenroder, *Confessions*, 1797
1775–1854   Friedrich Wilhelm Joseph von Schelling, *System of Transcendental Idealism*, 1800
1776–1822   Ernst Theodor Amadeus Hoffman, *Undine*, 1816
1776–1848   Johann Joseph von Görres, *Rheinischer Merkur* (ed.), 1814–16
1777–1811   Heinrich von Kleist, *The Prince of Homburg*, 1821
1779–1829   Adam Müller, *Elemente der Staatskunst*, 1808–9
1788–1860   Arthur Schopenhauer, *The World as Will and Representation*, 1819
1804–1872   Ludwig Andreas Feuerbach, *The Essence of Christianity*, 1841
1808–1874   David Friedrich Strauss, *The Life of Jesus*, 1835–6
1813–1855   Søren Aabye Kierkegaard, *Fear and Trembling*, 1843
1818–1883   Karl Marx, *German Ideology*, 1845–6
1820–1895   Friedrich Engels, *German Ideology*, 1845–6

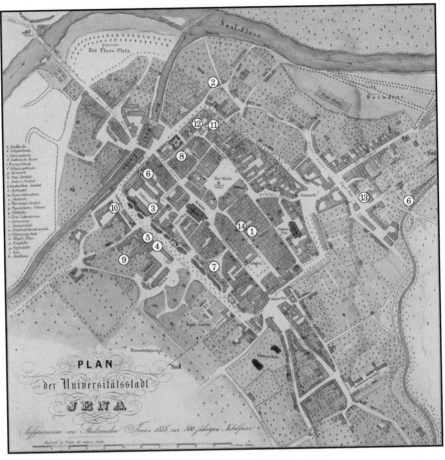

Plan of Jena, 1858, reproduced by permission of the Städtische Museen Jena.
Guide to the Jena residences of philosophers and other notable figures in the early 1800s

1. August Wilhelm Schlegel, professor of literature, Friedrich Schlegel, writer, Caroline (Bohmer) Schlegel, wife of August Wilhelm Schlegel, later, partner of Schelling [probably at the back court of the corner of Leutrastrasse and Brüdergasse]
2. Ludwig Tieck, writer [Fischergasse]
3. Johann Wolfgang Goethe, poet and government official [city palace; he also had a garden house in the botanical garden]
4. C. F. E. Frommann, publisher [Fürstengraben 18]
5. F. W. J. Schelling, philosopher [Fürstengraben 16]
6. Friedrich Schiller, poet [apartment in the Griesbach House, Schlossgasse 17, later a garden house on the Leutra, Schillergässchen 2]
7. Sophie Moreau, writer, feminist [behind the church, Jenergasse]
8. Friedrich Hölderlin, poet [probably Unterlauengasse 17]
9. J. W. Ritter, scientist [Fürstengraben 18; Zwätzengasse 9]
10. Henrik Steffens, scientist [Lutherplatz 2, the Schwarzer Bär]
11. J. G. Fichte, philosopher [Romantikerhaus]
12. G. W. F. Hegel, philosopher [Unterlauengasse 15, next to the Romantikerhaus]
13. C. G. Schuetz, editor of the *Allgemeine Literatur Zeitung* [Engelplatz]
14. G. Hufeland, judge, legal theorist [Leutragraben]

KARL AMERIKS

Introduction: interpreting German Idealism

I The idealist achievement

The period of German Idealism constitutes a cultural phenomenon whose stature and influence has been frequently compared to nothing less than the golden age of Athens. For this reason the era from the 1770s into the 1840s that we tend to call "the age of German Idealism" is often designated in Germany simply as the period of "classical German philosophy." This designation is meant to indicate a level of preeminent achievement rather than to characterize a specific style or content. It thus bypasses issues such as how philosophers of this era match up with the division in German literature between classicism and romanticism, and how strong a distinction is to be made between the "Critical" or "transcendental" idealism of Kant and the so-called "absolute" idealism that culminated in the work of the three most famous philosophers who came after him: Fichte, Schelling, and Hegel.[1]

Standard works on German Idealism, especially in English, still tend to focus on (at most) these four best-known philosophers and one or two of their main works. As a consequence, the philosophical complexity of the era as a whole is seriously misrepresented. Studies that compensate for this approach by attempting to indicate the full richness of the period are apt to get lost in historical detail and fail to set key philosophical distinctions in sharp relief. An additional problem arises from one of the most valuable features of German Idealism – the unique degree to which its works transcend standard boundaries between academic disciplines. The texts of German Idealism continue to be an enormous influence on other fields such as religious studies, literary theory, politics, art, and the general methodology of the humanities. Philosophy often generates applications of itself in other areas, but with German Idealism an extraordinarily close relation to other domains was built in from the start. The idealists were not only responding directly to major cultural upheavals such as the Enlightenment, the French Revolution, and the rise of romanticism; they were also determining the reception of these epochal events. In recognition of the

I

complexity of this period, this volume will cover a broader range of writers than readers might expect, although the focus will remain on the main *philosophical* arguments and themes that concern the era *as a whole*.

Two pairs of cities played a special role in the diffusion of idealism: Königsberg and Berlin, and Weimar and Jena. In these cultural capitals, the lectures of idealist philosophers were objects of pilgrimage for leading writers, scientists, and politicians. Although Kant remained in his remote hometown and let others come to him, his many contacts with other leaders of the Enlightenment kept him in close touch with developments in other cities, especially Berlin and its new Academy. He had no trouble in drawing an audience even before the publication of the first – and by far the most important – major work of the era, his *Critique of Pure Reason* (Riga, 1781). After formative experiences with Kant in Königsberg, Herder and Fichte took up residence near Goethe, who was in charge of the cultural institutions of the Weimar region. As a result of the enormously effective popularization of Kant by Reinhold,[2] who lectured in the nearby university town of Jena, the area had become a breeding ground for scores of apostles of the Critical philosophy.[3] When Reinhold left Jena in 1794, Fichte, Schelling, and Hegel took over in turn. They offered to improve on the "letter" of Kant's work in the name of its "spirit," and developed one system of German Idealism after the other, often within a span of a few months.[4]

In the very same town and era, the literary giants Schiller, Hölderlin, Novalis (Friedrich von Hardenberg), and Friedrich Schlegel worked with the greatest intensity on their own philosophical essays and notebooks. An unprecedented cultural revolution was taking place, fueled by the collaboration of Goethe and Schiller, the birth of German romanticism, and the arrival of a new and – at least for a while – radically non-conformist generation rich with aesthetic and scientific talent. In addition to those already named, its leading figures were Friedrich Heinrich Jacobi, Friedrich Schleiermacher, Ludwig Tieck, Jean Paul Richter, August Wilhelm Schlegel, Dorothea [Veit] Schlegel, Caroline [Böhmer] Schlegel, and Wilhelm and Alexander von Humboldt.[5] It was a relentlessly creative and interactive group and inevitably split into factions. It suffered from the early death of Novalis (1801), the retreat into madness of Hölderlin (1802), and the depression of Schelling after the death of Caroline Schlegel (1809). By the time of Napoleon's victory at Jena in 1806, Hegel, Schleiermacher, Schelling, and others had already dispersed in different directions. Most of the group eventually settled in Berlin to present later versions of their philosophies at the new university there. In the context of the recovery of Prussia, German Idealism in its later years contributed significantly to the rise of nationalism and conservatism within Germany – and also to the worldwide growth of liberalism and the philosophical underpinnings of the revolutionary movements of the 1840s and after.

In the latter half of the nineteenth century, the reputation of the movement suffered a noticeable setback. Schopenhauer and Marx, who were peripheral figures earlier, gained considerable philosophical attention largely because they appeared to be an alternative to the whole mainstream tradition. During this period Dilthey and historical scholars began to edit influential and more accurate editions of the writings of the classical German philosophers, but for the most part this research had a limited effect on regenerating first-rate systematic philosophy. Kant's work alone maintained a fairly constant significance, but usually in precisely those areas where his philosophy was sharply distinguished from that of his idealist successors. The tide began to turn again in the period around the First World War. Intense crises in art, theology, and politics brought about a renewal of interest in figures such as Hegel, Schleiermacher, and Hölderlin. Indicative of this shift is the fact that already in 1915 Heidegger turned from purely logical, scholastic, and phenomenological interests to an explicit concern with history, "spirit," and neo-Hegelianism. Very soon, however, idealism was eclipsed by Heidegger's other shifts, which dominated the continental philosophical scene after he came to prominence in the 1920s. The debacle of fascism and the Second World War left a temporary vacuum in German philosophy. Independent thinkers such as Walter Schulz, Dieter Henrich, Ernst Tugendhat, and Jürgen Habermas eventually managed to combine an appreciation for Heidegger's significance with a fruitful return to the classic themes of German Idealism. In addition, historical work became much more careful, and it has now reached a level of unparalleled detail, with meticulous thousand-page studies of the background of figures who had a direct influence on only brief and never before appreciated subperiods of the movement.[6]

In the last decades of the twentieth century, the outstanding work of a new generation of German philosophers (for example, Gerold Prauss, Ludwig Siep, Manfred Frank, and Otfried Höffe) has coincided with developments in philosophy outside of Germany to create an international influence for German Idealism that appears to have reached a new high point. "Analytic philosophy," which arose as largely a rejection of German Idealism (and its neo-Hegelian British variants), has for the most part given up any thought of being able to impose a substantial form or content that would wholly replace traditional philosophy. Anti-"idealist" movements such as logical positivism and ordinary language philosophy have themselves become historical curiosities. While the extremely clear and careful style of analytic philosophy has gained a universal and irreversible influence, its leading practitioners now often turn, without apology, not only to Kant, but also to Hegel, Fichte, and other idealists. Wilfrid Sellars's reminder that where Kant appears, Hegel cannot be far behind, has been taken up positively by contemporary philosophers as diverse as Charles Taylor, Stanley Cavell, Donald Davidson, Richard Rorty, John McDowell, and Robert

Brandom. At the same time, the study of German Idealism, especially in its interconnections with romanticism, has become central in the work of the most influential international scholars concerned with cultural studies in general – for example, in major books by Isaiah Berlin, Paul de Man, Jacques Derrida, Jean-Luc Nancy, Tzvetan Todorov, and Terry Eagleton.

In 1900, exactly one century after the high noon of German Idealism, it might well have seemed as if the passage of one more century would make the movement look like a much overrated phenomenon. Astonishingly, in the year 2000, the very opposite appears to have happened. The significance of German Idealism is here to stay, and our task is to begin to understand this fact in order to be able to appropriate it authentically for our own time – and not to imagine any longer, as Heidegger or the positivists did, that it can or should be "overcome."

German Idealism deserves the attention it has received. It fills an obvious gap generated by traditional expectations of philosophy and problems caused by the rise of the unquestioned authority of modern science. Unlike most of the philosophy of the later twentieth century, its works always demand that philosophy take on the traditional challenge of articulating a synoptic account of all our most basic interests. It holds that philosophy must be a deeply unified and autonomous enterprise, not a series of ad hoc solutions to abstract technical puzzles, or the mere application of findings taken from other disciplines. The main philosophers of the idealist era each constructed an extraordinarily broad and tightly connected system of their own. And those writers who did not go so far as to offer such a system, in any traditional sense, at least made it a major point of their writing to indicate how and why modern systematic philosophy must be limited.

Modern philosophy was developed in the shadow of the sharp decline of the hegemony of authoritarian thinking in theology, traditional science, and politics. This decline was brought about by the consequences of a series of momentous revolutions: the Reformation, the "new physics," and the political movements culminating in the French Revolution. A natural first response to the decline of the old authorities was an attempt to construct purely philosophical foundations for the new revolutionary perspectives. Descartes and Hobbes have been taken to be prime examples of this approach at the beginning of the modern era. The intensely self-critical tendency of modern philosophy itself soon led, however, to a skeptical perspective that threatened (in the aftermath of Hume) to undermine not only the claims of all the new philosophical systems but also the whole project of a rational justification of any common knowledge.

In the face of this challenge, Kant presented a system that at first seemed to offer an ideal reconciliation of all interests. He took it to be obvious that no modern rational person would want to turn back from either common sense or the fundamental claims expressed most powerfully by Newton and Rousseau. But there seemed to be a deep conflict between these claims. In so far as it had a clear metaphysics, Newton's science of "the heavens above" appeared, on the one hand, to entail a deterministic universe, with no need for the three basic claims of traditional philosophy – the existence of God, freedom, and immortality. On the other hand, Rousseau's reminder of the "law within," the overriding claim of morality upon all persons as free, equal, and practical beings, seemed to require – or so Kant and his older generation assumed – precisely these claims. And not only did these basic perspectives on nature and freedom appear to conflict with one another; they both seemed in tension with elementary common sense, which says nothing about either strictly universal physical laws or strictly universal moral laws, let alone the non-physical grounds that these were alleged to require.

Kant's Critical system attempted to deal with all these problems by arguing that a philosophical analysis of common judgment in theoretical and practical contexts can provide a consistent justification for the essential presuppositions of both of the structures that Newton and Rousseau had articulated. There was a price to the Critical solution: the laws of nature were given a universal and necessary but empirical and "merely phenomenal" significance, while the sphere of freedom was grounded explicitly in a metaphysical and not theoretically knowable domain, one revealed only by "pure practical reason." Knowledge had "made room for faith," albeit a strictly moral faith that did not rest on supernatural evidence or theological arguments.

Apparent weaknesses in Kant's system were heavily attacked from the first, even by its "friends." Reinhold introduced a demand for *premises* that were absolutely certain, *arguments* that were absolutely unified, comprehensive, and rigorously deduced, and *conclusions* that absolutely excluded unknowable transcendent features. The project of an *absolutely* "rigorous science" (*Fundament*) was taken up with a vengeance by Reinhold's successors in Jena. While holding on to the new ideal of a completely certain, thorough, and immanent system, Fichte modified Kant's balanced perspective on nature and freedom, and his sharp distinction of theoretical and practical philosophy. Fichte accepted the view of those who had concluded that modern *theoretical* philosophy led only to skepticism. He based his system entirely on the implications of the (allegedly) absolute certainty of our mere self-consciousness in its commitment to freedom and morality. Kant had argued for a highest "moral world" in a traditional transcendent sense (with happiness proportionate to virtue in some manner independent of space and time) as a domain supposedly required by the rational hopes underlying our commitment to morality. Fichte insisted instead that our moral conscience requires us to see the actual shape of the natural world as *already completely* fitting (in principle) the "revelation" of pure practical reason. He called this the one and only "moral world," and any transcendent domain was dismissed as not only unknowable but also meaningless. His insistence on preaching this doctrine on Sundays in Jena led to the famous "Atheism Controversy" of 1798 in which Goethe eventually chose to allow Fichte to be removed in order to avoid complications. This event had momentous implications; it opened the door for new teachers in Jena, and it taught them to express any radical implications of their idealism in a much more esoteric form.

Fichte's views had a profound impact on the Swabian trio of Schelling, Hegel, and Hölderlin, who all came to Jena after having studied together as seminarians in Tübingen. Schelling was the first to develop a post-Fichtean system, one that offered a more balanced approach to the relation of freedom and nature. In place of a foundation in reflections on morality and self-consciousness alone, Schelling argued that it is only rational to presume that there is a series of basic stages intrinsic to the development of nature, which is an organic whole embracing history and "spirit." (Not surprisingly, Marxists have looked back to Schelling's earliest views as an anticipation of their own critical naturalism and historical materialism.) These stages exhibit a necessary progressive sequence that can be explored independently and still leads to the same *conclusion* that Fichte reached, namely that the natural world is a domain (and the only domain) that provides for the ultimate realization of pure practical reason. Thus it is a moral world, a heaven on earth in the making – provided that human beings take up their capacity to be rational and reorder their society in line with the revolutions of modernity. For a while, this result came to be expressed by Schelling in terms of a "system of identity," for it asserted an underlying identity of nature as implicit rationality and of mind as explicit rationality. The structures that allow for humans to come explicitly to know the rationality of nature as a whole must be structures that are built into nature itself from the start.

Schelling's position was a radicalization of teleological ideas in Kant's later work. Kant supplemented the natural and moral perspectives of his first two *Critique*s with a third *Critique* on the power of judgment. He observed that in both aesthetic judgment and the regulative principles of natural science, especially biology, there is a phenomenon of purposiveness and systematicity that exceeds the minimal conditions that seem needed for human experience to take place. Kant noted that the appreciation of natural beauty in particular provides a "sign" of a deep harmony of nature and freedom, a harmony that he thought his moral argument for God alone rigorously justified. Unlike Fichte, Kant had stressed the apparent purposiveness of nature itself; unlike Schelling, he had stressed that this was a mere sign, not even a partial proof, of objective purposiveness – and, unlike both, Kant had stressed that it was, above all, a sign that freedom and nature had a transcendent ground and not merely an immanent unity.

Hegel took Schelling's philosophy of identity a step further by presenting detailed arguments, with a more intricate dialectical structure, for each of the stages in the development of nature and history, as well as in logic, metaphysics, and self-consciousness in general. In insisting on an "objective" rather than merely moral purposiveness as his starting point, Hegel's system had a problem that was the opposite of Fichte's. Where Fichte started with freedom alone and left the internal structure of nature to appear arbitrary, Hegel started with such a global focus on being, nature, and history that it became unclear how freedom in the sense of individual free choice could retain its full meaning. This problem became a dividing point after Hegel. Those more sympathetic to traditional religion, such as the later Schelling or Kierkegaard, insisted in going back, in a Kantian fashion, to a belief in a "fact" of absolute human freedom. Left wing Hegelians, in contrast, insisted on a thoroughly naturalized notion of freedom. They were no longer afraid of the difficulties of another "Atheism Controversy" but instead gloried in their radicalism. If he had only lived long enough, Kant would no doubt have been shocked by the ultimate consequences of his argument for a moral world – but no doubt he would have understood them too.

Parallel to these mainstream developments in theoretical and practical philosophy, an equally important tradition was developing in other areas opened by Kant. His third *Critique* – combined with the impact of Goethe's and Herder's work – stimulated the growth of aesthetics as an autonomous discipline, and this became one of the glories of the era. It made possible fundamental works on art by philosophers such as Schelling, Hegel, and Schopenhauer, and by philosophic writers who were also great poets, such as Schiller and Hölderlin. More importantly, it raised the whole issue of the relation of philosophy to aesthetic writing. Ultimately, it opened the door to the suspicion raised later by Nietzsche, and developed intensively by a wide range of thinkers at the end of the twentieth century (Heidegger, Derrida, Rorty, and Williams), that the future of philosophy lies more in a dissemination of something like aesthetic insights and values than in a pursuit of the traditional claim to be a rigorous science.

The key philosophical arguments of idealism are all examined in much more detail in the chapters that follow. In the remainder of this Introduction I will attend briefly to two issues that, left unattended, can lead to considerable misunderstanding: (1) the meaning of the notion of idealism itself in the German tradition and (2) the philosophical significance of the phenomenon of romanticism.

II What is the "Idealism" of German Idealism?

For a long time, the term "idealism" has had a largely negative and unattractive connotation for Anglo-American philosophers. This feature, combined with the difficult and speculative style of most German writers in the idealist era, has created a strong barrier to their appreciation in England and America. It is not possible to escape this problem by pointing to a single uncontroversial and appealing core-meaning for idealism throughout the period. Exactly what "idealism" means for Kant, Hegel, Fichte, etc., is precisely one of the main issues that dominates the work of the participants and interpreters of this era.[7] It is possible, however, to set aside some common and very misleading presumptions.

Because of the influence of philosophers such as Berkeley and G. E. Moore, "idealism" has tended in the English tradition to be associated primarily with negative metaphysical or epistemological doctrines: the thesis that matter, or the external world, is not independently real, or at least that it cannot be known, or known with certainty, as real. Given such quite distinct meanings, one would be better off substituting clearer and more specific terms, such as immaterialism and skepticism (or fallibilism). Unfortunately, "idealism" continues to be used for many ambiguous purposes, and the term is generally assumed from the start to have to indicate some kind of anti-realism, as if "ideal" must always mean "not-real." To be sure, the word has often been used precisely that way – and that is the problem. For it has also been used in other ways by very significant thinkers. Originally, for philosophers such as Plato, the "ideal" was precisely the real, the most real. In modern times, at least in many philosophical contexts, matters became reversed. Somehow, just as with the terms "subjective" and "objective," "ideal" has come to mean almost the opposite of what it did before.

In German philosophy, from Leibniz through Kant, Schelling, and Hegel, it is quite clear that the Platonic tradition had a much heavier influence, systematically and terminologically, than the skepticism of the British tradition. Therefore, anyone reading German Idealism should, at the very least, take note that the notion of idealism has carried with it both positive and not merely negative meanings, and that the negative sense dominant in contemporary English is by no means to be assumed. The negative meaning of "idealism" implies that most things that are commonly taken to be real are *not* so in fact, that is, they do not exist at all, or at least not in the manner that has been assumed. The positive interpretation of "idealism," in contrast, involves seeing the term as *adding* rather than subtracting significance, as emphasizing that, whatever we say about the status of many things that are thought to exist at a common-sense level, we also need to recognize a set of features or entities that have a higher, a more "ideal" nature.

"Ideal" features or entities thus need by no means be thought of as having to be projected into "another" world; on the contrary, they can be taken to be simply the purposive structure or ideal, in the sense of optimal, form of our one world of ordinary objects, once these are properly understood. In general, the *positive* exploration of such features is precisely what characterizes those later philosophers who are often assumed, by non-sympathetic "readers," to be *especially* negative in their idealism: Fichte, Schelling, Hegel. In fact, these philosophers started by repeatedly mocking the whole metaphysical tradition of opposing any fully transcendent (unknown, "in itself") realm to the world that we take ourselves to share and to be certain of through the latest forms of knowledge and social self-determination. The disputes among these German philosophers have to do primarily with *identifying* specific philosophical categories, the genuinely ideal structures that provide the most illuminating general account of how all experience, history, and nature hang together. In addition, like Marx (see below, chapter 13), they resisted a crude mechanistic epistemology that would attempt to explain cognition as simply a brute effect of receiving data in perception. Just as contemporary thinkers latch on to more complex notions such as "evolution" to suggest an intelligible pattern for everything from genetic and cosmological development to sensation and higher acts of mind, so too late eighteenth-century German philosophers welcomed the radical scientific strands of the late Enlightenment, and tried to elaborate dynamic, chemical, and organic models that aimed not at denying the existence of given natural forms but at affirming deep ("ideal") structures that make these forms comprehensible as a whole, and that force us to go beyond the meager passive vocabulary of mechanics. (Chomsky's appropriation of Humboldt is an example of one of the few contemporary American attempts to encourage a scientific appreciation of this side of German thought.[8])

In sum, the sad and ironic fact is that the "idealist" German thinkers in this period took themselves to mean something that is precisely the *opposite* of anything like negative metaphysical idealism – the philosophical view that, in its paradigm modern form, prides itself on a denial of public material objects. Yet it is precisely this negative kind of idealism that English readers have tended to presume is the core of the philosophical position that they have derisively rejected as "German Idealism."[9] It is not only English readers who have obscured matters. Very influential strands of left wing Hegelianism also tended to speak as if there was an anti-realistic metaphysical position in their predecessors that needed to be overturned – when it can be shown that in fact the genuine differences between figures such as Hegel and Marx had nothing to do with such a position (see below, chapter 13).

Even if one succeeds in comprehending that the idealism of the German idealists is not the negative kind, there remain difficulties enough in the positive aspects of their systems. The main problem is precisely that they are so elaborately systematic, that this is what their idealism largely consists in – a holism of a highly ambitious "idealizing" kind that refuses to take *any* particular, wholly contingent, and limited structure as the final story. Even if they in no way mean to deny nature and experience, they do frequently insist on offering an absolutely certain and purely philosophical framework to "ground" or complete "true" science. By itself, however, this systematic urge should not be regarded as a sin of German Idealism alone. It remained an even stronger influence in several branches of empiricism and the positivist movement into the twentieth century, from Mill to Schlick and Carnap. The systems of twentieth-century empiricist foundationalism and its radical pragmatist successors proved to be much more of a threat to ordinary realism than any philosophy that came from the "idealists" of Jena. Nonetheless, even without any misplaced worry about a threat to realism, the systematic ambitions of the German idealists were enough by themselves to create considerable and legitimate resistance from the very beginning. In the 1790s Jena gave birth not only to absolute idealism but also to a philosophical counter-movement generated by an unusual alliance of thinkers who shared a deep interest in views about the limits of reason that were stressed by both Kant and romanticism.

III Idealism and romanticism

It is no accident that in this era the *style* of philosophical writing itself became a *fundamental* problem for the first time. The question of style took on a special importance because of two developments. On the one hand, Kant and some of his immediate followers introduced a new kind of writing that required massive efforts of interpretation even for those who were specialists and close to the author in time, space, and language. Geniuses such as Mendelssohn and Goethe were sincere in professing difficulty in merely reading Kant's major works. (This problem was in part connected to the fact that Kant belonged to the first generation of philosophers who presented their major works in German alone and had to invent their own terminology.) An unprecedented number of digests, popularizations, and conflicting interpretations flooded the scene. Later systems, especially those developed by Fichte, Schelling, and Hegel, only exacerbated this problem. Every attempt of an author to present one more "crystal clear report" (*sonnenklarer Bericht*, a term in one of Fichte's titles) of the latest idealist system was met with curiosity that soon gave way to incredulity and incomprehension.

On the other hand, there was also, almost from the very start, and as a complementary movement to the growing esotericism accompanying the rise of German Idealism, the development of an intentionally anti-systematic, non-technical style of writing. This strand is internal to German Idealism itself. An anticipation of the ideas behind it can be found already in some of Kant's own work (his desire to overturn "the philosophy of the schools"), but it became a genuine movement only in the early romantic circles of mid-1790s Jena.

The "anti-systematic" strand of this period favored a specific *content* and *form* for philosophy. In its *content* this strand emphasized a distinctive feature of

Kant's work, its "Critical" orientation, that is, its claim to show, first and above all else, that there are basic limits to knowledge, and especially to theoretical philosophical claims. This "restrictive" tendency was quickly understood to be relevant to the Critical philosophy itself. That philosophy, and all the idealistic systems that followed it, had to face up to the possibility that their own claims might turn out to be in principle much more limited and uncertain than they at first appeared.

The theme of the self-limitation of philosophy went hand in hand with the nature of the unique *form* of writing that several of the anti-systematic idealists preferred. "Self-limitation" can be, and was, argued for in a fairly straightforward and prosaic way – for example, in an easy-to-read article on the importance of common sense presented by Friedrich Niethammer to inaugurate his extremely important *Philosophisches Journal* (Jena, 1795).[10] But there is an even more natural technique for indicating the self-limitation of philosophy, a method that was especially convenient for the poetic talents in Jena then. Hölderlin, Novalis, Friedrich Schlegel, and Schleiermacher all had a remarkable gift for creative writing, and they were deeply impressed by the (very Kantian) philosophical idea that an all-encompassing theoretical system seems both inescapably alluring and inevitably frustrating. When faced directly with the ambitious systems offered by their close neighbors and friends – Reinhold, Fichte, Schelling, and Hegel – these especially talented thinkers reacted in their own way. In a barrage of philosophic poems, revolutionary novels, gnomic essays, dialogues, extensive critical notebooks, literary journals, and writings that purposely fit no standard genre, they developed the unique German phenomenon now called Early Romanticism (*Frühromantik*). It was at once a literary sensation and a new kind of philosophy and anti-philosophy – a philosophy that made a point of emphasizing, often in more poetic than traditional philosophical style, the limits of philosophic systems as such and of rationality in general.

It is not surprising that this phenomenon emerged precisely at the moment of an intense and very prescient sense of the futility of the absolutist efforts to make philosophy a fully immanent and "rigorous science." Right at the time that the exact sciences were establishing themselves as paradigms of cognitive authority, philosophy after Kant fought a last-ditch battle to establish itself as the absolute foundation for all disciplines, as a subject with all the aura of the strongest claims of both the new physics and the old theology. The failure of this effort had an audience. It may be too controversial to say (although it has been vigorously argued of late) that this was the very moment at which "art" and "literature" were born[11] – the moment at which, with the simultaneous overturning of religious and political authoritarianism, writing as such, without any pretensions to rigor, dared to claim its complete independence. It does, however, appear to coincide with the moment that all "pure" philosophy that still presumed to make absolute claims as a genuine "science" was explicitly put on notice. For this reason alone Early Romanticism deserves much more attention than it has received within philosophy itself, especially in English.

History gives us many instances of deep disappointment with "systematic foundations" offered by philosophers. But this disappointment usually results in either skepticism (at least about philosophy) or yet another attempt to offer a better philosophical foundation. Early Romanticism resisted these extreme reactions and attempted to work out a new position, a position self-consciously still within the margins of philosophy. With his typical irony, Schlegel put the position this way: "It is equally fatal to have a system and to have none. One must decide to combine both."[12] The claim about having "both" is, of course, literal nonsense, but it is intended that way. It is memorable and provocative, and thus makes us think on our own about what is needed. The idea it is pointing to is not that one can literally have *a system and no system*. Rather, what one can do, and what some of these Jena writers were doing, each in their own way, is to advocate a modest respect for rationality and system, one exemplified, as some of them explicitly maintained, in a non-foundational system of a broadly Kantian variety that accepts a variety of given and not "absolutely" certain premises.[13] Such a system also explicitly leaves open the possibility for important truths beyond our theoretical knowledge, and even the natural domain altogether, and thus it contrasts sharply with the absolute claims of the post-Kantian systems.

The significance of Jena at this time has hardly been lost on literary historians and specialists in "romanticism." Nonetheless, Early Romanticism can be, and has been, very underappreciated *philosophically* for a number of reasons. Key texts have been falsified, kept long unknown, or simply misunderstood because of their complexity. Also, the very fact of the outstanding quality of these writers, and their close relations to figures such as Goethe, Schiller, and others, has made it very easy to treat them only under the heading of something like literature or aesthetics as *opposed* to philosophy. The "philosophy of German Idealism" can thus get narrowed down to a small set of recognizably academic textbooks by writers employed as philosophy professors – as if other writing must be peripheral to philosophy itself. This is to forget that the very notion of a sharp distinction of the philosophical and the non-philosophical is itself the result of a fairly recent phenomenon. Prior to Kant, none of the truly great modern philosophers had lived the life of a philosophy professor – not Descartes, not Leibniz, not Hume. Conversely, the early romantics all studied philosophy closely, and most of them showed serious interest in an academic career in philosophy.

Another problem with interpretations of figures such as the early romantics is that even when they are allowed to have writings that can be called philosophical, there is a tendency to understand them as valuable only in so far as they can be seen as anticipations or modifications of the systems of "pure" philosophers such as Fichte or Hegel. This is a double injustice. First, and most obviously, thinking of movements such as Early Romanticism as a mere "precursor" phenomenon destroys the possibility of appreciating them for their own ideas. Secondly, this approach can also be unfair to the "systematic" idealists. It can block recognition of the fact that the greatest value of their work may lie not in its claims to be "scientific" but in aspects of its cultural vision that it shares with, and even takes from, sources such as romanticism. If, for example, we feel closer now to Hölderlin than Hegel, and if we are open to recent evidence that on some major points it may have been Hegel who was influenced by Hölderlin rather than vice versa, then we can appreciate Hegel himself in a valuable new way that makes sense only once we stop thinking of Hölderlin as a mere stage on the road to Hegel.

The greatest problem for the philosophical appreciation of Early Romanticism may be simply the word romanticism itself. This term seems not only vague and unphilosophical, especially in English, but it also tends to bring with it all that is associated with the larger phenomenon of all forms of romanticism. The addition of the term "German" to Early Romanticism adds problems of guilt by association. It cannot be denied that there are many romantic writings that manifest highly irrational and reactionary doctrines. But although such doctrines are certainly found in German thought, they occur primarily in *Late*, rather than Early, Romanticism – and hence these two movements will be capitalized and sharply distinguished throughout this volume. Such distinctions have often been ignored, however, especially by readers swayed by the widespread presumption that there is a single pernicious and anti-rationalist strand in German thought that connects a whole line of figures from Hamann (or before) through the romantics of the Metternich era and after. The problem also arises for readers who may have no specific view about German writers but are put off by the mere mention of "romanticism" and associate it with conservative and anti-scientific traditions in cultures with which they are familiar. Yet, even if it might seem convenient to try to avoid these problems by finding another term altogether, the phrase Early Romanticism (*Frühromantik*) has a clear enough literal meaning, and impressive German scholarship has established its usage in a way that makes it impossible to ignore.[14] Like the more general philosophical term "idealism," the term "romanticism" should not be dismissed because of terminological difficulties and common misunderstandings; both terms can still be used effectively in phrases that designate quite specific and extremely valuable texts and doctrines in the German tradition.

IV Preview

For an overview of the era as a whole, especially as it emerges as a response to the period that preceded it, readers are advised to begin with the first chapter, by Frederick Beiser, "The Enlightenment and idealism." Beiser chronicles the idealist attempt to stress criticism without falling back into skepticism, and to make room for naturalism, in a broad sense, without falling back into a reductive materialism. The chapters that follow are arranged in roughly chronological order, and they take up in more detail each of the figures and movements touched on in Beiser's preview. (For more detail readers can consult several Cambridge Companions on individual philosophers.)

Kant's philosophy is discussed in two chapters linking it to problems in its reception in later idealism. Paul Guyer focuses on dualisms within Kant's theoretical philosophy that were criticized especially severely by Hegel. Guyer argues that a fundamental distinction between concepts and intuitions is Kant's major innovation, and that Hegel's absolute idealism can be understood as a not clearly persuasive attempt to roll back Kant's distinction. Allen Wood reviews the entire structure of Kant's practical philosophy. He emphasizes the importance, for both understanding and appreciating Kant's ethics, of not regarding as primary the initial formulation of the categorical imperative in terms of the universalizability test for maxims. In arguing that Kant's value theory needs to be understood in terms of his primary interest in the ends of reason and the ideal of an ethical community, Wood indicates ways in which Kant's project fits in well with the ultimate objectives of later idealism.

Daniel Dahlstrom discusses three important figures who developed as writers prior to studying the Critical philosophy. Hamann and Herder knew Kant personally and challenged his philosophy very directly, insisting that pure reason does not have the independence Kant claimed for it. Schiller joined this debate by arguing for a greater role for the satisfaction of our sensory interests, especially in aesthetics and the process of moral education. Despite the differences between Hamann's orthodox Christian commitments, Herder's liberal interest in cultural diversity, and Schiller's deeply moralistic but non-Christian approach, all three thinkers shared responsibility for a very influential "holistic turn in German thought." Paul Franks discusses another trio of early critics of Kant. He carefully reconstructs Jacobi's argument that all theoretical philosophy, precisely because of its systematicity, leads to the threat of nihilism. He then presents Reinhold's and Maimon's systems as significant attempts to improve on the Critical philosophy in developing a response to Jacobi's objections.

Rolf-Peter Horstmann offers a detailed reconstruction of the early systems of Fichte and Schelling. It is very hard to find treatments of these difficult systems that do not remain merely historical or fall back on oversimplifications of the

text. Horstmann's analysis provides a clear step-by-step discussion of the fundamental arguments of Fichte and Schelling, and in this way alone it is an important addition to the literature in English. In a chapter on Hölderlin and Novalis,
who were both reacting directly to Fichte, Charles Larmore gives a philosophical
assessment of their writings as well as of the influence of Schiller and Friedrich
Schlegel. Building on recent research by Dieter Henrich and Manfred Frank,
Larmore shows how, in different ways, both Hölderlin and Novalis challenged
the "goals of rational transparency and wholeness" that had come to dominate
early idealist systems.

Two essays are devoted to overviews of Hegel's philosophy. Terry Pinkard
traces the entire argument scheme of Hegel's *Phenomenology* and *Logic*. He puts
each of their main steps in the context of a conception of philosophy that is
aimed not at establishing traditional metaphysical or epistemological doctrines
but at giving an adequate reflective account of the whole human practice of
giving reasons and respecting normativity. Robert Pippin expands on this theme
in direct relation to Hegel's practical philosophy. He shows how the project of
Hegel's *Philosophy of Right* can be understood in terms of a radicalization of
Kant's notion of the "fact of reason." Hegel explains how "pure reason shows
itself actually to be practical" through a procedure that is "developmental, not
deductive," that is, through a series of uncoverings of the "partiality of some
prior attempt at self-imposed normative authority."

Günter Zöller discusses idealist systems less ambitious than Hegel's. He shows
how the later Fichte, Schelling, and Schopenhauer each argued, in very different
ways, for a fundamental "self-limitation of idealism." In this way they returned
to a more clearly "realist" position and one closer to Kant's doctrine of "the
bounds of reason." Dieter Sturma examines the sources and value of the "turn"
to Late Romanticism, as anticipated by Novalis and carried out in some aspects
of the late work of Friedrich Schlegel and Schelling. Sturma points out that the
"New Mythology" called for in the founding document of German idealism contains a progressive political component that parallels discussions of Kant's essay
on "Perpetual Peace" and retains a value independent of the backward-looking
uses to which it was put by some late romantic political writers. Andrew Bowie
begins his discussion of the relation between German Idealism and the arts by
noting Kant's emphasis on the fact that aesthetic values are not discernible by
mere concepts. This point helps to explain the special romantic interest in immediacy, feeling, and music, and the emphasis on aesthetics in the philosophies of
Schelling and Schleiermacher. The chapter concludes with a provocative evaluation of Hegel's history of art, which has the value of reminding us of the force
of sociopolitical influences but also illustrates the danger of forgetting the
romantic appreciation of the concrete and irreducible value of art as "world-
disclosing."

In a final chapter, I discuss ways in which the philosophies of Feuerbach, Marx, and Kierkegaard all remain closer to Hegel's dialectic and idealism than they explicitly acknowledge. The early writings of Feuerbach and Marx turn out to be especially close to Hegel's system because of numerous specific ways in which they share its rejection of transcendence and its commitment to a thoroughgoing rational structure of history. In contrast, Kierkegaard has an overriding concern with the problem of avoiding despair and with finding eternal satisfaction for the absolutely free individual self. His dialectic of "the stages on life's way" ends in a position that recalls the orthodox attitudes of Hamann and Jacobi at the onset of the idealist era.[15]

NOTES

1 Although "German Idealism" is a phrase generally used for philosophy right *after* Kant, it is also often used (as here) *simply* for convenience, to stand for the whole "age" of German Idealism, including Kant. Manfred Frank has stressed a contrast between the "idealism" of Fichte and Hegel and the "romanticism" of many of the other Jena writers. In this volume the term "romantic" is generally used only where its meaning is specified, e.g., as "early" or "late" (although Frederick Beiser, in ch. 1 below, prefers to speak of several of the idealists simply as "romantics"). See Frank, *"Unendliche Annäherung." Die Anfänge der philosophischen Frühromantik* (Frankfurt: Suhrkamp, 1997); and Beiser, *Enlightenment, Revolution, and Romanticism: The Genesis of Modern German Political Thought* (Cambridge, MA: Harvard University Press, 1992), and "Introduction," in *The Early Political Writings of the German Romantics* (Cambridge: Cambridge University Press, 1996).

2 Reinhold's "Letters on the Kantian Philosophy" (Jena, 1786–7) had an enormous effect on the interpretation of Kant. This effect is a main theme of my *Kant and the Fate of Autonomy: Problems in the Appropriation of the Critical Philosophy* (Cambridge: Cambridge University Press, 2000). See also ch. 5 below.

3 See Theodore Ziolkowski, *The Institutions of German Romanticism* (Princeton: Princeton University Press, 1990) and *Das Wunderjahr in Jena: Geist und Gesellschaft 1794/5* (Stuttgart: Klett-Cotta, 1997).

4 See *Between Kant and Hegel*, ed. and trans. George di Giovanni and H. S. Harris (Albany: State University of New York Press, 1985), and Rolf-Peter Horstmann, *Die Grenzen der Vernunft: Eine Untersuchung zu Zielen und Motiven des Deutschen Idealismus* (Frankfurt: Anton Hain, 1991).

5 See Nicholas Boyle, *Goethe: The Poet and the Age*, I (Oxford: Oxford University Press, 1992), and Ernst Behler, *German Romantic Literary Theory* (Cambridge: Cambridge University Press, 1993).

6 E.g., Dieter Henrich, ed., *Carl Immanuel Diez, Briefwechsel und Kantische Schriften* (Stuttgart: Klett-Cotta, 1997); *Konstellationen: Probleme und Debatten am Ursprung der idealistischen Philosophie (1789–1795)* (Stuttgart: Klett-Cotta, 1991); *Der Grund im Bewusstsein: Untersuchungen zu Hölderlins Denken (1794–1795)* (Stuttgart: Klett-Cotta, 1992); Frank, *"Unendliche Annäherung"*; and Marcelo Stamm, *Systemkrise: Die Elementarphilosophie in der Debatte (1789–1794)* (Stuttgart: Klett-Cotta, forthcoming).

7 See n. 1 above, and my "Kant, Fichte, and Short Arguments to Idealism," *Archiv für Geschichte der Philosophie*, 72 (1990), 63–85; "Hegel and Idealism," *Monist*, 74 (1991), 386–402; "Kantian Idealism Today," *History of Philosophy Quarterly*, 9 (1992), 329–42; and "Husserl's Realism," *Philosophical Review*, 86 (1977), 598–619. Kant's position contrasts with the other idealists in so far as he stresses the negative point that space and time are not real as independent things. See below, ch. 2.

8 Noam Chomsky, *Cartesian Linguistics* (New York: Harper & Row, 1966).

9 George Santayana's *Egotism in German Philosophy* (New York: Scribner, 1915) is but one striking expression of this sentiment. John Dewey provided a more accurate account in his *German Politics and Philosophy* (New York: Henry Holt, 1915), 82: "the idealism in question was not that of another world."

10 This article is stressed by Manfred Frank in K. Ameriks and D. Sturma, eds., "Philosophical Foundations of Early Romanticism," in *The Modern Subject*: *Conceptions of the Self in Classical German Philosophy* (Albany: State University of New York Press, 1995), 65–85. For its relation to Jena Kantians such as Johann Benjamin Erhard, see Frank, "*Unendliche Annäherung*", and cf. my *Kant and the Fate of Autonomy*, ch. 1, on Kant's "modest system." See also below, ch. 13, n. 15.

11 See Philippe Lacoue-Lebarthe and Jean-Luc Nancy, *The Literary Absolute: The Theory of Literature in German Romanticism*, trans. Philip Barnard and Cheryl Lester (Albany: State University of New York Press, 1988).

12 Friedrich Schlegel, "Fragmente," #53, *Athenäum*, vol. 1, 1798. See below, ch. 7.

13 See above, n. 10.

14 See especially M. Frank, *Einführung in die frühromantische Ästhetik* (Frankfurt: Suhrkamp, 1989).

15 In addition to thanking all the contributors for their very helpful assistance on this project, I would like to acknowledge a special debt to Patrick Frierson, Manfred Frank, Hilary Gaskin, Gary Gutting, and support from the University of Notre Dame. Alissa Branham provided essential help with the final stage of the project.

I

FREDERICK BEISER

The Enlightenment and idealism

I Introduction

It is a commonplace of intellectual history that any philosophical movement must be understood in its historical context. This dictum is especially true of German Idealism, whose aims and problems become intelligible only in the context of the culture of late eighteenth-century Germany. This culture was essentially that of the Enlightenment or *Aufklärung*, which had dominated intellectual life in Germany since the middle of the eighteenth century.

Toward the close of the eighteenth century, the Enlightenment began to show signs of a crisis. The more it extended its fundamental principles, the more they seemed to lead to dire consequences. The fundamental principles of the Enlightenment were rational criticism and scientific naturalism. While criticism seemed to end in skepticism, naturalism appeared to result in materialism. Both results were unacceptable. If skepticism undermines our common-sense beliefs in the reality of the external world, other minds, and even our own selves, materialism threatens the beliefs in freedom, immortality, and the *sui generis* status of the mind. There were few *Aufklärer* in Germany ready to admit such disastrous consequences; but there were also few willing to limit the principles of criticism and naturalism.

German Idealism grew out of this crisis of the Enlightenment. All its various forms – the *transcendental idealism* of Kant, the *ethical idealism* of Fichte, and the *absolute idealism* of the romantics – were so many attempts to resolve these *aporiai* of the Enlightenment. For all their criticisms of the Enlightenment, the German idealists were true to its two fundamental principles: rational criticism and scientific naturalism. Though German Idealism assumes such different, even incompatible forms, what all its forms have in common is the attempt to save criticism from skepticism, and naturalism from materialism.

The dynamic behind the development of German Idealism, the source of all its transformations, consisted in the long and bitter struggle to save these principles of the Enlightenment. One form of idealism succeeds another as each later form finds an earlier one inadequate to preserve these principles. Kant would insist that only his transcendental idealism avoids the dangers of skepticism and materialism. Fichte would complain that Kant's transcendental idealism, if it were only consistent, collapses into skepticism, and that the only escape from skepticism and materialism lies with his ethical idealism. The romantics would also object that Fichte's ethical idealism has no response to skepticism, and they would insist that only their absolute idealism could provide a basis for naturalism without materialism. Behind all these permutations, there remains the constant attempt of the German idealists to preserve the legacy of the Enlightenment.

II The inner tensions of enlightenment

What is enlightenment? The *Aufklärer* themselves had no single answer to this question, which became the subject of intense debate among them in the 1780s.[1] But all would have agreed that the age of Enlightenment was "the age of reason." The phrase was indeed accurate since the Enlightenment had made reason into its highest authority, its final court of appeal, in all moral, religious, and political questions. Reason provided the criterion to judge all beliefs, laws, works of art, and sacred texts; but it could not be judged by any higher criterion. Nothing was sacred or infallible before the tribunal of critique – except, of course, that tribunal itself.

What did the Enlightenment mean by reason? What was this faculty to which it had attributed such awesome powers? There were many definitions of reason during the Enlightenment, but two conceptions were fundamental and widespread. First, reason is a *faculty of criticism*, the power to examine beliefs according to the evidence for them. Second, reason is a *power of explanation*, the capacity to understand events by seeing them as instances of general laws. The Enlightenment had a specific paradigm of explanation, namely *mechanism*, which it derived from the new physics of Galileo, Descartes, and Newton. According to this paradigm, the cause of an event is not its purpose or final cause but its efficient cause, some prior event in time. Since the effect of such a cause can be measured in terms of impact, by how much a body changes place in a given amount of time, the laws of mechanism are quantifiable. Hence one of the great advantages of mechanism was that it led to a mathematical conception of nature where all laws could be formulated in precise mathematical terms.

The crisis of the Enlightenment grew out of each of these concepts of reason. Each concept, if universalized and pushed to its limits, led to unacceptable consequences. But the crisis was inescapable since the Enlightenment *had to* radicalize each of them. For to limit them in any form would be a form of "unreason": it would be either obscurantism or "dogmatism," the limitation of reason by authority.

Radical criticism seemed to lead of necessity to skepticism. The skeptic had always claimed that doubt is the necessary result of criticism, the demand that we have sufficient evidence for all our beliefs. For it seems inevitable that the more we examine the reasons for our beliefs, the more we find they are inadequate. We discover that the evidence is doubtful, or that it does not imply its alleged conclusions. This seems to be the case especially with regard to our beliefs in the reality of the external world and other minds. We find that we have no reason to trust our senses, or that even if they are reliable they are not sufficient in number or in kind to give us complete knowledge of the object in itself. These kinds of skeptical arguments, which go back to Sextus Empiricus and the Pyrrhonism of antiquity, were revived in the seventeenth century by Montaigne and Charron, and in the eighteenth century by Bayle and Hume. They would have been familiar to any *Aufklärer*.

This dialectic from criticism to skepticism only seemed confirmed by the development of epistemology in the seventeenth and eighteenth centuries. The Enlightenment concern with epistemology grew directly out of its demand for criticism. For if we are to be systematic and thorough in examining the reasons for our beliefs, we should investigate the sources, conditions, and limits of knowledge in general. The epistemology of Locke, Berkeley, and Hume in Britain, of Descartes, Malebranche, and Condillac in France, and of Leibniz, Tetens, and Kant in Germany, all came from the need for a more systematic and rigorous form of criticism. But the more epistemology advanced, the more it seemed to lead to the conclusion that *what* we know – the object of cognition – is conditioned by *how* we know – the act of cognition. Nowhere is this conclusion more apparent than in the theory of ideas, which is endemic to the epistemology of the Enlightenment. According to this theory, the role of sensory organs and perceptual activities in cognition makes the immediate objects of perception not things themselves but the ideas we have of them. It was just this theory, however, that seemed to lead directly to skepticism. It seemed to bring down "a veil of perception," so that the subject directly knew only its ideas; it was then necessary *to infer*, somewhat hazardously, the existence of the external world.

If radical criticism seemed to end in skepticism, a radical naturalism appeared to lead to materialism. This seemed to be the inevitable result of universalizing the Enlightenment's paradigm of explanation, of claiming that *everything that exists* is explicable, at least in principle, according to mechanical and mathematical laws. If something falls under mechanical and mathematical laws, then it must be quantifiable or measurable. But to be quantifiable or measurable it must be extended, having a determinate size, shape, and weight; in other words, it must be material. Hence the mechanical-mathematical paradigm of explanation applies only to matter; and if it explains everything, everything must be material.

The only escape from such materialism seemed to be a form of dualism, a sharp distinction between the material and the mental. Such dualism admits that the mechanical-mathematical paradigm explains everything in nature, but it denies that everything that exists is within nature. It makes a distinction between extended substance, which falls inside nature, and mental or thinking substance, which falls outside it. But such dualism also has its price: the realm of the mental becomes something mysterious, inexplicable according to scientific laws. Hence the Enlightenment's mechanical-mathematical paradigm of explanation seemed to lead to an *aporia* in the philosophy of mind where the only possibilities were materialism and dualism. But both are unacceptable. For if materialism explains the mind, it also denies its distinctive status, reducing it down to a machine; and if dualism recognizes the unique qualities of mind, it makes it into a mysterious entity. Hence the mind becomes either a machine or a ghost; on no account is it possible to explain its characteristic qualities according to natural laws.

The crisis of the Enlightenment went even deeper. Its problem was not only that each of its concepts of reason had unacceptable consequences, but also that these concepts were in conflict with one another. Criticism and naturalism, when universalized, undermine one another. Since criticism ends in skepticism, it undermines naturalism, which is committed to the independent reality of nature and the necessity of scientific laws. Since naturalism results in materialism, it undermines criticism, and more specifically its claim to be in possession of universal and necessary standards of reason. For materialism ends in relativism, given that it claims that everything, including human rationality, is the product of material forces at a specific time and place.

The conflict between these concepts of reason appears time and again in the epistemologies of the Enlightenment. The epistemologies of Descartes, Locke, Hobbes, and Hume attempted to provide some foundation for the new natural sciences; yet they also ended in a skepticism that completely undermined scientific naturalism. This tension was apparent in Descartes, who could resolve his doubts about the reality of the external world and the applicability of mathematics only by a question-begging demonstration of the existence of God. It was also plain in Hobbes, who affirmed materialism only to question whether "the phantoms" of perception have any resemblance to things outside them. It was no less clear in Locke, who wanted his epistemology to be a handmaiden of the new natural philosophy, but who also made the perceiving subject directly aware only of its own ideas. Finally, it was also evident in Hume, who doubted the reality of the external world and induction, but who also wanted to develop a science of human nature.

These problems with the Enlightenment concepts of rationality were already fully apparent in Germany by the 1770s, the decade Kant wrote his *Critique of Pure Reason*. The dangers of materialism were widely felt. The writings of Holbach, Helvétius, and Diderot had a wide clandestine circulation in Germany; and the views of La Mettrie and Maupertuis were notorious, not least because these *philosophes* were prominent in the Prussian Academy of Sciences in Berlin. The writings of the English free-thinkers – John Toland, Anthony Collins, and Matthew Tindal – had been translated into German and were widely read.[2] Although materialism was more advanced in France and Britain, there were also some notable German materialists, such as Friedrich Wilhelm Stosch, Theodor Ludwig Lau, and Gabriel Wagner, who were inspired by Spinoza to develop mechanistic explanations of human actions.[3] Spinozism was a notorious doctrine in Germany, but it was so not least because it represented a mechanistic materialism. The threat of skepticism was also widely recognized. Skepticism became known chiefly in the form of Berkeley's and Hume's idealism, which was interpreted as a form of solipsism or "egoism," as doubt about the reality of everything except one's own self.[4] So well known were Berkeley's and Hume's versions of idealism that they became a favorite subject of refutation in lectures on metaphysics. That Humean skepticism is the inevitable result of the way of ideas was a well-known doctrine in Germany, especially from the writings of Thomas Reid and the Scottish philosophers, who had a large following among the *Popularphilosophen*.[5]

III Transcendental idealism and the Enlightenment

It has sometimes been said that the crisis of the Enlightenment began with the publication of the *Critique of Pure Reason* in May 1781.[6] Without doubt, Kant was one of the harshest critics of the Enlightenment, and few of its enemies could match his ruthless and relentless dialectic. Still, Kant came to save the Enlightenment, not to bury it. His aim was to give a lasting foundation to its fundamental article of faith: the authority of reason.

No one saw more clearly than Kant, however, that the Enlightenment had to keep its house in order. If reason is not aware of its limits, he taught, then it undermines itself, turning into unreason by lapsing into all kinds of fallacies. The sleep of reason breeds monsters: amphibolies, antinomies, paralogisms. Kant was confident that a fully aroused and alert reason, properly disciplined through the critique, could stay firmly within its own limits and so save the Enlightenment from self-destruction.

In the 1770s Kant could already see that the Enlightenment was heading for trouble. Before he wrote the *Critique of Pure Reason* he was unsettled by the dangers of skepticism and materialism. Kant was well aware that criticism could end in skepticism, given his appreciation of Hume, who had awakened him from his "dogmatic slumbers." Kant was also fully conscious that naturalism, if radicalized, presents the danger of materialism, and it was for just this reason that he believed it necessary to deny knowledge to save room for faith. His early concern to refute skepticism and materialism is apparent from several sources: his 1755 *Nova dilucidatio,* his 1766 *Dreams of a Spirit Seer,* his 1770 Inaugural Dissertation, and his lectures on metaphysics during the 1760s and 1770s.[7]

To prevent the impending crisis of the Enlightenment – to save reason from self-destruction – was a central motive behind Kant's development in the 1770s. Kant had two fundamental tasks to rescue the Enlightenment. The first was to prevent criticism and naturalism from self-destruction. He wanted to establish criticism without skepticism, and naturalism without materialism. A criticism without skepticism would provide an account of our knowledge of the external world that is resistant to Cartesian and Humean doubts. A naturalism without materialism would insist that everything in nature is explicable by mechanical laws, yet it would forswear the claim – crucial to materialism – that everything that exists is in nature. Kant's second task was to disarm the conflict between criticism and naturalism, so that each could be universalized without destroying the other. He wanted to create a criticism immune from the dangers of naturalism, and a naturalism free from the threat of skepticism. A criticism immune from materialism would ensure that reason is an autonomous faculty, a source of universal laws, independent of the causality, and hence the relativism, of the historical and natural world. A naturalism free from skepticism would show that the laws of physics apply to nature itself and do not simply consist in our habit of associating impressions. The Critical philosophy intended to avoid, therefore, that tension between naturalism and criticism that had so marred Enlightenment epistemology.

Kant's solution to all these problems was nothing less than his famous Copernican Revolution. As Kant describes that Revolution in the preface to the second edition of the *Critique of Pure Reason,* it consists in a reversal of the normal externalist conception of truth (Bxvi–xvii). According to that conception, truth consists in the conformity of concepts with objects, in the correspondence of our representations with things that exist independent of them. While Kant is willing to accept such a conception of truth within ordinary experience, he thinks that it is profoundly misleading if it becomes an account of truth in general or the possibility of experience itself. Such a conception of truth aids skepticism because it is impossible to get outside our representations to see if they conform to an object in itself. To avoid such problems, Kant proposes that we see truth as the conformity of objects with our concepts, as the agreement of our perceptions with certain universal and necessary concepts that determine the form or structure of experience. If we adopt this conception of truth, it is no longer necessary to get outside our own representations to see if they conform to objects in themselves. Rather, the standard of truth will be found within the realm of consciousness itself by seeing whether a representation conforms to the universal and necessary forms of consciousness itself.

Kant's transcendental idealism grew out of the new conception of truth behind his Copernican Revolution. Since Kant held that we do not create the objects of our cognition, and since he also claimed that we know these objects only insofar as they conform to the conditions of our cognizing them, he concluded that we know these objects only as they appear to us but not as things in themselves. Hence Kant would explain transcendental idealism in terms of two fundamental doctrines: the distinction between appearances and things in themselves, and the claim that we know things only as appearances and not things in themselves.[8] Accordingly, in the *Critique of Pure Reason* Kant defines his transcendental idealism in contrast to a *transcendental realism* that makes just the opposite assumptions: it conflates appearances with things in themselves and assumes we know things in themselves.

Transcendental idealism was Kant's solution to the imminent crisis of the Enlightenment. It was a very strategic doctrine because it allowed him to avoid the dangers of both skepticism and materialism. Through its new conception of truth, transcendental idealism could escape the snares of skepticism. Kant could now argue that the skeptic's doubts were based upon a false conception of truth, for they presuppose the externalist conception of truth according to which truth consists in the correspondence of a representation with a thing in itself.[9] The skeptic's doubts are based upon the possibility that such a correspondence might not take place, that we cannot determine whether our representations conform to something completely independent of them. While Kant admits that such a standard of truth is unrealizable, he also doubts its necessity. The truth of all empirical judgments would still be preserved, he maintains, if we explain it in terms of the conformity of representations with the universal and necessary forms of consciousness.[10] It was the great merit of his transcendental idealism over Descartes's and Hume's skeptical idealism, Kant contended, that it could maintain an empirical realism within itself. While skeptical idealism doubts the reality of the external world, transcendental idealism is committed to its reality because it shows that objects in space must exist outside us. The reality of these objects in space consists not in their existence as things in themselves, to be sure, but in their conformity to universal and necessary forms of consciousness, which is sufficient to establish that they are not illusory.

Through its distinction between appearances and things in themselves, transcendental idealism also secured the possibility of naturalism without materialism. Kant maintained a universal naturalism, so that everything that occurs in nature must be subject to universal laws; yet this does not entail materialism since he limited nature to the realm of appearances, denying that the laws of nature are applicable to things in themselves. Kant therefore undermined the central contention of materialism: that *everything that exists* must be in nature. Such a contention simply conflated appearances with things in themselves, assuming, wrongly, that what is true of the phenomena of nature must also be true of reality itself.

It was in virtue of his distinction between appearances and things in themselves that Kant could also resolve the classical conflict between criticism and naturalism. Criticism would not undermine but support naturalism since it would show how the fundamental principles of natural science apply without exception to *all* appearances, to *any* object of experience. Conversely, naturalism would not undermine criticism because transcendental idealism would show how naturalism operates *only* in the sphere of appearances and cannot be extended to things in themselves. Transcendental idealism would ensure the autonomy of reason, its freedom from the determination of experience and history, by showing how the standards and activities of reason do not operate in the natural realm at all.

It is important to see that Kant's transcendental idealism rejects both idealism and realism in the traditional sense. Kant insisted on describing his transcendental idealism as *critical* idealism because it limits knowledge to experience alone and makes no claims about reality in itself.[11] This means that it must reject idealism as well as materialism insofar as both make claims about the nature of all reality. From the standpoint of critical idealism, the idealist claim that the essence of an object is perception is no better than the materialist claim that the essence of an object is its occupation of space. Both are metaphysical propositions that go beyond the realm of possible experience. Hence Kant indignantly rejected the imputation of many of his early critics that his idealism was essentially the same as Berkeley's.

IV The pantheism controversy

Despite its brilliant strategy, the *Critique of Pure Reason* could not prevent the crisis of the Enlightenment. The issues that had been simmering for decades – the skepticism and materialism implicit in a radical rationalism – finally burst on the public stage in the late 1780s. Ironically, no one played a greater role in their transmission than Kant himself. For all his good intentions toward the Enlightenment, Kant had posed its fundamental problems in a way that made them impossible to ignore. When his critics complained that Kant himself could not resolve these problems, the crisis had become public and seemed utterly irresolvable.

If there is any single year that marks the beginning of the crisis of the Enlightenment it would have to be 1786. On 16 August Frederick II, the king of

Prussia, died after more than forty years on the throne. Since Frederick was "the philosopher king," who had advocated such enlightened policies as toleration and freedom of the press, his death seemed very symbolic, like the demise of the Enlightenment itself. Sure enough, his successor, Frederick William II, was not so liberal. Fearful of the effects of free-thinking upon his subjects, his minister C. G. Wöllner began in 1788 to lay down decrees imposing censorship and greater control over religious consistories.[12] Some of the foremost journals of the *Aufklärung*, such as Nicolai's *Allgemeine deutsche Bibliothek*, were forced to stop their presses in Prussia. The halcyon days of the *Aufklärung*, which came from the blissful alliance of throne and philosophy, were truly over.

The year 1786 is also significant because it marks the onset of the "pantheism controversy" between Moses Mendelssohn and F. H. Jacobi. No other controversy had a greater effect upon the fate of the Enlightenment. This dispute had been brewing for over a year in the increasingly bitter correspondence between Mendelssohn and Jacobi; but in early 1786 it erupted into a storm that captured the public imagination. Of the impact of this controversy upon its age Goethe later wrote of "an explosion" and Hegel of "a thunderbolt out of the blue." Almost every notable thinker of the 1790s developed his philosophy as a response to this controversy. Herder, Reinhold, Kant, Rehberg, Hamann, and Wizenmann all wrote contributions to the dispute; and the notebooks of the young Schlegel, Hegel, Schleiermacher, Novalis, and Hölderlin reveal their intense involvement in it.

Prima facie the dispute concerned little more than Lessing's Spinozism. Jacobi had shocked Mendelssohn and many *Aufklärer* by claiming that Lessing had confessed to him in the summer of 1780 that he was a Spinozist. Since Spinozism was synonymous with atheism and fatalism in eighteenth-century Germany, publicizing Lessing's confession would besmirch his reputation as the most revered thinker of the *Aufklärung*. But these biographical issues were only of secondary importance. Lessing was really only a vehicle for Jacobi, a means of drawing attention to, and indeed dramatizing, his own critique of the *Aufklärung*. For years Jacobi had harbored the deepest animosity for the *"morgue berlinoise"* – the clique of Berlin *Aufklärer* consisting in Mendelssohn, Nicolai, Biester, Eberhard, and Gedike – because, unlike Lessing, they were unwilling to admit the ultimate consequences of all rational inquiry: atheism and fatalism. Hence Lessing was a symbolic figure for Jacobi, the only *Aufklärer* he could admire, because he alone was willing to take his reason to its limits and to confess its atheistic and fatalistic consequences.

That rationalism ends in atheism and fatalism was an old pietist complaint. In the 1740s pietists like Andreas Rüdiger and J. F. Budde had leveled this charge against Wolff's philosophy, insisting that its rationalism made it nothing more than a half-way house on the road to Spinozism. While any *Aufklärer* could grumble that he had heard this refrain before, there was still something new and deeply disturbing about Jacobi's criticisms. For Jacobi had equated rationalism not with the old geometric method of Spinoza's philosophy, which had been discredited even before Kant, but with the mechanistic paradigm of the new sciences. These sciences had been making remarkable progress, extending this paradigm into new areas, such as physiology and cosmology. The more they advanced, the less room there seemed to be in the world for the supernatural, for God, freedom, and immortality. So what Spinozism represented for Jacobi was a radical naturalism. He said that the spirit of Spinozism was epitomized in the dictum "*ex nihilo nihil fit*," from nothing comes nothing, because Spinoza extended the series of natural causes to infinity. Spinoza admitted no exception to the principle of sufficient reason, so that there had to be a cause for every event, such that the event could not be otherwise. Like Kant, Jacobi concluded that given such a principle there cannot be God or freedom, which presuppose spontaneity, a first cause not determined by a prior cause.

The sum and substance of Jacobi's polemic was thus to renew the threat of a radical naturalism, a materialism in Spinozistic dress. The *Aufklärer* were presented with a dramatic dilemma: either a rational atheism and fatalism or an irrational leap of faith; either a rational materialism or a *salto mortale* affirming the existence of God, providence, and freedom. There was no middle path, however, which would attempt to prove faith through reason.

V The meta-critical campaign

The crisis of the Enlightenment grew out of the critique of Kant's philosophy as much as the pantheism controversy. This critique began in earnest in the late 1780s when a horde of polemics, books, reviews, and even journals, appeared attacking Kant. The net effect of this attack was to further weaken the Enlightenment. While the pantheism controversy had revived the danger of materialism, the criticism of Kant's philosophy had resurrected the threat of skepticism.

One of the central themes of the criticism of Kant's philosophy in the 1780s was the widespread interpretation of Kant as a skeptical idealist. The threat of egoism, which had troubled the *Aufklärer* in the 1760s and 1770s, had now returned more potent than ever. It seemed to many of Kant's early critics that he had not refuted but radicalized Hume's skepticism. Kant was a "Prussian Hume" because his philosophy, if it were only consistent, ends in a complete skepticism which gives us no reason to believe in the existence of anything beyond our own passing representations. Such skepticism seemed to be the inevitable consequence of two often repeated statements of Kant: that external things are only appearances, and that appearances consist in nothing but representations. These critics duly noted Kant's commitment to the existence of things in themselves; but they countered that Kant had no right to assume their existence on his own premises, given that he limited all knowledge to experience and that things in themselves are not in experience. They were also not impressed with the "Refutation of Idealism" of the second edition of the *Critique*, where Kant attempted to prove the existence of objects in space outside us; for they pointed out that Kant also held that space is nothing but a form of representation itself. By implication, if not intention, then, Kant had revived the specter of a skepticism that had haunted the *Aufklärung*.

One of the most interesting results of the criticism of Kant's philosophy in the late 1780s and early 1790s is the rise of a neo-Humean skepticism in Germany. Among these neo-Humean skeptics were G. E. Schulze, Solomon Maimon, Ernst Platner, and A. W. Rehberg; Jacobi, Hamann, Justus Möser and Thomas Wizenmann were also very sympathetic to and influenced by Hume's skepticism. The central theme of their neo-Humean skepticism is that Kant's Transcendental Analytic cannot refute Hume, and that the critique of knowledge, if it is consistent, must end in a total skepticism.

These neo-Humean critics make many objections to Kant, which vary greatly in quality and force. But there is one objection in their complex polemic that stands out for its central role in the later development of German Idealism. This objection stresses the problematic status of the Kantian dualisms. Kant had famously insisted that knowledge requires the most intimate interchange between understanding and sensibility – "intuitions without concepts are blind and concepts without intuitions are empty" – but he had made such a sharp distinction between these faculties that it seemed impossible for them to interact with one another. The understanding was active, formal, and intellectual, while sensibility was passive, material, and empirical. Maimon claimed that the dualism between these faculties was analogous to the old Cartesian dualism beween the mind and body, and that all the problems of the older dualism should hold *mutatis mutandis* for the new one. Such was the heterogeneity between understanding and sensibility, Maimon further argued, that there could be no criterion to determine how the concepts of the understanding apply to the intuitions of sensibility.[13]

By thus pointing out these problematic dualisms, Maimon and the neo-Humean critics left a foothold open for skepticism *within the framework of Kant's own philosophy*. For now the question arose how two such heterogeneous realms as the intellectual and the sensible could be known to correspond with one another. The problem was no longer how we know that our representations correspond with things in themselves but how we know that a priori concepts apply to a posteriori intuitions.

VI Fichte's ethical idealism

The net effect of the crisis of the Enlightenment was the return of its old enemies: skepticism and materialism. Now that Jacobi had resurrected Spinoza and the meta-critique of Kant had revived Hume, these monsters seemed stronger than ever. It was the task of the later idealists to slay them, to succeed where Kant had failed.

Fichte's early philosophy – the so-called 1794 *Wissenschaftslehre* (*Science of Knowledge*) – grew directly out of the crisis of the Enlightenment. In fundamental respects the young Fichte's ideals were still very much those of the Enlightenment. Like Kant, Fichte too wanted to uphold the authority of reason, which he saw as the ultimate standard of truth and value. He also shared Kant's basic philosophical ideals: a criticism without skepticism, a naturalism without materialism. But in the early 1790s, after the revival of Spinoza and the criticism of Kant, these ideals seemed even more impossible to achieve. Transcendental idealism no longer seemed to be the surest safeguard against skeptical idealism and mechanistic materialism.

For the young Fichte, the main challenge of philosophy was to defeat the traditional enemies of the Enlightenment: the skeptical idealism of Hume and the mechanistic materialism of Spinoza. Fichte famously stated that there were only two possible positions in philosophy: the "dogmatism" of Spinoza and the "criticism" of Kant; but he also understood the problematic versions of these positions to be materialism and skepticism. For Fichte, dogmatism represented materialism, the complete denial of human freedom and the overturning of all moral responsibility (I, 431).[14] And the degenerate form of criticism was Hume's skeptical idealism. Fichte was painfully aware of, and profoundly influenced by, the neo-Humean skeptics, who convinced him that Kant's philosophy, at least in its present exposition in the *Critique of Pure Reason*, ends in "a skepticism worse than Hume's."[15] After reading Schulze and Maimon in early 1794 he vowed to rebuild the critical philosophy on a new foundation.

The central task of Fichte's 1794 *Wissenschaftslehre* was to defeat the materialism of Spinozism, and the skepticism of the neo-Humeans. To combat skepticism, Fichte had to grapple with the problematic dualisms of Kant's philosophy, which had made it vulnerable to doubt. Somehow, he had to establish that understanding and sensibility, the form and content of experience, stem from a single source and unifying principle. Hence in his first exposition of the *Wissenschaftslehre* – his 1794 *Foundations of the entire Wissenschaftslehre* – Fichte postulated an absolute ego, of which the ego and non-ego, the subject and object of experience, are only parts or aspects (I, 105–23). This absolute ego would also be the antithesis of Spinoza's single universal substance. Just as

Spinoza's substance has the mind and body as its modes, so Fichte's absolute ego has the subject and object of empirical consciousness as its parts.

No one knew better than Fichte, however, that this postulate created more problems than it solved. It was hardly likely to convince the skeptic. For where was this absolute ego, and how could we know of its existence, if it were not within experience? Such an hypothesis was transcendent, going beyond possible experience, which Fichte too saw as the limits of knowledge. Even worse, the postulate also could not explain the basic structure of experience. For if there were an absolute ego, why did it limit itself by positing a non-ego outside itself? To assume that the absolute ego posits the world outside itself is not only meta-physically extravagant but logically absurd, since it presupposes that something completely active somehow makes itself passive, or that something infinite somehow makes itself finite. For all these reasons Fichte refused to give the absolute ego a constitutive status and insisted instead that it could be no more than a regulative idea (I, 260–1, 270, 277).

Rejecting the constitutive status of the absolute ego still left Fichte with the tricky task of explaining experience. His problem took the form of a dilemma: he had both to affirm and deny the dualism between subject and object of our ordinary experience. He had to affirm this dualism because it is just a basic fact of our experience that the object is given to us, and that its qualities appear inde-pendent of our will and imagination. He also had to deny this dualism, however, because knowledge required some correspondence or interaction between the subject and object. Furthermore, if there were a dualism, there would also be a foothold for the skeptic, who could ask why our representations correspond with things.

Fichte's solution to this dilemma is his concept of striving (*Streben*), which he expounds in the third section of his 1794 *Grundlage*. This concept is the very heart of the early *Wissenschaftslehre*, which Fichte even called "a philosophy of striving" (*Strebensphilosophie*). According to this concept, the absolute ego, which creates all nature, is not a reality but only an idea, the goal for the striv-ing of the finite ego. All that is left for the finite ego is constant striving, the cease-less struggle to make nature conform to the demands of its rational activity. If the finite ego strives to control nature, it approaches, even though it never attains, the ideal of the absolute ego. This concept then resolves the dilemma regarding dualism. Doing justice to each horn of the dilemma, it both affirms and denies the dualism. It affirms this dualism because the subject never gains complete control over nature, which continues to resist its efforts. It also denies this dualism because the subject gains some control over nature, making it conform to the demands of reason. Hence Fichte could do justice to the fact that we are finite beings who have a world independent of our control, and to the demand that there be some correspondence between the subject and object of knowledge.

This concept of striving was Fichte's weapon to slay the monsters of skepticism and materialism. Both fail to appreciate the role of human activity in knowledge. The problem with skepticism is that it presupposes a contemplative model of knowledge, according to which the subject's representation must somehow correspond to an object given independently of it. What it fails to see, however, is that the subject can *act* upon the object, making it conform to the standards of its activity. To an extent the skeptic is indeed right: *if* the object remains simply given, if it cannot be acted upon, then we cannot know it; but there is no reason for such an assumption in the first place. It is just a fact that we change the world, making it into something we can know. The problem with materialism is analogous. The materialist too underrates the role of activity in knowledge, for he hypostatizes the laws of nature, thinking that they represent forces that govern us, when in truth they too are our own creation. If the materialist only paid sufficient attention to the role of our activity in the creation of nature, he would see that we are indeed its lawgivers, and that there are no given objects to whose laws we must submit.

Such, in crude summary, was the spirit of Fichte's early 1794 *Wissenschaftslehre*. This philosophy is best described as an *ethical* idealism for two reasons. First, it maintains that the world *ought* to be ideal, but not that it *is* so. Idealism thus becomes a goal of our moral activity, our ceaseless striving to make the world conform to the demands of reason. Second, it gives priority to our activity in the production of knowledge, so that *what* we know, and even *that* we know, depends upon our efforts to conquer nature according to our moral ideals. Fichte went beyond Kant in giving practical reason priority over theoretical reason, for he made the activity of will central to the very foundation of knowledge itself. It was not only the understanding but the will that became the lawgiver of nature.

VII Absolute idealism

For all its brilliance, the *Wissenschaftslehre* had a brief life. Like a rocket, it quickly rose to the heights but only to explode in mid air. The young romantics – Hölderlin, Schelling, and Hegel, Novalis, Schlegel, and Hülsen – were deeply impressed by Fichte, whose lectures some of them attended in Jena in 1795. But no sooner had they heard "the titan of Jena" than they began to topple him. As early as the winter of 1796, Hölderlin, Novalis and Schlegel began filling their notebooks with criticisms of Fichte's idealism.[16] It is in these notebooks that we can trace the beginnings of *absolute idealism*.[17] This new standpoint will find its more systematic exposition in Schelling's and Hegel's writings in the early 1800s.

The romantic critique of Fichte is complex and wideranging, but their objections against his idealism reduce down to a few points. First, Fichte does not escape Hume's skeptical idealism after all. The concept of striving traps the ego inside the circle of its own consciousness, so that it knows either itself or nothing. Insofar as the ego succeeds in controlling nature, it knows only the products of its own activity; but insofar as nature resists its control, it becomes an unknowable thing in itself. Fichte himself admitted that this was a circle he could not avoid but only extend to infinity; but, to the romantics, this was tantamount to an admission of failure. Second, Fichte does not surmount Kant's dualisms but only restores them in new form. The Fichtean subject is active, noumenal, and purposive, while the Fichtean object is inert, phenomenal, and mechanical. How, then, can there be any correspondence between the subject and object required for all knowledge? To be sure, Fichte, unlike Kant, thinks that the striving subject makes some progress in reducing the dualism; but insofar as its striving is an infinite task the dualism must remain; and the question remains how it makes any progress at all, given that this would require some interaction between completely heterogeneous entities. Third, Fichte's absolute ego cannot be an ego at all, because something absolute transcends all finite determinations, and the subjective and objective, the ideal and the real, are finite determinations. It is only possible to say that the absolute is pure being or the indifference point of the subjective and objective.

The romantic critique of Fichte did not ease their problems but only exacerbated them. For now they faced anew the very dilemma that had once troubled Fichte. On the one hand, it was necessary for them to overcome the dualism between the subjective and objective, the ideal and the real, for there had to be some correspondence and interaction between them to explain the possibility of knowledge. On the other hand, however, it was also necessary for them to preserve that dualism, because this alone would explain the reality of an external world. The problem was then how to have both some identity and some non-identity of the subjective and objective, the ideal and the real. As Hegel later formulated the point, the task of philosophy was to establish the identity of identity and non-identity.

The romantic solution to this problem came with *Naturphilosophie*, their philosophy of nature, which had been developed by Schelling, Novalis, Schlegel, and Hegel. The central strategy behind the philosophy of nature was to surmount the persistent dualisms of modern philosophy by reexamining the nature of matter itself. According to the romantics, the source of these dualisms arose from the Cartesian conception of matter as inert extension. Since neither mind nor life are conceivable in spatial or mathematical terms, this made it impossible to explain them according to the laws of nature. As long as this concept of matter prevailed, there could be only those two unsatisfactory options in the philosophy of mind: dualism or materialism.

The only escape from these extremes, the romantics believed, lay in going back to a competing concept of matter, namely, the concept of matter as living force, *vis viva*. It was this concept that Leibniz had once cited against Cartesianism, and that the *Naturphilosophen* now intended to revive. They saw Leibniz not as the founder of the pre-established harmony, which made the dualism between the mental and physical a perpetual mystery, but as the father of a vitalist physics, whose conception of living matter surmounted that dualism. The great strength of the Leibnizian concept of matter, in their view, is that it overcomes the dualism between the subjective and objective while still accounting for the differences between them. Rather than heterogeneous substances, they now become different degrees of organization and development of a single living force. There is indeed a difference in *degree* or *form* between them; but there is not a difference in kind or substance. There is a single force of which the subjective and objective, the ideal and the real, are simply different expressions, embodiments and manifestations. The mind and body now become completely interdependent. The mind is the highest degree of organization and development of the living forces of the body, while the body is the lowest degree of organization and development of the living forces of the mind. The subjective and ideal is the *internalization* of living force, while the objective and the real is the *externalization* of living force. As Schelling put it in some poetic lines: "[M]ind is invisible nature, while nature is visible mind."[18]

It was this concept of matter that lay behind the organic conception of nature, the central and characteristic concept of romantic *Naturphilosophie*. The romantics saw all of nature in terms of a living organism, which they understood in a Kantian sense. In paragraph 65 of the *Critique of Judgment* Kant had defined an organism or natural purpose by two central characteristics: the idea of the whole precedes its parts; and the parts are mutually the cause and effect of one another. This second characteristic did not just mean reciprocal causality, which is also characteristic of inorganic matter, but that an organism is self-generating and self-organizing, having the cause of its motion within itself. While the romantics endorse the Kantian conception of an organism, they also differ fundamentally from Kant in insisting upon dropping the regulative constraints he had placed upon it. They insisted that nature *is* an organism, and not only that we must proceed in our inquiries *as if* it were one. It was only by giving this concept constitutive status, the romantics believed, that they could overcome the outstanding Kantian dualisms, which had made the solution of Kant's own problem impossible.

This organic conception of nature is the basis of the romantic doctrine of absolute idealism. This doctrine consists in three fundamental propositions. First, there is a single universal substance in nature, which is the absolute. Second, this absolute consists in living force, so that it is neither subjective nor objective, but the unity of them both. Third, through its organic structure all of nature conforms to a purpose, plan, or design, which is not created by God but inherent in matter itself. The first proposition makes absolute idealism a form of monism; the second makes it a form of vitalism; and the third makes it a species of idealism. In sum, absolute idealism is a form of vitalistic monism or monistic vitalism.

It should be clear that absolute idealism is not an idealism in the same sense as Kant's transcendental idealism or Fichte's ethical idealism. Unlike Kant's and Fichte's idealism, absolute idealism does not understand the ideal in terms of the realm of subjectivity or consciousness. Rather, the ideal is conceived as the underlying purposiveness and rationality of nature itself. It is the archetype, form, or structure of nature, which both the mental and the physical, the subjective and objective, instantiate or exemplify in equal degrees.

It is important to see that absolute idealism involves a profound break with what it called the "*subjective idealism*" of Kant and Fichte. It would be a serious mistake, as is often done, to interpret the "absolute" of absolute idealism in terms of some universal and impersonal ego or subject. The romantics decisively reject such a subjectivist interpretation of their absolute, which they insist transcends all finite determinations, such as the subjective and objective. Hence they persistently define the absolute in terms of *the unity* or *indifference* of the subjective and objective. The break of absolute idealism with subjective idealism becomes very apparent as soon as one recognizes that it permits a much greater degree of realism and naturalism – a realism and naturalism that Kant and Fichte would have rejected as "dogmatism" or "transcendental realism." Absolute idealism allows a greater realism because it permits the existence of nature independent of any consciousness whatsoever, even the activities of the transcendental ego; and it permits a greater naturalism because it claims that all self-consciousness, even that of the transcendental subject, derives from the laws of nature.

The romantics understood absolute idealism as a synthesis of idealism and realism, as the union of Fichte and Spinoza. Their doctrine involves a form of Spinozism because of its greater realism and naturalism; but it also contains an element of Kant's and Fichte's idealism because it continues to understand the subjective or ideal as the purpose of nature itself. They maintain that the self-consciousness of the ego is the highest organization and development of all the organic powers of nature. The mistake of Kant and Fichte came in failing to see that self-consciousness is only the purpose of nature and not its cause, that it is first in order of explanation but not first in order of being.

While absolute idealism involved a fundamental break with Kant and Fichte, it could also claim to be the final realization of their goals. This seemed to be the final victory over skeptical idealism and materialism. Absolute idealism was in no danger of lapsing into skeptical idealism because it allowed for a much greater degree of realism and naturalism than subjective idealism. Nature existed completely independently of all consciousness, which was the product of its organic development. Absolute idealism also provided for a naturalism without materialism because, although it understood everything as a mode of a single universal substance, it was the product not of mechanism but a living force. Hence the romantics never broke the Enlightenment's ideal of a complete explanation of all of nature. They did, however, transform the paradigm of explanation: to understand an event is not to explain it as the result of prior events in time but to see it as a necessary part of a whole. Their paradigm is thus holistic rather than mechanistic.

Absolute idealism would thus claim to be the apotheosis of the idealist tradition, the final achievement of its goals, a criticism without skepticism, a naturalism without materialism. But, naturally, like any philosophy it too had its weaknesses. For how did it know that nature exists independent of our consciousness? And how could it establish that nature is an organism except by analogy with our own human ends? It was not surprising that the neo-Kantians would accuse absolute idealism of metaphysical speculation and a relapse into dogmatism. It was one of the deeper ironies of the history of philosophy that the neo-Kantians attacked absolute idealism and *Naturphilosophie* in the name of Kant and a return to the Enlightenment.

NOTES

1 For a translation of some of the contributions to the debate, see James Schmidt, ed., *What is Enlightenment? Eighteenth Century Answers and Twentieth Century Questions* (Berkeley: University of California Press, 1996), 47–85.

2 On the influence of the free-thinkers in Germany, see Hermann Hettner, *Geschichte der deutschen Literatur im achtzehnten Jahrhundert* (Berlin: Aufbau Verlag, 1979), I, 350–1.

3 On the early German materialists, see Gottfried Stiehler, ed., *Beiträge zur Geschichte des vormarxistischen Materialismus* (Berlin: Dietz Verlag, 1961), which contains useful accounts of their lives and philosophies. Also see Gottfried Stiehler, ed., *Materialisten der Leibniz-Zeit* (Berlin: Deutscher Verlag, 1966), which contains selections from their writings.

4 On the problem of idealism or egoism in German philosophy before Kant, see Henry Bracken, *The Early Reception of Berkeley's Immaterialism: 1710–1733* (The Hague: Nijhoff, 1959), 1–39, 83–4; Manfred Kuehn, "Kant and the Refutations of Idealism in the Eighteenth Century," in Donald Mell, Theodore Braum, and Lucia Palmer, eds., *Man, God, and Nature in the Enlightenment* (East Lansing, MI: Colleagues Press, 1988), 25–35; and Dietmar Heidemann, *Kant und das Problem der metaphysischen Idealismus* (Berlin: de Gruyter, 1998) (*Kant-Studien Ergänzungsheft* 131), 15–46.

5 On the influence of the Scottish philosophers of common sense in Germany, see Manfred Kuehn, *Scottish Common Sense in Germany, 1768–1800* (Kingston and Montreal: McGill-Queen's University Press, 1987).

6 See Reinhard Koselleck, *Kritik und Krise* (Frankfurt: Suhrkamp, 1973), 90.

7 On Kant's early opposition to idealism, see *Nova dilucidatio*, 1:411–12; the Inaugural Dissertation §11–12, 2:397–8; *Metaphysik L1*, 28:207; and *Metaphysik Herder*, 28:43. On his opposition to materialism, see *Dreams of a Spirit Seer*, 2:327, and again *Nova dilucidatio*, 1:411–12. References to Kant's works are cited by volume and page number of *Kant's gesammelte Schriften*, edited by the Royal Prussian (later German) Academy of Sciences (Berlin: Georg Reimer, later Walter de Gruyter & Co., 1900–).

8 See *Critique of Pure Reason*, A369, 490–1.

9 See Kant's argument in the *Critique* of the Fourth Paralogism, A369, 372.

10 See Kant's argument in the first edition of the Transcendental Aesthetic, A26, 37, 39.

11 See *Prolegomena*, 4:374–5.

12 For a good introductory account of the edicts and the controversies leading up to them, see Klaus Epstein, *The Genesis of German Conservatism* (Princeton: Princeton University Press, 1966), 112–75.

13 See Solomon Maimon, *Versuch über die Transcendentalphilosophie*, in *Gesammelte Werke*, ed. V. Verra (Hildesheim: Olms, 1965), II, 62–5, 182–3, 362–3.

14 All references in the text are to *Johann Gottlieb Fichtes sämmtliche Werke*, ed. I. H. Fichte (Berlin: Veit & Co., 1845–6).

15 The influence of these skeptics upon Fichte is apparent from his early fragment "Wer Hume, Aenesidemus und Maimon noch nicht verstanden hat . . .," in *J. G. Fichte-Gesamtausgabe der Bayerischen Akademie der Wissenschaften*, ed. Reinhard Lauth, Hans Gliwitzky, and Hans Jacob (Stuttgart-Bad Cannstatt: Frommann-Holzboog, 1962ff.), II/3, 389–90 (henceforth abbreviated AA for Akademie Ausgabe). Also see his November 1793 letter to L. W. Wloemer, AA III/2, 14; his mid-December 1793 letter to Heinrich Stephani, AA III/2, 28; and his 15 January 1794 letter to F.V. Reinhard, III/2, 39.

16 These notebooks consist in Novalis, "Fichte-Studien," in *Novalis Schriften*, ed. Richard Samuel, Hans Joachim Mähl, and Gerhard Schulz (Stuttgart: Kohlhammer, 1960–88), II, 104–296; Schlegel's *Philosophische Lehrjahre*, in *Kritische Friedrich Schlegel Ausgabe*, ed. Ernst Behler, Jean Jacques Anstett, and Hans Eichner (Munich and Paderborn: Schöningh, 1958f.), XVIII, 3–15, 31–9, 505–16, 517–21; Hölderlin's important fragment "Über Urteil und Seyn," in *Hölderlin: Sämtliche Werke, Grosser Stuttgarter Ausgabe*, ed. Friedrich Beissner (Stuttgart: Cotta, 1946), IV/1, 216–17.

17 This term is not anachronistic, as is sometimes said. The first to use it appears to have been Friedrich Schlegel, who applies it frequently in his notebooks. See his *Philosophische Lehrjahre*, *Kritische Friedrich Schlegel Ausgabe* XVIII, 33, 65, 80, 85, 90, 282, 396. On Schelling's use of the term, see his *Fernere Darstellungen meines Systems der Philosophie*, in *Friedrich Wilhelm Joseph von Schellings sämmtliche Werke*, ed. K. F. A. Schelling (Stuttgart: Cotta, 1856–61), IV, 112; his "Über das Verhältniß der Naturphilosophie zur Philosophie überhaupt," V, 112; "Zusatz zugleich Einleitung" to the *Ideen zur einer Philosophie der Natur*, II, 67, 68; and *Bruno*, IV, 257, 322. On Hegel's use of the term, see *Enzyklopädie der philosophischen Wissenschaften*, §160 Zusatz, 32 Zusatz, and §45 Zusatz.

18 See Schelling's introduction to his *Ideen zur einer Philosophie der Natur*, II, 56; *Ideas for a Philosophy of Nature*, trans. Errol Harris and Peter Heath (Cambridge: Cambridge University Press, 1988), 42.

2

PAUL GUYER

Absolute idealism and the rejection of Kantian dualism

I Hegel on the sources of Kantian dualism

Absolute idealism, the philosophical movement that culminated with the work of Hegel, defined itself by its attempt to transcend the various dualisms that pervaded the philosophy of Kant. In Hegel's only complete, even if highly schematic, exposition of his system, the *Encyclopedia of the Philosophical Sciences* (1817, further editions in Hegel's lifetime in 1827 and 1830), Hegel defined absolute idealism by contrast to what he called the "subjective idealism" of Kant, which he described thus:

> Objectivity of thought, in Kant's sense, is again to a certain sense subjective. Thoughts, according to Kant, although universal and necessary categories, are *only our* thoughts – separated by an impassable gulf from the thing, as it exists apart from our knowledge. But the true objectivity of thinking means that the thoughts, far from being merely ours, must at the same time be the real essence of the things, and of whatever is an object to us.[1]

Kant's idealism, in spite of Kant's own protests at the association of his philosophy with the idealism of Bishop Berkeley,[2] is a subjective idealism because even our most secure knowledge reflects the nature of the human subject rather than the essence of the objects of knowledge themselves. Hegel's absolute idealism, by contrast, holds that human thought reflects the nature of reality itself, not its own subjectivity, although since the deepest fact about the nature of reality is that it is a product of God's thought this absolutism is still, in Hegel's view, a form of idealism rather than any kind of absolute realism or materialism. Indeed, Hegel even goes so far as to claim that the fact that objects appear to human beings in a particular way, as phenomena, is a reflection of the essential nature of those objects and of their origin in a divine intelligence rather than in our own. Thus, Hegel does not simply reject Kant's dualisms, above all that between the form of human thought and the real nature of being, *ab initio*; rather, he thinks that the dualisms Kant identified are themselves manifestations of the real nature of being. He also thinks that these manifestations are ultimately transcended by this real nature, and that we can know them to be so transcended by means of our own capacity for absolute knowing. In Hegel's eyes, Kant was thus a Moses who brought philosophy to the border of the promised land but could not cross the Jordan into absolute knowing.

In addition to this distinction Hegel emphasizes that Kant's subjective idealism includes a contrast between sense and intellect. He maintains that "though the categories, such as unity, or cause and effect, are strictly the property of thought, it by no means follows that they must be ours merely and not also characteristics of the objects." In his view, Kant's mistake is to fail to see that the forms of thought must also be the nature of real being; and Kant fails to see this for the forms of intellectual thought as well as for the forms of sensible perception:

> Kant however confines them to the subject-mind, and his philosophy may be styled subjective idealism: for he holds that both the form and matter of knowledge are supplied by the Ego – or knowing subject – the form by our intellectual, the matter by our sentient ego.[3]

Here Kant's dualism between sense and intellect seems to be just one manifestation among several of his general tendency to dualism.

In one of his earliest statements of his emerging philosophical position, however, the 1802 essay on *Faith and Knowledge or the Reflective Philosophy of Subjectivity*, Hegel took a stronger position, and suggested that Kant's distinction between sense and intellect was not just one instance of a more general tendency to dualism but rather the fundamental dualism in which all of Kant's other dualisms were rooted. Here Hegel claimed that the various oppositions that are central to Kant's philosophy can all be traced back to the fundamental opposition between intuition and concept, the objects of sensibility and understanding respectively, but also implied that Kant was wrong to think that this opposition, any more than any of those founded upon it, is insuperable – the task of philosophy is not to attempt the impossible, that is, to show how insuperable oppositions can be superseded, but rather to show how the appearance of opposition itself arises from a fundamental or absolute unity.[4] Hegel praises Kant for having discovered the problem of the synthetic *a priori*, but faults him for having conceived of the solution to this problem as lying in a demonstration that two essentially different cognitive capacities can nevertheless work together. Instead, Hegel says, "This original synthetic unity [is] a unity that must not be conceived of as the product of opposites, but rather as a genuine necessary, absolute, original identity of opposites, and is a principle of productive imagination,"[5] while the productive imagination in turn "is a genuine speculative idea in the form of sensible intuiting as well as in the comprehension of intuition or experience,"[6] that is, not the source of a unity that can be imposed upon two essentially different faculties but rather a unity that is more fundamental than those two apparently diverse faculties while at the same time also somehow the source of the appearance of their difference. As he says a few pages later, the "imagination must not be understood as a middle term that is shoved in between an existing absolute subject and an absolute existing world, but must rather be understood as that which is first and original and out of which the subjective I as well as the objective world first separate themselves into a necessarily bipartite appearance and product."[7]

In *Faith and Knowledge*, Hegel develops a catalogue of distinctions that Kant holds to be insuperable because of their derivation from the fundamental insuperable distinction between intuition and concept. This list includes Kant's distinction between appearance and reality;[8] the distinction between understanding and theoretical reason, with Kant seeing the former as a source of substantive, informative judgments but the latter as only a capacity for the formal and basically empty organization of the judgments that are supplied by the former;[9] and even the distinction between theoretical and practical reason. Kant begins by taking its complete isolation from intuition as the source for the emptiness and formality of theoretical reason, but then, in Hegel's view, also uses the independence of reason from intuition as the explanation of the autonomy of practical reason. In fact, Hegel's general polemic against all of the Kantian distinctions based on Kant's supposedly erroneous conception of the insuperable difference between intuition and concept can be regarded as nothing less than the generalization of his attack upon the supposedly empty formalism of Kant's ethics, separately enunciated at the same time in his essay on *The Scientific Treatments of Natural Right, its Position in Practical Philosophy and its Relation to the Positive Juridical Sciences*.[10]

Almost two decades later, in the *Encyclopedia*, Hegel extends this line of criticism by arguing that Kant's rejection of all theoretical proofs of the existence of God is another product of his insistence upon the insuperable distinction between intuition and concept and the claim that knowledge can only arise from superimposing an external combination upon these two essentially different elements. Thus Hegel says that "the main force of Kant's criticism on this process" – attempting to prove the existence of God, that is – "attacks it for being a syllogizing, i.e., a transition," which Kant regards as "checked by the argument of Hume . . . according to which we have no right to think sensations, that is, to elicit universality and necessity from them." On the contrary, he holds, the validity of proofs for the existence of God can only be understood once we understand "[t]he rise of thought beyond the world of sense, its passage from the finite to the infinite, the leap into the supersensible which it takes when it snaps asunder the chain of sense . . . Say there must be no such passage, and you say there is to be no thinking."[11] Kant's insistence upon the radical distinction between intuition and concept is once again precisely what keeps him from entering into the promised land.

Hegel was entirely correct to think that the distinction between intuition and concept is indeed the foundation of Kant's philosophy, and the source of so many of the other distinctions that are characteristic of it. An introduction to the whole critical philosophy could thus be neatly structured on the basis of Hegel's insight that it is founded entirely on this fundamental distinction. I will not have space here to provide such an introduction in its entirety, and will confine myself to showing how Kant derived the distinction between appearance and reality from that between intuition and concept. However, I will also suggest, as Hegel does not, that Kant did not simply pull this most basic distinction out of thin air, or accept it uncritically from Hume, but slowly reached it by means of arguments that he thought could demonstrate its inescapability. Yet Kant also recognized that there are limits to these arguments, and himself recognized that at the deepest level the distinction between intuition and concept may be an inexplicable brute fact of the human condition. If that is so, then the issue between Kant and Hegel becomes one that is not likely to be decided by any single argument or its refutation, but only by considering which philosophy taken as a whole seems to give a more accurate picture of the sources and limits of human cognition as we experience them.

II Intuition and concept

In this section, I will consider Kant's arguments for the fundamental distinction between intuition and concept. Section III will treat Kant's direct argument from the distinction between intuition and concept to the distinction between appearance and reality, an argument to which Hegel so strongly objected. Here I will argue, which Hegel did not, that Kant's argument for his objectionable idealism could be rejected without rejecting the fundamental distinction between intuition and concept. In section IV, I shall consider but reject Hegel's view that Kant himself suggested how the distinction between intuition and concept could itself be superseded.

Kant defines an intuition as a singular representation that is in immediate relation to its object, while a concept is a general representation that can be related to many objects but is not in immediate relation to any, and for that reason can be related to an object only through an intuition. Kant's contrast between intuition and concept in his late logic handbook (the so-called *Jäsche Logic*) stresses only the contrast between singular and general, defining an intuition as "a *singular* representation (*representatio singularis*)" and a concept as "a universal (*representatio per notas communes*) or *reflected* representation (*representatio discursiva*)," that is, "a representation of what is common to several objects, hence a representation *insofar as it can be contained in various ones.*"[12] His initial definition of intuition in the *Critique of Pure Reason* stresses the immediacy of intuition: "In whatever way and through whatever means a cognition may relate to objects, that through which it relates immediately to them, and at which all thought as a means is directed as an end, is *intuition*" (*CPuR*, A 19/B33). Later in the *Critique*, Kant uses both contrasts to define intuitions and concepts: an intuition "is immediately related to the object and is singular"; a concept "is mediate, by means of a mark, and is common to several things" (*CPuR*, A320/B377). There has been considerable debate about whether Kant needs two criteria for his contrast, but for our present purposes we do not need to decide whether the two criteria for the distinction between intuition and concept are fundamentally distinct or not: it will suffice to observe that over the course of his various arguments for the necessity of this distinction, Kant sometimes appealed to the immediacy criterion to establish the necessity of intuitions for cognition and at other times appealed to the singularity criterion to establish that a representation is an intuition rather than a concept.

The first arguments that began to push Kant towards the distinction between intuition and concept – and thus to the fundamental rejection of the philosophy of Gottfried Wilhelm Leibniz and Christian Wolff in which he had been raised – may be thought of as bringing out the need in all cognition for an immediate relation to objects that cannot be satisfied by concepts alone. Among these arguments, the first that Kant developed was his critique of the ontological argument for the existence of God, which he expounded in his earliest philosophical work, the *New Elucidation of the First Principles of Metaphysical Cognition* of 1755, and which was to remain central to his major works. In its original form, the argument is simply that because a concept can be formed from any combination of predicates in the mind, as long as there is no logical or internal contradiction among those predicates, the construction of a concept cannot itself be the proof of the existence of any object outside the mind corresponding to such a concept:

> Of course, I know that appeal is made to the concept itself of God; and the claim is made that the existence of God is determined by that concept. It can, however, easily be seen that this happens ideally, not really. Form for yourself the concept of some being or other in which there is a totality of reality. It must be conceded that, given this concept, existence also has to be attributed to this being . . . But if all those realities are only conceived as united together, then the existence of that being is also only an existence in ideas. The view we are discussing ought, therefore, rather to be formulated as follows: in framing the concept of a certain Being, which we call God, we have determined that concept in such a fashion that existence is included in it. If, then, the concept which we have conceived in advance is true, then it is also true that God exists.[13]

Kant's point here is not about generality versus singularity: he is not claiming that because we can form the concept of God in our own minds it could apply to more than one God. He seems willing here to allow that we can perfectly well form a concept of a single being in which all perfections are united. His claim is quite simply that because we can voluntarily form such a concept in our own mind, the formation of the concept alone cannot prove the existence of its referent, and we have to appeal to something other than our formation of the concept to prove the reality of its existence. To be sure, in 1755 Kant had not yet formulated the distinction between intuition and concept, and he does not say that we must always appeal to an intuition to prove the extramental reality of a concept considered as a mental representation. Instead, at this point he appeals to a principle that all possibilities require a ground, which is certainly not itself an intuition or derived from intuition. By the time of the *Critique of Pure Reason*, however, he had rejected that principle too as the basis for a revised ontological proof, and instead argued that the ontological argument is completely hopeless because "*Being* is obviously not a real predicate, i.e., a concept of something that could add to the concept of a thing" (*CPuR*, A598/B626). Instead, being is simply what is posited when I "posit the *object* in relation to my *concept*" (*CPuR*, A599/B627). The existence of an object of a concept must be *given* by something other than the concept itself: "Thus whatever and how much our concept of an object may contain, we have to go out beyond it in order to provide it with existence" (*CPuR*, A601/B629). And the only medium that Kant can find in which existence could be given is perception, pure perception in the case of the objects of mathematics and sense perception in the case of all other objects. This is why all cognition must ultimately relate immediately to an intuition.

During the 1760s, Kant developed several other arguments that persuaded him that something in addition to concepts is necessary to anchor our concepts to reality. These arguments have the form of showing that we recognize relationships that cannot be captured by purely logical relations of identity, compatibility or contradiction among the marks that can be combined to constitute a concept, but are instead immediately given by sense perception, thus proving a difference between perception and conceptualization that would eventually be canonized in the form of the contrast between intuition and concept. These arguments might be thought of as proceeding in the opposite direction from Kant's critique of the ontological argument: instead of starting from an obvious gap in what can be shown by the analysis of a concept and thus specifying a role for an immediate presentation of an object, which turns out to be unfulfilled in the case of the concept of God, they instead start out from an indisputable cognitive accomplishment that on analysis turns out to be inexplicable given merely conceptual resources. What I have in mind here are the argument for the contrast between logical and real relationships that Kant developed in his *Attempt to*

Introduce the Concept of Negative Magnitudes into Philosophy of 1763 and the argument that we can recognize features of the spatial structure and orientation of objects that cannot be contained in the concepts of those objects that he advanced in his 1768 essay *On the Ultimate Ground of the Differentiation of Regions in Space.* In the first essay, Kant argues that as far as logic is concerned, to attempt to combine opposed predicates in a concept or a proposition is simply to deprive the latter of any sense at all, and thus to say nothing, but that this is clearly not what happens when we say that a ship is acted upon by opposed forces or a mind by opposed desires. To say that a ship is acted upon by a westerly current of five knots and an easterly wind of five knots and is therefore making no headway is not to say nothing at all, as would be the case in the assertion of a logical contradiction, but is to explain informatively why the ship is not moving.[14] Kant still does not formulate the concept of intuition, and thus does not explicitly say that mathematical or real rather than logical opposition must be based on differences immediately given in intuition, like the differences between east and west. But he is surely moving in this direction when he concludes the essay by stating that in the end "all our cognitions of this relation" – real relations such as real repugnancy but also such as relations of cause and effect as opposed to merely logical ground and consequence – "reduce to simple, unanalysable concepts of real grounds, the relation of which to their consequences cannot be rendered distinct at all."[15] The point of this remark is that the basis for such relationships, relationships of real opposition leading to equilibrium or of causation leading to actual change, cannot be revealed by the logical analysis of the composition of complex concepts, but must be immediately given and reflected in concepts that cannot themselves be analyzed by logical means. It would not be much of a further step for Kant to argue that such concepts can only reflect what is immediately given in some medium other than concepts, which is what he would come to call intuition.

Kant took at least half of the final step toward this position in the 1768 essay on the *Differentiation of Regions in Space.* Here he argued that there are a variety of distinctions of direction or orientation in space that cannot be captured by any "complete description" of the "proportion and position" of the parts of an object in relation to each other, and thus must be given in some way other than such a description.[16] He argued that whether the thread of a screw is left- or right-handed, or whether a glove would fit a left or a right hand, is not something that can be discerned from a complete description of the size and shape of the parts of such things, but can only be immediately perceived by perceiving their positions in space and their relations to the left and right sides of our own bodies. Again, Kant does not yet quite say that the fundamental perception of our own body on which other determinations of direction or orientation are based is an intuition, thus that it is only intuition that gives concepts an immediate relation to objects. Rather, he says that these arguments show that "[t]he ground of the complete determination of a corporeal form does not depend simply on the relation and position of its parts to each other; it also depends on the reference of that physical form to universal absolute space, as it is conceived by the geometers."[17] It will be a further step, finally taken only in the inaugural dissertation *On the Form and Principles of the Sensible and Intelligible Worlds* of two years later, to argue that the "universal absolute space" of the geometers is itself the immediate object of an intuition, thus that the concept of such a space, to which Kant here refers without further explanation,[18] can only be justified and used on the basis of an intuition of it. But he clearly intended to establish by the present arguments that our most ordinary and secure cognition of objects – for who can doubt that we know the difference between right and left, thus between a right- and left-handed glove or screw? – depends on something we are directly given in some way other than by the analysis of complex concepts of the parts and relative positions of such objects. This is surely meant to establish that we have a fundamental source of cognition of objects other than the analysis of concepts, and indeed that this other source of cognition is more direct or immediate than the analysis of concepts.

Beginning with the inaugural dissertation and continuing up to and including the *Critique of Pure Reason*, Kant added to these arguments for the necessity of a kind of immediacy in cognition that cannot be provided by concepts further arguments for the singularity of this alternative source of cognition, which he would now finally come to call intuition. Two years after the essay on the *Differentiation of Regions of Space*, Kant's inaugural dissertation, given on the occasion of his appointment to the chair in metaphysics at Königsberg, formally introduced the distinction between intuition and concept, and in so doing transformed the previous article's single argument for the geometers' concept of absolute space into an elaborate theory of space and time as both pure forms of all intuition of ordinary particular objects and also themselves singular objects of pure intuitions. Kant's argument for the first of these points may be considered as an extension of the considerations in behalf of the immediacy of intuition already hinted at in his earlier works: the key claim is that the representations of space and time cannot be concepts abstracted from repeated experience of particular objects, because such objects, and presumably the experience of them, can only be individuated by separating them from each other through their location in different positions in space and/or time. Thus the representations of space and/or time are presupposed by all representations of particular objects, and in this sense can be said to be immediate relative to any such particular representations, *a fortiori* immediate relative to all further judgments about objects that will be based on these representations of them. Kant also makes the point even more generally by describing space and time as forms within which sensations of particular objects can be ordered and positioned, and then maintaining: "Since that within which the sensations can alone be ordered and placed in a certain form cannot itself be in turn sensation, the matter of all appearances is only given to us *a posteriori*, but its form must all lie ready for it in the mind *a priori*" (*CPuR*, A20/B34). As such a form in the mind, Kant supposes, the representations of space and time themselves must be more immediately accessible to us than any others; the doctrine of space and time as the pure forms of intuition is thus a doctrine of their immediacy as well.

Kant's second thesis is that the representations of space and time must be not merely pure forms of intuition but also pure intuitions because they represent space and time each as singular. The *Critique of Pure Reason* makes the point somewhat more elaborately, arguing first that particular spaces or times are not independent entities that can be combined into larger spaces or times, but are rather particular regions of a single, larger space or time that are carved out of the single all-embracing space or time by the introduction of boundaries or limits between them. He then takes the further step of arguing that this actually implies not only the singularity but also the infinitude of space and time, because we can only represent any determinate region of space or time as bounded by more space and time, and thus cannot represent any ultimate boundary to space or time themselves. Kant takes this argument to establish that our representations of space and time are intuitions rather than concepts: concepts may have an indefinite number of instances *under* them, but they do not represent their instances also as parts *within* them, let alone determine by themselves that they actually have an infinite number of instances.

As Kant makes clear in the inaugural dissertation, his two main lines of argument, that the representations of space and time are presupposed by all representations of particular objects and that regions of space and time are represented as parts of something single and all-embracing rather than merely as instances of general concepts, together show that the representations of space and time are intuitions rather than concepts by showing that the two requirements of immediacy and singularity have been fulfilled. "*The concept of space is thus a pure intuition*, for it is a singular concept, not one which has been compounded from sensations, although it is the fundamental form of all outer sensation."[19] What makes the "concept of space" not a concept at all, but a pure intuition – although of course we can form a concept of space on the basis of our pure intuition of it – is both that it is singular and that its singularity is presupposed by the representation of particular objects, which is what makes it immediate.

During the quarter-century from the *New Exposition* to the *Critique of Pure Reason*, then, Kant gradually developed an array of arguments that first showed in very general ways that we must have sources of knowledge other than concepts and the logical analysis of them, and then more particularly that space and time are distinctive representations that do not have the logic of ordinary general concepts, but have the form and function that Kant captured by calling them intuitions.

III From intuition and concept to appearance and reality

In this section, I will show why Kant thought that the distinction between intuition and concept gives rise to his pervasive contrast between appearance and reality, or between the character that the objects of our experience appear to us to have and how they and other objects that we cannot experience at all – such as God – may be in themselves. In the preface to the second edition of the *Critique of Pure Reason*, Kant suggests that the work will provide both a direct and an indirect proof of this distinction (see especially Bxix–xxi). Both forms of proof turn on the character of our representations of space and time as intuitions. In the Transcendental Aesthetic, Kant argues not only that our representations of space and time are pure intuitions rather than concepts, but also that space and time themselves are nothing but the pure forms of our own intuition. In the Transcendental Dialectic, Kant argues that there are conflicts between the limits of spatial and temporal representation and the demands of reason that will condemn reason to incoherence unless the spatial and temporal characteristics of objects are recognized as merely features of how they appear to us, leaving open at least the possibility that as long as reason refrains from interfering within the realm of sensible appearance itself, it can formulate indemonstrable but coherent conceptions of how objects such as God or our own wills are in themselves.

In the *Science of Logic*, Hegel directly engages Kant's "indirect" argument for transcendental idealism, presented in the section of the *Critique* entitled "The Antinomy of Pure Reason." But he never directly engages Kant's initial, direct argument for the distinction between appearance and reality, so a rejection of Kant's resolution of the antinomies alone would not justify him in his confidence that Kant's transcendental idealism can be superseded. I will focus on Kant's direct argument in this section. This direct argument itself divides into separate parts. The main distinction is between an argument that there is something inherently subjective about our basic forms of sensible representation, on the one hand, and a line of argument on the other that purports to show that there are difficulties in the supposition of the independent reality of space and time, and that spatiality and temporality can therefore be nothing more than the subjective forms of our representations.

The first line of argument is in fact clearly expounded only in the inaugural dissertation and not in the *Critique of Pure Reason*. Kant's argument in the earlier work is that "*[s]ensibility* is the *receptivity* of a subject in virtue of which it is possible for the subject's own representative state to be affected in a definite way by the presence of some object," and then that "whatever in cognition is sensitive is dependent upon the special character of the subject in so far as the subject is capable of this or that modification by the presence of objects";[20] when space and time are then shown to be universal and fundamental characteristics of the sensible representation of objects, it is inferred that they must also reflect the "special character of the subject," that is, of the human being as cognitive subject, rather than of objects themselves. This argument seems open to a glaring objection, however, namely that just insofar as sensibility is described as a kind of *receptivity*, that is, a form of *passivity*, it is not obvious why it should in any way *modify* the appearance of the objects that affect it rather than pass them on to consciousness unchanged.

Be that as it may, Kant's chief direct argument in the *Critique* for the claim that the fundamental forms of representation are features of appearance rather than of things as they are in themselves is founded on the claim that what have been shown to be the indispensable forms of representation, namely space and time, *cannot* be features of things as they are in themselves at all, and for that reason must *therefore* be nothing more than the indispensable but subjective forms of our representation (see *CPuR*, A26/B42 and A32–3/B49–50). This line of argument itself further divides into two, what we may call metaphysical and epistemological arguments. The metaphysical line of argument is meant to establish that space and time fit none of the ontological categories available for objects conceived to exist independently of our representations of them: space and time cannot be conceived of as substances, as properties of substances, or as relations among substances that exist independently of those relations (see *CPuR*, A23/B37–8). It would be incoherent to conceive of space and time as substances that contain other substances. Nor, Kant seems to suppose although he does not explicitly argue, would it make any sense to conceive of space and time as real properties of any particular substances, when they so obviously concern relations among substances. Yet, as such relations, they cannot be thought to be independent of our representation of them. Kant's reasons for this last claim seem to be partly metaphysical and even theological: he maintains that while space and time are obviously relational in nature, "through mere relations no thing in itself is ever cognized" (*CPuR*, B67), apparently precisely because a thing in itself is supposed to be what it is on its own rather than in virtue of its relation to anything else; and he claims that if space and time were relations of things in themselves, then "as conditions of all existence in general they would also have to be conditions of the existence of God" (B71) – that is, God would not only have to represent spatial and temporal relations among things as they are in themselves, but he would even have to possess spatial and temporal characteristics himself.

Neither of these arguments seems very compelling: the first is question-begging, for instead of defining things in themselves as things considered independently of their relations to *us* and then attempting to show that space and time are not just relations but relations to us, it simply defines things in themselves as things devoid of all relations and thereby simply defines away their spatiality and temporality; and the second argument makes a naked appeal to theology of the sort that Kant everywhere else disallows in theoretical philosophy.

Kant's main objection against the supposition that space and time are real relations among things in themselves is epistemological. In both the inaugural dissertation and the *Critique*, he objects that Leibnizians, who believe space and time to be a system of relations supervening on independently existing subjects, "cast geometry down from the summit of certainty, and thrust it back into the rank of those sciences of which the principles are empirical."[21] Or as he puts it in the *Critique*:

> If they . . . hold space and time to be relations of appearances (next to or successive to one another) that are abstracted from experience though confusedly represented in this abstraction, then they must dispute the validity or at least the apodictic certainty of *a priori* mathematical doctrines in regard to real things (e.g., in space), since this certainty does not occur *a posteriori*, and on this view the *a priori* concepts of space and time are only creatures of the imagination . . . (*CPuR*, A40/B57)

Just why *a priori* cognition of spatiality and temporality is incompatible with their reality independent of our representation of them is not immediately apparent. Often Kant seems simply to suppose that the fact that we can have a representation of an apparent property or relation of objects without having a representation of the objects themselves, for instance when we represent space or time devoid of any objects in them (see *CPuR*, A24/B38–9, A31/B46), is enough to prove that what we are representing cannot be any property or relations that the objects have independently of our representing them. But this does not seem obviously true – why couldn't we be created with innate ideas that we can be aware of without the presence of any external object but that also veridically represent the real character of external objects, as indeed Descartes supposed was the case with the idea of God? It is clear that Kant does not like the idea of a pre-established harmony between our *a priori* representations and reality (see, e.g., *CPuR*, B166–8), but the real basis for his objection comes out only once in the *Critique*: it is that even if a characteristic that we know to be true of our representation *a priori* were also to be a characteristic of objects independent of our representations, it could at best be a *contingent* characteristic of such objects, which would in turn undermine what Kant takes to be the universal and necessary validity of any *a priori* cognition, for he supposes that what is known *a priori* must be *necessarily* true of any object of which it is true at all. As Kant reveals this crucial presupposition in his discussion of *a priori* cognition in geometry:

> If there did not lie in you a faculty for intuiting *a priori*; if this subjective condition regarding form were not at the same time the universal *a priori* condition under which alone the object of this (outer) intuition is itself possible; if the object ([e.g.] the triangle) were something in itself without relation to your subject, then how could you say that what necessarily lies in your subjective conditions for constructing a triangle must also necessarily pertain to the triangle in itself? . . . If therefore space (and time as well) were not a mere form of your intuition that contains *a priori* conditions under which alone things could be outer objects for you, which are nothing in themselves without these subjective conditions, then you could make out absolutely nothing synthetic and *a priori* about outer objects.
>
> (*CPuR*, A48/B65–6)

It's as if by supposing that you could have an *a priori* representation of a property such as triangularity that could also be realized by triangular objects existing independently of your representations of them you would be supposing the existence of two triangles, one of which necessarily has the features you represent in it but the other of which has them only contingently, which would in turn undermine the original supposition that your knowledge of the nature of all triangles is always *a priori*.

This argument is not as obviously question-begging as Kant's more purely metaphysical objections to the supposition that space (or time) is a real relation among independently existing objects. Nevertheless, it depends upon a specific interpretation of the implications of *a priori* cognition that can certainly be controverted, although to my knowledge none of the German idealists ever did identify, let alone criticize, this specific objection.[22] At the same time, it must also be noted that weaknesses in the arguments by means of which Kant derived the distinction between appearances and things in themselves from his initial distinction between intuition and concept do not cast any doubt on that distinction itself: the flaws in Kant's arguments for transcendental idealism are not flaws in the arguments for distinguishing between intuitions and concepts, but problems in his interpretation of the epistemological *consequences* of the specific supposition that we have *a priori* intuition or in independent metaphysical assumptions.

IV The transcendence of Kantian dualism?

I will conclude by considering two claims that Hegel made about Kant's fundamental distinction between intuition and concept: that it had no basis except an apparently not very secure basis in "experience and empirical psychology," but also that Kant himself pointed to the way to supersede this distinction by means of his own concept of "intellectual intuition." I will argue that Kant in a way acknowledged the first charge, although without thereby either meaning or having to undermine his own arguments for the primacy of this distinction, but that he would by no means have accepted Hegel's second suggestion, for he never intended to use the concept of intellectual intuition to overcome the fundamental duality of human cognition, but only to drive it home.

Hegel claims that:

> Kant has no other ground than simply experience and empirical psychology for [holding] that the human cognitive faculty essentially consists in the way it appears, namely in that progress from the universal to the particular or back again from the particular to the universal; but insofar as he himself thinks an intuitive understanding and is led to it as an absolutely necessary idea, he himself establishes the opposite experience of the thinking of a non-discursive understanding and demonstrates that his cognitive faculty knows not only the separation of the possible and the real in it, but also reason and the in-itself.[23]

This passage makes both of the claims I want to examine: first, the charge that Kant has nothing but an empirical basis – a basis that Hegel clearly thinks is inadequate – for his distinction between intuition and concept; but second, that Kant himself shows the way to supersede this dichotomy by means of his concept of intellectual intuition or a "non-discursive understanding," that is, an understanding that would not be restricted to applying general and partial concepts to objects given to it from some other source, but that is instead capable of immediately presenting objects through representations that are concepts but yet are singular and fully rather than partially determinate.

In a well-known remark that was not included in the first edition of the *Critique of Pure Reason* but that was added to the "Transcendental Deduction" of the categories in the second, Kant seemed to anticipate and accept Hegel's first charge:

> But for the peculiarity of our understanding, that it is able to bring about the unity of apperception *a priori* only by means of the categories and only through precisely this kind and number of them, a further ground may be offered just as little as one can be offered for why we have precisely these and no other functions for judgment or for why space and time are the sole forms of our possible intuition.
>
> (*CPuR*, B145–6)

In its suggestion that we can trace the table of the categories back to a tabulation of the logical functions of judgment – the basic aspects of the structure of all judgments the specifications of which determine the logical form of any particular judgment – but that we cannot derive the latter from anything more basic, this is precisely the kind of passage which drew Hegel's ire, leading him to claim that Kant's deduction of the categories was just as arbitrary as the Aristotelian listing of categories which Kant himself rejected on grounds of arbitrariness (see *CPuR*, A80–1/B106–7). Thus Kant's similar resignation about the two forms of intuition would seem to suggest that he has no argument for the distinction between them and for the even more fundamental distinction between intuition and concept.

Yet Kant hardly gives a hint in this remark that he means it to retract all of the arguments that he had developed over the previous quarter of a century for the fundamental distinction between what is given and what is thought, what is intuition and what is concept. Instead, I would suggest that he only means to acknowledge that these arguments are not *completely specific* and are not *explanatory*. That is, all of Kant's arguments prior to the inaugural dissertation and the *Critique* as well as the arguments in the latter two works show *that* we must be immediately given certain information that cannot be derived from the analysis of concepts, and *that* our representations of space and time are immediate and singular in a way that none of our general concepts are; but they do not attempt to explain *why* we are so constituted as to need intuitions as well as concepts nor *why* space and time should be the particular forms of our intuitions. To attempt to explain *why* space and time are our forms of intuition would be beyond the limits of any form of argument that Kant can conceive, but that by no means undercuts the force of the arguments by which Kant has shown *that* we need intuitions as well as concepts and *that* space and time are the forms of our intuitions. Or at least Hegel's observation that there's something of brute fact about Kant's supposition that space and time are what play the role of intuition for us hardly shows that there's any flaw in Kant's battery of arguments for the necessity of the fundamental distinction between intuition and concept itself.

I turn now to Hegel's claim that Kant himself established the idea of a "non-discursive understanding" or "intellectual intuition" in order to demonstrate that the "cognitive faculty knows not only the separation of the possible and the real in it, but also reason and the in-itself." Whether Hegel was right to think that human reason can ever overcome the distinction between the real and the possible I will leave to others in this volume to argue, but he was certainly wrong to hold that Kant thought this distinction could be overcome. Kant introduced the idea of "intellectual intuition" in the *Critique of Pure Reason* in order to drive home the point that we possess a discursive understanding, that is, one that is confined to applying general concepts to particular intuitions given to it from elsewhere by sensibility, and he does not so much as hint at an abandonment of this contrast in the *Critique of the Power of Judgment* but rather develops it precisely by arguing that the fundamental distinction between intuition and concept also entails that by intellect alone we only know possibility, not actuality: the concepts of a discursive understanding, he argues, unlike those of an intuitive intellect, merely define possibilities that we can know to be realized only on the basis of the additional evidence of our intuitions.

Kant's distinction between our own discursive understanding and the concept of an intuitive intellect was anticipated in his famous letter to Marcus Herz of 21 February 1772, in which he announced the project that would ultimately become the *Critique of Pure Reason*. Here Kant distinguished between "an *intellectus archetypus* (an intellect whose intuition is itself the ground of things)" and "our understanding, [which] through its representations is neither the cause of the object (save in the case of moral ends), nor is the object the cause of our intellectual representations in the real sense."[24] It is precisely because we do not possess an *intellectus archetypus* that the puzzle Kant proposes to explain arises, namely, how can we be certain that concepts that arise in our own minds necessarily apply to objects that are *not* caused to exist by our own representations of them? or, in other words, why do the concepts that are products of our active intellect necessarily apply to the representations of the objects that we receive from our passive sensibility?

In the letter to Herz, to be sure, Kant used the term *"intellectus archetypus"* rather than his later terminology of intellectual intuition or intuitive understanding. But his very first uses of the latter language in the *Critique of Pure Reason* make it clear that he has in mind the same point that he had made to Herz. In the first edition of the *Critique*, Kant's first mention of the idea of an intuitive intellect comes in the chapter on the distinction between phenomena and noumena, when he maintains that the concept of a noumenon is not the concept of a "special *intelligible object* for our understanding," but only "a concept setting limits to sensibility": "an understanding to which" the positive concept of a noumenon would belong "is itself a problem, namely, that of cognizing its object not discursively through categories but intuitively in a non-sensible intuition, the possibility of which we cannot in the least represent" (*CPuR*, A256/B311–12). This statement needs to be unpacked, because by Kant's own lights if we can even form the *concept* of an intuitive rather than discursive understanding we must be able to conceive of its *logical* possibility, which is simply the freedom of a concept from internal contradiction; but his point is clear enough, namely that we have no basis for an assertion of the *real* possibility of such an understanding, for real possibility requires some connection of a concept to the possibility of evidence for its existence in intuition as well as freedom from self-contradiction (see *CPuR*, B265, A220–1/B267–8) – but the distinct functions of understanding and sensibility are all that we can find evidence for in our own experience and the conditions of its possibility.

In the second edition of the *Critique*, Kant introduces the contrast between discursive and intuitive understanding into his argument earlier, namely in his revised version of the transcendental deduction of the categories. Commenting upon the first part of his new exposition, he says:

> In the above proof, however, I still could not abstract from one point, namely, from the fact that the manifold for intuition must already be *given* prior to the synthesis of understanding and independently from it . . . For if I wanted to think of an understanding that itself intuited (as, say, a divine understanding, which would not represent given objects, but through whose representation the objects would themselves at the same time be given, or produced), then the categories would have no significance at all with regard to such a cognition. (*CPuR*, B145)

Kant's point is that the use of the categories for cognition of objects is necessary precisely because we need to organize intuitions of objects that are given to us by sensibility in order to make judgments about those objects. Thus, without the distinction between intuitions and concepts we would no more know why we need to conceive of objects by means of categories that make them fit subjects of judgment than we would know why we must represent those objects as existing in determinate positions in space and/or time (see B145–6).

Kant's distinction between discursive and intuitive understanding thus reflects his most fundamental distinction between intuition and concept. There is no hint that Kant means to surrender or supersede either of these distinctions in the *Critique of the Power of Judgment*. On the contrary, Kant reintroduces the concept of an intuitive understanding only in the course of developing the further argument that because necessary connections for us are always expressed by concepts (here he omits the synthetic *a priori* cognition of mathematical necessities, which are based in intuition rather than understanding), but concepts define only possibilities and we must always appeal to intuition to establish the actuality of the possible objects defined by our concepts, there must always remain an element of contingency in our cognition of the actual – that is, the empirical intuition of objects always presents us particular determinations of those objects not foreseen in our general concepts of them. Here is Kant's initial statement of this argument:

> It is absolutely necessary for the human understanding to distinguish between the possibility and the actuality of things. The reason for this lies in the subject and the nature of its cognitive faculties. For if two entirely heterogeneous elements were not required for the exercise of these faculties, understanding for concepts and sensible intuition for objects corresponding to them, then there would be no such distinction (between the possible and the actual). That is, if our understanding were intuitive, it would have no objects except what is actual. Concepts (which pertain merely to the possibility of an object) and sensible intuition (which merely gives us something, without thereby allowing us to cognize it as an object) would both disappear. Now, however, all of our distinction between the merely possible and the

actual rests on the fact that the former signifies only the position of the representation of a thing with respect to our concept and, in general, our faculty for thinking, while the latter signifies the positing of the thing in itself (apart from this concept).[25]

Kant revisits this distinction in the *Critique of the Power of Judgment* because he supposes that recognition of the necessary truth of all scientific generalizations, no matter how fine-grained and particular, is a natural objective of human reason, indeed an objective defined for us by the very concept of a law of nature itself;[26] but he also wants to make it clear that because of the very nature of our cognitive faculties such an objective is ultimately unobtainable for us, no matter how much scientific progress we make, although the very idea of such a goal can stimulate us to make progress toward it, and the idea of the kind of necessity that could be recognized by an intuitive intellect – "even if not ours"[27] – is therefore a useful regulative ideal, but not a constitutive idea of theoretical reason. By revisiting the concept of an intuitive intellect in the context of his most sustained treatment of regulative ideals, Kant means to make it as clear as he can that such an idea can never be an object of human knowledge, but only a guide for human conduct, though in this case the conduct of inquiry itself.

The idealists who followed Kant vigorously objected to every aspect of his dualistic conception of human nature. Hegel was profoundly right to suggest that virtually all of Kant's dualisms could be traced back to his fundamental distinction between intuition and concept. But he was certainly wrong if he thought that this distinction was an inherited or unthinking prejudice on Kant's part. Rather, the distinction was a product of everything in the quarter-century of philosophical work that led to the *Critique of Pure Reason* as well as the foundation for the two further decades of philosophical work that followed it, and was deeply entrenched in a large body of philosophical argument. Whether this distinction could really be rejected or superseded by equally well-founded arguments must thus be the fundamental question for a serious evaluation of the theoretical pretensions of absolute idealism.

NOTES

1 *The Logic of Hegel*, from *The Encyclopedia of the Philosophical Sciences*, trans. William Wallace, 2nd edn. (Oxford: Oxford University Press, 1892) (henceforth *Logic*), §41, p. 86.

2 See Immanuel Kant, *Prolegomena to any Future Metaphysics that shall come forth as Scientific* (1783), Appendix, 4:374–5. References to Kant's works are cited by volume and page number of *Kant's gesammelte Schriften*, edited by the Royal Prussian (later German) Academy of Sciences (Berlin: Georg Reimer, later Walter de Gruyter & Co.,

1900–). Translations used are cited on the first occasion of their use. The one excep-
tion to this method of citation will be the *Critique of Pure Reason*, where references
will be cited, parenthetically, by the pagination of Kant's own first ("A") and second
("B") edition rather than by volume and page number of the Academy edition.
Translations are from Immanuel Kant, *Critique of Pure Reason*, ed. and trans. Paul
Guyer and Allen W. Wood (Cambridge: Cambridge University Press, 1998).

3 *Logic*, §42; Wallace, p. 90.

4 Hegel, *Glauben und Wissen oder die Reflexionsphilosophie der Subjektivität in der
Vollständigkeit ihrer Formen als Kantische, Jacobische und Fichtesche Philosophie*, in
G. W. F. Hegel, *Werke in zwanzig Bänden*, Band II: *Jenaer Schriften 1801–1807*, ed.
Eva Moldenhauer and Karl Markus Michel (Frankfurt am Main: Suhrkamp, 1970),
287–433, at 302–3; G. W. F. Hegel, *Faith and Knowledge*, tr. Walter Cerf and H. S.
Harris (Albany: State University of New York Press, 1977), 67–8.

5 Hegel, *Jenaer Schriften*, II, 305; Cerf and Harris, 70.

6 Hegel, *Jenaer Schriften*, II, 306; Cerf and Harris, 71.

7 Hegel, *Jenaer Schriften*, II, 308; Cerf and Harris, 73.

8 Hegel, *Jenaer Schriften*, II, 312; Cerf and Harris, 76.

9 Hegel, *Jenaer Schriften*, II, 316; Cerf and Harris, 80.

10 "Über die wissenschaftlichen Behandlungsarten des Naturrechts, seine Stelle in der
praktischen Philosophie und sein Verhältnis zu den positiven Rechtswissenschaften,"
Kritisches Journal der Philosophie, vol. II, parts 2–3 (1802–3), in *Jenaer Schriften*, II,
434–530; G. W. F. Hegel, *Natural Law*, trans. T. M. Knox (Philadelphia: University of
Pennsylvania Press, 1975).

11 *Logic*, §50; Wallace, 102–3.

12 *Immanuel Kant's Logic: A Manual for Lectures*, ed. Benjamin Gottlob Jäsche, §1 and
note 1; in *Immanuel Kant: Lectures on Logic*, ed. and trans. J. Michael Young
(Cambridge: Cambridge University Press, 1992), 589.

13 *New Elucidation of the First Principles of Metaphysical Cognition*, Proposition VI,
1:394. Translation from Immanuel Kant, *Theoretical Philosophy, 1755–1770*, ed. and
trans. David Walford (Cambridge: Cambridge University Press, 1992), 15.

14 See *Negative Magnitudes*, 2:176; *Theoretical Philosophy, 1755–1770*, 216.

15 *Negative Magnitudes*, 2:204; *Theoretical Philosophy, 1755–1770*, 241.

16 *On the Ultimate Ground of the Differentiation of Regions in Space*, 2:381;
Theoretical Philosophy, 1755–1770, 370.

17 *Differentiation of Regions in Space*, 2:381; *Theoretical Philosophy, 1755–1770*, 369.

18 See 2:383; *Theoretical Philosophy, 1755–1770*, 371.

19 *Form and Principles*, §15.C, 2:402; *Theoretical Philosophy, 1755–1770*, 396.

20 *Form and Principles*, §§3–4, 2:392; *Theoretical Philosophy, 1755–1770*, 384.

21 *Form and Principles*, §15.D, 2:404; *Theoretical Philosophy, 1755–1770*, 397.

22 For a discussion of Jacobi's critique of Kant's conception of the thing in itself, see
Frederick Beiser, *The Fate of Reason: German Philosophy from Kant to Fichte*
(Cambridge, MA: Harvard University Press, 1987), 122–5. Cf. ch. 5 below.

23 *Glauben und Wissen*, 325–6; *Faith and Knowledge*, Cerf and Harris, 89.

24 Letter to Marcus Herz of 21 February 1772, 10:130; translation from Immanuel Kant,
Correspondence, trans. and ed. Arnulf Zweig (Cambridge: Cambridge University
Press, 1999), 133.

25 *Critique of the Power of Judgment*, §76, 5:401–2; translation from Immanuel Kant,

Critique of the Power of Judgment, ed. Paul Guyer, trans. Paul Guyer and Eric Matthews (Cambridge: Cambridge University Press, 2000).

26 See *Critique of the Power of Judgment*, published Introduction, section IV, 5:179–80, and section V, 5:184–5.

27 *Critique of the Power of Judgment*, Introduction, section IV, 5:180.

3

ALLEN W. WOOD

Kant's practical philosophy

Kant's mature writings about morality and right fall into four different categories. (1) There are the foundational writings, which include *Groundwork of the Metaphysics of Morals* (1785) and the Analytic of the *Critique of Practical Reason* (1788). (2) There are the writings that attempt to ground a morally motivated answer to metaphysical or religious questions. Kant deals with this concern toward the end of all three Critiques: in The Canon of Pure Reason, The Dialectic of Practical Reason and the Methodology of Teleological Judgment. (3) There are the writings in which Kant applies ethical principles. The central work here is the final product of Kant's ethical thought, the *Metaphysics of Morals* (1797–8), but this category also includes other works on politics and religion of varying lengths, including *On the Common Saying: That May Be Correct in Theory but Will Not Work in Practice* (1793), *Religion Within the Boundaries of Mere Reason* (1794), and *Perpetual Peace* (1795), as well as a number of short occasional pieces, such as *Answer to the Question: What Is Enlightenment?* (1784), *What Does It Mean To Orient Oneself in Thinking?* (1786), *The End of All Things* (1794), *On A Presumed Right to Lie from Philanthropy* (1797), and *Conflict of the Faculties* (1798), as well as part of the Methodology of the *Critique of Practical Reason* and part of the Methodology of the *Critique of Pure Reason* (1781) ("The Discipline of Pure Reason in its Polemical Use"). (4) There are writings that deal specifically with the human nature to which moral principles are to be applied and with the methods of studying human nature. These include *Idea Toward A Universal History With a Cosmopolitan Aim* (1784), *Conjectural Beginning of Human History* (1786), *Anthropology from a Pragmatic Standpoint* (1798), and a considerable portion of the contents of the *Critique of Judgment* (1790).

Kant's direct and acknowledged influence, from the German idealists down to the present day, rests almost exclusively on (1). Where the other three categories of writings are considered at all, they are interpreted (if necessary, with some violence) to bring them into line with the impressions gained from reading (1). The result is to give chief emphasis to Kant's most formalistic statements of the moral principle, and to treat the opposition of the motive of duty or reason to that of feeling or inclination as a consequence of Kant's ethical "formalism." For the German idealists, Fichte, Schelling, and Hegel, two corollaries of reading Kant in this way are that the Kantian principle is regarded as "empty" of content, and the opposition between duty and inclination is treated as a pernicious "dualism," which is to be bridged by going beyond Kant to a more unified picture of our moral nature.

The great German idealists were also significantly influenced by (2), which they bring under the general heading of "the primacy of the practical." Fichte sometimes presents his entire system as if it were grounded on a kind of "moral faith" in freedom, leading to what Hegel was to call an entire "moral *Weltanschauung*." In so doing, however, he blurs or ignores Kant's fenceposts between "theoretical" and "practical" philosophy, as well as between "constitutive" and "regulative" principles. The same tendency is even more pronounced in Schelling and Hegel, for whom speculative philosophy is an attempt to overcome Kantian "dualisms" and "antinomies" by blending all standpoints, principles, and modes of cognition into a seamless whole.

It is not my purpose here to decide whether Kant's followers were right in making these revisions in what they saw as the Kantian project. I will be concerned instead to point out how they, as well as many others who think themselves much farther from German Idealism than they are even from Kant, have misconceived Kant's theory itself, as well as to highlight the parts of Kant's practical philosophy whose influence on the German idealists has not been sufficiently appreciated. For this reason, I will begin by discussing (4) (Kant's philosophy of human nature and history), moving only later to (1) and (2), and saying just a little about (3) at the very end.[1]

Practical anthropology and the philosophy of history

In the *Groundwork of the Metaphysics of Morals*, Kant divides ethics into two parts: the *metaphysics of morals*, consisting in moral principles valid a priori for every rational being, and *practical anthropology*, an empirical study of the human nature to which the principles are to be applied (G 4:388). It is too seldom appreciated that Kant there treats practical anthropology as a necessary part of ethics, without which it would not be possible to specify determinate duties. Perhaps this is because Kant never wrote a work specifically on practical anthropology, despite the fact that his lectures on anthropology, begun in 1772 and continuing to the end of his teaching career, were the most popular and most frequently offered lecture course he gave. Kant's various remarks about the present state of our sciences of human nature show him to believe both that, despite the importance of this study, there are severe limitations on our capacity to treat it scientifically, and also that the present state of the study of human nature is very poor even in relation to its limited possibilities. It is also less often appreciated than it should be that when he finally came to write a *Metaphysics of Morals* at the very end of his career, Kant recast the distinction between "metaphysics of morals" and "practical anthropology," integrating the empirical "principles of application" into "metaphysics of morals itself" and restricting "practical anthropology" to the study of the "subjective conditions in human nature that hinder people or help them in fulfilling the laws of a metaphysics of morals" (*MS* 6:217).[2]

The only approach to the study of human nature that Kant works out with confidence is to be found in his writings on the philosophy of history, chiefly in *Idea toward a Universal History with a Cosmopolitan Aim* (1784) and in the *Critique of Judgment* (1790), where Kant works out the theory of natural teleology which grounds his approach in the *Idea toward a Universal History*. Once we appreciate this point, we can see how Kant's philosophy of history is also operative in his *Anthropology from a Pragmatic Standpoint*, and is especially explicit in the concluding section on the "character of the species" (*VA* 7:321–33). In brief, Kant's thesis is that human history can be made theoretically intelligible to us only by finding in it a natural end, which is the full (hence temporally endless) development of the natural predispositions of the human species (*I* 8:18). This end does not belong to the conscious intentions of people, but is a natural end, posited by reflective judgment as a regulative idea for maximizing the intelligibility of the data to us (*I* 8:17; cf. *KU* §§75–9, 5:397–417). Since in a rational species, these predispositions do not belong to any individual specimen but only to the entire species as it develops through time, the ends which make human history intelligible must be collective ends of the whole species through time, which individuals serve unintentionally and of which they can become conscious only through the philosophical study of history (*I* 8:17–20).

There is no space here to expound this theory of history in detail, but even the above provides us with enough to make two points that controvert common misunderstandings of Kant and his relation to his idealist followers. First, Kant's conception of human nature is fundamentally historical. It is not only oversimplified but fundamentally erroneous to represent Kant as having a "timeless" or "ahistorical" conception of reason, and Hegel (for example) as correcting it by introducing a "historical" conception. Second, the thesis that human history is grounded on an unconscious collective purposiveness, which is quite rightly associated with German Idealism and more specifically with Hegel, was already fully present in the philosophy of Kant (though for him it was not to be regarded as a dogmatic principle of speculative metaphysics, but a regulative principle of judgment, adopted because it is a necessary heuristic device for making the empirical facts of history intelligible to us).

A third point, relating to the way the German idealists (and most of Kant's readers since) have understood the opposition of duty and inclination in Kantian moral psychology, becomes clear when we look at Kant's execution of his theoretical project in the *Idea Toward a Universal History*. In seeking for natural purposiveness in the development of our rational predispositions in history, Kant posits "social antagonism" or "unsociable sociability" as the principal mechanism through which nature cultivates human nature and develops its collective capacities (*I* 8:20–2). In other words, human nature develops itself in history chiefly through a competitiveness, in which each individual seeks to "achieve a rank among his fellows, whom he cannot stand, but also cannot stand to leave alone" (*I* 8:21). The natural history of human reason is therefore a process driven by people's natural inclinations, behind which lurks a propensity to "self-conceit," a desire to be superior to other rational beings, hence to use them as mere means to one's ends and to exempt oneself from general rules one wants others to have to obey.

"The human being feels within himself a powerful counterweight to all commands of duty, which reason represents to him as so deserving of the highest respect – the counterweight of his needs and inclinations" (*G* 4:405). Kant's critics (beginning with Schiller, but including Hegel and countless others down to the present day) read such remarks as the one just quoted in a shallow and shortsighted manner when they attribute them to an artificial metaphysical "dualism," or to an unhealthy (stoical or ascetical) hostility to "nature" or "the senses" or "the body." As Kant makes quite clear, the counterweight to reason and duty is nothing so innocent. The opponent that respect for morality must overcome is always "self-conceit" (*KpV* 5:73), which arises not out of our animal nature but from our humanity or rationality (*R* 6:27). The enemy of morality within us is not "to be sought in our natural inclinations, which merely lack discipline and openly display themselves unconcealed to everyone's consciousness, but is rather as it were an invisible enemy, one who hides behind reason and hence is all the more dangerous" (*R* 6:57).

Our ironic predicament, in Kant's view, is that the natural device of social antagonism is required to develop our rational faculties, which (like all human faculties) belong more to the species than the individual, and show themselves chiefly through our capacity for self-criticism through free communication with others (*KrV* Axi–xii, A738–9/B766–7; *O* 8:144–6; *KU* 5:293–8). When reason develops, however, it recognizes a moral law whose fundamental value is the dignity (or absolute, incomparable worth) of rational nature in every rational being, hence the absolute equality of all rational beings (*G* 4:428–9, 435; *MA* 8:114; *MS* 6:314, 435–7, 462–6). Reason must therefore turn against the very propensity in our nature that made it possible. Kant therefore thinks that the most adequate conception of our human nature that we can form is a historical one, centered on the task of converting ourselves from competitive and antagonistic beings into beings capable of uniting with one another on terms of mutual respect: "What is characteristic of the human species in comparison with the idea of possible rational beings on earth is that nature has put in them the seed of *discord*, and willed that from it their own reason should produce *concord*, or at least the constant approximation to it" (*VA* 7:322). Our destiny, then, is to be engaged in an endless struggle between "nature" and "culture," whose object is the moral perfection of the human character.

Kant is no more opposed than his critics to understanding this aim as that of cultivating our natural desires so as to bring them into harmony with the demands of reason. "Natural predispositions," he says, "since they were set up in a mere state of nature, suffer violation by progressing culture and also violate it, until perfected art once more becomes nature, which is the ultimate goal of the moral vocation of the human race" (*MA* 8:117–18). Kant's philosophy of history, however, gives him reason to think that this reconciliation will be an extremely long and difficult social process. It is not to be accomplished merely through a philosophical conversion – by the adoption of more "healthy" (that is, less critical and mistrustful) attitudes toward our natural propensities, or by "going beyond" the "artificial dualisms" of those who are sober enough to see an endless, painful historical task for what it is.

The fundamental principle of morality

Now it is time to turn to the part of Kant's practical philosophy that usually gets the most attention. Kant's aim in the *Groundwork* is to "seek out and establish the fundamental principle of morality" (*G* 4:392). In the First Section of the *Groundwork*, Kant attempts to derive a formulation of the principle from what he calls "common rational moral cognition," or the moral know-how he thinks every human being has just in being a rational moral agent. Kant's chief aim here is to distinguish the principle he derives from the kinds of principles that would be favored by moral sense theorists and by those who would base morality on the consequences of actions for human happiness. This attempt is not very success-ful, because Kant underestimates the extent to which the competing theoretical standpoints are capable of alternative interpretations of the issues and examples he discusses, yielding reactions to them which call into question the responses he regards as self-evident. Thus the opening pages of the *Groundwork*, especially its famous attempt to persuade us that actions have moral worth only when they are done from duty, has seldom won converts to Kant's theory and has more often simply distracted attention from what is really important in Kant's ethical theory. Kant is more successful when he makes a second, more philosophically motivated attempt to expound the moral principle in the Second Section.

Kant thinks that if correct moral judgments are to constitute a well-grounded and consistent whole, they must ultimately be derivable from a single fundamental principle. But in the Second Section of the *Groundwork*, Kant considers this one principle from three different standpoints, and formulates it in three distinct ways. In two of the three cases, he also presents a variant formulation that is supposed to bring that formulation "closer to intuition" and make it easier to apply. The system of formulas can be summarized as follows:

First formula:

FUL *The Formula of Universal Law*: "Act only in accordance with that maxim through which you can at the same time will that it become a universal law" (*G* 4:421; cf. 4:402);

with its variant,

FLN *The Formula of the Law of Nature*: "Act as if the maxim of your action were to become by your will a **universal law of nature**" (*G* 4:421; cf. 4:436).

Second formula:

FH *The Formula of Humanity as End in Itself*: "So act that you use humanity, whether in your own person or that of another, always at the same time as an end, never merely as a means" (*G* 4:429; cf. 4:436).

Third formula:

FA *The Formula of Autonomy*: ". . . the idea of the will of every rational being as a will giving universal law" (*G* 4:431; cf. 4:432) or "Choose only in such a way that the maxims of your choice are also included as universal law in the same volition" (*G* 4:439; cf. 4:432, 434, 438);

with its variant,

FRE *The Formula of the Realm of Ends*: "Act in accordance with the maxims of a universally legislative member of a merely possible realm of ends" (*G* 4:439; cf. 4:432, 437, 438).

FUL (and FLN) consider the principle of morality merely from the standpoint of its *form*, FH considers it from the standpoint of the *value* which rationally motivates our obedience to it, and FA (and FRE) consider it from the standpoint of the ground of its *authority*.

The Formula of Universal Law

In the first formula, Kant considers the principle from the first standpoint, that of its *form*. The earliest characterization of Kantian ethics adopted by his German idealist followers and critics is that Kantian ethics is "formalistic." The use of this epithet is due largely to the mistaken emphasis Kant's readers place on the first formulation of the moral principle at the expense of the other two formulations, whose aim is precisely to complement and hence remedy any such "formalism." From this first standpoint, however, the principle is what Kant calls a "categorical imperative." Kant's terminology here is derived from grammar, but that is misleading, because grammatical forms are not what he is interested in. An *imperative* is any principle through which an agent constrains itself to act on the basis of objective rational grounds. An imperative is *hypothetical* if the rational constraint is conditional on the agent's adoption of an optional end, and *categorical* if the constraint is not conditional in this way. Since some hold that all rationality is "only instrumental," it is controversial whether there are (or could be) any categorical imperatives. Kant's procedure in the *Groundwork* is to assume provisionally that there are, and to inquire, in the Second Section, what their principle would be. Then in the Third Section Kant attempts to argue that as rational beings we must in effect presuppose that there are such imperatives, which therefore in effect establishes the validity of the formulas derived provisionally in the Second Section.

Because FUL is supposed to be derived from the very idea of a categorical imperative, it is easy to fall into simply using the term "the Categorical Imperative" to refer to it. But this often leads to the unjustifiable privileging of FUL as the principle definitive of Kant's theory, and the consequent neglect of FH and FA. As a matter of fact, Kant regards his argument in the Second Section of the *Groundwork* as a developing exposition of the principle, which ought to lead us to think of FUL as the starting point of the process, thus the most abstract, most provisional and (in that sense) the least adequate of the three formulas. And this thought turns out to be right; for it is FH, not FUL, which is Kant's formula of choice for applying the moral principle in the *Metaphysics of Morals*, and it is FA, not FUL, which is used in his attempt to establish the principle in the Third Section of the *Groundwork* (and also in his somewhat different attempt to achieve the same goal in the *Critique of Practical Reason*). The same thought gets confirmed in another way by Kant's critics when, erroneously privileging FUL and virtually excluding FH and FA from their consideration, they then accuse Kant's theory of being satisfied with an "empty formalism." This charge, however, when properly understood, is an indictment less of Kant's theory than of their mistaken way of reading it.

FUL is derived from the mere concept of a categorical imperative in the sense that it tells us simply to obey all "universal laws," that is, practical principles which apply necessarily to all rational beings. In order to make this a bit more informative, Kant includes in FUL a test on *maxims* (subjective practical principles, formulating an agent's policies or intentions), which is supposed to determine which maxims conform to universal laws. FUL says that a maxim violates a universal law if it cannot be willed as a universal law. FLN tries to bring this test closer to intuition by inviting us to imagine a system of nature of which the maxim is one of its universal laws, and asking us whether we can, without contradiction or conflicting volitions, will to be a part of that system. Kant attempts (I think prematurely) to illustrate his moral principle by applying these tests to four maxims. Each of the four maxims Kant considers is supposed to be a way in which someone might violate a determinate kind of moral duty. The first maxim, about suicide, violates a perfect duty to oneself. The second maxim, about making false promises to get out of difficulty, violates a perfect duty to others. The third maxim, of letting one's talents rust, violates an imperfect duty to oneself. The fourth maxim, of refusing help to those in need, violates an imperfect duty to others.

Kant's attempt to show that these four maxims violate the universalizability tests proposed by FLN have been an object of endless controversy. The principal effect of these controversies has been to obscure the moral point of FUL and FLN, and to concentrate attention on their failure to perform a task for which they were never intended. Kant states that point quite explicitly: "If we now attend to ourselves in any transgression of duty, we find that we do not really will that our maxim should become a universal law, since that is impossible for us, but that the opposite of our maxim should instead remain a universal law, only we take the liberty of making an exception to it for ourselves (or for just this once) to the advantage of our inclination" (G 4:424).

FUL and FLN are therefore best understood in light of Kant's anthropology and philosophy of history. Their point is to oppose our unsociable propensity to self-conceit, which makes us want to see ourselves and our inclinations as privileged exceptions to laws we think all other rational beings should follow. The formulas presuppose that we have already identified "the opposite" of our immoral maxim as such a law. As Kant's earliest critics were quick to perceive, FUL and FLN by themselves are inadequate to specify what these laws are. But the result of dwelling on this point (which some misguided Kantians still waste their time disputing) is only to distract readers from the remainder of the Second Section of the *Groundwork*, in which Kant returns from this ill-fated digression and continues his development of the formulation of the supreme principle of morality, arriving at the two thoughts which, in addition to the concept of a categorical imperative, are really crucial to his ethical theory, namely the worth of rational nature as end in itself and autonomy of the will as the ground of obligation.

Humanity as end in itself

Another side of the charge of "formalism" is the complaint that the Kantian conception of a categorical imperative is nonsensical because there could be no conceivable reason or motive for an agent to obey such a principle. They have seldom even noticed that Kant's derivation of FH addresses this objection quite directly, by inquiring after the rational motive (*Bewegungsgrund*) for obedience to a categorical imperative (G 4:427). His answer is that such a motive cannot be any desire or object of desire, but can only be the objective worth of rational nature regarded as an end in itself (G 4:428). Rational nature is an "end in itself" (or an "objective end") because it is an end we are rationally required to have irrespective of our desires (though Kant holds that when we have this end on rational grounds, this will produce in us various desires, such as love for rational beings, and a desire to benefit them [*MS* 6:401–2]).

Rational nature is also an *existing* (or "self-sufficient") end, not an "end to be produced" (G 4:437). That is, it is not something we try to bring about, but something already existing, whose worth provides us with the reason for the sake of which we act. The value of rational nature is ultimate, not based on any other value. Kant thinks that the argument that something has this character can take only the form of showing us that insofar as we set ends we regard as having objective value, we already regard the rational nature that set them as having value, and we are committed to regarding the same capacity in others in the same way (G 4:428–9).

Because the end in itself is to provide a rational ground for categorical imperatives, it cannot be something whose value depends on contingencies about rational beings (such as the degree to which they exercise their rational capacities); its value must be whole and unconditional in every rational being, which entails that the worth of all rational beings is equal. Kant calls rational nature (in any possible being) "humanity" insofar as reason is used to set ends of any kind; humanity is distinguished from "personality," which is the rational capacity to be morally accountable. To say that "humanity" is the end in itself is to accord worth to all our permissible ends, whether they are enjoined by morality or not.

Kant illustrates FH using the same four examples to which he earlier tried to apply FLN. Few readers have appreciated the fact that the arguments from FH are much more straightforward and transparent than the earlier ones, and even shed new light on the earlier arguments. Whatever objections one might raise to Kant's arguments illustrating FH, the claim that Kant's formula is empty of practical consequences is far less plausible in the case of FH than in the case of FLN. When he turns to the derivation of ethical duties in the *Metaphysics of Morals*, Kant appeals only once to anything like FUL, but well over a dozen times to FH.

Autonomy and the realm of ends

Kant now puts together the thought of a categorical practical law and the thought of the rational will as a ground of value, deriving a new formula, "the idea *of the will of every rational being as a will giving universal law*" (G 4:431).

Although Kant's German idealist followers tend to overemphasize the importance of FUL for his theory, they were all profoundly influenced by the idea of autonomy as the ground of morality. The most creative aspect of the ethical thought of both Fichte and Hegel is their attempts to employ and (in some respects) to reinterpret this Kantian idea.

In the Second and Third Sections of the *Groundwork*, Kant himself states FA in a variety of ways, and his "universal formulations" of the moral law in the *Groundwork* (G 4:437), the *Critique of Practical Reason* (KpV 5:30) and the *Metaphysics of Morals* (MS 6:225) are all statements of FA (*not* of FUL).[3] FUL and FLN contain only tests for the permissibility of individual maxims. No positive duty (such as the duty never to commit suicide or positively to help others in need) can be derived from them. (The most their universalizability tests permit us to show is, for example, that it is impermissible to commit suicide *on one specific maxim.*) FA, however, tells us positively that every rational will is actually the legislator of an entire system of such laws, hence that the duties prescribed by these laws are binding on us. FA says of a plurality of maxims that they collectively involve the positive volition that they (again considered collectively) *should actually be* universal laws. The universalizability tests contained in FUL and FLN provide no criterion for deciding which set of maxims, considered collectively, involves such an actual volition. (Nor does Kant ever pretend that the thought experiments involved in the four examples discussed at G 4:421–3 would ever be adequate to determine which maxims belong to this set. From Kant's procedure in the *Metaphysics of Morals*, the most reasonable surmise is that he thinks FH provides the best criterion for that.)

Kant argues that only autonomy of the rational will can be the ground of moral obligation. If anything external to the rational will were the ground of moral laws, then that would destroy their categorical character, since they could be valid for the will only conditionally on some further volition regarding this external source. (If happiness is the ground of the laws, they are conditional on our willing happiness; if the ground of moral laws is the will of God, then their obligatoriness is conditional on our love or fear of God.)

The idea of an entire system of moral laws legislated by our will leads Kant to another idea: that of a "realm of ends" – that is, of an ideal community of all rational beings, which form a community because all their ends harmonize into an interconnected system, united and mutually supporting one another as do the organs of a living thing in their healthy functioning. FRE tells us to act according to those principles which would bring about such a system. If FH implies the equal status of all rational beings, FRE implies that morally good conduct aims at eliminating conflict and competition between them, so that each pursues only those ends that can be brought into harmony with the ends of all others.

Establishing the moral law

FA is used both in Kant's deduction of the moral law in the Third Section of the *Groundwork*, and in his alternative account in the *Critique of Practical Reason* (*KpV* 5:28–33). Both involve the claim that the moral law and freedom of the will reciprocally imply each other (*G* 4:447, *KpV* 5:29). This claim rests on Kant's conception of practical freedom as a causality according to self-given (hence normative) laws. To think of myself as free is to think of myself as able to act according to self-legislated principles. Kant has shown in the Second Section that if there is a categorical imperative, then it can be formulated as FA, in other words, as a normative principle self-given by my rational will. Thus if there is a moral law that is valid for me, it is so if and only if I am (in this sense) free. In the *Groundwork*, Kant argues that to regard oneself as making even theoretical judgments is to regard oneself as free, since to judge (even on theoretical matters, such as the freedom of the will) is to see oneself as following logical or epistemic norms. This means it would be self-refuting to judge that one is not free, and to represent oneself as making this judgment on the basis of good reasons. This argument is not a theoretical proof that we are free, but it does show that freedom is a necessary presupposition of any use of reason at all, and this means that any use of reason at all commits one to the validity of the principle of morality as Kant has formulated it in the Second Section of the *Groundwork*.

Note also that this entire line of argument is quite independent of Kant's (more controversial) idea that the causality of freedom is incompatible with natural causality, and his inference from this idea that we can presuppose ourselves to be free only by regarding ourselves as members of an unknowable noumenal world (*KrV* A538–58/B566–86; *G* 4:450–63; *KpV* 5:42–57, 95–106). You might agree entirely with Kant's view that freedom and the moral law are presuppositions of reason while holding, contrary to Kant, that our freedom (our capacity to act according to self-given norms) is a natural power we have in virtue of the operation of natural causal laws.

The metaphysical system of duties

Readers of the *Groundwork* tend to emphasize FUL at the expense of Kant's later (hence better developed and more adequate) formulations of the moral law. This leads them to a picture of how Kant thinks the moral law should be applied, a picture that involves formulating maxims and ratiocinating about whether they can be thought or willed as universal laws (or, following FLN, laws of nature). When Kant finally got around to writing the *Metaphysics of Morals* (for which the *Groundwork*, as its name implies, was intended merely to lay the foundation), he provided a very different account of ordinary moral reasoning from the one suggested by this picture.

Right and ethics

The *Metaphysics of Morals* (*Sitten*) is divided into two main parts: the first is a Doctrine of Right (*Rechtslehre*), the second deals with "ethics" (*Ethik*), which is a Doctrine of Virtue (*Tugendlehre*). Right, which is the basis of the system of *juridical* duties, is concerned only with protecting the external freedom of individuals, and is indifferent to the incentives that lead them to follow its commands. The duties of ethics, concerned with the self-government of rational beings, not only require actions but also have to do with the ends people set and the incentives from which they act. The principle of right is:

> R: "Any action is right if it can coexist with everyone's freedom according to a universal law, or if on its maxim the freedom of choice of each can coexist with everyone's freedom in accordance with a universal law." (*MS* 6:230; cf. *TP* 8:289–90)

R bears a superficial verbal similarity to FUL, but the differences between it and all forms of the principle of morality are far more significant than the similarities. R does not directly command us what to do (or not to do). It tells us only what is *right* (*recht*) or externally just. To say that an act is "right" (i.e. externally just) is only to say that, by standards of right, it may not be coercively prevented. This juridical standard of permissibility is not a moral standard but is determined by what a system of right (of external justice, as coercively enforced by a legitimate authority) demands in the name of protecting external freedom according to universal law.

R no doubt *suggests* (though it does not directly state) that right, as external freedom according to universal law, is something valuable. This value is also obviously an expression of the principle of morality, as we can see most easily if we consider FH. Respect for humanity requires granting people the external freedom needed for a meaningful use of their capacity to set ends according to reason. That is why Kant says that the "innate right to freedom" which is the sole ground of all our rights, "belongs to every human being by virtue of his humanity" (*MS* 6:237). For this reason, Kant holds that we also have a *moral* (i.e. ethical) duty to limit ourselves to actions that are right, but that duty is no part of R itself. For juridical duties the incentive may be moral, but it may equally be prudential or (more often) something even more direct and reliable – namely, the immediate fear of what a legal authority will do to us if we violate its commands. An action fulfilling an ethical duty has greater moral merit if it is performed from duty, but the incentive from which we perform a right action makes no difference to its juridical rightness.

Ethical duties

The *Metaphysics of Morals* conceives of ordinary moral reasoning as deliberation based on the bearing on one's action of one's various *ethical duties*. The
material of one's ethical duty is constituted by "duties of virtue" or "ends that
are at the same time duties" (*MS* 6:382–91). In other words, for Kant, ordinary
moral reasoning is fundamentally *teleological* – it is reasoning about what ends
we are constrained by morality to pursue, and the priorities among these ends
we are required to observe.

Thus in the *Groundwork*'s four examples, what tells us most about moral reasoning as Kant's theory presents it is not the formulation of maxims or the use
of a universalizability test, but instead the taxonomy of duties through which
Kant organizes the examples. The basic division is between duties toward oneself
and duties toward others. Within duties toward oneself, Kant distinguishes
perfect duties (those requiring specific actions or omissions, allowing for no latitude in the interests of inclination so that failure to perform them is blame-
worthy) from imperfect duties (where one is required to set an end, but there is
latitude regarding which actions one takes toward the end, and such actions are
meritorious). Perfect duties to oneself are further divided into duties toward
oneself as an animal being and as a moral being (*MS* 6:421–42). Imperfect duties
toward oneself are divided into duties to seek natural perfection (to cultivate
one's powers) and duties to seek moral perfection (purity of motivation and
virtue) (*MS* 6:444–7). Duties toward others are subdivided into duties of love
(which correspond to imperfect duties) and duties of respect (which correspond
to perfect duties) (*MS* 6:448). Duties of love are further subdivided (*MS* 6:452),
as are the vices of hatred opposing these duties (*MS* 6:458–61). Regarding duties
of respect, there is a subdivision only of the vices that oppose them (*MS* 6:465).
Metaphysical duties of virtue are distinguished from duties arising out of particular conditions of people or our relations to them. Kant holds that there are
many important duties of the latter sort, but their detail falls outside a "metaphysics" of morals, which deals only with the application of the supreme principle of morality to human nature in general (*MS* 6:468–74).

In German idealist ethics, duties grounded on determinate social relations
assume increasing importance. Fichte's *System of Ethics* includes a taxonomy of
them (and the attendant social analysis required for this) under the heading of
"particular duties." Hegel goes so far as to hold that a "doctrine of duties" can
be entirely replaced by a "development of those [social] relationships that are
necessitated by the idea of freedom."[4]

In the *Groundwork*, Kant tries (unsuccessfully) to ground the distinction
between perfect and imperfect duties on two kinds of universalizability test
involved in FLN (*G* 4:423–4); he never even tries to use FUL or FLN to draw the

more basic distinction between duties (those to oneself and those to others). Both distinctions, however, are easily explicated in terms of FH (cf. *G* 4:429–30). A duty *d* is a duty toward (*gegen*) *S* if and only if *S* is a rational being and the requirement to comply with *d* is grounded on the requirement to respect humanity in the person of *S*. A duty is wide or imperfect (or, if toward others, a duty of love) if the action promotes a duty of virtue (an end it is a duty to set); an act is required by a strict or perfect duty (or a duty of respect to others) if the failure to perform it would amount to a failure to set this obligatory end at all, or a failure to respect humanity as an end in someone's person. An act violates a perfect duty (or duty of respect) if it sets an end contrary to one of the ends it is our duty to set, or if it shows disrespect toward humanity in someone's person (as by using the person as a mere means).

Ends that are duties

Imperfect or wide duties should guide us in setting the ends of our life. Not all ends need be duties or contrary to duty (some ends are merely permissible), but morally good people will include duties of virtue among the central ends that give their lives meaning. Kantian morality thus leaves a great deal of latitude in determining which ends to set and how much to do toward each end. The pursuit of our ends, once they have been decided upon, is constrained only by juridical duties, perfect duties to ourselves and duties of respect to others. (In this respect, Kant's theory contrasts sharply with the terrifying rigorism of Fichte, who allows no actions to be merely permissible: every possible act is either obligatory or forbidden.[5])

There are two sorts of ends that it is our duty to have: our own perfection and the happiness of others (*MS* 6:385). "Perfection" includes both our natural perfection (the development of our talents, skills, and capacities of understanding) and moral perfection (our virtuous disposition) (*MS* 6:387). A person's "happiness" is the greatest rational whole of the ends the person set for the sake of her own satisfaction (*MS* 6:387–8). Because we naturally have our own happiness as an end, it cannot be a duty except insofar as we need to be constrained to pursue it from grounds of reason (e.g. in order to promote one's own perfection). Because we must respect the autonomy of others, their perfection is a duty only insofar as it belongs to their ends (hence their happiness) (*MS* 6:386, 388).

For Kant all ethical duties whatever are grounded on ends. The general formula is that an action is a perfect ethical duty if omitting it means refusing to set a morally required end, or setting an end contrary to a morally required one. The analogous perfect ethical duties not to behave with contempt toward others, to defame, mock or ridicule them, would be based on the claim that such behavior involves an end contrary to morally required ends (*MS* 6:463–8). Contrary to its familiar image, therefore, Kantian ethics conceives of moral reasoning as fundamentally *teleological*. But Kant's theory conceives of our pursuit of obligatory ends in a less restricted way than most consequentialist theories do. Standard devices of prudential rationality, such as summing and averaging, maximizing and satisficing, do not apply directly to our moral reasoning about these ends. My duty to promote the happiness of others is *not* a duty to maximize the collective happiness of others. My duty to promote my own perfection is not a duty to achieve any specific level of overall perfection, much less a duty to make myself as perfect as I can possibly be. This makes it possible for duties of virtue all to be in their concept wide, imperfect, and meritorious duties (*MS* 6:390–1). I behave meritoriously insofar as I act to promote an end falling under the concept of the required ends. But I deserve no blame for failing to promote the end, and hence no blame for not promoting it maximally. In general, it is up to me to decide whose happiness to promote, and to what degree. Ethics allows me latitude or "play-room" (*Spielraum*) in deciding such matters (*MS* 6:390). Thus moral agents themselves, as free agents, and not the theory or moral principles or duties, are responsible for the design of their individual life-plans.

Ethics as virtue

The title of Kant's system of ethical duties is the "Doctrine of Virtue." His name for the obligatory ends of pure practical reason is "duties of virtue." In the *Critique of Practical Reason*, Kant describes "virtue" as "a naturally acquired faculty of a non-holy will" (*KpV* 5:33), or, more specifically, as "the moral disposition in the struggle" (*im Kampfe*) (*KpV* 5:84). In the *Metaphysics of Morals*, virtue is characterized as "the moral strength of a human being's will in fulfilling his duty" (*MS* 6:405; cf. 6:394). "Moral strength" is an "aptitude" (*Fertigkeit*, *habitus*) in acting and a subjective perfection of the power of choice (*MS* 6:407). Obligatory ends are called "duties of virtue" because virtue is required to adopt and pursue them. There is only a single fundamental *disposition* of virtue, but because the ends which it is our duty to have are many, there are many different virtues (*MS* 6:383, 410). I can have one virtue and lack another if my commitment is strong to one obligatory end but weak to another.

Kant holds that we have a duty to cultivate feelings and inclinations that harmonize with duty and to acquire a temperament suitable to morality (*MS* 6:457). But he does not equate *virtue* with success in fulfilling that duty (*MS* 6:409). Virtue is needed precisely to the extent that good conduct is hard for us, since it consists in the strength we need to perform a difficult task. A person might have a temperament so happily constituted that their feelings and desires make duty easy and pleasant to do. Such a temperament is not virtue, but only makes virtue less often necessary. The person may still be virtuous too, but virtue is a quality of *character* (of the active strength of rational maxims), not of temperament (of the feelings and desires we passively experience).

This conception of virtue follows naturally from Kant's theory of human nature. For according to this theory, in society our inclinations, as expressions of competitive self-conceit, are inevitably a counterweight to the moral law, which requires strength to overcome it. Therefore, there can be no reliable fulfillment of duty without (some degree of) virtue. The theory of ethical duties is called a "Doctrine of Virtue" only because human nature is such that virtue is the fundamental presupposition of all reliable ethical conduct. In the civilized condition, where our feelings and desires are corrupted by social competition and self-conceit, it would be not only dangerous, but blamably irresponsible, to rely (as Hutcheson and Hume would have us do) on natural feelings and desires to motivate us to morally good conduct.

Politics and religion

In the Doctrine of Virtue, Kant applies the *a priori* principle of morality systematically to his empirical theory of human nature in determining ethical duties. But his moral vision, combining moral principle with anthropology and the philosophy of history, is displayed more grippingly in his writings on politics and religion. For in these he attempts to bring together his theory of history with his conception of the ends human beings should try to pursue together as enlightened and self-conscious historical agents.

Enlightenment: the idea of a just civil society; the need for perpetual peace

The foundation for our pursuit of any such ends, in his view, is "enlightenment" (*Aufklärung*) itself. Enlightenment is "release from self-incurred minority" (WA 8:35). Minority is the condition in which one uses one's understanding only under the direction of another. It is "self-incurred" (*selbstverschuldet*, i.e. something for which the person in question is responsible or to blame) when it is due not to the immaturity or impairment of our faculties, but to the lack of courage or resolve to use them. When, as in the entire historic past, most people have remained in a condition of minority (under the degrading subservience to holy books, religious dogmas, priests, and other pernicious traditional authorities), Kant thinks it is very difficult for any individual to break out of this condition and think for himself. It is easier for an entire public to do this, if only it has, and is not discouraged from using, the capacity to communicate freely about matters of universal human concern.

One important historical aim of the species for Kant is the achievement of a just form of political constitution, which (he holds) can truly be found only in some form of *republic*. But Kant thinks this aim can be fully achieved only when states are no longer in a condition of war with respect to one another, and so another necessary collective aim for humanity is the achievement of a federation between states which is capable of securing peace between them. He articulates this thought in the *Idea Toward a Universal History* (1784), but gives it its fullest expression in *Perpetual Peace* (1795).

The ethical community; religion; the highest good

The historical goals of the just state and perpetual peace, ambitious though they may seem, are not in Kant's view our highest historical aims, because they concern only external freedom, and do not have directly to do with our moral vocation. Because the ground of moral evil in human beings, arising from our unsociable sociability, is social in origins, the struggle against it cannot be successful if it is limited to the private struggle of each individual with his own evil tendencies. In that sense, Kant repudiates "individualism" in morality, regarding both the cause of moral evil and the remedy for it.

To achieve the final moral end of the species, Kant thinks, we must join together in an *ethical community*, which differs from a political or civil society in that it is entirely free, voluntary, and non-coercive, and can therefore deal with our ethical disposition – something regarding which external coercion in any form would be wrongful (*R* 6:93–102). The political state, even in the existing form of the unjust despotisms Kant sees around him, must serve as the historical vehicle humanity uses to achieve external justice through its enlightened reform. In the same way, Kant thinks organized religion or the church, despite the superstitious and unenlightened ideas and practices that characterize existing churches, must be the historical vehicle through which the human race unites in an ethical community to actualize its final moral vocation.

A political community, in Kant's view, rests solely on a common coercive power protecting external freedom. An ethical community, however, must rest on freely shared *ends*, as represented by the moral ideal of a *realm of ends*. Kant concludes each of the three critiques with an account of an ideal moral teleology, culminating in a final end or *highest good* (*summum bonum*). This end is then made the basis for a practical argument for religious faith in God (and sometimes also of faith in a future life) (*KrV* A795–831/B823–59; *KpV* 5:107–48; *KU* §§82–91, 5:425–85). These arguments, as already mentioned, exercised a powerful influence on the German idealists, even though they were never accepted without modification and often worked on subsequent thinkers by inciting them to criticize and rethink Kant's entire conception of the "primacy of the practical." To Kant's immediate followers, and also to subsequent generations, his discussions of the highest good have often seemed artificial and strained, pieces of high-flown metaphysics having little about them that is immediately compelling.

Yet we may gain a new perspective on this side of Kant's thought if we consider the ideal of the highest good, and the religious faith that he associated with it, from another standpoint. The ethical community or church, in the enlightened shape Kant hopes it will assume, must unite all in pursuit of a shared end. That is the sort of end Kant intends the highest good to be. He thinks of the moral faith arising out of our commitment to it as one that would be suitable to a free ethical community.

Kant's hopes for such a community no doubt seem hopelessly unrealistic to us. But it at least served his immediate followers as something worth criticizing and reworking. If we see it as the highest expression of Kant's hopes for a better human future, perhaps it can still serve us in the same way.

NOTES

1 For a fuller account of Kant's theory of the "practical postulates" and moral faith, see my book *Kant's Moral Religion* (Ithaca: Cornell University Press, 1970) or "Rational Theology, Moral Faith, and Religion," in Paul Guyer, ed., *The Cambridge Companion to Kant* (Cambridge: Cambridge University Press, 1992), pp. 394–416.

2 Kant's writings will be cited according to the following system of abbreviations:

Ak   *Immanuel Kant's gesammelte Schriften.* Ausgabe der königlich preussischen Akademie der Wissenschaften (Berlin: W. de Gruyter, 1900–). Unless otherwise footnoted, writings of Immanuel Kant will be cited by volume:page number in this edition.

Ca   *Cambridge Edition of the Writings of Immanuel Kant* (New York: Cambridge University Press, 1992–). Most English translations now include Ak pagination, and all writings of Kant available in English are (or presently will be) available with the marginal Ak volume:page citations. Specific works will be cited using the following system of abbreviations (works not abbreviated below will be cited simply as Ak volume:page).

EF   *Zum ewigen Frieden: Ein philosophischer Entwurf* (1795), Ak 8
    Toward Perpetual Peace: A philosophical project, Ca *Practical Philosophy*

G   *Grundlegung zur Metaphysik der Sitten* (1785), Ak 4
    Groundwork of the Metaphysics of Morals, Ca *Practical Philosophy*

I   *Idee zu einer allgemeinen Geschichte in weltbürgerlicher Absicht* (1784), Ak 8
    Idea Toward a Universal History with a Cosmopolitan Aim, Ca *Anthropology, History and Education*

KrV   *Kritik der reinen Vernunft* (1781, 1787). Cited by A/B pagination.
    Critique of Pure Reason, Ca *Critique of Pure Reason*

KpV   *Kritik der praktischen Vernunft* (1788), Ak 5
    Critique of Practical Reason, Ca *Practical Philosophy*

KU   *Kritik der Urteilskraft* (1790), Ak 5
    Critique of the Power of Judgment, Ca *Aesthetics and Teleology*

MA   *Mutmaßlicher Anfang der Menschengeschichte* (1786), Ak 8

Conjectural Beginning of Human History, Ca Anthropology, History and Education

MS Metaphysik der Sitten (1797–8), Ak 6
Metaphysics of Morals, Ca Practical Philosophy

O Was heißt: Sich im Denken orientieren? (1786), Ak 8
What Does it Mean to Orient Oneself in Thinking?, Ca Religion and Rational Theology

R Religion innerhalb der Grenzen der bloßen Vernunft (1793–4), Ak 6
Religion within the Boundaries of Mere Reason, Ca Religion and Rational Theology

SF Streit der Fakultäten (1798), Ak 7
The Conflict of the Faculties, Ca Religion and Rational Theology

TP Über den Gemeinspruch: Das mag in der Theorie richtig sein, taugt aber nicht für die Praxis (1793), Ak 8
On the Common Saying: That May Be Correct in Theory But It Is of No Use in Practice, Ca Practical Philosophy

VA Anthropologie in pragmatischer Hinsicht (1798), Ak 7
Anthropology from a Pragmatic Standpoint, Ca Anthropology, History and Education
Vorlesungen über Anthropologie, Ak 25
Lectures on Anthropology, Ca Lectures on Anthropology

WA Beantwortung der Frage: Was ist Aufklärung? (1784), Ak 8
An Answer to the Question: What Is Enlightenment?, Ca Practical Philosophy

3 With regard to the *Critique of Practical Reason*, this point has been noted by both H. J. Paton, *The Categorical Imperative* (New York: Harper & Row, 1949), 130, and Lewis White Beck, *A Commentary on Kant's Critique of Practical Reason* (Chicago: University of Chicago Press, 1960), 122 and note 22.

4 Fichte, *System of Ethics*, *Fichtes sämmtliche Werke*, ed. I. H. Fichte (Berlin: De Gruyter, 1971), IV, 325–65. Hegel, *Elements of the Philosophy of Right*, trans. Hugh Barr Nisbet and ed. Allen Wood (Cambridge: Cambridge University Press, 1991), §148R.

5 See Fichte, *System of Ethics*, *Fichtes sämmtliche Werke* IV, 156, 204, 264.

4

DANIEL O. DAHLSTROM

The aesthetic holism of Hamann, Herder, and Schiller

Johann Georg Hamann (1730–88), Johann Gottfried Herder (1744–1803), and Friedrich Schiller (1759–1805), two sons of Prussian pietists and a Swabian poet, are among a handful of thinkers most responsible for initiating *a holistic turn* in German thought in the second half of the eighteenth century. If this era is generally associated with the end of the Enlightenment, the writings of Hamann, Herder, and Schiller represent the German "Counter-Enlightenment," dedicated to the premise that the genuine meanings of things derive from their interactive functions in a developing, self-determining whole. Hamann and Herder are also known to historians of German culture as prime movers of the so-called "Storm and Stress" (*Sturm und Drang*) movement epitomized in the theater – its artform of choice – by the early plays of Schiller (*The Robbers*) and Goethe (*Götz of Berlichingen*).[1] This highly self-reflective movement derives from an identity crisis that is both national and philosophical, because the effort to establish a distinctively German literature in the face of France's cultural hegemony coincides with the question of the nature of reason itself.[2] Not surprisingly, the work of all three thinkers feeds off sustained polemics with the likes of Rousseau, Kant, Mendelssohn, and members of the Berlin Academy reconstituted by Frederick the Great.[3] As in any battle, the adversaries meet on some common ground. Yet Hamann, Herder, and Schiller set themselves apart by their insistence on understanding human nature holistically and thereby dismantling walls erected between reason, on the one hand, and language, history, or nature (including human sensuous nature) on the other. In keeping with this insistence and perhaps, too, with their own humble origins, all three thinkers sharply criticize what they regard as an oppressive and autocratic state machinery, its alienating social arrangements, its impoverishing economic structure, and the bad faith of its defenders.[4] Far from being opponents of reason, they share a commitment to a reason sufficiently robust and self-conscious to embrace and promote the spontaneity, individuality, and geniality of human life in all its different historical, linguistic, and cultural expressions.

It would be wrong, however, to portray the thinking of these three men with a single brushstroke. Hamann is, after all, fifteen years older than Herder and almost thirty years older than Schiller. Yet even if age-differences are set aside, no one would mistake any pair of them for twins. Despite Hamann's life-long friendship with Herder and their common antipathy toward their contemporaries' idolizing of reason, Hamann is unsparing in his criticism of the humanist tendencies informing Herder's studies of language.[5] So, too, despite occasional collaborations, Herder and Schiller essentially part ways midway through the 1790s. While an insistence on understanding human beings as living wholes and a deep appreciation of culture's transforming potential are common to the two former medical students turned historians, it is not easy to square Herder's sense of providential heterogeneity with Schiller's vision of an ideal apotheosis of ancient naïveté and modern sentimentality.[6] Similarly, though Schiller's objections to Kant's views of reason and aesthetics echo Hamann's criticisms, Schiller does not share Hamann's intensely ironic and deliberately enigmatic religiosity.[7] At the same time neither Hamann nor Schiller seems to have harbored anything like Herder's theoretical ambitions and pretensions.

Despite such differences, each member of this trio shares a common preoccupation that is the catalyst of their holism: aesthetics. Each regards art and literature (developing in continuity with language itself) as ways that individuals and societies jointly express and define themselves as wholes across the divide of nature and history. Characterization of this triumvirate as authors of an "aesthetic holism" in the second half of the eighteenth century must, however, be qualified. Baumgarten's *Aesthetica*, published in 1750, might well be considered something of a subversive work, judging from the amount of print the author devotes to this science of so-called "inferior" faculties of cognition (namely, the sensory) and their perfection (namely, beauty) in contrast to the study of the "superior" faculties. Yet even if Baumgarten's work is subversive in the sense suggested, the aesthetics of Hamann, Herder, and Schiller are even more so, since they undo the very economy of faculties divided into superior and inferior. Subverting that economy is, of course, not the same as inverting it, a move clearly inconsistent with a thoroughgoing holism. Yet herein lies precisely the difficulty presented by the new meaning given by Hamann, Herder, and Schiller to the young science of aesthetics. Because art in their view is continuous with life in all its historical particularity as the real synthesis of experience and thought, they take art's holistic character as the critical paradigm (criterion and goal) of philosophy itself. In the final analysis, however, the reason why supposedly holistic considerations, even ones tempered with the humble awareness of the aesthetic finitude of life, override others in matters of knowledge and action is something that can be shown but not said – or only said poetically. This is the challenge presented by Hamann, Herder, and Schiller to German idealists who share their holistic concerns, their sense of the continuity of human life with nature and of reason with history, but remain unwilling to give aesthetics – metaphor – the final word.

Hamann and the aesthetics of the Incarnation

"The whole historical puzzle of our existence, the impenetrable darkness of its *terminus a quo* and its *terminus ad quem*, is resolved and explained by the first and primal message of the Word become flesh" (N III, 192). At the center of Hamann's thinking is the Incarnation, not as an event in the past, but as an historical and eschatological revelation in word and body. Little wonder that Herder's reasons for championing the "human" hypothesis of language's origin amount in Hamann's mind to a deist refusal to countenance God's efficacy, not only in nature but even in human linguistic activity.[8] "The *communicatio* of divine and human *idiomatum* is a fundamental law and the chief key of all our knowledge and the entire visible economy" (N III, 27).

The unique but holistic character of God-becoming-Human (*Menschenwerdung*) challenges several distinctions dear to the Enlightenment, preeminently that between the natural and the supernatural, but also distinctions between such natural phenomena as language or experience, on the one hand, and reason on the other. Herein lies the source of Hamann's complaint, echoed by Herder and Schiller, about their contemporaries' pretentious personification of "universal reason," as though it were an actual person or a separate power or faculty, detached (or, in Kant's case, capable of purification through critique) from tradition and use, capable of speaking other than in allegories and telling human beings what to do. "Even if I were as eloquent as Demosthenes," Hamann declares, "I would do nothing but repeat one thing three times: reason is language, logos. I gnaw on this bone full of marrow, and will do so until I die" (ZH V, 177). One of Hamann's more influential formulations of this thesis is his *Metacritique of the Purism of Reason*, finished in January 1784, in which Hamann takes Kant to task for, among other things, his "mystical love of form," expressed in the "mystery" of a pure sensible intuition (space and time as the forms of sensibility), in the "transcendental superstition" of pre-linguistic logical principles (the categories as the forms of understanding), and in the onanist synthesis of those forms that Kant deems knowledge. (Though Hamann was not satisfied with the work, Herder and Jacobi circulated it until its publication in 1800 by Herder's foes in an effort to expose the alleged plagiarism of his own 1799 *Understanding and Experience: A Metacritique of the Critique of Pure Reason.*[9])

Nor is history, any more than reason, to be understood as something discontinuous with nature. On the contrary, prefiguring Herder's own concentration on nature in the first two parts of his *Ideas for a Philosophy of the History of Mankind*, Hamann declares: "[T]he entire physical nature of man from his conception to his ceasing to be is a type of history, and is in itself a key to the notion of history" (N I, 228). The import of the Incarnation is patent: all philosophical knowing must flow from God the historian.[10] Yet, while there is a privileged and indispensable word, God's "Memoirs for the Sake of the History of Heaven and Earth" (N II, 394; I, 308), the divine word is by no means confined to scripture: "Every phenomenon of nature was a word – the sign, symbol, and promise of a new, secret (and at that time) unrepresentable union which was all the more wonderful" (N III, 32). Reason is once again not left out of this equation, but placed squarely in the context of nature as a theophany: "God, nature and reason have as intimate a relation to one another as light, the eye, and all that the former reveals to the latter, or like the centre, radius, and periphery of any circle, or like author, book, and reader" (ZH V, 272).

Hamann apparently came to this incarnational perspective through the experience of a kind of conversion in the aftermath of a prodigal episode in London as a young envoy of the family firm of his friend, Johann Berens. The exact nature of the experience has been a subject of some puzzled conjecture[11] but no more so than Hamann's ability to incorporate Hume's philosophy into his incarnational holism. Like Hume, Hamann holds that existence (including our own) and causality are matters of immediate impressions and belief. Impressions and belief are apparently not identical in his view, but they are on a par inasmuch as there are no more grounds or reasons for belief than there are for taste and sight.[12] Immediate impressions are God's way of appearing to us in nature, while beliefs are the stuff of tradition. With his penchant for an earthy metaphor, Hamann observes that "the *stamina* and *menstrua* of our *reason* are properly only *revelation* and *tradition*" (N III, 39). At the same time, existence, a matter of sensual and passionate revelation, is always a step ahead of reason: "Our own existence and the existence of all things outside us must be believed and cannot be determined in any other way."[13] So, too, Hamann declares: "Do not forget, for the sake of the *cogito*, the noble *sum*." He rejects any Cartesian or Kantian pretensions to a capacity for self-knowledge – in contrast to God – as the foundation of understanding (ZH VI, 230; G, 497; N I, 300f.).

Hamann's strategy, it bears emphasizing, is not bent on debunking putatively universal and theoretical claims in favor of just any sort of empirical and practical knowledge. The knowledge privileged is the knowledge that comes to the rightly disposed person, though it is knowledge allegedly available to anyone who opens her mind to the voice of God speaking immediately to her in and through nature. Generalizations are accordingly construed by Hamann in Berkeleyan fashion as fabrications at odds with the particularity and contextuality of experience.[14] The refusal to accept accidental truths of history, physical facts, and political appearances is interpreted as a vain display of human hubris, the very antithesis of the divine humility of the Incarnation. In this same spirit, he assigns emphatic roles to passions and sexuality; as he puts it to Herder: "[M]y coarse imagination has never been able to picture a creative spirit without *genitalia*" (ZH II, 415; V, 167). Further revealing Hume's influence, Hamann insists that passions are like limbs, the source of understanding, something that philosophy can only guide (ZH I, 442; N II, 201–8, 162). Radically anti-dualist most of the time,[15] Hamann regards attempts to differentiate appearances or experience from reality, be it with respect to nature or politics, as a human conceit, an artifice designed largely to evade reality and responsibility and to control others. In this spirit he construes Kant's *Critique of Pure Reason* as part of the metaphysical legacy promising "that universal and infallible Philosopher's Stone, so indispensable for Catholicism and despotism" (N III, 284). Similarly, Mendelssohn's *Jerusalem: A Plea for the Toleration of the Jews*, a plea based upon a distinction between natural and civil orders, is rejected by Hamann as an apostate ruse to neutralize religion.[16]

Hamann's dispositional epistemology, his refusal to separate the claims of thinking from the character of the thinker, is prominent in his initial contribution to the "Storm and Stress" movement, indeed, by some accounts "the first manifesto" of it: the *Socratic Memorabilia* of 1759.[17] Hamann attempts to show that Socrates, far from being a precursor of Enlightenment thinking (left or right, religious or secular), represents its very antithesis.[18] With his self-effacing yet ironic humility and confessions of ignorance, with his pained acknowledgment of his vices (readily excusable in someone with such an eye for natural beauty, Hamann notes, by way of excusing Socrates' homosexuality), with his humorous exposure of the sophistry among putative experts of his time and, not least, with the genius of his capacity to believe an inner voice and his brave indifference to an unjust death-sentence, Socrates is, if anything, the forerunner of the Apostle Paul and even Christ himself.[19] (The interpretation of Socrates' genius, *daimon*, and striking similarities with Jesus is, it bears noting, a crucial and recurrent preoccupation of Hegel.)

One of Hamann's most important works, *Aesthetica in nuce* (1762), is a critique of contemporary biblical scholarship for failing to recognize the essentially poetic nature of scripture and interpretation. But this poetic character of scripture also has unmistakable implications for both theology and philosophy, implications that Hamann crafts into an argument for the superiority of "the beautiful, creative, imitative spirit" of poetry to philosophy (N II, 210). God himself is "the poet at the beginning of days" (as well as "the thief at the end of days"), as Hamann puts it, undermining in the process any attempt to isolate the sacred from the profane (N II, 206). Grace and revelation are the stuff of scripture and nature. "Every impression of nature on the human being is not only a reminder, but also a pledge of the fundamental truth: who the Lord is. Every counter-effect of the human being in creatures is a letter and seal of our share in the divine nature, and that we are his family" (N II, 207).

For all the radicalness of Hamann's incarnational thought and its implications in his mind about the primacy of poetry over philosophy, he conceives poetry in traditional terms as a form of mimesis. Senses and passions speak and understand nothing but images; indeed, all the riches of human knowledge and happiness consist in images. God speaks through these images and poets, as God's imitators of nature, translate these images. Given the poetic character of this incarnational revelation, poets, not philosophers, are the real students of nature. The passion of poetry does not drown "the text of nature like the deluge," turning "all its beauties and riches into water," or "make nature blind" in order then miraculously to be guided by her (N II, 207f., 197ff.; I, 157f.). The poet's task is not simply to interpret the various parts of nature (that is philosophy's task) but to imitate them "or – even more audaciously – to bring them to their destiny."[20] Thus, far from merely picturing an already finished reality, the truth of poetic mimesis consists in creative words that mimic the creator and participate in the creation itself.

Further underlying the subordination of philosophy to poetry is Hamann's basic conviction that "speaking is translating," that from the beginnings of humanity "every phenomenon of nature was a word," a conviction canceling any philosophical pretensions to being able to distinguish rigorously between sign (spirit) and signified (nature).[21] This conviction entails, too, that Hamannian "reason" or understanding is always intersubjective and volitional, that is to say, other persons are what we primarily understand. Even when we understand nature or events, it is always in view of someone's willing them (creating or making them). "The complication of speech is a history, a phenomenon, an unending wonder, and a likeness by which God always comes forth to speak with us."[22]

Hamann's influence on German Idealism is formidable but indirect, not merely because of the often ironic play of metaphor that marks the style of his writings but also because of their sheer unavailability, a point Hegel himself emphasizes in his 1828 review of Hamann's writings.[23] All the idealists, however, are directly engaged with the work of F. H. Jacobi who, after Herder, was the most effective promulgator of Hamann's ideas (though both Hegel and Schelling take pains to distinguish Jacobi's thinking from what they take to be the profounder level attained by Hamann). The spirit of Hamann resonates unmistakably in the young idealists' common dissatisfaction with dogma and the state, the preeminent role that the Tübingen seminarians, Schelling and Hegel, assign to aesthetics, and their refusal to accept Kantian dichotomies, even if in the end they can no more accept Hamann's appeals to belief and metaphor than they can Kant's categories. But the primary conduit of Hamann's aesthetic holism for the

German idealists is the work of Herder, to whom Hamann himself writes: "Your theme of language, experience, and tradition is my favorite idea, the egg I brood upon . . . my one and all . . . the idea of mankind and its history" (ZH V, 501).

Herder and the aesthetics of the force of history

Herder became an influential Lutheran chaplain, court preacher, and superintendent of schools in Weimar, while Hamann lived out his days as a low-level tax and customs official.[24] Yet the churchman is much more willing to engage the Enlightenment on its own turf and, perhaps for that reason, the foundational role played by the Incarnation in Hamann's thought is replaced by a flexible conception of force (*Kraft*), an amalgam of notions drawn from Shaftesbury, Spinoza, and Leibniz that Herder insists on understanding in terms of analogies between God and humanity, nature and history. "What we know, we know only from analogy, from the creature to us and from us to the creature," he maintains as he attempts to unite psychology and physiology in *On Knowing and Feeling* (1778).[25] Six years later, in the first part of the *Ideas for the Philosophy of the History of Mankind*, he claims that all the physiological forces masterfully unpacked by Haller are, at bottom, one and the same force, and that the chief purpose behind all the organizations formed by nature on earth is "a certain analogous sensing and knowing."[26] Just as "all substances are sustained by divine force," and all differences in reality are merely different forces,[27] so terms like "'sensibility' and 'instinct,' 'imagination' and 'reason' are merely determinations of a single force" (S V, 31). Auspiciously, in his earliest ruminations on art, he reasons that what space is for painting and time for music, force is for poetry (S III, 137).

It is primarily Herder's endeavor to understand the historical working of these forces that sets him apart from his peers and has a particular impact on German idealists. With Herder, Leibniz's notion of living force enters history and, indeed, does so in all its magnificent, empirical variety. A concern for historical differentiation of linguistic style, coupled with a rejection of universal standards of taste and a plea for a renewal of homegrown German literature, is a hallmark of his thought from the outset. In *Fragments on Recent German Literature* (1766), the work that launches his career, poetic language is said to belong to a youthful stage before merging with prose in adulthood and ultimately giving way to the old age of philosophical prose. At the same time the vividness of poetry's language is said to require the closest connection between word and thought, a connection, Herder adds, that can hardly be attained by translation or imitation of other languages.[28] In the *Critical Groves* (1769), after declaring Homer inimitable and "the most successful poetic mind of his century and nation," Herder adds that Homer's poetic genius is not to be found "outside his nature or the age that formed him" (S III, 202). But neither is genius, for all its dependency upon a distinct historical and linguistic context, fully explicable by that context.[29]

Herder repeatedly sets for himself the gargantuan task of doing justice to the claims of genius and those of tradition as well as other discontinuities and continuities across nature and history. But his pursuit of this goal is not without conscious and, indeed, aesthetic precedent: Shakespeare. In a seminal essay on the English bard (1773) Herder describes him as the dramatist of a people (*Volk*) with no desire to ape Greek genius, let alone soulless French imitations of it. Contrasting Sophocles and Shakespeare, Herder observes that, while the Greek remained true to nature by treating one action in one time and place ("all these things lay at that time in *nature*, without which the poet could do nothing"), the Englishman could only do so by unrolling "world-historical events and human fates through all the times and places where they happened."[30] Nevertheless, for all Shakespeare's dependence upon historical conditions and theatrical traditions, his genius also produced something "new, first, completely different" (S V, 218). What Herder particularly treasures in Shakespeare is his ability to capture characters, families, customs, situations, and the like at a particular time and place – and no other. "When I read him, theater, actor, curtains disappear! only individual pages from the book of events, providence, the world, blowing in the storm of the times! individual marks of peoples, classes, souls," yet "filled with one soul breathing through, animating everything" (S V, 219ff.). The individuals cooperate in the direction of the whole, not in a direct and conceptual way (no cunning of reason), but rather as "obscure, little symbols outlining a theodicy," grasped by feeling (S V, 220).

The way in which Herder extends his interpretation of Shakespearean drama to history epitomizes his aesthetic holism. There are ample insinuations of that extension in the Shakespeare essay itself as when he rhapsodizes about Shakespeare: "Here is no poet! here is the creator! here is the history of the world!"[31] Eleven years after the Shakespeare essay Herder makes a valiant attempt to transfer this genetic yet also organic conception of art, beginning with its natural basis, to history itself as he devotes the first two parts of his monumental *Ideas for a Philosophy of the History of Mankind* (1784–91) to the study of the cosmic, physical, and biological basis of humanity and its presence in diverse cultures before turning in the final two books to recorded history proper. Placing human beings at the nexus of nature and a spiritual world, he observes: "The principles of this philosophy are as simple and unmistakable as the fact that it is a natural history of human beings: *tradition and organic forces*."[32] The need to join the philosophies of nature and history in some fashion is not lost on Schelling and Hegel, both of whom take their cues from the notion of reason that emerges from the *Ideas*, namely, a self-developing reason continuous with nature and history.[33]

Herder's *Ideas* is not, however, his first work on the philosophy of history after his Shakespeare essay nor arguably the work most consistent with its insights. In *Yet Another Philosophy of History* (1774), Herder describes history as a theater piece in which we are all players in a chain of events that only the divine playwright can oversee (S V, 558f.). Here the empirical theodicy described in the Shakespeare essay takes shape as Herder attempts to steer a course between progressivism and skepticism, each of which in his view not only neglects the uniqueness of historical individuals and events, but also puts in question divine omnipotence as the ultimate source of meaning. At the same time *Yet Another Philosophy of History* throws down the gauntlet at the Enlightenment: "'In Europe there is supposed to be more virtue now than there has ever been in the entire world?' – And why? because there is more *enlightenment* in it – I believe that precisely for that reason there would have to be less" (S V, 554). Anticipating Schiller and the young idealists among others, Herder lampoons his own age's infirmity: its alienation of theory from practice and mind from heart, its narcissistic detachment combined with philosophical abstractness, all of which play into the hands of theoretical and political absolutism by rendering uniformity and arbitrary mechanization not only possible but plausible (S V, 535–9).

A combination of parody and sermon most associated with Herder's "historicism," *Yet Another Philosophy of History* was conceived by him as a prelude to the larger project that became the *Ideas*. Yet, while the *Ideas* occasionally echoes the earlier work in remarks about the completeness of each age in itself and the role played by negation in historical change, it also sets forth a kind of organic progression in which, with temporary exceptions, the later surpasses the earlier. In short, a principle of continuity, an ordered, even teleological development overrides discontinuities – as it does in Fichte's *Characteristics of the Present Age*, in Schelling's *System of Transcendental Idealism*, and Hegel's *Lectures on the Philosophy of History*.[34]

Hamann's criticisms of Herder's prize-winning *Treatise on the Origin of Language* (1772) have already been mentioned, but the treatise warrants separate attention for its holistic view of language. The treatise won the essay contest of the Berlin Academy on the question: "In supposing humans left to their own natural faculties, are they in a position to invent language?"[35] Herder's aim in the treatise is to give an adequate account of the human origin of human language. But in the process of pursuing this rather straightforward-sounding goal, Herder does more than dispute attempts to locate the origin in God (Süßmilch's thesis) or in the aspects of human nature that are continuous with those of other animals (a thesis purportedly advocated by Rousseau and Condillac). He also impishly and nervously exposes the meaninglessness of the question posed by the Academy, a point not lost on Hamann.[36] For in the course of the *Treatise* Herder rejects key presuppositions of the Academy's question, namely, that human beings and their use of language can be clearly distinguished, that human beings have "natural faculties" that allow them to "invent" language, or even that an explanation can be given at all, if that is to mean looking outside the phenomenon of human language itself for its origin.

In regard to the first of these presuppositions, it bears noting that both Süßmilch and Condillac maintain – as Herder does in the *Treatise* and in his critique of Kant some thirty years later – that human language and human reason are equivalent.[37] Yet, despite considerable and largely unacknowledged overlap with explanations that he opposes, Herder charges that they beg the question of what is distinctive about human language. A considerable controversy has arisen regarding the novelty and the precise meaning of Herder's claim.[38] In Herder's own mind, however, it is patent that, in order for a sign to be able to designate a thought or object, someone has to recognize that it does so. The capacity for this sort of recognition is a natural gift akin to instinct in animals, namely, the power of reflection (*Besonnenheit*). By "reflection" Herder means a force (*Kraft*) saturating all conscious bodily activity in a human being ("the whole undivided human soul") and thus not separate from any sensation yet capable of both distinctly (not merely clearly) attending to an "object" by distinguishing a mark (*Merkmal*) of the object and recognizing that it is doing so.[39] Herder thinks that non-human animals are incapable of having distinct ideas, though it is hardly clear that they are, if distinctness consists only in distinguishing a part of the object (e.g., the sheep's bleating) on the basis of which the object can be reidentified. Herder is, however, also claiming that this reidentifiability or recognizability is bi-conditionally related to some level of self-consciousness, a claim that lends his theory about the human distinctiveness of this use of signs some warrant. In any event, the mark of reflection is "the word of the soul," a claim entailing the inseparability of reflection, the capacity for distinct apperception, and language (though something akin to a private language is countenanced).[40] Herder thus makes his own Leibniz's conception of *apperceptio*, which he translates "recognition" (*Anerkennung*). The recognition of this power as one's own is also the basis of self-determination: "No longer an infallible machine in the hands of nature, he becomes himself the purpose and aim of the work" (S V, 28). In sum, Herder is arguing that, in order for language to serve as an instrumental system of conventional signs designating thoughts and objects, it is necessary for human beings to agree to this arrangement, and the basis of that agreement is the distinctively apperceptive and self-determining character of human consciousness. What distinguishes humans from other animals is, Herder submits, the fact that a human being alone "knows that it knows, wants, and acts."[41]

The second part of Herder's treatise opens with the line: "Nature gives no forces in vain" (S V, 93). Humans are endowed with reflection, a capacity of human language, in the interest of preservation and progress. After iterating that "there is no condition in the human soul that is not capable of words or actually determined by words of the soul," he declares:

> As bold as it might sound, it is true: the human being feels with the intellect and speaks because he thinks. And because he thus always thinks further then as well and, as we say, holds each thought in stillness with the previous one and the future, then each condition that is connected by means of reflection, must think better, thereby also speak better. (S V, 100)

This declaration aptly captures Herder's aesthetic holism and the difficulties that it bequeaths to German Idealism. One such difficulty is presented by the synthetic character assigned by Herder to language. Language may well be a synthesis of sensibility and understanding but if they cannot be distinguished, it is not clear how that claim itself can be meaningfully sustained or how, indeed, any criterion for distinct reflection, the supposed hallmark of humanity, can be given. In a thoroughgoing holism, there is no *primus inter pares*. A cognate difficulty is the patent appeal to an "intuitive understanding," something that Kant rejects but Hegel later applauds, and its cousin, the "intellectual intuition" also rejected by Kant but affirmed by Fichte as well as by Schelling and Hegel at early stages in their thinking.[42] A final, related difficulty has already been mentioned but resurfaces here when Herder affirms the progressive character of language, in keeping with mankind's inherently social make-up and the "chain of culture."[43] This view remains in apparent contradiction with his insistence elsewhere on the relativeness of any earthly standpoint and the divine presence in every age.[44]

Schiller and the aesthetics of play

In addition to corresponding with Kant occasionally, Hamann, Herder, and Schiller developed their respective views through critical contrasts with those of Kant who, at least in the case of Herder and Schiller, responded publicly in kind. Mention has already been made of Kant's harsh reviews of Herder's historical writings, leading to a breach in their relationship.[45] Between Kant and Schiller matters proceeded more amicably, as the center of gravity shifted from theoretical to practical reason and aesthetic judgment. When Schiller endorsed Kant's moral principles but objected to his way of presenting obligatoriness in the absence of grace, Kant suggested that there need be no disagreement among them as long as duty, the dignity of which was in his view necessarily independent of grace, was distinguished from virtue which was not. Schiller was not persuaded but he retained an enthusiasm, not shared by Herder, for the transcendental turn introduced into philosophy by Kant.[46]

Schiller's relation to the German idealists was not a one-way street, as it was for Hamann and Herder. While Hamann died before Fichte had published a single word, and Herder was generally dismissive of Fichte's and Schelling's work, Schiller openly acknowledged his debt to Fichte's efforts to rethink Kant's transcendental philosophy. In 1794, the year of Fichte's move to Jena, he and Schiller served on the same editorial board of the new philosophical journal in which Fichte contributed his essay on language mentioned earlier.[47] In that same year Fichte provided Schiller with an advance copy of the *Science of Knowledge* (*Wissenschaftslehre*), and its theme of the reciprocity of drives found its way, a year later, into Schiller's pivotal account of beauty and the unifying play-drive (*Spieltrieb*) in his *Letters on the Aesthetic Education of Humanity*.[48] Perhaps in part because of his interaction with Fichte, Schiller was also a clear favorite of Schelling and Hegel, each of whom cut his teeth on Fichte's thought.[49] Though all three idealists were laboring in different ways to establish a systematic conception of the sort of self-developing reason or spirit in history projected by Herder, none of them addressed his work in any sustained way. But the same cannot be said for Schiller's writings, especially his *Letters* and *Naïve and Sentimental Poetry*. Together these works provide a model of dialectic that manages to be historical, logical, and aesthetic at once and yet, for that very reason, also provides a challenge to philosophy itself – or at least to the sorts of philosophy that Schelling and Hegel found themselves compelled to elaborate.

Schiller's differences with Kant are particularly telling for the German idealists. One such difference, his resistance to the foundational claims made by Kant for an allegedly pure practical reason, that is to say, a moral reason defined independently of moral sense ("grace"), has already been mentioned.[50] In keeping with Schiller's aesthetic holism, this difference is intimately related to his refusal to accept what he took to be the overly subjectivistic character of Kant's aesthetics. After initially construing a "critique of taste" to be hopeless since its principles are empirical, Kant manages to arrive at transcendental principles for aesthetics – but they are principles merely for reflection upon forms given to a knowing subject (spatial and temporal configurations that are themselves dependent upon the imagination). Schiller continues this move from an empirical to a transcendental conception of beauty, and he also joins Kant in regarding the contemplation of beauty as a means for effecting a transition from nature to morality. In these respects at least, his aesthetics has more affinities with Kant's than with those of Herder or Hamann. However, in Kant's understanding of the aesthetic transition from nature to morality, each of these domains retains its self-sufficiency and validity independent of the other. In Schiller's eyes there is, by contrast, a higher, aesthetic unity to nature and morality, a unity that completes the human being, by integrating a person's identity with her changing conditions, her dignity with her happiness (*Essays*, 158). This completeness of a human being is an aesthetic state, the play of reason and sensibility, directed at beauty. Thus, while he takes Kant to construe beauty in subjective terms, namely, as the form of an object that, when represented, sets our cognitive capabilities into a state of "free play," Schiller defines beauty objectively as a "living form," the object corresponding to the play-drive that completes human nature by freeing it from the constraints of both the sensual and the rational drives. Schiller accordingly observes that "with beauty man shall only play and it is with beauty only that he shall play. For, to mince matters no longer, man plays only when he is in the full sense of the word a human being, and he is wholly a human being only when he plays" (*Essays*, 131; translation slightly altered).

Far from merely completing Schiller's critique of the subjective orientation of Kant's aesthetics, this conception of objective beauty and an organic play-drive has – once again in the tradition of aesthetic holism – epistemological and moral implications as well. For both truth and morality require a countenancing of objectivity that reason alone cannot provide. Acceptance of the objectivity of the world and others requires the ecstatic perspective of an aesthetic state where human beings put themselves in a position "outside themselves," no longer relating to everything else as potential master or slave, but as an object of wonder and contemplation ("the first liberal relation to the surrounding universe") (*Essays*, 162).

But is this aesthetic state, then, means or end – "a middle state" and "necessary precondition," or "the consummation of humanity" and "supreme reality" (*Essays*, 137, 152, 129, 148)? Conceived as a response to the French Revolution's failures, Schiller's *Letters* aim to demonstrate that "if man is ever to solve the problem of politics in practice he will have to approach it through the problem of the aesthetic, because it is only through beauty that man makes his way to freedom" (*Essays*, 90). In the course of the *Letters*, however, beauty and an aesthetic state are also described as constituting freedom itself, the objective self-determination in oneself and others that alone can beckon genuine honor and respect. Thus, claims that beauty has no say in the separate workings of the understanding or the will, and that it serves as a means of moving from a state of nature to a moral state, are offset by observations that "the aesthetic [state] alone is a whole in itself," the necessary intersection of a human being's active, rational and passive, sensuous determinations (*Essays*, 149, 153–6, 176f.). The apparent discrepancy between transitional and consummative conceptions of the aesthetic state, for which Schiller is often criticized, is resolved, at least to some degree, by his doctrine of aesthetic semblance ("the very essence of fine art") at the end of the *Letters*. The aesthetic realm is an independent world of semblances ("ornamentation and play") which, precisely by displaying the ideal harmony of the whole in contrast to the divisiveness of the real world, holds the key to the transformation of the latter.[51]

From the *Letters*' opening apologies for favoring aesthetic over direct political engagement and Rousseauian laments about the wounds inflicted by culture on modernity ("the artist is indeed the child of his age") to its concluding account of the moral promise and indispensability of the aesthetic realm for society, it is evident that Schiller, like Hamann and Herder before him, is preoccupied with the role of art in history and history in art. In keeping, too, with the practice, common to aesthetic holism, of drawing analogies between art and nature, individual and society, cognition and morality, Schiller hits upon a remarkably elastic developmental structure that resurfaces in the Hegelian dialectic. "Nature (sense and intuition) always unites, the understanding always divides, but reason unites once more," he observes (*Essays*, 139n.). The structure of immediacy, its negation, and their unity (negation of the negation) is at work throughout the *Letters* but a particularly pregnant expression of its aesthetic and historical significance is given in *Naive and Sentimental Poetry* (1796). The concept of the naïve captures the ancient and childlike immediacy of nature, belief, and sentiment, while the concept of the sentimental draws on the modern and adolescent preoccupation with itself, mediated by its capacity to understand and remake itself (by its science and art). As in the *Letters*, the resolution of these two divergent and separately limited tendencies is an ideal in which art returns to nature, though the *Letters* ends on a rueful note that it is only achieved in the "finely attuned souls" of a "few chosen circles."[52]

Schiller's enormous impact on German Idealism is registered in no uncertain terms in Hegel's *Lectures on Aesthetics*. "Schiller must be paid the great tribute," he declares, "of having broken through Kantian subjectivity . . . and of having dared to move beyond it, grasping unity and reconciliation" as the ultimate truth of things (*Werke* XIII, 89). Schiller's concept of art, he maintains, comes closest to his own. As if these kudos are not enough, Hegel uses the conclusion to his review of Schiller's essays as a segue to remarks on how science arrived at an absolute standpoint. Hegel is referring specifically to Schelling, but the observation applies equally to his own philosophy.

> This unity of universal and particular, freedom and necessity, spirituality and the natural, what Schiller grasped in a scientific way as the principle and essence of art and relentlessly tried to call into actual life through art and aesthetic education, was then made *as the idea itself* into the principle of knowledge and existence and recognized as what is alone true and actual. (*Werke* III, 91)

In the process, Hegel adds, the scientific place of art was found.

This last remark is particularly telling inasmuch as both Schelling and Hegel respond to aesthetic holism by according art a foundational place within their scientific systems, though they do so in markedly different ways. In the *System of Transcendental Idealism* Schelling construes poetry as the alpha and omega of philosophy in the course of making his argument for an absolute identity of opposites, available through an intellectual, but non-objective, intuition. That identity becomes objective only in art, "the sole true and eternal organon and at the same time document of philosophy," the union of "what is separate in nature and history" (*SW* III, 628). Schiller's differentiation of naïve and sentimental is recast by Schelling as a contrast between the beautiful and the sublime, the objective and the subjective, a contrast that is overcome by "poetry in its absoluteness" (*SW* V, 468–74). Hegel's mature work also elaborates the concept of art as an absolute, though Hamann's incarnate whole – iterated systemically by Schelling – is replaced, in a reinterpretation of the third person of the trinity, by the idea of an absolute spirit. As "the supreme truth . . . the dissolution of the ultimate opposition" between freedom and necessity, spirit and nature, the individual ("subjective spirit," nature becoming self-conscious) and the community ("objective spirit," the self-consciousness of a shared ethical life), absolute spirit recapitulates the aesthetic holism of Hamann, Herder, and Schiller. But art is only the first stage of absolute spirit, superseded historically and systematically by philosophy and, indeed, in the prosaic form of an *Encyclopedia of Philosophical Sciences*. Hegel is, of course, under no illusion that to appropriate aesthetic holism in this way is also to subvert it. He thus brings idealism to a close with words that not even Schelling, let alone Hamann, Herder, or Schiller could endorse: art "has ceased to be the highest need of the spirit."[53]

NOTES

1 On the connection between pietism and the *Sturm und Drang* movement, see M. Mann, *Sturm-und-Drang-Drama* (Berne: Francke, 1974), 42–7. The primary sources cited in the following chapter include: J. G. Hamann, *Sämtliche Werke*, ed. J. Nadler, 6 vols. (Vienna: Herder, 1949–57) (hereafter = N); *Briefwechsel*, ed. W. Ziesemer and A. Henkel, 6 vols. (Wiesbaden: Insel, 1955–75) (hereafter = ZH); *Hamanns Briefwechsel mit F. H. Jacobi*, ed. C. H. Gildemeister (Gotha: Perthes, 1868) (hereafter = G); J. G. Herder, *Sämtliche Werke*, ed. B. Suphan, 32 vols. (Berlin: Wiedmannsche Buchhandlung, 1877–1913) (hereafter = S); F. Schiller, *Werke*, Nationalausgabe, ed. B. von Wiese, 43 vols. (Weimar: Hermann Böhlhaus Nachfolger, 1962) (hereafter = NA) and *Essays*, trans. and ed. W. Hinderer and D. O. Dahlstrom (New York: Continuum, 1993).

2 Cf. Schiller, NA XX, 99: "If we would experience having a national theater, then we would also experience having a nation."

3 Nor is Frederick himself spared; see Hamann's *Au Salomon de Prusse* (1772) in N III, 57ff.; on Frederick and the Academy, see L. W. Beck, *Early German Philosophy: Kant and His Predecessors* (Cambridge, MA: Harvard University Press, 1969), 308–16, 374–92.

4 See R. Koselleck, *Kritik und Krise*, 2nd edn. (Frankfurt am Main: Suhrkamp, 1976), 85 and J. Habermas, *Strukturwandel der Öffentlichkeit* (Neuwied: Luchterhand, 1962), 68.

5 Herder's fear of anthropomorphism, one of the bases of his critique of the divine origin of language, is immediately challenged by the line "I believe, therefore I spoke" (2 Cor. 4:13) on the title page of Hamann's *The Last Will and Testament of the Knight*

of the Rose-Cross on the divine and human origin of language, one of several reviews of Herder's essay on the origin of language.

6 Criticizing Schiller's classification of naïve and sentimental poets, Herder prefers "to leave each flower in its own context and from here to study it from its roots to its top just as it is, in reference to its own time and nature" (S XVIII, 138). Herder and Schiller became acquainted with one another in Weimar and in 1787 discussed their common interest in the concept of nemesis or Andrastea.

7 Isaiah Berlin claims that Hamann's "doctrine of the need for total self-expression as the object of natural human craving for freedom" gave rise to Schiller's "liberation . . . from the despotism – moral as well as aesthetic – of the laws of fanatical eighteenth century rationalism"; *The Magus of the North: J. G. Hamann and the Origins of Modern Irrationalism*, ed. H. Hardy (New York: Farrar, Straus and Giroux, 1993), 66f., 105.

8 For a balanced review of Hamann's criticisms of Herder, see F. Beiser, *The Fate of Reason: German Philosophy from Kant to Fichte* (Cambridge, MA: Harvard University Press, 1987), 135–41.

9 For Hamann's *Metacritique*, see N III, 283–9; see, too, N III, 225; N I, 157f.; ZH VII, 26; for a precis of Hamann's "verbalism," see Beck, *Early German Philosophy*, 376f. Among those cognizant of the challenge that Hamann's work represented to a transcendental philosophy is Fichte; see his 1794 essay "On the Linguistic Capacity and the Origin of Language," translated together with a valuable interpretive essay in J. P. Surber, *Language and German Idealism: Fichte's Linguistic Philosophy* (New Jersey: Humanities, 1996).

10 ZH I, 437; N I, 5, 8; II, 247; each section of history (Egyptian, Carthaginian, Roman) is special just as each has its own "present fate"; see *Hamanns Schriften*, ed. F. Roth (Berlin: Riemer, 1821–5), I, 303; ZH III, 218.

11 J. C. O'Flaherty, *Johann Georg Hamann* (Boston: Twayne, 1979), 21ff. and Beiser, *Fate of Reason*, 19f., 331n.10f.

12 N III 29; II, 73f.; ZH VII, 460; for Hamann's criticisms of Hume see ZH I, 379; N III, 28; II, 208.

13 N II, 73; also ZH VII, 167; G 504: "Faith has need of reason just as much as reason needs faith."

14 N III, 191; ZH IV, 59; "if data are given, why use ficta?" (ZH VI, 331); by ficta Hamann has in mind words, numbers, and systems, "castles in the sky" as he calls them (ZH V, 265; cf. ZH VII, 441; N III, 285); see also ZH V, 264 on the error of confusing words with things.

15 Cf. N I, 24; however, he also distinguishes "the invisible nature shared with God" from "the veiled schema of the body," the image of "the hidden human being in us" (N II, 198).

16 Rejected, too, in the polemic with Mendelssohn – the substance of *Golgotha und Schlebimini!* (1784) – is the unhistorical and, from Hamann's anti-dualist perspective, illogical notion that an intellectual act of assent legitimates the state (N III, 300f.); for an English translation, see S. Dunning, *The Tongues of Men: Hegel and Hamann on Religious Language and History* (Missoula: Scholars Press, 1979).

17 For a useful bi-lingual edition with commentary, see J. C. O'Flaherty, *Hamann's Socratic Memorabilia: A Translation and Commentary* (Baltimore: Johns Hopkins University Press, 1967). The *Sokratische Denkwürdigkeiten* was a reply to an attempt by two friends – Christoph Berens, Hamann's former employer, and Kant – to win him

back to the tenets of the Enlightenment. See too, G. G. Dickson, *Johann Georg Hamann's Relational Metacriticism* (Berlin: de Gruyter, 1995), 28–75.

18 For Hamann's own survey of interpretations of Socrates, see N I, 75.

19 Cf. O'Flaherty, *Hamann's Socratic Memorabilia*, 88ff.

20 N II, 199. Reconceiving distinctions made by J. G. Wachter (kyriological, symbolic or hieroglyphic, and characteristic), Hamann distinguishes poetic, historical, and philosophical forms of speaking.

21 N II, 199; III, 32; I, 308: "the book of nature."

22 N I, 220; herein lies the source of the "expressionism" that Berlin urges is, along with populism and pluralism, a hallmark of Herder's thought; cf. I. Berlin, *Vico and Herder: Two Studies in the History of Ideas* (London: Hogarth, 1976), 153, 165–80 and *The Roots of Romanticism*, ed. H. Hardy (Princeton, NJ: Princeton University Press, 1999), 59f.

23 Hegel says, in fact, that Hamann's writings are style "through and througth"; on their unavailability, see S. Jørgensen, "Hamann und seine Wirkung im Idealismus," in *Idealismus und Aufklärung*, ed. C. Jamme and G. Kurz (Stuttgart: Klett-Cotta, 1988), 153–61.

24 The standard intellectual biographies of Herder in English (which have the scholarly advantage of disagreeing with one another) are A. Gillies, *Herder* (Oxford: Blackwell, 1945) and R. T. Clark, Jr., *Herder, His Life and Thought* (Berkeley: University of California Press, 1955).

25 S VIII, 170; see also S V, 92 and S IX, 301; as with many other notions in Herder, his conception of analogy is articulated by Hamann; cf. N II, 206f.: "This analogy of the human to the creator imparts its stamp and content to all creatures."

26 S XIII, 81f., 126f. Parts one and two of Herder's *Ideas* are panned by Kant precisely for their appeal by way of analogy to a basic force. "This is still metaphysics, and what is more, very dogmatic metaphysics, even though our author renounces it, as fashion demands," Kant concludes; cf. I. Kant, *On History*, ed. L. W. Beck (Indianapolis: Bobbs-Merrill, 1963), 38. On the ways Kant's critique of teleological judgment is influenced by his continuing debate with the position of Herder and his circle, see J. Zammito, *The Genesis of Kant's "Critique of Judgment"* (Chicago: University of Chicago Press, 1992), 178–88.

27 See S XVI, 441 (*God, Some Conversations*, 1787); ibid., 541, 566.

28 S I, 151f., 179, 240, 414f.

29 A similar concern for native genius motivates his ground-breaking publication of *Folk Songs* and *Songs of Love* in 1778 and popular defense of the Old Testament in *The Spirit of Hebrew Poetry, an Introduction for Lovers of the Same and of the Most Ancient History of the Human Spirit* of 1782–3.

30 S V, 221, 226; see also 225: "Take from this plant its soil, water, and force and plant it in the air; take from these human beings place, time, individual constitution – you have taken breath and soul from them and it is a mere picture of the creation."

31 S V, 223; see ibid., 230f.: "Each [theater] piece is history in the widest sense . . . testimony to a world event, a human fate"; see *Friedrich Wilhelm Joseph von Schellings sämmtliche Werke*, ed. K. F. A. Schelling (Stuttgart/Augsburg: Cotta, 1859) (hereafter = *SW*) III, 602f. for a similar exploitation of the way history is a drama.

32 S XIII, 347.

33 S XIII, 145: "Theoretically and practically, reason (*Vernunft*) is nothing else but something heard (*Vernommenes*), a learned proportion and orientation of ideas and forces,

to which a human being is educated according to his organization and manner of living." See *SW* I, 4, 66f.

34 S XIV, 207: "If God meanwhile is in nature, then he is also in history . . ."; 213: "All the destructive forces in nature must not only submit to the preserving forces in the course of time, but also even themselves serve ultimately for the development of the whole"; see, too, 239: "In keeping with the laws of their inner nature, reason and equity must also acquire a larger place among men in the course of time and promote an enduring humanity."

35 "En supposant les hommes abandonnés à leurs facultés naturelles, sont-ils en état d'inventer le langage?" This question is only the first of two questions set by the Berlin Academy.

36 S V, 147; Clark, *Herder, His Life and Thought*, 136: ". . . the *Treatise* shows a Voltairean or Swiftian gall."

37 See S V, 40: "Without language a human being has no reason and without reason no language"; see ibid., 100; S XXI, 9, 88; for a linguistic critique of the thing in itself, see ibid., 173f.

38 On Herder's appropriation of themes from his predecessors and unfairness to them, see H. Aarsleff, "The Tradition of Condillac: The Problem of the Origin of Language in the Eighteenth Century in the Berlin Academy before Herder," in D. Hymes, ed., *Studies in the History of Linguistics* (Bloomington, IN: Indiana University Press, 1974), 93–156; and C. Taylor, "The Importance of Herder," in E. and A. Margalit, eds., *Isaiah Berlin: A Celebration* (Chicago: University of Chicago Press, 1991), 40–63.

39 For this emphasis on distinctness in reflection and the role of the distinguishing feature, see S V, 35f., 39, 46f., 50f., 64, 79, 94f., esp. 96: "Animals combine their thoughts obscurely or clearly, but not distinctly."

40 Or the equivalence of reflection and what in the twentieth century might be called the "intentionality" underlying the semantic use of signs. S V, 35: "This first distinguishing mark of reflection was the word of the soul! With it, human language is invented!"

41 S V, 31; following Shaftesbury (as well as Reimarus and Rousseau), Herder develops a principle, common to humans and other animals, of the respective interaction between environment and native powers; the power of sensations and instincts is inversely related to their range and herein lies the basis of human freedom; see S V, 22–8, 110f. Nevertheless, reflection implies not merely lively or clear knowledge but the capacity to recognize distinguishing features: "the first act of this recognition yields distinct conception; it is the first judgment of the soul" (S V, 35).

42 Kant, *KrV* B138f. and *Kritik der Urteilskraft*, in *Kants Werke* (Berlin: de Gruyter, 1968), V, 406; Fichte, *Zweite Einleitung in die Wissenschaftslehre*, in *Fichtes Werke* (Berlin: de Gruyter, 1971), I, 463; Schelling, *System des transzendentalen Idealismus* (*SW* III, 369f.); Hegel, *Glauben und Wissen* (*Werke in zwanzig Bänden*, ed. E. Moldenhauer and K. M. Michel (Frankfurt am Main: Suhrkamp, 1969–71), II, 325).

43 S V, 116: "No individual human being is here for itself; he is inserted into the whole of the species, he is only one for the progressing succession."

44 S V, 557ff., 584ff. Herder apparently had little contact with Fichte (at least one conversation took place in August, 1795) but Herder wrote a letter that played an important role in the "Atheism Controversy" and Fichte's later dismissal from Jena in 1799.

45 See note 26.

46 Just as research on Hamann struggles to recover the rationality of his thought ignored by early commentaries, so there is a tendency among researchers on Schiller to reinstate the deliberately rhetorical dimension of his aesthetic writings in the wake of previous attempts to read them primarily as philosophical tracts; cf. J. Sychrava, *Schiller to Derrida: Idealism in Aesthetics* (Cambridge: Cambridge University Press, 1989).

47 See note 9.

48 Fichte, *Grundlage der gesamten Wissenschaftslehre*, in *Fichtes Werke* I, 287–90, 293f., 319f. Schiller acknowledges debts to Fichte in the fourth and thirteenth letters: see H-G. Pott, *Die schöne Freiheit* (Munich: Fink, 1980). In 1795 Schiller and Fichte had a falling-out when Schiller rejected Fichte's essay "On the Spirit and Letter in Philosophy" for confusing philosophical and non-philosophical styles.

49 Schelling paid Schiller a visit in 1796; for Schelling's views on Schiller's aesthetics, see his *SW* V 470–7, 463n.

50 See the first paragraph of this section.

51 See *Essays* 168f., 176f.; A. Gethmann-Siefert, *Die Funktion der Kunst in der Geschichte* (Bonn: Bouvier, 1984), 61n. and D. C. Durst, *Zur politischen Ökonomie der Sittlichkeit bei Hegel und der ästhetischen Kultur bei Schiller* (Vienna: Passagen, 1994).

52 *Essays* 178, 233n.

53 *Werke* XVIII, 141f.: "For us art is no longer the supreme way in which truth procures existence for itself."

5

PAUL FRANKS

All or nothing: systematicity and nihilism in Jacobi, Reinhold, and Maimon

If one looks to Fichte, Schelling, and Hegel for illumination of the problems addressed by other philosophers – such as the nature of things, the freedom of the will, and the existence of God – one may experience at least initial frustration. They seem to write as though the completion of "the system" were philosophy's principal problem, under which all others are subsumed. Not only do they appear mostly to take this view for granted, they also assume a particular view of systematicity, requiring the whole of philosophy to articulate a single principle. Why interpret systematicity in this monistic fashion, and why ascribe it such importance? Why must it be all or nothing?

Reading Kant only raises further questions. Since he attaches neither the same meaning nor the same value to philosophical systematization, how could the German idealists think that systematization in accordance with a single principle was necessary to complete Kant's revolution?

To answer these questions, we must study figures who, although less famous today, established the philosophical context within which Kant was first read and within which Fichte, Schelling, and Hegel formed their views – figures such as Friedrich Heinrich Jacobi (1743–1819), Karl Leonhard Reinhold (1757–1823), and Salomon Maimon (1753/4–1800).

All these figures regarded human reason as under threat. Each gave a distinct diagnosis, yet monistic systematicity was always at the centre of discussion – sometimes as the cause of the crisis, sometimes as its cure. Moreover, Kant's view of the threat and of its resolution differed fundamentally from the views of those who shaped his reception. Hence Kant was widely misunderstood at first, and soon parted from those who sought to complete his work.

I Jacobi's defense of reason against rationalism

Jacobi was the gadfly of his age, who provoked or exacerbated three major controversies on a single, complex theme: the controversy over Lessing's alleged Spinozism,[1] the controversy over Fichte's alleged atheism,[2] and the controversy over Schelling's alleged pantheism.[3] The first put the issue of monistic system-aticity at the center of philosophical debate and established the context in which the German idealists interpreted Kant.[4]

Jacobi has been difficult to understand, both for his contemporaries and for later readers. This is mainly because his ideas cut against the grain of the Enlightenment age in which he began to write and whose death-knell he sounded. Jacobi challenged rationalist assumptions which went without saying for his contemporaries and which seemed so inseparable from reason that Jacobi was taken to be an *irrationalist*.[5] I will argue, however, that his project was intended to *rescue* reason from *rationalism*. Indeed, Jacobi himself was so entangled in the rationalist conception of reason, that he did not succeed in clarifying his position until the end of his life.[6] I will draw upon Jacobi's later writings to explain his earlier writings, hoping to bring to his position a clarity for which he himself struggled.

Reasons were conceived by Jacobi's contemporaries, not as context-dependent responses to specific episodes of puzzlement, but as the conditions explaining why things existed at all, and why things were as they were and not otherwise. Behind, as it were, a given thing's existence or properties, stretched a series of explanatory reasons. If one thinks of reasons in this way, it is natural to wonder where, if anywhere, a series of reasons might end. Could there be an infinite series, and would that mean that one would never reach a stable resting place from which to fully understand the thing in question? Or could there be a finite series? And, if there could be a finite series, could it simply end, for no reason, and would that not render the thing in question intelligible only to a limited or finite degree? Or could a finite series end with a self-explanatory reason, and would that not render the thing in question intelligible to an unlimited or infinite degree? According to the rationalist position so rigorously articulated by Leibniz, reason demanded this latter kind of infinite intelligibility.

Jacobi's attitude to these questions was coloured, I believe, by an experience he had at the tender age of eight or nine:

> That *extraordinary* thing was a representation of endless duration, quite independent of any religious concept. At the said age, when I was pondering on eternity *a parte ante*, it suddenly came over me with such clarity, and seized me with such violence, that I gave out a loud cry and fell into a kind of swoon. A movement in me, quite natural, forced me to revive the same representation as soon as I came to myself, and the result was a state of unspeakable despair. The thought of annihilation, which had always been dreadful to me, now became even more dreadful, nor could I bear the vision of an *eternal forward duration* any better.
>
> . . . I gradually managed not to be afflicted by this trial so often, and finally managed to free myself from it altogether . . .
>
> This representation has often seized me again since then, despite the care that I

constantly take to avoid it. I have reason to suspect that I can arbitrarily evoke it in me any time I want; and I believe that it is in my power, were I to do so repeatedly a few times, to take my life within minutes by this means.[7]

The vision that made Jacobi faint was of an infinite series of conditions. But he found no relief in the thought of a finite series of conditions that simply ended, bordering on nothingness. Jacobi was at once horrified and fascinated, both by the idea of an infinite series and by the idea of an annihilated series. Originally occasioned by the thought of a series of temporal moments, this experience of dread seems later to have become associated with the idea of a series of reasons or explanatory conditions. Jacobi sought a stable standpoint, as though his very life depended upon it. Hence the title page of his Spinoza book bore the motto: "δος μοι που στο" ("Give me a place to stand").[8] I suspect that he must have been powerfully attracted by the rationalist idea of infinite intelligibility, of a finite series ending in a *causa sui*. But he came to believe that this idea was exactly as good as nothing. Since he could not live with any of the other options, his radical solution was to abandon the very idea of reasons as explanatory conditions and of human reason as the capacity to understand why things existed and were as they were.

We are now ready to understand the significance of the Spinozism controversy, which Jacobi provoked by letting it be known that Lessing, a recently deceased hero of the Enlightenment, had intimated to Jacobi in conversation that he was a Spinozist. Since Spinozism was generally regarded as untenable and irreligious, it seemed important at the time for Mendelssohn and other friends of Lessing to determine whether Lessing actually had been a Spinozist and, if so, whether his Spinozism was defensible and consistent with theism. But Jacobi's deeper point was that *anybody* who, like Spinoza and Lessing, developed a maximally *consistent* version of the rationalist conception of reasons as explanatory grounds, would be led inexorably to a system that was (A) monistic, (B) atheistic, (C) fatalistic, and (D) nihilistic.[9] Why did Jacobi believe that rationalism led to these consequences, and what alternative did he offer?

Jacobi gave no fully explicit argument for his view of rationalism, and I doubt a rigorous argument is possible, but the framework of an argument may be reconstructed from his scattered remarks. The argument for (A) begins with (1) the Principle of Sufficient Reason, which Jacobi prefers to formulate as "Nothing comes from nothing."[10] Two consequences are tacitly assumed to follow from the Principle, as they would have been by many contemporary readers: (2) for any series of explanatory reasons, there is some self-explanatory reason, and (3) for every series of explanatory reasons, there is a unique self-explanatory reason: the First Cause.[11] Spinoza's central claims, in Jacobi's view,[12] are that (4) the First Cause cannot be an entity that is (a) transcendent and (b) rational, and (5) the

First Cause must instead be identified with being: the infinite totality of which entities are modifications or parts. The argument for (4a) is that, if the First Cause transcended the totality of series of conditions, temporally (by existing prior to creation) or modally (by being capable of existing without creation), either there would be some *prior* reason for creation (whether regarded as a temporal act or as an eternal actuality) and the First Cause would not be first, or the First Cause would be conditioned by nothingness, contravening the Principle.[13] The argument for (4b) is that rationality involves representation and will, but representation involves relation to an object, while will involves self-relation, and the First Cause cannot have relational properties, for its relatedness would require prior reason or else be conditioned by nothingness.[14] However, (5) the First Cause can (therefore must) be the totality of the series of conditions, regarded as an infinite whole prior to its finite parts, or the *ens realissimum* of which all realities are limitations.[15] Therefore, infinite intelligibility requires all finite realities to be modifications of one infinite substance: in short, the Principle of Sufficient Reason entails that reality be a monistic system, which philosophy should mirror.

Consistent rationalism is (B) atheistic, not because it cannot call the infinite substance "God," but because, for Jacobi, only belief in a transcendent, divine person (with intellect and will) is genuinely theistic.[16] Connected to this claim is the thesis that consistent rationalism is (C) fatalistic insofar as it excludes the purposive, free acts of both infinite *and finite* personality altogether, recognizing only the blind operations of fate. For to be a person is to be an entity capable of initiating finite series of conditions. Consistent rationalism can at best allow us to be *observers* of activity, not *agents*.[17] This entails (D) nihilism in one sense, for nihilism goes beyond idealism in denying, not only the independent subsistence of material entities, but also the independent subsistence of spiritual entities. Consistent rationalism is also nihilistic in the further sense that it denies the existence of entities altogether. To be an entity is to be the individual locus of organic activity, determined both in contrast with other entities and in terms of some positive internal nature. Rationalism's infinite substance is not an entity, for it has no contrast, and the finite modifications of substance also fail to be entities, because they are determined only through contrast. For Jacobi, the lesson was clear: the Principle of Sufficient Reason led inexorably to an All that was One and therefore Nothing.[18]

Jacobi came to believe that, prompted by his Spinoza interpretation, Fichte and Schelling had developed still more thoroughgoing rationalisms. By characterizing the infinite substance as "the absolute I," Jacobi thought that Fichte had made explicit rationalism's self-deification. To comprehend something, Jacobi contended, was to represent the conditions under which it became as it is, and we best comprehended what we could construct. The quest for infinite intelligibility therefore led to the annihilation of the actual, external things we wished to comprehend, for which we substituted our own idealized construc-tions.[19] By rigorously pursuing the quest for explanation, Fichte had shown Spinoza's infinite substance to be a divinized version of our own capacity to understand. Breaking with Fichte, Schelling argued that the infinite substance had to be understood, not as an I, but rather as an absolute indeterminacy dynamically generating finite things. For Jacobi, this showed that rationalism led ultimately, not to a self-grounding ground, but to what Schelling himself called an "abyss" or "non-ground": a chaos that was, and explained, nothing.[20]

As an alternative, Jacobi recommended a *salto mortale* or life-risking leap to "faith."[21] Mendelssohn and others understandably thought that Jacobi was invoking *Christian* faith in opposition to reason.[22] But Jacobi was invoking a faith into which "we are all born . . . just as we are all born in society,"[23] not a faith with a specific history, requiring conversion. Although he used Christian language, Jacobi's conception of faith was inspired by Spinoza, "who drew a clear distinction between being certain and not doubting,"[24] and by Hume, who saw that, although skepticism may be irrefutable, "men are carried, by a natural instinct or prepossession, to repose faith in their senses."[25]

Systematic monism, atheism, fatalism, and nihilism were irrefutable, because they were inevitable results of the rationalist project of demonstrating, compre-hending or explaining everything without limitation. Indeed, to refute rational-ism by *demonstrating* its falsehood or inadequacy would only be to continue the project! Since rationalism arose from a loss of faith, one could escape only by changing one's life and returning to pre-philosophical faith in the existence of things, oneself, and God.

Far from being opposed to reason, this was "the *natural faith of reason*."[26] Jacobi came to believe that what rationalism called "reason" was actually an abstraction from the capacity for *understanding* (*Verstand*), which was sub-ordinate to reason proper (*Vernunft*).[27] First, understanding (grasping the condi-tions of a thing) was only a means for achieving the true goal of intellectual research, which was not explanation, but "to unveil *existence* (*Dasein*), and to reveal it."[28] Second, understanding was never self-sufficient, because every explanation had unexplained presuppositions.[29] Properly speaking, reason was the capacity, not to comprehend the explanatory conditions of things, but to per-ceive the infinite,[30] which remained ineluctably mysterious.[31] Reason perceived those places where explanation ended: human personality and the personality of God. The rationalist quest for infinite intelligibility undermined the ground on which explanations stood, a ground that we could feel but not comprehend.

"The natural faith of reason" involved commitment to the existence both of things as individual organisms, determined both reciprocally and through their teleologies,[32] and of human persons as determining themselves in relation to the divine person who is "the 'More than I!' the 'better than I!' – Someone entirely Other."[33] Jacobi never developed these influential ideas into a metaphysical, epistemological or ethical theory. Nor, by his own lights, could he have consistently done so. Opposed to the rationalist project he discerned in the entire philosophical tradition since Aristotle,[34] his was an "unphilosophy."[35]

In light of Jacobi's position, we can understand his famous criticism of Kant, "that *without* [the presupposition that things in themselves affect the senses] I could not enter into the system, but *with* it I could not stay within it."[36] Particular explanations presupposed faith in the explanatory factor they invoked, but the rationalist project of total explanation presupposed a *loss* of faith. Kant's natural faith was manifest in his assertions that things in themselves existed and that sensibility was genuinely receptive, distinct from the spontaneous faculties of understanding and reason.[37] But this dualistic residue was incompatible with his rationalist thesis that knowable objects were mere appearances. If we could know only appearances, how could we know that sensibility was receptive and that things in themselves existed? Kant faced a dilemma. Either he could be a consistent rationalist by confessing "transcendental ignorance" of the existence of things in themselves, and developing "the strongest idealism ever professed."[38] Or he could abandon rationalism and return to natural faith. Jacobi's criticism is sometimes cited as pointing toward idealism. But Jacobi himself endorsed faith in things in themselves.

II Kant's dualism

Like Jacobi, Kant was troubled by the rationalist conception of infinite intelligibility. But the differences between their concerns, neglected by many readers under Jacobi's influence, meant that Kant's project was misunderstood and transformed.

Kant's concerns were motivated neither by the mind's demand for respite from reflection nor by the dread of nothingness. They were initially driven by the tensions between the admirable achievements of Newtonian physics and Leibnizian metaphysics.

Newton's success was sufficient to vitiate skepticism about natural science. But, as Leibniz argued, Newton's physics conflicted with reason's demand for infinite intelligibility. First, Newtonian space was an infinite manifold of homogeneous points. This meant that any determinate location and orientation of the totality of objects was a brute fact, for which not even God could give sufficient reason.[39] Second, Newtonian laws explained every event in terms of prior sufficient conditions. This apparently entailed that there could be no first causes, whether of the world or of free actions.

Dualism[40] was Kant's hard-won solution. About the world as known by God,

Leibniz had been largely correct: reason demanded that it be an infinitely intelligible realm of things in themselves, completely determined by their inner principles. But, about the world as known by us, Newton had been largely correct: it was a finitely intelligible realm of things possessing formal features for which there was no sufficient reason, although those forms could themselves be known by us a priori, because they were brute facts about *our* cognitive capacities. In the first *Critique*, Kant argued that the phenomenal world was *finitely* – but nonetheless *genuinely* – intelligible. In the second, he argued that, although only phenomena were *knowable*, reason legitimately demanded the infinite intelligibility of a free and autonomous life, and "rational faith" in a personal God.

The dualism was threefold. Kant distinguished the finitely intelligible realm of phenomena from the infinitely intelligible realm of things in themselves. He also distinguished the capacity of sensibility, which was capable of receiving data only in the finitely intelligible form of Newtonian space and time, from the spontaneous capacity of reason, which demanded the infinite intelligibility of Leibniz's Principle of Sufficient Reason. Finally, with respect to the intermediate cognitive faculty of understanding, Kant distinguished the *matter* of human understanding's cognition – received through the finitely intelligible form of sensibility – from understanding's *forms* – which could be *either* applied to matter for cognition of phenomena *or* employed independently of matter for thinking things in themselves.

Kant's insistence on systematicity[41] did not undermine his dualism. Systematicity was intended to demonstrate the necessary *harmony* within each of Kant's dualities, not to show that phenomena and noumena, receptivity and spontaneity, form and matter, were really *one*. Furthermore, systematization was not required in order to *ground* intelligibility against doubt or dread. Finite science and infinite morality were already secure. But harmonization was necessary if we were to inhabit *both* realms without *despair*. Kant argued in the third *Critique* that it was rational to hope for the cooperation of phenomena with the human pursuits of natural science, virtue, and happiness, because it was rational to assume the ultimate harmoniousness of our finitely intelligible condition with God's infinitely intelligible *purpose*. Someone like Spinoza, who lacked commitment to the infinite purposiveness of finitude, could be virtuous (and scientific), but would despair in a world where things happened without sufficient reason.[42]

Read in the context created by Jacobi, Kant's response to the crisis of reason was little understood and less appreciated. Kantian dualism was sometimes assimilated to Jacobi's very different dualism, which distinguished the finitely intelligible realm of understanding from the infinitely *un*intelligible realm of faith. And Kant's demand for systematicity was sometimes assimilated to the Spinozist demand that finite intelligibility be grounded as a modification of infinite intelligibility. Readers formed by Jacobi, who did *not* abandon rationalism, could not be satisfied by Kant's harmonization of the finite and the infinite. For them, Kantianism could become consistent only if transformed into a monistic system, while rationalism could avoid fatalism and nihilism only if synthesized with Kantian freedom.

III Reinhold's quest for systematic reconciliation

Kant's *Critique of Pure Reason* first gained widespread appreciation in 1786–7, when Reinhold's *Letters on the Kantian Philosophy*[43] presented Kant's philosophy as the solution to problems raised in the Spinozism controversy. As a result, Reinhold was appointed in 1787 to the new chair in Kantian philosophy at Jena. But in 1789, the man widely regarded as Kant's spokesman published the first attempted completion of Kant's revolution through monistic systematization.[44]

If Reinhold was the first *post*-Kantian, it was because he read Kant within the problematic established by Jacobi.[45] Reinhold became a Kantian to address the need, brought out by Jacobi, for a uniquely stable standpoint that adequately connected reason with faith. But he had also been convinced by Jacobi that such a standpoint would have the monistic systematicity of Spinozism. And this led Reinhold to unwittingly undermine Kant's dualism through the very procedure he developed to defend it.

Reinhold had personally experienced the need for stability as he moved, in the course of a decade, from religious supernaturalism to atheism, then to rationalist theism, and then to skepticism.[46] None of these systems, he told Kant, could unite his head with his heart.[47] A Jesuit novice-master at Vienna, he became a Mason and Illuminatus before fleeing to Weimar, where he became a Protestant in 1784. But there was no stable standpoint of reason even in the heartland of Reformation and Enlightenment, where the Spinozism dispute soon broke out. It was a time of unprecedented, "general shuddering of all our previous doctrinal structures,"[48] in which "hot-headed fanatics" waged intellectual war against "cold-hearted sophists."[49] Jacobi, Mendelssohn, and Wizenmann had set the conflict of head and heart on a new level, by raising the question of the very nature of reason. But none of them had realized that, before the Spinoza controversy, Kant had already answered the question, establishing the unique standpoint sought by all. Discovering Kant, Reinhold experienced a "salutary revolution."[50] His letters were intended to create readers for Kant's neglected work.[51]

Reinhold's conception of how to achieve the uniquely stable standpoint was to stay constant, despite later changes in philosophical affiliation. When each side could refute the other without demonstrating its own validity,[52] instability was unavoidable. But stability could be achieved by articulating an unsuspected "middle-concept,"[53] through which the partial truth and partial falsehood on each side would be revealed, reconciling all parties. Jesus had once reconciled Jewish religion with Greek morality through the concept of a universal, divine Father.[54] Now Christian faith had to be reconciled with philosophical reason, if philosophy was to ground political freedom and natural rights.[55] Without consensus on principles, philosophy would be "a mere thought-game."[56] But reconciliation and consensus could be achieved through Kant's conception of "rational faith." Kant was the "second Immanuel,"[57] Reinhold the preacher of "the gospel of pure reason."[58]

However, when Reinhold prepared to teach his first introduction to Kant, he found that many had read Kant without becoming reconciled. Reviewers and critics had either misunderstood Kant or found him wholly unintelligible. In his *Letters*, Reinhold had emphasized Kant's *results*, addressing a general audience, but, in a series of works beginning in 1789, he turned to Kant's *premises*, addressing future professional philosophers.[59] Reinhold argued that, although Kant's results possessed "universal validity," they had not yet attained the "universal acknowledgment"[60] required for reconciliation, because the initial premise of his arguments remained unstated. Kant had justified a priori knowledge of the forms of sensibility and understanding by showing them to be necessary conditions of, respectively, the possibility of synthetic a priori mathematical knowledge and the possibility of experience. But, first, Kant had *specified* the forms of sensibility and understanding through "a complete induction," not a genuine deduction.[61] Second, Kant had not forestalled objections to his deductions of our *knowledge* of those forms: rationalists could deny that mathematics was synthetic, while empiricists could deny the actuality of experience in Kant's sense: "empirical knowledge" involving universality and necessity.[62] Third, Kant's explicit premises were not only too *weak*, they were also too *narrow*.[63] At best, Kant had founded a complete account of our access to the finite, phenomenal world, not a complete account of our access to the infinite, noumenal world. Without a complete and universally acknowledged system, the disputes would continue: dogmatists would propose competing theories about things in themselves and skeptics would doubt that *any* views about the infinite were rational.

Reinhold offered a cure as well as a diagnosis. He formulated the initial premise unstated by Kant as a definitive clarification of "representation," the "middle-concept" through which empiricists and rationalists could be reconciled. From that premise,[64] Reinhold claimed to derive the forms of sensibility and understanding, and to demonstrate conclusively that theistic faith was theoretically unattainable, yet practically rational. Responding triumphantly to Jacobi, one of Reinhold's works bore the same motto as Jacobi's Spinoza book: "δος μοι που στο."[65] The uniquely stable standpoint of reason, discovered by Kant, had been vindicated by Reinhold.

However, convinced that Spinozism was the maximally consistent version of rationalism,[66] Reinhold misread Kant's conception of systematicity as monistic.[67] Moreover, his own procedure – deducing the forms of sensibility, understanding and reason from a highest first principle – is charitably interpreted as monistic. For his procedure faces an apparent dilemma: either the first principle expresses a concrete but particular state of consciousness, or it expresses an abstract generalization about all states of consciousness; in the former case, no universal consequences follow; in the latter, universal consequences follow, but only at an equally abstract level of generality, not about more specific features of consciousness.[68] Construed monistically, however, the procedure is coherent: the first principle expresses the substance of the totality of states of consciousness, of which every particular state is a derivative modification.

If successful,[69] Reinhold's derivations would have undermined the Kantian dualism they were intended to support. First, the dualism of sensibility and understanding could not be maintained if the formal features of both faculties were derivable from a single principle expressing their common root. Second, Reinhold explicitly denied the dualism of cognitive form and matter. He derived cognitive form and matter as merely *notional* abstractions from the concrete actuality of representational consciousness, thereby arriving at a new argument for the unknowability of things in themselves.[70] For Kant, things in themselves were *thinkable* through the forms of the understanding, which were radically distinct from the finite forms of sensibility. Indeed, they were *necessarily* to be thought as the ground of the matter of cognition given through the forms of sensibility. Yet things in themselves were *unknowable*, because knowledge required form and matter, and because cognitive matter was *only* available to us via sensibility, rendering all our knowledge finite and all our thoughts of things in themselves empty. For Reinhold, however, things in themselves were *unrepresentable*, because cognitive forms were merely notional abstractions from representations of phenomena and could not alone constitute even empty representations.[71] Reinhold still maintained that things in themselves had to be invoked as the ground of cognitive matter[72] but, unlike Kant's, his things in themselves were *unthinkable limits* with which thinking necessarily *collided*.

Ultimately, Reinhold's methodological monism undermined Kant's dualism of finite and infinite intelligibility. By proposing to derive the specific formal features of all the faculties from a single first principle, Reinhold was placing in question the finitude of the human mind. Perhaps the human mind, on Reinhold's conception, was finite insofar as its representational structure always pointed beyond the mind, but it was not finite in Kant's sense because its formal features were intelligible without residue. By deriving the unrepresentability of things in themselves, Reinhold was placing in question the *intelligibility* of the infinite. If rational faith involved commitments about an infinite realm that was unrepresentable and hence *incomprehensible*, how did Reinhold's dualism differ from Jacobi's?

These difficulties may explain how, in 1797, Reinhold could espouse Fichte's systematic monism,[73] which developed Reinhold's post-Kantian conception of finitude, and how, in 1799, Reinhold could criticize Fichte from a position close to that of Jacobi,[74] from whose faith in the infinite he had never been far. However, throughout these and later changes, Reinhold remained committed to his goal of grounding religion, morality, and politics through an enlightened consensus that reconciled conflicting parties.[75] Subsequent post-Kantians had to consider, not only whether reason required a uniquely stable set of commitments and whether those commitments constituted a monistic system, but also whether reason's systematic claims needed universal acknowledgment – beyond refutation, doubt or misunderstanding.

IV Maimon's system (or non-system)[76]

Maimon's background was very different from those of Jacobi and Reinhold. Born in Polish Lithuania, he was educated as a Talmudist.[77] Transformed by Maimonidean rationalism, he migrated westwards, encountering the modern philosophy of Spinoza, Leibniz, Newton, Hume and, finally, Kant. The issue of divine personality, which made the Spinozism controversy so torturous for Jacobi and Reinhold, was less important to Maimon, because it was less central to Judaism than to Christianity. Through Maimonides' radical anti-anthropomorphism, Maimon had already experienced a revolution entailing the belief that, "[r]eason could continue on its way to perfection and faith could become ever more rational."[78] Moreover, in his transition from Maimonides' medieval philosophy, which axiomatized Aristotelian physics,[79] Maimon was especially struck by the modern *mathematization* of physics. His focus on the exact sciences distinguished him from both Jacobi and Reinhold and, along with his rationalist background, helped him to a deeper understanding of Kant. However, Maimon redoubled the connection between the crisis of reason and the problem of monistic systematicity.

Jacobi's influential portrayal of comprehension – as involving the construction of ideal mechanisms of generation that are substituted for the annihilated real things for which they are intended to account – was not based on a detailed examination of natural science.[80] But Maimon's detailed examination produced a similar account and even produced that "most powerful idealism" which Jacobi had both feared and longed for.[81]

Maimon discerned a single structure in the fundamental problems of medieval, early modern, and Kantian philosophy: "[T]he question *quid juris* [i.e., the question of the legitimacy of applying the forms of the understanding to what is sensibly given, addressed in Kant's transcendental deduction] is one and the same as the important question that has been treated by all previous philosophers, namely the explanation of the community between soul and body, or even as the explanation of the origination of the world (with respect to its matter) from an intelligence."[82] For the problem of mind and body reduced to "How is it conceivable that a priori forms should agree with things given a posteriori?" and the problem of creation versus eternity to "How is the origination of matter as something merely given, but not thought, conceivable through the assumption of an intelligence, since they are so heterogeneous?"[83] Both reduced to the problem of the *heterogeneity* of a priori intelligible or universal and necessary *form*, and a posteriori given or particular and contingent *matter* – the very problem raised by Kant.

Maimon believed that Kant's methodological advance was to address this problem transcendentally, by investigating the a priori conditions of science or of the comprehension of real objects.[84] But he argued that Kant's dualism, expressed in his radical distinction between sensibility and understanding, made the problem *insoluble*, whereas the problem could be solved on two monistic assumptions: that sensibility and understanding were quantitatively distinct faculties with a single cognitive source,[85] and that the finite understanding was formally (notionally) but not really distinct from the infinite understanding.[86] Maimon's first assumption explicitly revived a Leibnizian view of sensibility. His second – as Kant recognized – tended towards Spinozism.[87]

These assumptions arose through a medieval's engagement with modern physics. For Maimonides, the divine mind was best characterized by the thoroughgoing unity of intellect, act of intellection, and object comprehended, a unity also attained by the human intellect when *in actu*.[88] Following Kant, Maimon argued that the act of intellection was adequately understood, not only as Aristotelian a posteriori abstraction of specific forms or analytic universals, but also as the a priori synthesis of reality through forms, without which abstraction and analysis would be impossible.[89] However, this criticism enabled a deeper validation of Maimonides: formal synthesis was exemplified by mathematical construction, in which the intellect, the formal activity, and the constructed object were one. Mathematics was the paradigm of infinite intelligibility, in which we accomplished something like *creatio ex nihilo*[90] and were similar to God.[91] Only this constructive interpretation of mathematics, Maimon believed, could explain the modern physicist's ability to comprehend the sensibly given by treating sensible qualities as infinitesimal quantities whose relations could be represented as law-governed ratios.[92] The procedure's predictive and explanatory use demonstrated its legitimacy, which was conceivable only if the sensations passively received by our finite minds were regarded as infinitesimal degrees of an infinite mind's intellectual activity, and if our finite minds regarded themselves as limited expressions of the same infinite mind. The ultimate identity of sensible qualities or their relations with infinite intellectual syntheses explained both how those qualities appeared to us as passively given – because our finite minds could not pre-scientifically comprehend their origination – and how they were nevertheless mathematically intelligible – because our finite minds could progress *toward* infinite understanding by regarding themselves as *modifications of* the infinite mind.

In effect, Maimon repudiated Kant's account of finite intelligibility and reformulated the rationalist conception of infinite intelligibility as a transcendental condition for the possibility of mathematical physics. He was led in turn to reconceive things in themselves in ways that Jacobi would surely brand nihilistic. For Maimon, as for Kant, things in themselves were infinitely intelligible things, comprehended in terms of their sufficient reasons or inner principles. However, since Maimon rejected Kant's dualistic commitment to the independent finite intelligibility of form applied to cognitive matter, he rejected Kant's idea that things in themselves were the grounds of cognitive matter, toward which finite minds could make no cognitive progress whatsoever. Instead, every step in the mathematization of the given moved closer to infinite understanding, or to the understanding of things in themselves. The concept of the thing in itself was the concept, not of an unknowable thing beyond the limits of our understanding, but of a cognitive goal, to which we could increasingly approximate in a striving that could not be completed as long as we remained finite.[93] Maimon acknowledged that attaining perfect wisdom would involve losing individuality and merging with the infinite.[94] From Jacobi's viewpoint, Maimon's rationalistic reason annihilated the comprehension-resistant felt things and free persons of everyday life, substituting for them an infinite ego that was identical with everything, had no contrast,[95] and therefore amounted to nothing.

Yet Maimon did not encourage Reinhold's hopes for reconciliation through the one true system. He was a sharp critic of both Reinhold's first principle and his deductive procedure.[96] Most importantly, Maimon's diagnosis of Kant's failure to win universal acknowledgment motivated a different program that claimed to dash the hope for philosophical consensus.

Like Reinhold, Maimon saw that the fundamental role of the possibility of experience in Kant's transcendental deduction left it vulnerable. Kant had answered the question *quid juris* by showing that the application of a priori forms to the sensibly given was a necessary condition for the possibility of experience. But he had simply assumed an affirmative answer to the question *quid facti*, which Maimon understood as the question whether we actually have experience.[97] For Kant understood experience to be empirical knowledge, claiming universality and necessity. But, whereas Reinhold saw that Humeans *could* deny Kantian experience, Maimon argued that its actuality *should* be denied.[98]

The form of, say, causality, was neither sufficient nor necessary for the possibility of everyday causal judgments. Kant had argued that, unless we presupposed the formal principle of causality – that every event must proceed from some prior event according to a law – we could not distinguish between subjective successions of perceptions and perceptions of objective successions. But, as Maimon pointed out, this distinction presupposed only the universal principle that every event has *some* cause, and did not presuppose the capacity to apply that principle in judgments attributing events to *particular* causes. So the form of causality was insufficient to explain particular causal judgments.[99] Furthermore, the form was unnecessary, because our actual causal judgments could be *psychologically explained*, through a developed account of the effect of repetition on the imagination, a faculty governed by non-rational principles of apprehension and association.[100]

Thus the dualism of form and matter persisted in everyday life, where skepticism remained unrefuted. However, Maimon's skepticism differed from Hume's. For Maimon acknowledged the universality and necessity of knowledge secured through mathematical synthesis.[101] Even in mathematics, however, the dualism of form and matter confronting the finite mind created room, if not for skepticism, then for infinite progress. We could fully comprehend only what we could generate independently of the limits of the intelligibility of space and time, but we could only demonstrate the actuality of our concepts by constructing them *within* space and time.[102] If the actualization of experience required the mathematization of what is given in empirical intuition, then the mathematization of mathematics required the conceptualization of what is constructed in a priori intuition.

The problematic dualism confronting Kant's philosophy called for a program quite different from Reinhold's. If there were a highest principle of all forms, it would be maximally indeterminate and would not enable the derivation of subordinate forms. Nor would it address the problem of the forms' *applicability*.[103] Needed, instead, was a lowest principle to bridge the gap between form and matter.[104] Maimon proposed such a principle, within his version of transcendental logic – the investigation of the necessary conditions of the specification of mathematical reality – which was conducted alongside the investigation of mathematical practices in the exact sciences.[105]

But, insofar as our understanding remained finite, dualism would always infect everyday judgments. Psychological explanations would never become redundant. And room for doubt would always remain about whether everyday judgments could be mathematized. The answer to the question *quid juris* became problematic or hypothetical: *if* the sensibly given was intelligible, then its intelligibility necessarily had a certain formal structure. Thus the relationship between transcendental philosophy and skepticism resembled that of man and snake after the fall: "He will strike at your head, but you will strike at his heel."[106] On Maimon's interpretation, "the critical philosopher will always disturb the skeptical philosopher with the necessity and universality of principles required for scientific knowledge . . . the skeptic will always tease the critical philosopher with the fact that his necessary and universal principles have no use."[107] Hence Reinhold's hopes for consensus would remain unrealized.

The *dynamic* character of Maimon's monism illuminates the relation between his monistic "rational dogmatism" and his dualistic "empirical skepticism." First, Maimon was committed to the idea of the infinite intellect as the goal of infinite striving, which finite minds could near but never attain. He frequently repeated that the idea of God was regulative, not constitutive.[108] Second, under the influence of medieval Aristotelianism and Bruno – to whom Jacobi apparently introduced him![109] – Maimon suggested the hypothesis of a world-soul: a principle of form-actualization immanent within matter and determining its dynamic development.[110] Although monistic,[111] his view was not Spinozist, because the world-soul, as principle of the totality of *actualizations*, was distinct from God, as principle of the totality of *real possibilities*.[112]

One might conclude that Maimon made no ontological commitment to God, only a pragmatic commitment for the sake of scientific progress. But this would underestimate the role of practice in Maimon's view. In his last book, Maimon proposed a proof of the "existence" or "actuality"[113] of God: since God was the necessary condition of all objective and universally valid knowledge, and since we actually had objective and universally valid knowledge (at least in mathematics), God had to be objective and universally valid or actual.[114] Maimon judged the rationality of scientific practice by the standards of infinite intelligibility, and the actuality of infinite intelligibility by the practice of the exact sciences. As he strikingly put it, "Without the *Godhead* the world cannot be *thought* but, without the world, the *Godhead* cannot be *known*. Without *philosophy*, no *science in general* is possible, because it determines a priori the form of a *science in general*. Without presupposing some other science, *philosophy* can have no significance whatsoever for us."[115] Ontological commitment to God was necessitated by the pragmatic significance of the idea of infinite understanding in the exact sciences, together with the idea's consistency, which distinguished it from the useful but contradictory fiction of an infinitesimal quantity.[116] Although finite minds could find no resting place,[117] they could enjoy immortal unity with God in this life.[118]

Maimon was thus genuinely committed *both* to dynamically monistic rationalism and to dualistic skepticism. His dogmatism was unreserved about exact science, but was problematic about everyday life, where skepticism was therefore justified. If Maimon's dogmatism fulfilled Jacobi's worst fears, his skepticism fulfilled Reinhold's. Insofar as the world *was* intelligible, individuality and personality were annihilated; insofar as the world was *not* intelligible, philosophical consensus was unattainable.

V Conclusion

Philosophers formed by the Spinozism controversy and its aftermath were confronted by the following questions. (1) Could reason find a uniquely stable standpoint? If so, would it be *through* philosophy or *against* it? (2) Would such a standpoint have to attain universal acknowledgment? If not, how would the failure be explained? (3) Did philosophy require monistic systematization? If so, would room be left for everyday things, individual persons, and God? Or would the overcoming of dualisms within philosophy open an unbridgeable gap between philosophical reason and ordinary reasoning?

Various answers were available. One approach, familiar from the famous German idealist philosophies, was to view reason's vindication as depending upon the construction of the one true, monistic system, within which alone the solution to problems about thinghood, freedom, and divinity could be resolved. At first, Reinhold and others believed their project to be Kant's. After 1799, when Kant repudiated Fichte,[119] it was clear that Kant did not share the monistic interpretation of his philosophy. Fichte, Schelling, and Hegel found this to be proof that Kant did not understand himself, while others found it to be proof that *they* did not understand Kant.

My purpose has not been to indict German idealists for misunderstanding Kant, but to illuminate the historical and philosophical sources of the misunderstanding. Underlying the continuing debates between strict Kantians and creative, post-Kantian misreaders are questions about how to understand the finitude of human reason: can the rationalist conception of infinite intelligibility be salvaged? Or can finite intelligibility supply reason enough? The intricate variety of answers given by Kant, Jacobi, Reinhold, Maimon, and other post-Kantians must be appreciated, along with the differences in their underlying assumptions, if we are to draw upon their work in continuing investigation of these persisting questions.

NOTES

1 F. H. Jacobi, *Über die Lehre des Spinoza in Briefen an den Herrn Moses Mendelssohn* (Breslau: Loewe, 1785), henceforth *S1785*; second revised edition, 1789, henceforth *S1789*, critically edited and annotated in Jacobi, *Werke*, ed. Klaus Hammacher and Walter Jaeschke (Hamburg: Meiner, 1998). For translations, see *Friedrich Heinrich Jacobi: The Main Philosophical Writings and the Novel Allwill*, trans. and ed. George di Giovanni (Montreal: McGill-Queen's University Press, 1994), henceforth *MPW*. For analysis, see Alexander Altmann, *Moses Mendelssohn* (Alabama:

University of Alabama Press, 1973), 582–759, and *Die trostvolle Aufklärung* (Stuttgart-Bad Canstatt: Frommann-Holzboog, 1982), 28–83; Frederick Beiser, *The Fate of Reason: German Philosophy from Kant to Fichte* (Cambridge, MA: Harvard University Press, 1987); Hermann Timm, *Gott und die Freiheit* (Frankfurt am Main: Klostermann, 1974).

2 F. H. Jacobi, *Jacobi an Fichte* (Hamburg: Perthes, 1799); *MPW* 495–536. See J. G. Fichte: *Introductions to the Wissenschaftslehre and Other Writings*, trans. and ed. Daniel Breazeale (Indianapolis: Hackett, 1994), xv–xviii, 141–176; George di Giovanni, "From Jacobi's Philosophical Novel to Fichte's Idealism: Some Comments on the 1798–99 'Atheism Dispute,'" *Journal of the History of Philosophy*, 26 (1989), 75–100.

3 See Wolfgang Weischedel, ed., *Streit um die göttlichen Dinge. Die Auseinandersetzung zwischen Jacobi und Schelling* (Darmstadt: Wissenschaftliche Buchgesellschaft, 1967).

4 Jacobi's influence was hardly second to Kant's, according to Arthur O. Lovejoy, *The Reason, the Understanding, and Time* (Baltimore: Johns Hopkins University Press, 1961), 5. Beiser (*Fate of Reason*, 44) calls the Spinozism dispute the most significant event in late eighteenth-century Germany, along with the publication of Kant's first *Critique*.

5 See Immanuel Kant, "What Does it Mean to Orient Oneself in Thinking," in *Religion and Rational Theology*, trans. and ed. Allen Wood and George di Giovanni (Cambridge: Cambridge University Press, 1996), 7–18, esp. 15–16. Jacobi tried to correct Kant's interpretation, for which he blamed Reinhold. See Immanuel Kant, *Correspondence*, trans. and ed. Arnulf Zweig (Cambridge: Cambridge University Press, 1999), 318–20, 323–5. Beiser (*Fate of Reason*, 83) describes Jacobi as believing "that we have but two options, a rational nihilism or an irrational faith."

6 See Jacobi's 1815 preface to his collected works, in F. H. Jacobi, *Werke*, ed. J. F. Köppen and C. J. F. Roth (Leipzig: Gerhard Fleischer, 1812–25; repr. Darmstadt: Wissenschaftliche Buchgesellschaft, 1968), II, 7–11; *MPW*, 539–41. Jacobi had already distinguished two senses of "reason" in *S1789*, Supplement VII.

7 See *S1785*, 8; *S1789*, 328–34, *MPW*, 183, 362.

8 Descartes had used the phrase, associated with Pythagoras' boast that the science of levers could move even the earth, in his second *Meditation*.

9 Jacobi first spoke of "nihilism" in *Jacobi an Fichte*, 39; *MPW*, 519. Jenisch had accused transcendental idealism of nihilism in 1796. See Otto Pöggeler, "Hegel und die Anfänge der Nihilismus-Diskussion," in Dieter Arendt, ed., *Der Nihilismus als Phänomen der Geistesgeschichte* (Darmstadt: Wissenschaftliche Buchgesellschaft, 1974), 307–49; Wolfgang Müller-Lauter, "Nihilismus als Konsequenz des Idealismus," in Alexander Schwan, ed., *Denken im Schatten des Nihilismus* (Darmstadt: Wissenschaftliche Buchgesellschaft, 1975), 113–63. However, Jacobi had already said in *S1789*, Supplement VII that comprehension of quality involves its "annihilation" (*MPW*, 374–5n.).

10 See, e.g., *S1785*, 14; *MPW*, 187.

11 (1) is motivated by the claim, discussed above, that only a finite series of conditions terminating in a self-conditioned condition would be infinitely intelligible. Various arguments for (2) are derivable from ancient and medieval proofs of the First Cause's uniqueness. E.g., if there were two series, each ending in a distinct first condition, a

prior reason for the actuality of two *distinct* conditions would be required, so the regress would continue. See Aristotle, *Metaphysics Λ*, 107a, 31–8.

12 I will not examine the accuracy of Jacobi's interpretation here.

13 *S1785*, 118–29; *MPW*, 217, based on Spinoza, *Ethics*, I, P28. Compare Kant's argument for the antithesis of the third antinomy in I. Kant, *Critique of Pure Reason*, trans. Paul Guyer and Allen Wood (Cambridge: Cambridge University Press, 1998), A445–7/B473–5.

14 *S1785*, 61–72; *MPW*, 205–7.

15 *S1785*, 121–31; *MPW*, 217–20.

16 See *S1789*, 335–41; *MPW*, 363–4. Note Jacobi, *Jacobi an Fichte*, 41; *MPW*, 520: "the (I believe correct) judgment of natural reason that calls a God who is *non-personal* a God *who is not*, a non-entity."

17 *S1785*, 29; *MPW*, 193–4. *S1789*, xxxvi–xlviii; *MPW*, 341–9.

18 Although Jacobi does not explicitly draw this conclusion, one might say that rationalism thereby contradicts itself, for the attempt to avoid deriving something from nothing leads precisely to the derivation of everything from nothing.

19 *S1789*, 415–22; *MPW*, 372–5.

20 Jacobi, *Werke* (1812–25), II, 81–98; *MPW*, 572–9.

21 *S1785*, 17; *MPW*, 189.

22 Consciously risking misunderstanding, Jacobi ended his Spinoza book by quoting Lavater, who had tried to publicly convert Mendelssohn to Christianity. See *S1785* 212–13; *MPW*, 250–1. He further muddied the waters by appearing to affirm the views of his deceased friend, Thomas Wizenmann, who had argued in *Die Resultate der Jacobischen und Mendelssohnschen Philosophie* (Leipzig: Göschen, 1786; repr. Hildesheim: Gerstenberg, 1984) that the Spinozism dispute had shown Christian faith based on revelation and history to be the only firm standpoint. See Jacobi, *Werke* (1812–25), IV, 174.

23 *S1785*, 162; *MPW*, 230.

24 *S1785*, 28; *MPW*, 193.

25 David Hume, *Enquiries concerning Human Understanding and concerning the Principles of Morals*, ed. L. A. Selby-Bigge, rev. P. H. Nidditch (Oxford: Clarendon Press, 1975), 151, cited in *MPW*, 268.

26 Jacobi, *Werke* (1812–25), II, 36; *MPW*, 552.

27 See, e.g., Jacobi, *Werke* (1812–25), II, 7–14; *MPW*, 539–42.

28 *S1785*, 31–2; *MPW*, 194.

29 *S1785*, 172; *MPW*, 234. See F. H. Jacobi, *David Hume über den Glauben oder Idealismus und Realismus* (Breslau: Löwe, 1787; repr. New York: Garland, 1983), 20; *MPW*, 264.

30 Jacobi, *Werke* (1812–25), II, 9; *MPW*, 230.

31 See, e.g., Jacobi, *Werke* (1812–25), II, 30; *MPW*, 376, 515.

32 Jacobi, *David Hume*, 158–77; *MPW*, 310–19.

33 Jacobi, *Werke* (1812–25), II, 30; *MPW*, 515.

34 Jacobi, *Werke* (1812–25), II, 11; *MPW*, 541.

35 Jacobi, *Jacobi an Fichte*, 9; *MPW*, 505.

36 Jacobi, *David Hume*, 223; *MPW*, 336.

37 Cf. Jacobi, *Werke* (1812–25), II, 22; *MPW*, 546.

38 Jacobi, *David Hume*, 229; *MPW*, 338, cf. Jacobi, *Werke* (1812–25), II, 22; *MPW*, 552.

39 See Leibniz's argument in H. G. Alexander, ed., *The Leibniz–Clarke Correspondence* (Manchester: University of Manchester Press, 1956), 26.

40 Kant, *Critique of Pure Reason*, A370.

41 See, e.g., Kant, *Critique of Pure Reason*, A840/B868.

42 Immanuel Kant, *Critique of Judgment, Including the First Introduction*, trans. Werner Pluhar (Indianapolis: Hackett, 1987), Ak 452–3. After the Spinozism controversy, Kant sometimes presented his dualism as the only alternative to Spinozism. See I. Kant, *Lectures on Metaphysics*, trans. and ed. Karl Ameriks and Steven Naragon (Cambridge: Cambridge University Press, 1997), 368: "If we consider space as real, we assume Spinoza's system. He believed in only one substance and all substances in the world he held for – its divinely inhering determinations (he called space the phenomenon of the divine omnipresence). A dialectician said – if nothing *is*, then being and not-being are the same. Thus if I say that space remains if I take everything away, then a nothing exists. But space is only ideal, only a relation of things, so if the things are gone, then naturally there is also no relation of them possible, thus also no space."

43 Citations are from K. L. Reinhold, "Briefe über die Kantische Philosophie," published in four installments in *Der Teutsche Merkur*, ed. Christoph Wieland (Weimar: 1786–7), not from K. L. Reinhold, *Briefe über die Kantische Philosophie I–II* (Jena: Mauke, 1790–4), which contains new letters on practical philosophy and revises the earlier letters to reflect Reinhold's development.

44 K. L. Reinhold, *Versuch einer neuen Theorie des menschlichen Vorstellungsvermögens* (Jena: Widtmann and Mauke, 1789).

45 Cf. Timm, *Gott und die Freiheit*, 405.

46 Reinhold to Nicolai, 1789, cited in K. L. Reinhold, *Korrespondenz 1773–1788*, ed. Reinhard Lauth, Eberhard Heller, and Kurt Hiller (Stuttgart-Bad Canstatt: Frommann-Holzboog, 1983), 10, n. 3.

47 Reinhold to Kant, 1787, in Kant, *Correspondence*, 265.

48 Reinhold, "Briefe über die Kantische Philosophie," I, 111.

49 Reinhold, "Briefe über die Kantische Philosophie," I, 101.

50 Reinhold to Kant, 1787, in Kant, *Correspondence*, 265.

51 Reinhold to Voigt, 1786, in Reinhold, *Korrespondenz*, 153.

52 Reinhold, "Briefe über die Kantische Philosophie," I, 112.

53 Reinhold, "Briefe über die Kantische Philosophie," III, 116.

54 Reinhold, "Briefe über die Kantische Philosophie," III, 116.

55 K. L. Reinhold, *Über das Fundament des philosophischen Wissens* (Jena: Mauke, 1791; repr. Hamburg: Meiner, 1978), vi; K. L. Reinhold, *Beyträge zur Berichtigung bisheriger Missverständisse der Philosophen I–II* (Jena: Mauke, 1790–4), II, 95.

56 Reinhold to Maimon, 1791, in Salomon Maimon, *Gesammelte Werke*, ed. Valerio Verra (Hildesheim: Olms, 1970), IV, 222.

57 Reinhold to Kant, 1787, in Kant, *Correspondence*, 265.

58 Reinhold, "Briefe über die Kantische Philosophie," III, 39.

59 Reinhold, "Briefe über die Kantische Philosophie," I, 125; Reinhold, *Versuch einer neuen Theorie*, 57; Reinhold, *Briefe über die Kantische Philosophie I–II*, I, iv.

60 See Reinhold, *Versuch einer neuen Theorie*, 18–19, 22, on Newton's failure to win universal acknowledgment immediately. Compare Reinhold, "Briefe über die Kantische Philosophie," I, 126.

61 Reinhold, *Über das Fundament*, 73; Reinhold, *Briefe über die Kantische Philosophie I–II*, I, 275.

62 See, e.g., Kant, *Critique of Pure Reason*, B166. Schulze argued in 1785 that Kant begged the question against Hume. See Beiser, *Fate of Reason*, 206.

63 Reinhold, *Über das Fundament*, 127–9.

64 The Principle of Consciousness: "that in consciousness representation is distinguished through the subject from both object and subject and is referred to both." See, e.g., Reinhold, *Über das Fundament*, 78.

65 "Über die Möglichkeit der Philosophie als strenge Wissenschaft," in Reinhold, *Beyträge zur Berichtigung bisheriger Missverständnisse der Philosophen I–II*, I, 341–72.

66 See, e.g., Reinhold, "Briefe über die Kantische Philosophie," IV, 137: "Spinozism is, in the field of metaphysics, what Catholicism is in the field of hyperphysics [i.e. non-rational faith in the infinite] – the most systematic version." See also Reinhold, *Versuch einer neuen Theorie*, 254.

67 See, e.g., Reinhold, *Über das Fundament*, 116–17, where Reinhold argues that Kantian critique is not scientific by Kant's own standards because it lacks "a single founding principle."

68 For contemporaneous criticisms, see Manfred Frank, *"Unendliche Annäherung." Die Anfänge der philosophischen Frühromantik* (Frankfurt: Suhrkamp, 1997), 152–661, esp. 320 and 340–2. For recent criticism, see Beiser, *Fate of Reason*, 245–6.

69 I explain why Reinhold's proposed principle is not, as claimed, a *causa sui* in "Transcendental Arguments, Reason, and Skepticism: Contemporary Debates and the Origins of Post-Kantian Idealism," in Robert Stern, ed., *Transcendental Arguments: Problems and Prospects* (Oxford: Oxford University Press, 1999).

70 See Reinhold, *Versuch einer neuen Theorie*, 230–64; Reinhold, *Beyträge zur Berichtigung I–II*, I, 182–5. For criticism of Reinhold's argument and discussion of its influence, see Karl Ameriks, "Reinhold and the Short Argument to Idealism," in G. Funke and T. Seebohm, eds., *Proceedings of the Sixth International Kant Congress 1985* (Center for Advanced Research in Phenomenology and the University Press of America, 1989), vol. II, part 2, 441–53; Karl Ameriks, "Kant, Fichte, and Short Arguments for Idealism," *Archiv für Geschichte der Philosophie*, 72 (1990), 63–85; Karl Ameriks, *Kant and the Fate of Autonomy: Problems in the Appropriation of the Critical Philosophy* (Cambridge: Cambridge University Press, 2000).

71 Reinhold, *Versuch einer neuen Theorie*, 235.

72 Reinhold, *Versuch einer neuen Theorie*, 248–9.

73 Reinhold had revised his position to respond to criticism in 1792. See Frank, *"Unendliche Annäherung,"* 396–406, 485–511; Marcelo Stamm, *Systemkrise: Die Elementarphilosophie in der Debatte (1789–1794)* (Stuttgart: Klett-Cotta, forthcoming). In 1797, he endorsed Fichte. See Frank, *"Unendliche Annäherung,"* 212–13.

74 See K. L. Reinhold, *Sendschreiben an J. C. Lavater und J. G. Fichte* (Hamburg: Perthes, 1799) for his response to Fichte's alleged atheism.

75 See Sabine Roehr, *A Primer on the German Enlightenment with a Translation of Reinhold's Fundamental Concepts and Principles of Ethics* (Columbia: University of Missouri Press, 1995), and Paul Franks, review of Roehr 1997, *Philosophical Review* 106:1 (1997), 141–4.

76 See Maimon, *Gesammelte Werke*, II, 438: "my system (or non-system) . . ."

77 See Maimon's autobiography in *Gesammelte Werke*, I.

78 Maimon, *Gesammelte Werke*, VII, 639.

79 See Moses Maimonides, *Guide of the Perplexed*, trans. S. Pines (Chicago: University of Chicago Press, 1963), Part II, Introduction.

80 See di Giovanni's comments, *MPW*, 162–3.

81 See Frank, *"Unendliche Annäherung,"* 91–132.

82 Maimon, *Gesammelte Werke*, II, 62, 362.

83 Maimon, *Gesammelte Werke*, II, 63.

84 See, e.g., Maimon, *Gesammelte Werke*, IV, 35.

85 Maimon, *Gesammelte Werke*, II, 63.

86 Salomon Maimon, *Giv'at ha-Moreh*, eds. S. H. Bergman and N. Rotenstreich (Jerusalem: Israel Academy of Sciences and Humanities, 1965; repr. 2000) (Maimon's commentary to Maimonides' *Guide*), 107.

87 For Kant's suggestion that, although unfaithful to Leibniz' intentions, Maimon's arguments might refute Leibniz *ex concessis*, see Kant, *Correspondence*, 311–16. For Maimon's monistic interpretation of Leibniz' pre-established harmony, see Maimon, *Gesammelte Werke*, III, 457; IV, 41–8.

88 Maimonides, *Guide of the Perplexed*, Part I, ch. 68; Maimon, *Giv'at ha-Moreh*, 101–8.

89 Maimon, *Giv'at ha-Moreh*, 101.

90 Maimon, *Gesammelte Werke*, III, 55.

91 Maimon, *Gesammelte Werke*, IV, 42.

92 See, e.g., Maimon, *Gesammelte Werke*, I, 75–83, 226–38, 265–332, 348–56; IV, 39–40, 51–2. This difficult doctrine deserves discussion elsewhere.

93 See, e.g., Maimon, *Gesammelte Werke*, III, 185–7.

94 Maimon, *Gesammelte Werke*, VII, 249–50, 277–9. This was the view of Averroists like Moses Narboni, whose commentary on Maimonides' *Guide* was first printed with Maimon's.

95 Maimon, *Gesammelte Werke*, VII, 250.

96 See Maimon's acrimonious correspondence with Reinhold in Maimon, *Gesammelte Werke*, IV, and his letters to Kant in Kant, *Correspondence*, 387–9, 440–4.

97 See Maimon, *Gesammelte Werke*, I, 70–2, 174, 186, 193; III, 42–8; V, 437.

98 Maimon, *Gesammelte Werke*, IV, 465: "in the sense that the Kantian gives to the concept of experience, I have no experience."

99 Many Anglo-American commentators would think Kant should readily concede Maimon's point, since he does not intend to refute Hume's skepticism about particular causal laws. But on the interpretation developed by Michael Friedman, "Causal Laws and Natural Science," in Paul Guyer, ed., *The Cambridge Companion to Kant* (Cambridge: Cambridge University Press, 1992), 161–99, Maimon is indicating a genuine difficulty, for which Kant offers a solution in his 1786 *Metaphysical Foundations of Natural Science*, where he seeks to ground Newton's laws *a priori* in principles of understanding.

100 See Maimon, *Gesammelte Werke*, II, 72; III, 42–8; V, 437. Maimon co-edited a pioneering journal of empirical psychology.

101 Maimon, *Gesammelte Werke*, IV, 214–16.

102 Maimon, *Gesammelte Werke*, III, 47–8.

103 Maimon, *Gesammelte Werke*, III, 18–23; V, 389–90, 401.

104 Maimon, *Gesammelte Werke*, VI, 449–50.

105 See Maimon, *Gesammelte Werke*, V. Maimon's Principle of Determinability states that in any real synthesis, the subject must be capable of being an object of consciousness in itself, while the predicate must be capable of being an object of consciousness only in combination with the subject.

106 Genesis 3:15.

107 Maimon, *Gesammelte Werke*, IV, 80.

108 See, e.g., Maimon, *Giv'at ha-Moreh*, 53, 81; Maimon, *Gesammelte Werke*, IV, 51.

109 In *S1789*, Supplement I, Jacobi translated excerpts from Bruno, presumably to illustrate the pitfalls of monism. See *MPW*, 359–60 and Giordano Bruno, *Cause, Principle and Unity*, eds. Richard J. Blackwell and Robert de Lucca (Cambridge: Cambridge University Press, 1998). Maimon translated Jacobi's excerpt into Hebrew in *Giv'at ha-Moreh*, 109–10, and commented in *Gesammelte Werke*, III, 203–32; IV, 611–52.

110 Maimon, *Gesammelte Werke*, III, 205, 218. Some medieval Aristotelians combined Aristotle's active intellect with Plato's world-soul.

111 See Maimon's letter in Kant, *Correspondence*, 351–3.

112 Maimon might reply to Jacobi's Spinozist objection, that any temporal or modal difference between the possibility of realities in God and their actualization would require a *prior* cause, by saying that the modal difference is merely notional, although necessary for the finite mind; thus it requires, not explanation, but overcoming through infinite progress.

113 Maimon uses the terms *Dasein* and *Wirklichkeit*, but elsewhere he follows Maimonides in denying that such predicates may be ascribed to the idea of God in the same sense in which they may be ascribed to other ideas. See Maimon, *Giv'at ha-Moreh*, 89–90; Maimon, *Gesammelte Werke*, III, 49–51. He already claims in *Gesammelte Werke*, I, 196–200 and III, 124–5 that the idea of God signifies a real synthesis with real consequences.

114 Maimon, *Gesammelte Werke*, VII, 248–9, 278–9.

115 Maimon, *Gesammelte Werke*, VI, 19.

116 Maimon emphasizes the consistency of the idea of God in, e.g., *Gesammelte Werke*, III, 49–51.

117 See Maimon, *Gesammelte Werke*, I, 444 and *Giv'at ha-Moreh*, 40 on Babylonian Talmud, Berakhoth, 68a (see Eidels' commentary ad loc., which Maimon probably knew).

118 Maimon, *Gesammelte Werke*, VII, 279.

119 Kant, *Correspondence*, 559–60.

6

ROLF-PETER HORSTMANN

The early philosophy of Fichte and Schelling

German idealistic thinking can be approached in many different ways, each of which has peculiar advantages and problems. According to the standard view, the German idealist movement is best looked at as a philosophical program that was developed in the wake of Kant's Critical philosophy with the intention of improving his transcendental idealism in various directions.[1] The now-dominant version of this view has it that, starting with K. L. Reinhold, a whole generation of young German philosophers embarked on the project of arriving at new foundations for Kant's philosophy, of distinguishing what was taken to be the highly promising spirit of his philosophical conception from its rather poor literal expression by Kant himself, and of providing the missing premises for the conclusions of his theory.[2] Although this project was approached from very different points of view by each of the main figures of that movement – J. G. Fichte, F. W. J. Schelling, and G. W. F. Hegel – there were some convictions that they shared.

Three of these convictions deserve to be mentioned. (1) They were all convinced that Kant had succeeded in establishing the most resourceful philosophical system to be found in modern times, a system that was deeply committed to the idea of the unity of reason and that permitted a coherent picture of the world in all its different aspects. It was this conviction that made them followers of Kant, or Kantians. (2) At the same time, however, they were also convinced that Kant had not really succeeded in developing adequately his systematic approach because he was hopelessly entangled in a dualistic mode of thinking which was fundamentally at odds with his proclaimed goal of unity. This conviction made them opponents of Kant. (3) The third belief they shared was the opinion that, in order to avoid Kant's dualism, one has to supplement his philosophy with a monistic basis and accept that monism is the only viable alternative to dualism. It is this belief that made them German idealists.

Up to this point, the standard view of German Idealism is relatively uncontroversial, although it gives at best a very fragmentary and one-sided picture of all the different motives and considerations that played a role in the formation of that movement.[3] But even if one is prepared to think of German Idealism primarily as a reaction to Kant's influence, problems emerge. This can be seen especially when the question arises of how the different protagonists of that philosophical enterprise have to be related to one another with respect to what they wanted to achieve. It is, after all, one thing to agree on shared convictions and quite another to consent to what one can claim about the implications of these convictions. Concerning this question, the traditional idea has been that one has to conceive of the different philosophical theories of the leading German idealists as a sequence of systems in which each is an improvement on its immediate predecessor. The idea was that Fichte somehow managed to supersede Kant, that Schelling did the same to Fichte, and that everything culminated in Hegel. This conception has proved to be so powerful that up to now almost every handbook on the history of philosophy is indebted to it either explicitly or at least implicitly.[4]

It is seriously misleading, however, to look at the various philosophical theories presented by these German idealists in this way. There is no 'from . . . to . . .,' if by this is meant some kind of organic process of complementation. Rather, each of the German idealists pursued a very individual project that was guided by very special assumptions concerning what philosophy is all about. This does not imply that there were no connections between these projects – they were, after all, all based on shared beliefs – or that there were no common points of interest between their inaugurators – for example, they were all highly fascinated by holistic approaches in philosophy. It just means that there was no common project. In order to substantiate this claim, one only has to look at the early works of Fichte and Schelling, which will be discussed in turn in the following sections.

I Fichte

The public philosophical career of Johann Gottlieb Fichte (1762–1814) started in 1793, when he was offered a professorship at the university in Jena in succession to the then well-known Kantian Reinhold.[5] He accepted the offer and began teaching at that university in 1794. Up to that time his philosophical reputation was based mainly on two publications: a book published anonymously on a topic in the philosophy of religion, which was strongly influenced by Kantian views (*Attempt at a Critique of All Revelation*), and a review of G. E. Schulze's *Aenesidemus*, in which he presented a very original assessment of problems connected with Reinhold's so-called *Elementary Philosophy* (*Elementarphilosophie*).[6] In order to sharpen his philosophical profile, he introduced himself to the Jena intellectual community by publishing immediately before his arrival, in 1794, a short programmatic essay entitled *Concerning the Concept of* the *Science of Knowledge*, which presented philosophy as a "Science of Knowledge" (*Wissenschaftslehre*). This text was followed by his most influential philosophical treatise, *Foundations of the Entire Science of Knowledge*, whose first part appeared in the summer of 1794 and which was published in full in 1795. Although this has become his best-known philosophical work, it was only the first version of a project he was engaged in all his life. In addition to this first version, Fichte wrote quite a number of different expositions of the *Science of Knowledge* in the following years, but he managed to publish only one of them during his lifetime.[7] During the following years he published widely regarded books on *The Foundation of Natural Right According to the Principles of the Science of Knowledge* (1796/7) and *The System of Ethical Doctrine According to the Principles of the Science of Knowledge* (1798). At about the same time he produced a series of articles designed to give a better understanding of his project. They appeared in 1797/8 under the title *An Attempt at a New Presentation of the Science of Knowledge* and included the two *Introduction[s] to the Science of Knowledge*. In 1799 Fichte was dismissed from his post as professor because of his involvement in what became known as the "Atheism Controversy."[8] He then started a second career which eventually led him to Berlin, where in 1810 he became one of the founding members of the university of Berlin. During that period he mainly published books that addressed a wider public and that powerfully presented his views on the culture of his era, religion, and (national) education. Although he still gave semipublic lectures on the *Science of Knowledge* as well, he dealt with that subject in ways very different from his approaches before 1800.

In order to gain an understanding of the initial problems that led Fichte to his early conception of a *Science of Knowledge*, one has to go back to the debate between Reinhold and Schulze mentioned above. In this debate it was Schulze who tried to show that Critical, that is, Kantian, philosophy – and in particular Reinhold's purportedly improved version of it, which relied on the concept of a first principle of philosophy – had not succeeded in refuting skepticism. Schulze maintained that the very idea of a first principle as the basis of philosophy is ill-conceived, because there is no way even to formulate such a principle in a manner that does not give rise to skeptical objections. This, he claimed, can be proved particularly well when one has a closer look at Reinhold's candidate for this principle, the so-called "principle of consciousness."[9]

Fichte had at least three reasons for being concerned about this attack on Reinhold. The first was that he considered himself to be committed to Kant's philosophical views. This meant that everything that could seriously discredit Kant's position had to be carefully examined and, if possible, refuted in order to restore the credibility of Critical philosophy. The second reason was that Fichte was initially inclined to think that Reinhold had succeeded in the attempt to give a new and better foundation for Critical philosophy by means of the introduction of the principle of consciousness as a first principle. This assessment had to be reevaluated in the light of Schulze's criticism. The third reason eventually consisted in the fact that Schulze was not the only one who expressed lack of faith in the ability of Critical philosophy to deal successfully with skeptical challenges. Similar suspicions were articulated quite forcefully by Maimon.[10]

As can be seen from the review of Schulze's *Aenesidemus*, Fichte reacted to this situation in a rather cautious way. He tried to avoid giving the impression that Reinhold's position is easy to defend and that Schulze's criticism has no point at all; instead, he agreed with Schulze that Reinhold's principle of consciousness poses severe problems and ultimately has no chance of being accepted as the first principle of philosophy. At the same time, however, he insisted that Reinhold is right in claiming that there does have to be a first principle which functions as the foundation for all philosophy. The interesting point here is not Fichte's agreement with Schulze about the untenability of the principle of consciousness as a first principle[11] – what is much more important is Fichte's endorsement of the idea of a first principle as the necessary basis of philosophy. So the question arises: why did Fichte think a first principle is necessary? The answer, which concerns the threat of skepticism and how to deal with it, can be inferred in part from the "Review of *Aenesidemus*," and in part from the early essay, "Concerning the Concept of the Science of Knowledge."

Aware of, and perhaps even influenced by, F. H. Jacobi's criticism of Kant's theoretical philosophy,[12] Fichte agrees with Jacobi that it is a futile endeavor to meet the skeptical challenge by presenting arguments which aim to prove that skeptical claims rest on bad reasoning. According to Jacobi, such an approach is ill-conceived because it already shares with the skeptic a fundamental assumption that ultimately makes skepticism irrefutable: it shares the assumption that there is, for example, something to prove with respect to the existence of an outer world, or the reality of freedom, or the existence of God. But in fact there is nothing to prove in those cases because there is nothing to doubt. Up to this point Fichte follows Jacobi. They disagree, however, on the conclusions to be drawn from this assessment. Whereas Jacobi insists on belief as the proper attitude with respect to the claims that the skeptic doubts, Fichte takes a different course. He wants to overcome skepticism by showing that most of the judgments that are subject to skeptical attacks have the status of indisputable truths because they all have in common the characteristic of certainty. Thus, what has to be done in order to refute skepticism is to dispute not skepticism's material claims but rather its assumption that there is a basis for doubt about the propositions it challenges.

It is in this context that the conception of a first principle becomes important to Fichte. This is so because he thinks that the certainty of a judgment,[13] which ultimately guarantees its indubitability, is the result of the judgment's being deducible from another judgment whose certainty is beyond question.[14] In order to avoid an infinite regress in the chain of judgments that give certainty to other judgments, and thus in order to avoid the collapse of the whole idea of the transmission of certainty from one judgment to another, Fichte has to endorse the possibility of a particular judgment that is (1) immediately certain by and through itself, and (2) such that the certainty of other judgments can be accounted for by their standing to it in a relation of deducibility. This judgment would be the first and highest principle because it would be the sole basis for all claims to certainty of judgments. Thus, for Fichte, having access to a first principle is a necessary and perhaps even a sufficient condition[15] for the possibility of knowledge in general, and in particular for the possibility of knowledge that is resistant to skeptical doubts. And this is the main reason why he thinks Reinhold was right in insisting on a first principle in philosophy.

Fichte's first attempt to find a first principle, and to derive from it in a systematic fashion the essential claims of theoretical and practical knowledge, is documented in his *Science of Knowledge*. His thoughts about how a first principle has to look are found in the first three sections of this treatise. He starts with two basic assumptions; the first assumption is that a first principle has to express a truth concerning the structure of the I, or of self-consciousness; the second assumption consists in the claim that although there is only one absolutely first principle, there are two other truths that also have the status of principles, so that in the end we have to account for three principles. Whereas Fichte never really argues for the first assumption,[16] he does argue for the second. Here the argument is based on three assertions. The first is that every judgment is characterized by a certain form and certain contents.[17] The second assertion is that a judgment can be conditioned or unconditioned with respect to its form, or its contents, or both. "Unconditioned" here means that at least one of these characteristics is not derivable from anything else. The third assertion is that a judgment that is unconditioned with respect to either of these characteristics has to be called a principle. Given these assumptions, it is easy to see that we have to be prepared to accept up to three principles. The first would be a judgment that is unconditioned with respect to its form and its content. Fichte calls it the absolutely first principle. The second would be a judgment that is unconditioned with respect to its form – Fichte's second principle. And the judgment as unconditioned with respect to its contents is the third principle of the *Science of Knowledge*.[18] It is within this rather formal framework that Fichte starts his search for his first principle.

Now, finding such a principle poses several problems. The most serious and immediate one is determining a method that necessarily leads to the principle. Fichte chooses a procedure that he calls "abstracting reflection," which is described as a process that has as its starting point a so-called "fact of empirical consciousness." By that he means something that can be an object of knowledge for a conscious being and is taken by such a being to be certain. According to this description, ordinary facts of empirical consciousness would be indubitable propositions or judgments. Reflection then proceeds to abstract from the empirical features of such a fact in order to arrive at the characteristics that account for its being a fact of consciousness, that is, for its being something which is indubitable or certain. Fichte obviously believes that these characteristics reflect the structure of the I, or of self-consciousness, which can then be said to be the ultimate basis of all claims to certainty.[19] The whole process that eventually leads to the concept and the structure of the I, or of self-consciousness, is not supposed to be an argument that proves something in a demonstrative way; it is rather conceived of by Fichte in terms of an analysis of the necessary and sufficient conditions for the certainty of a judgment.

As a starting point for his abstracting reflection, Fichte takes the law of identity as known from logic. His consideration is roughly the following: (1) The judgment "A is A" is rightly claimed to be certain unconditionally (*schlechthin*), without any further reason. To claim such a thing already presupposes the ability to posit (*setzen*) something unconditionally. (2) The meaning of the judgment "A is A" must be interpreted as stating a hypothetical relation between the first A and the second A. It thus means "if A is, then A is," understood in the sense "if A exists, then A exists." This interpretative move, which transforms a categorical judgment about the identity of A with itself into a hypothetical judgment about the existence of A, is important because it allows Fichte to claim that what is involved in the assertion of "A is A" are existence-claims, or, to be more specific, claims to different modes of existence of A, depending on whether A is considered to be part of the antecedent or of the consequent. In the first case, A is said by Fichte to exist in a conditioned way, in the second, A is claimed to exist unconditionally.[20] (3) Because this judgment is certain unconditionally, the relation it states indicates a necessary connection between the antecedent and the consequent.[21] Fichte characterizes this connection by the term "X," and he goes on to focus on its possibility. (4) Due to the fact that according to (1) "A is A" must be taken as an expression of an unconditional positing, everything implied in the meaning of that judgment must also be something that is posited unconditionally. Thus the possibility of X depends on its being posited in such a way. (5) Because X, according to (4), is a relation that holds between something, A, existing unconditionally and the same thing, A, existing as conditioned, the unconditional positing of X implies the unconditional positing of A as existing. (6) X, and consequently A as existing, are posited within and by the I, or the self-conscious mind, because it is for such a mind that X and A are given unconditionally. (7) Thus we must take the I to be responsible for the unconditional positing of something as existing, and this simply means, according to Fichte, that we must accept the I as underlying all claims to unconditional certainty, because it is the I in whose unconditional positing the very notion of something existing is founded. Clearly, for Fichte, to settle claims about the certainty of judgments is to settle claims about the existence of what a judgment is.

This result does not yet provide us with the first principle of all knowledge because it would rest the claim to unconditional certainty of a judgment on the I understood as an empirical fact of consciousness. This is so because we arrived at the I by reflecting on the empirical fact that "A is A" is unconditionally certain for us. The conditions of the empirical fact that a judgment is unconditionally certain, however, are themselves empirical facts, which depend on something's being the case contingently, in this instance that there happens to be an I around. In other words, what we have reached so far is merely the assertion that if "A is A" is unconditionally certain, then the judgment "I am" is unconditionally certain too. This clearly places the "I am" under a condition and thus does not make it an expression of a first principle. Therefore, in order to arrive at the first principle we are seeking, we have to start over again and answer the question: what makes the empirical fact of consciousness expressed by the judgment "I am" possible? Fichte's answer goes roughly like this: we already know (see (1) and (6) above) that the I has the ability to posit something unconditionally within the I. However, in order to do such a thing, the I itself has to be posited. Now, we have also seen that the unconditional positing of the I consists in its activity of positing existence (*Sein*). All this together indicates, according to Fichte, that we have to think of the I as being the product of its own positing activity if we want to account for its existence at all. This in turn is supposed to mean that the I must be conceived of as an activity which, in being active, posits its own existence. In order to express this situation, Fichte chooses the following formulation: The I "is at the same time the acting (*das Handelnde*) and the product of the act; the active (*das Tätige*) and that which is generated by the activity; act and deed (*Tat*) are one and the same." The I viewed under this description Fichte calls *Tathandlung* (deed-act). A *Tathandlung* is not a *Tatsache* (fact) because this deed-act is logically and ontologically prior to all facts in that it ultimately posits or constitutes them. It is an unconditioned entity because it posits itself, and it is an existing entity because its positing itself consists in its positing its existence. Thus we have an entity here whose very concept includes its existence. Hence this entity, in virtue of the fact (which we saw in (1) to (7) above) that it is the ultimate basis of all claims to unconditional certainty, has all the characteristics needed to make it the appropriate candidate for being the subject of the first principle of all knowledge. Fichte makes several suggestions as to what the best formula for the first principle could be. The most accessible is the last one he gives in the first section of the *Science of Knowledge*. It says: "The I originally posits its own being unconditionally."[22]

This summary of what Fichte himself took to be merely an outline of a convincing consideration is not intended to cover the details of his reasoning. Nevertheless, it should be sufficient for hinting at the general strategy he is pursuing in order to reach his goal, namely, an insight into the I as a self-positing activity. For Fichte, this insight is not only important and fundamental in its own right; it is at the same time the basis for a vindication of the validity of logical laws and, more importantly, for a much sounder derivation and thus justification of the categories than Kant was able or willing to give to them. As for the vindication of logical laws, Fichte is of the opinion that in our having been witnesses to the very process which led to his theory of the I as a *Tathandlung*, we have seen the reasons for our having to take as certain the logical law of identity "A is A." Thus as soon as we come to think of the I as a *Tathandlung*, we have to accept the validity of the law of identity. Because, according to Fichte, there is no way to avoid thinking of the I as a *Tathandlung*, the logical law of identity is vindicated.[23]

The connection which Fichte sees between his theory of the I and the Kantian deduction of the categories is a little less obvious. The background to it is as follows: one of the most heavily criticized pieces of Kant's *Critique of Pure Reason* has been, and still is, his derivation of the categories – that is, the most elementary concepts which guide our epistemic access to reality, from the so-called forms of judgment.[24] Fichte subscribed to that criticism up to a certain point. But unlike his fellow-critics, who took Kant's general access to this question of the derivation of the categories to be seriously flawed, Fichte thought that the problems connected with this deduction were easy to overcome within his own approach to a theory of knowledge, by showing that both the forms of judgment and the categories have a common ground in the I understood as a *Tathandlung*.

That this indeed is the case can be demonstrated, according to Fichte, in a paradigmatic way simply by considering what the first principle, understood as the exclusive expression of the I as a *Tathandlung*, means if one is to interpret it in Kantian terms. In order to arrive at (Kantian) categories and forms of judgments, one need only look at the implications connected with that *Tathandlung*. If the I is an activity that posits its own existence, it thereby constitutes reality – because, without that positing activity, which consists in nothing other than making something real, it would be impossible to attach any meaning to the very concept of reality. Thus the category of reality, as Fichte sees it, is founded in the very manner of acting (*Handlungsart*) of the human spirit. A similar consideration, if we are to follow Fichte, would lead to the form of what he calls a "thetic" judgment. Here the idea would be that the adequate expression of the

Tathandlung, because of its intrinsic characteristics, allows only for a judgment that states something to be the case in such a way that it claims positively that something is or exists.[25]

As we mentioned above, Fichte considers that the establishing of his first principle of all knowledge claims is only the first, though most important, step toward the realization of a sound anti-skeptical program in epistemology. He is well aware that he has to add some further elements in order to make his solution convincing or at least plausible. Within his approach as described so far, there are two questions in particular that need an answer. The first is that if Fichte's first principle is valid, how can we think of our epistemic environment as a world of interrelated objects that are distinguished from us and to which we have cognitive access? In other words: if all we have by now is a self–positing I, how can the very concept of an object known as something which is different from a knowing subject be accommodated within this approach? The second question concerns the possibility of an epistemic relation between a subject and an object: how do we have to conceive of the I and of the object respectively if we want them to be epistemically connected?

Fichte tries to answer these questions by introducing his second and third principles. The considerations which lead to these principles are supposed to establish that there are two other unconditioned positing acts of the I. According to Fichte the I, over and above its positing itself, has the ability (1) to posit unconditionally the Not-I, that is, it has the power, by what Fichte calls "an absolute act," to counter-posit something that is exactly the opposite (*das Entgegengesetzte*) of, or in opposition to, the I. This act of counter-positing is the object of the second principle. The I is also in the position (2) to posit unconditionally the divisibility (*Teilbarkeit*) of the I and the Not-I. This idea of divisibility is taken to be the third principle.[26]

It is easy to see what Fichte wants to account for with the second principle. It is supposed to give a foundation for our common-sense belief that there are objects outside and different from us, to which we can refer in our capacity as epistemic and acting subjects. According to Fichte, this belief is justified not because we can trace it back to the way in which a subject-independent reality forces us to think of its constitution, but because it belongs to the very nature of the I to organize its world in terms of the subject–object distinction, or the I/Not-I opposition. Things are not so easy with respect to the third principle, of divisibility. The motive for introducing it consists in the conviction that we have to guarantee that the Not-I is thought of as having a certain amount of positive reality itself, and not as being merely the negation of the reality that the I is claimed to posit in positing its own being. The rather strange presupposition implicit here seems to be that we have to take reality or existence to be a quantity that comes in portions or in degrees. If one shares this presupposition, then something like the third principle is indeed unavoidable, because within the Fichtean framework the idea of some fixed amount of reality or existence, together with the idea that objects should have some independent existence, implies the idea of reality as being something distributable, and the claim that there is an instance which distributes reality between the I, or knowing subject, and the Not-I or known object.

With his three principles in hand, Fichte is convinced that he has successfully achieved his twofold goal: he believes (1) that he has succeeded in giving a non-dualistic account of the most fundamental operations and concepts constituting reality for us, thereby presenting a new basis for Kantian claims, and (2) that he has established a sound anti-skeptical strategy in epistemology by relying on the notion of an I that can act spontaneously in the mode of positing. Although he never gave up these beliefs explicitly, he transformed their presentation and their justification considerably in later years. The most obvious of his modifications concerns methodology. Starting with lectures in 1796 (*Wissenschaftslehre nova methodo*) and publications in 1797/8 (*Second Introduction*), Fichte comes forward with a new procedure for how we can attain an insight into the structure of the I, that is, into its being a self-positing activity. This procedure he calls "intellectual intuition" (*intellektuelle Anschauung*), a term that was to play a somewhat unfortunate role in the assessment of German idealistic philosophy in general.[27] It is designed to replace the method of abstracting reflection characteristic of his writings in 1794/5. Whereas the process of abstracting reflection leads to the specific features of the I by starting from an unconditionally certain claim like the law of identity, and by then proceeding to conditions necessary and sufficient to account for the unconditional certainty of this claim, the method of intellectual intuition is intended to arrive at the I as a self-positing activity by analyzing the act a thinker performs in thinking of the I. Here the underlying idea seems to be that when I choose to think of myself – in Fichte's terminology, to make my I the object of my thinking activity – I thereby become immediately aware of the I's being nothing other than that activity which is directed toward itself in a self-reflective and self-constitutive way. This act that I, the thinker, perform on myself results in an intellectual intuition, because for Fichte, to be immediately aware of something is to have an intuition of that entity, and the immediate awareness of an intellectual activity cannot be a sensible (*sinnliche*) intuition that presupposes material existence (*materielles Bestehen*).[28] Whatever might be the merits or the shortcomings of this new attempt to give some plausibility to his theory of the I, Fichte succeeds in getting rid of the restraints which were connected with his explanation of the peculiar nature of the I within the framework of first principles.

Having thus established the absolute I, or the I understood in the sense of *Tathandlung*, as the very foundation for all that can be real for us, Fichte goes on to develop on that basis his ethical theory and theory of natural right. In both of these theories he is no longer concerned with the I in an absolute sense, but rather with what he calls an empirical self-conscious being, a person. His aim in both cases is to show that a rational justification of legal rights and moral duties follows directly from his conception of the I.[29] Although the application of the main results of this conception, and the transformation of its central categories like activity, self-positing or reflectivity to legal and moral contexts, are highly original, his positive doctrines as to what natural rights consist in and what we are morally committed to are not especially revolutionary. In questions concerning natural right and ethical theory, Fichte's deep commitment to Kant's philosophy shows up much more clearly than in his theory of knowledge. Thus one can characterize his *Foundation of Natural Right* as the attempt to give a new derivation of Kant's concept of right under the condition of freedom, and the objective of his *System of Ethical Doctrine* consists in nothing other than proving that Kant's categorical imperative is valid. This is not to say that there are no innovative ideas or new aspects to be found in these writings; it simply means that the material results of these theories are very close to those of Kant.[30]

These are the main elements of Fichte's philosophical project as presented by him in his major writings before 1800.[31] As we mentioned earlier, at the beginning of the new century Fichte developed a totally different approach to the realization of his foundationalist program in epistemology and ethics. The most significant distinguishing characteristic of this new approach is the replacement of the (absolute) I as the ultimate and only basis for all our different conceptions of cognitive, moral, and legal reality by what Fichte calls absolute being (*Sein*). The reasons for and the consequences of this conceptual change are still a matter of controversy, as is the question of whether this change really contributes to a better understanding of his overall concern.[32] The details of these discussions do not concern us, however, because it was Fichte's system as expounded in his pre-1800 writings that was influential on the German idealistic movement in general, and in particular on the early Schelling.

II Schelling

Almost at the same time as Fichte published his first *Wissenschaftslehre*, the nineteen-year-old Friedrich Wilhelm Joseph Schelling (1775–1854) began to emerge as a major philosophical writer with a series of highly remarkable publications which showed him to be a very original thinker, deeply influenced and encouraged in his views by Kant's theory and its problems. Schelling's approach to philosophy was formed and guided by his being a member of a group of young Swabian students who studied theology at the Protestant seminary of Tübingen university, the so-called "Tübinger Stift." This group, which also included Hölderlin and Hegel, became interested in Kant's Critical philosophy in the wake of its revolt against the orthodox, anti-Enlightened tendencies of its professors who taught Protestant theology at Tübingen. Schelling and his friends at the Stift were convinced that they could profit from Kant's philosophical enterprise in their attempt to give a rational foundation for religion, and this conviction led them to study Kant's Critical system in detail, to take notice of the debates it inaugurated, and to participate in the project of improving Kant's philosophy by suggesting either new founding principles or other remedies.[33]

But Kant's thought was not all that was highly influential for the young Schelling. Ancient philosophy, particularly that of Plato, also had an enormous impact on his more general views. This is documented by a number of texts from the early nineties, the best known of which is a commentary on passages from Plato's *Timaeus*. Although never published by Schelling himself, these texts already deal with topics that were to become central to his own philosophical teachings, that is, with topics concerning aesthetics and the philosophy of nature.[34] It is clear that he was also well aware of Jacobi's criticism of Kant's position – which led him to think of Spinoza in a very unconventional way – and that he had some acquaintance with Reinhold's and Fichte's early systematic efforts.

Schelling's first published essays almost immediately made him famous all over Germany, and are best understood as reactions against and responses to the ongoing discussions of questions concerning the basis and the justification of knowledge. These essays all appeared between 1794 and 1797, and were followed by a couple of essays on the philosophy of nature.[35] In 1798 he became a professor at Jena, which made him not only the youngest philosophy professor of his time but also a close colleague of Fichte for about a year.[36] In 1800 he published his *System of Transcendental Idealism*, in which he gives a unified account of what he calls theoretical and practical philosophy in the form of a history of self-consciousness. When viewed from an architectonic perspective, this book shows many similarities to Fichte's early *Science of Knowledge*,[37] and when viewed from a methodological point of view, it foreshadows Hegel's *Phenomenology of Spirit* (1807).

In 1801 Schelling started a new project that became known as "identity philosophy." It is quite likely that Hegel played a considerable role in motivating Schelling to give up his transcendental idealist approach and to replace the absolute I as the foundation of his system by a structure he describes as the point of indifference of the ideal and the real, or of the subject and object.[38] This new project was central to Schelling's philosophical concern until roughly 1810, and is documented in several important publications.[39] In 1803 he left Jena and moved to Bavaria (Würzburg, Erlangen, Munich), where he stayed until 1841, holding leading positions at different academic institutions. After 1810 he almost completely stopped publishing his major philosophical works, and from about 1810 until the late 1820s he was mainly concerned with what became known as the philosophy of the Ages of the World (*Die Weltalter*), producing texts that discuss fundamental questions about the ultimate constitution of the world and its intelligibility. During the very last period of his intellectual activity, from 1827 to his death, he was working on a huge project dealing with topics in the philosophy of religion. His aim here was to give a philosophical explanation of why there is a world at all. This explanation is the subject of his *Philosophy of Mythology* and his *Philosophy of Revelation*. It is during this period that Schelling moved to Berlin to become Hegel's successor at the university of Berlin (1841). Although he was not very successful in this role, he remained philosophically productive till the end of his life.

Although the later Schelling was critical of the success of his earlier philosophical attempts, there is no doubt that his basic motives for becoming involved in philosophy at all were rooted mainly in his being drawn into the discussions about the shortcomings of Kant's philosophical theory and the possible ways of overcoming them. This is clear from two programmatic statements that he made in his early letters to Hegel: in the first, he states that philosophy is not yet finished because Kant's philosophy has given only conclusions, for which the premises are still missing; the second holds that he has converted to Spinozism.[40] Both these statements are the results of his conviction, first, that in order to achieve anything philosophically important, we have, in one way or another, to rely on Kantian insights, and second, that what is philosophically important is to find a monistic foundation, that is, a foundation à la Spinoza, for Kant's philosophy. These convictions in turn owe much to the influence of Fichte on the one hand and Jacobi on the other.[41]

Thus it comes as no surprise that Schelling's first two philosophical essays – the writings *On the Form of Philosophy* (1794) and *On the I* (1795) – deal with problems in the theory of knowledge from the perspective posed by the skeptical threat. This Fichtean perspective on epistemology, however, is applied to a thoroughly Jacobian way of conceiving the goal that an anti-skeptic has to reach. For Jacobi, the skeptical problem in epistemology arises because of our conception of knowledge. According to him our concept of knowledge has to do with our understanding of something as being conditioned, but the idea of something being conditioned leads necessarily to the assumption of the unconditioned. Thus it is in the unconditioned that all our claims to knowledge are founded. Because of the impossibility of knowing the unconditioned – knowledge, after all, is restricted to conditioned states of affairs – we can never know what is at the basis of our knowledge claims, and this means that we can never refute the skeptic, who doubts that there is such a basis, by relying on arguments. According to Jacobi, this situation leaves us with only one choice: in order to avoid skepticism we have to accept the insight that although we cannot know the unconditioned, we have to believe in it.[42] In his attempt to fight skepticism Schelling agrees with Jacobi that we have to account for the reality of the unconditioned, but, contrary to Jacobi, he insists on our having to have an epistemic relationship (and not just one of belief) to the unconditioned. Thus he proceeds in his early writings to establish a non-trivial relation between knowledge and the unconditioned. He does this by offering an analysis of what he calls "the I," implying that it is this I which can carry the burden of relating knowledge and the unconditioned. The very title of his second philosophical essay – *Of the I as a Principle of Philosophy, or on the Unconditional in Human Knowledge* – is witness to such a program.

However, Jacobi's influence on Schelling not only shows up in his manner of framing the skeptical problem, but, more importantly, is also present in his way of dealing with questions concerning the scientific explanation of nature. This topic eventually brings him into conflict with Fichte's views, and leads directly to his early positions in the philosophy of nature. In Jacobi's view, one of the main problems that a philosophical theory which relies on Kantian premises has to face is that it gives a privileged status to causal-mechanical explanations of natural phenomena and thus rejects the validity of teleological explanations in natural sciences. This crucial point of Jacobi's refers to the then famous distinction between objective and subjective validity put forward by Kant, most prominently in the second part of his *Critique of Judgment*. Here Kant holds that we have to acknowledge two different types of physical objects, namely those whose constitution is the result of mechanical processes and those whose formation seems to be the effect of processes that are guided by purposes or ends. Paradigms of the former type are non-living objects, which allow for causal-mechanical explanations, and prototypes of the latter are living objects or organisms, which are in need of so-called teleological explanations. But whereas, according to Kant, causal-mechanical explanations of natural phenomena are objectively valid because of their being somehow grounded in or at least related to the real constitution of objects, this is not true of teleological explanations. These explanations are peculiar in that they have to explain their objects by relying on ends, purposes, or aims.

However, if we have to refer to purposes and ends in order to explain the constitution of a natural phenomenon, we are committed to subscribe to the idea of what Kant calls the "technic of nature." With this term he characterizes the ability of nature to create natural objects according to purposes or ends. For Kant, the idea of a technique of nature is a necessary condition for our making sense of the concept of an organism as a distinct type of entity. Although this result does not seem to be very provocative in itself, it has a number of quite disturbing aspects as soon as one realizes that the very idea of a technique of nature brings with it a couple of conceptual house guests that are difficult for Kant to accommodate in his philosophical framework: "the supersensible [*Übersinnliche*]" and "the primordial rational being [*verständiges Urwesen*]." These concepts are introduced because talk about natural purposes or ends presupposes an idea of nature as related to a subject having purposes and ends, and because such a subject has to be situated in the realm of the supersensible. According to Kant, neither of these implications of the assumption of a technique of nature can be taken to refer to entities or states of affairs of which we can have knowledge. They are examples of what Kant calls "problematic ideas," that is, ideas that are inevitable although they do not designate a possible object of knowledge. Ultimately this means, for Kant, that we have no objectively valid reasons to think of (physical) nature as having aims or ends. Thus teleological explanations, which are framed in terms of purposes and ends, do not give us insight into what is really going on in nature; they are heuristic devices that we use whenever we cannot figure out what really is the case. It is for this reason that they are only subjectively valid.[43]

For Jacobi Kant's position is totally unacceptable for many reasons. The most serious is that it implies the abandonment of the idea that organisms and other forms of living nature have an ontological status of their own. Abandoning that idea has far-reaching consequences, because it leads to a conception of reality that conceives of the world in its totality as a huge mechanism. It is here that Schelling gets involved in the Critical discussion about the achievements of Kant's philosophy. He shares with Jacobi the opinion that the concept of life is ontologically indispensable and irreducible, and that it is a mistake to envision the world as constituted solely by mechanical processes and governed exclusively by mechanical laws. He also agrees with Jacobi that a successful philosophy of nature has to be able to give a convincing account of teleological judgments and their (objective) validity. But he differs significantly from Jacobi in his conviction that one can solve this task in a Kantian spirit, that is, without putting into question Kant's general approach to organic nature, its phenomena, and their teleological explanation.

According to Schelling, all that is needed in order to reach a satisfactory solution of the problem of how to deal with organisms as natural phenomena is to come up with an alternative interpretation of Kant's teachings concerning the implications of the idea of what he calls the "technic of nature." This can be achieved by a different interpretation of Kant's conception of the supersensible, an interpretation which liberates this idea from the status of being a merely problematic item, and thus opens the way for giving a different account of the validity of teleological judgments. Schelling's first attempt to reinterpret the Kantian idea of the supersensible consists in claiming on epistemological grounds that the world of objects to which subjects are epistemically related is not to be identified with reality in its most fundamental and comprehensive sense. This is because reality in this basic sense must transcend the realm of experience, which is always subject to some condition or other. Hence, the epistemically accessible world of objects has to be understood as a manifestation of what is ultimately or unconditionally real. Because ultimate reality, which has to be conceived of as something unconditioned, is distinguished from the world of objects, and because only objects are epistemically accessible to us, reality in its proper sense, or the unconditioned, is something beyond our epistemic grasp; it is equivalent to the Kantian supersensible. This interpretation of the idea of the supersensible succeeds in giving it a non-subjectivistic reading by introducing a conceptual distinction between the world of objects and reality proper, but, as Schelling soon was to realize, the distinction is ultimately unproductive because it leads to insoluble problems concerning the determination of the relation that holds between the world of objects and reality proper. Schelling therefore gave up on this approach.[44]

A different and, in Schelling's view, more promising solution to the problem of how to give objective validity to the idea of a technique of nature is presented for the first time in his *Essays in Explanation of the Idealism of the Doctrine of Science* and is elaborated in his early writings on natural philosophy from 1797 to 1799. Here, too, he starts with an analysis of (necessary) conditions of knowledge. In order for something to be known, it has to be real. Something is real in knowledge if there is "an absolute correspondence between an object and its representation,"[45] where "absolute correspondence" is supposed to mean identity of object and representation. Now, the only concrete paradigm of such a correspondence is what Schelling calls self-consciousness, because only in this case do we have identity of "the representing and the represented, of the intuiting and the intuited."[46] Self-consciousness is taken to be the essence of spirit (*Geist*). According to Schelling, these stipulations allow for the claim that, strictly speaking, knowledge presupposes a relation of a spirit to itself. He thus declares: "Only in the self-intuition of a spirit is identity of representation and object. Consequently [if knowledge is possible at all] one would have to prove that spirit in intuiting objects intuits only itself. If this can be proved, the reality of our knowledge is guaranteed too."[47]

In order to arrive at the idea of a technique of nature as a concept that has objective reality, Schelling goes on to maintain that we have to think of nature as being a self-organizing entity if self-intuition of spirit (that is, knowledge) is to be possible at all. He supports this claim with a number of rather obscure arguments which amount to the following: knowledge or identity of representation and object, that is, self-intuition of spirit, can be achieved only if there is a structural isomorphism between the represented object and the representing spirit. According to Schelling, spirit has to conceive of itself as an entity that is organized according to purposes or ends. Hence if spirit is to know or intuit itself, it has to be related to something that is a structural counterpart to itself. Thus there has to be an organized object if there is knowledge at all. Schelling takes this to warrant the conclusion: "Because in our spirit there is an infinite tendency [*Bestreben*] to organize itself, such a general tendency towards organization must reveal itself in the outer world too. And this really is the case. The system of the world is a kind of organization . . ."[48]

Whatever the intellectual merits of such a consideration may be, the message Schelling wants to convince us of is quite clear: if we are to hold that our knowledge has something to do with reality, or that knowledge claims are founded in a relation to something real, we have to accept the objective reality of the idea of a technique of nature, and consequently we have to allow for the objective validity of teleological explanations. In pursuing this line of thought, Schelling goes even further than he would have to go in order to accommodate Kant's approach to teleology in nature to Jacobi's worries. Instead of being content with a rehabilitation of teleological explanations, he declares them to be epistemologically more fundamental than causal-mechanical explanations.

In his *System of Transcendental Idealism* (1800), Schelling sets out to combine the essential elements of his anti-skeptical considerations and the guiding principles of his approach to nature as an organized entity into a comprehensive account of how to conceive of reality if it is to be an object of knowledge.[49] He does this by identifying the notion of the unconditioned, which played the role of reality proper in his early attempts to dissolve the skeptical challenge, with his concept of a self-conscious spirit that has to objectify itself in order to know itself. The resulting story of how to make sense of the idea of an objective reality that can be known centers on the conception of a history of self-consciousness, and goes roughly like this: self-conscious spirit comes to realize its own objectivity in a process which aims to demonstrate that all the different phenomena we encounter in reality are nothing but products of its own activity. This process is divided into three main steps. The first consists in an account of the emergence of an outer world of (physical) objects by means of the self-limiting activity of spirit. This account Schelling calls theoretical philosophy. The second deals with the ability of spirit to determine itself under the condition that there is an objective world. This is Schelling's version of a practical philosophy. The third step eventually tries to answer the question of how the process of the self-objectification of spirit can be witnessed by human beings who are not philosophers. It is here that Schelling outlines his philosophy of art.

There are two points that are of special interest in connection with this version of transcendental idealism. The first is Schelling's way of using the notion of intellectual intuition. According to Schelling, intellectual intuition is founded in the capacity of spirit to have an immediate epistemic relation to itself. What is given in intellectual intuition, however, is not something objective, or something as an object; it is the pre-objective identity of spirit with itself. It is this pre-objectively intuited or, in Schelling's terminology, absolute identity which is then supposed to objectivize itself and thus to allow a distinction between subject and object that is not in an intellectual but rather in an experienced, "real" mode. The concept of an intellectual intuition was already introduced by Schelling in his essay *On the I* in order to characterize the specific manner in which the unconditioned can represent itself. In this essay it was barely more than a skillful terminological move on Schelling's part, giving a new and positive meaning to a conception that Kant had already discussed and dismissed as epistemologically meaningless. In the *System of Transcendental Idealism*, however, the situation has changed. Here Schelling attributes the faculty of intellectual intuition to the philosophizing subject as something it employs as a means for relating to the Absolute in a non-objectifying or non-objective fashion. Intellectual intuition thus emerges as a new epistemic faculty of human beings, a faculty whose sole purpose consists in somehow enabling us to contemplate the Absolute.

Although the very idea of an intellectual intuition, its function and its object, clearly has a number of inherent problems, Schelling makes the situation even worse by using the idea in a rather confused way. This is especially noticeable in connection with a point relating to the work of art. According to the *System of Transcendental Idealism*, it is not philosophy but the work of art that is given the distinction of being the most adequate objective expression of the absolute identity of subject and object. This distinction arises from Schelling's rather strange interpretation of intellectual intuition. He starts with his standard assumption, already hinted at, that what is given in intellectual intuition is given in a non-objective mode. "Non-objectivity" here is supposed to mean "beyond the subject–object distinction"; it is this meaning of non-objectivity that is constitutive for his concept of an intellectual intuition. However, in order to arrive at the supremacy of art, Schelling shifts to an interpretation according to which "non-objective" means "(exclusively) subjective," although such a move does not seem to be warranted by any of his own initial stipulations. At any rate, he employs this reinterpretation in order to substantiate the claim that the true constitution of reality finds its ultimate manifestation in works of art. This view of the epistemic function of art was to become one of the cornerstones of late eighteenth- and early nineteenth-century romanticism. Soon after the publication of his *System of Transcendental Idealism* Schelling abandoned the project of a history of self-consciousness, although he never gave up on the conviction that in philosophy one has to account for the unconditioned or the Absolute, and that in order to do so one has to acknowledge a non-discursive mode of knowledge in the form of an intellectual intuition.[50]

The aim of this outline of certain aspects of the philosophy of Fichte and Schelling has been to clarify what these philosophers took to be the intellectual challenge which has to be faced in the wake of Kant's philosophy. Although there was a common assessment of the shortcomings and the deficiencies of Kant's actual teachings, there was at the same time a shared belief in the significance of his philosophical program. Thus for philosophers like Fichte and Schelling it became imperative to develop a new basis for what would presumably be Kantian results. They differed considerably on questions concerning what this basis should be, and what conceptual and methodological means would be required in order to establish it. Nonetheless, ultimately they had a common vision of what philosophy is all about, and they were willing to explore new ways of reasoning that could support their views. They were very well aware that it was difficult to reconcile these ways of reasoning with traditional patterns of rationality. However, they were acutely aware that the most advanced philosophy of the time – Kantian philosophy – showed serious weaknesses in its conceptualization of the world and our place in it, and this left them with no alternative but to embark on the project of investigating alternative conceptions of rationality.[51]

NOTES

1 This view goes back ultimately to Hegel, who introduced it for the first time in his *Lectures on the History of Philosophy*. It became the standard view because some of the earliest historians of the philosophy of that time picked it up, for example, H. M. Chalybaeus (1837) and C. L. Michelet (1837/8). Concerning some of the problems connected with that view as Hegel presented it, see Rolf-Peter Horstmann, *Die Grenzen der Vernunft. Eine Untersuchung zu Zielen und Motiven des Deutschen Idealismus*, 2 Aufl. (Weinheim: Anton Hain, 1995), 22ff.

2 This formulation is meant to capture some of the more explicit motives put forward by Reinhold, Fichte, and Schelling when explaining in public and private writings what their philosophy is all about.

3 Other important factors include the debate over skepticism initiated by Schulze's *Aenesidemus*, the question of how to deal with first principles which goes back to Reinhold, and the exchange on Spinoza between Lessing, Jacobi, and Mendelssohn, as well as political and theological topics and broader issues such as the consequences of the eighteenth-century Enlightenment for modern life. Until now no really comprehensive study of the development of German Idealism has been available, though there are quite a number of very informative accounts of aspects of that development.

4 These handbooks are not alone in conveying that notion. Books such as those by Chalybaeus and Michelet do the same, as do the treatises of K. Fischer (1852–77) and R. Kroner (1921–4). This notion underlies the popular distinction between subjective, objective, and absolute idealism which is used to characterize the positions of Fichte, Schelling, and Hegel respectively.

5 The history of that offer is an interesting story in itself. It can be traced back to an initiative of Goethe, who wanted to make sure that a representative of Kant's philosophy would be present at Jena.

6 Fichte had also published two writings on the French Revolution which showed him to be a fervent admirer and defender of its goals and, to a certain extent, even its

means. This gave rise to the suspicion that he was a Jacobite and a radical in political matters.

7 Depending on how one counts, one can distinguish up to twenty different versions of the *Science of Knowledge*. The other exposition, published by Fichte himself in 1810, is a very short (twenty-page), very cryptic piece entitled *The Science of Knowledge in its General Outline*.

8 The literature on the Atheism Controversy (*Atheismusstreit*) and Fichte's role in it is quite extensive. For some of the more important titles, see the bibliography in the edition of Fichte's *Introductions to the Wissenschaftslehre and Other Writings* by D. Breazeale (Indianapolis: Hackett, 1994), xlvff.

9 For a discussion of Reinhold's philosophical position at this time, see the comprehensive study of his philosophy in all its different forms by M. Bondeli, *Das Anfangsproblem bei Karl Leonhard Reinhold. Eine systematische und entwicklungsgeschichtliche Untersuchung zu Philosophie Reinholds in der Zeit von 1789 bis 1803* (Frankfurt am Main: Klostermann, 1995). The Reinhold–Schulze debate and its influence on the early Fichte is very well analyzed by D. Breazeale, "Fichte's 'Aenesidemus' Review and the Transformation of German Idealism," *The Review of Metaphysics*, 34 (1980/1), 545ff. and "Between Kant and Fichte: K. L. Reinhold's 'Elementary Philosophy,'" *The Review of Metaphysics*, 35 (1981/2), 785ff.; and by R. Lauth, *Transzendentale Entwicklungslinien von Descartes bis zu Marx und Dostojewski* (Hamburg: Meiner, 1989), 155ff.

10 See R.-P. Horstmann, "Maimon's Criticism of Reinhold's 'Satz des Bewußtsein,'" in L. W. Beck, ed., *Proceedings of the Third International Kant Congress* (Dordrecht: Reidel, 1972), 330ff., and also P. Franks, ch. 5 in this volume.

11 That principle was soon abandoned by Reinhold himself, not because Schulze's intervention was completely convincing but mainly because of critical arguments developed by some of Reinhold's own pupils in Jena. See D. Henrich, "Die Anfänge der Theorie des Subjekts" (1789), in *Zwischenbetrachtungen im Prozeß der Aufklärung*, ed. A. Honneth *et al.* (Frankfurt: Suhrkamp, 1989), 106ff.

12 See a short essay by Jacobi entitled "On transcendental Idealism," added as an appendix to his *David Hume on Faith or Idealism and Realism* (1787).

13 In what follows I don't distinguish between judgments, propositions or sentences. Fichte normally uses just the term "sentence" (*Satz*) in order to refer to what we would call, depending on the context, either "proposition" or "judgment."

14 It should be noted here that this conception of transmission of certainty by derivation or deduction is reminiscent of Spinoza's project of proceeding in philosophy *more geometrico*. Though Fichte is indebted to Spinoza, or at least to Jacobi's version of his philosophy, he would disagree with Spinoza on what a deduction or derivation consists in and on his theory of substance.

15 Whether it is just a necessary or at the same time a sufficient condition depends largely on the interpretation one gives to Fichte's candidate for a first principle.

16 There might have been different reasons for Fichte not to address this topic explicitly. Among them could have been the following: (1) The first principle we are looking for is supposed to be a first principle of knowledge. After all, we are dealing with the "Science of Knowledge." Knowledge (*Wissen*) is a product and an activity which can be described as a mode of consciousness. (2) One of the essential insights of Kant, following the Cartesian tradition, has been that all knowledge claims have their foundation in what he calls the "transcendental unity of apperception" or the "tran-

scendental I." Although this insight is quite correct, Kant did not succeed in making the connection between knowledge and the I sufficiently transparent.

17 What the distinction between the form and the contents of a judgment exactly amounts to is hard to decide, especially in the case of his principles. Fichte explains the distinction with respect to judgments in general in GA(= Fichte, *Gesamtausgabe der Bayerischen Akademie der Wissenschaften*, ed. R. Lauth, H. Gliwitzky, and H. Jacob [Stuttgart-Bad Cannstatt: Frommann-Holzboog, 1962ff.]), I:2, 121 and 257.

18 There are quite a number of questions left open with respect to this taxonomy of principles, some of which Fichte never chose to address. However, he tries to answer the most obvious of these, namely, the question why there could be only one absolutely first principle, in GA I:2, 114ff. (*Über den Begriff der Wissenschaftslehre*). But this answer does not necessarily apply to related questions, such as why it is that there could be no more than one judgment which conforms to the criteria that a second or a third principle has to satisfy.

19 The very fact that Fichte is primarily concerned with questions about the certainty, and not, say, the truth or verifiability, of a proposition already indicates that his approach is deeply committed to an anti-skeptical project. The method of abstracting reflection as proposed in the *Science of Knowledge* in its 1794/5 version does not figure prominently in his later writings. One reason might have been that even in this early version of the *Science of Knowledge*, the procedure Fichte actually uses in order to arrive at his first principle is hard to reconcile with the description that he gives of it.

20 This distinction might sound strange to us, and it even seems to be at odds with some of Fichte's remarks concerning what the relation between subject and predicate in categorical judgments means in terms of modes of existence (especially with the first footnote of section one of the *Science of Knowledge*). This, however, is irrelevant to the consideration at hand because all Fichte needs is the notion of an unconditioned existence.

21 Fichte seems to think that unconditional certainty implies necessity, because otherwise one would have to allow for contingent unconditional certainty. This would make no sense to Fichte, because everything contingent must have a reason, and thus could not be unconditioned.

22 This way of introducing the I as a *Tathandlung* is relatively uncontroversial. Fichte himself soon became critical of such an approach, as his correspondence shows. He seems to have been dissatisfied with the attempt to connect the conception of the I as a *Tathandlung* with the discussion of the characteristics of first principles of knowledge. Quotations in this paragraph are from *Science of Knowledge* §1; GA I:2, 259.

23 This argument again makes it quite clear that Fichte's primary concern is with questions of certainty rather than with questions of, say, truth.

24 This line of criticism started with Reinhold in the eighteenth century and continues to Bennett and Strawson in the twentieth century.

25 GA I:2, 261. Here it should be noted that in the context of section 1, Fichte himself does not claim explicitly that the form of the "thetic" judgment is necessarily related to the first principle.

26 The second and the third principles are said to give the (Kantian) categories of negation and limitation respectively. Fichte also claims that these two principles are formally subordinated to the first because they are only in part unconditioned. This claim seems to rest on the assumption that on the one hand there is no strict conceptual relation between the acts of positing and counter-positing, only a material one, and that,

on the other hand, for introducing the notion of divisibility there is a conceptual necessity, but no material reason – that is, a reason founded in the very nature of these two acts. It is because of this assumption that Fichte characterizes his second principle as conditioned with respect to content, and his third as conditioned with respect to form. This somewhat artificial explanation of the respective status of his principles shows once again how difficult it is for Fichte to explain the basic moves of his antiskeptical program within the (Reinholdian) framework of first principles.

27 Kant's critical remarks, in his first and third *Critiques*, concerning our ability to acquire knowledge by relying on intellectual intuition or an intuiting understanding (*anschauender Verstand*) gave rise to a very intense debate as to the possibility and feasibility of such a faculty. Almost all German idealistic thinkers were engaged in this discussion at some point or other in their philosophical careers. Although the term "intellectual intuition" is already used by Fichte in his "Review of *Aenesidemus*" (1793) in order to characterize the way in which the I comes to know about itself, he does not mention either the term or the method connected with it in his writings on the Science of Knowledge in 1794/5. It is likely that he was encouraged by the example of the young Schelling to think again of intellectual intuition as an appropriate methodological device. See J. Stolzenberg, *Fichtes Begriff der intellektuellen Anschauung. Die Entwicklung in den Wissenschaftslehren von 1793/94 bis 1801/1802* (Stuttgart: Klett-Cotta, 1986).

28 This line of reasoning is presented mainly in sections 4, 5, and 7 of the Second Introduction. It should be noted that, in order to arrive at his concept of an intellectual intuition, Fichte obviously takes for granted that every intuition is either a sensible or an intellectual one.

29 A comprehensive account of the complicated relations between Fichte's theory of the I and his ethical thinking in particular is given by G. Zöller, *Fichte's Transcendental Philosophy. The Original Duplicity of Intelligence and Will* (Cambridge: Cambridge University Press, 1998).

30 Thus, for example, it is widely acknowledged that Fichte puts much more emphasis than Kant did on the importance of interpersonal relations in the process of the constitution of our legal and moral reality.

31 Studies which deal with this period of Fichte's thought in a much more extensive way include P. Rohs, *Johann Gottlieb Fichte* (Munich: Beck, 1991); P. Baumanns, *Fichte. Kritische Gesamtdarstellung seiner Philosophie* (Freiburg/Munich: Alber, 1990); F. Neuhouser, *Fichte's Theory of Subjectivity* (Cambridge: Cambridge University Press, 1990); and W. Martin, *Idealism and Objectivity: Understanding Fichte's Jena Project* (Stanford: Stanford University Press, 1997).

32 See, for example, M. Gueroult, *L'évolution et la structure de la doctrine de la science de Fichte*, 2 vols. (Paris: Société de l'édition Les Belles Lettres, 1930); W. Janke, *Fichte. Sein und Reflexion. Grundlagen der kritischen Vernunft* (Berlin: de Gruyter, 1979); L. Siep, *Hegels Fichte-Kritik und die Wissenschaftslehre von 1804* (Freiburg/Munich: Alber, 1970); and U. Schlösser, *Fichtes Paradox. Über die These von der uneinholbaren Voraussetzung des Wissens in Fichtes später Wissenschaftslehre* (forthcoming).

33 See D. Henrich, *Konstellationen: Probleme und Debatten am Ursprung der idealistischen Philosophie (1789–1795)* (Stuttgart: Klett-Cotta, 1991), on the general intellectual situation of the philosophically active students at the Tübinger Stift. On Schelling in Tübingen see W. G. Jacobs, *Zwischen Revolution und Orthodoxie? Schelling und*

seine Freunde im Stift und an der Universität Tübingen (Stuttgart: Frommann-Holzboog, 1989).

34 On Schelling and ancient philosophy, see M. Franz, *Schellings Tübinger Platon-Studien* (Göttingen: Vandenhoeck & Ruprecht, 1996).

35 These early essays include the following titles which are listed here in their standard English translation: *On the Possibility of an Absolute Form of Philosophy* (1794), *Of the I as the Principle of Philosophy or on the Unconditional in Human Knowledge* (1795), *Philosophical Letters on Dogmatism and Criticism* (1795), *Essays in Explanation of the Idealism of the Doctrine of Science* (1796–7), *Ideas for a Philosophy of Nature* (1797), *Of the Worldsoul, a Hypothesis of Higher Physics* (1798), *First Plan of a System of the Philosophy of Nature* (1799).

36 As in the case of Fichte, it was Goethe who was instrumental in getting Schelling to Jena.

37 Concerning the development in relation to Fichte, see Lauth, *Transzendentale Entwicklungslinien*.

38 Hegel joined Schelling at the university of Jena in 1801. They collaborated quite closely over the next two years – Schelling thinking of himself as being the senior partner in that relationship. Together they edited a journal and were its sole contributors. In 1801 Hegel published an essay in which he sets out to explain the difference between Fichte's and Schelling's systems of philosophy. It is in this essay that he ascribes a position to Schelling which already contains essential elements of the philosophy of identity, although at that point Schelling had not yet presented this new conception in writing. This strange fact (together with some others) led people to suspect that Hegel might have been more than just Schelling's junior partner in Jena. Concerning this question of their mutual influence, see K. Düsing, *Schellings und Hegels erste absolute Metaphysik (1801–1802)* (Cologne: Dinter, 1988).

39 Two works in particular have to be mentioned: *Presentation of My System of Philosophy* (1801) and *System of the Whole of Philosophy and the Philosophy of Nature in Particular* (1804).

40 Letters no. 7 (6 January 1795) and no. 10 (25 February 1795), in G. W. F. Hegel, *Briefe von und an Hegel*, ed. J. Hoffmeister, 3rd edn. (Hamburg: Meiner, 1969).

41 The nature and the intensity of this influence is quite difficult to determine exactly in Fichte's case, partly because there is almost no time gap between the publication of Fichte's first *Science of Knowledge* and the first series of philosophical essays by Schelling, thus making a close knowledge rather unlikely, and partly because there are reasons to believe that at the beginning of his career as a philosopher Schelling was not very familiar with the specific features of Fichte's early position. See, for example, F. W. Schelling, *Briefe und Dokumente*, ed. H. Fuhrmans (Bonn: Bouvier, 1962), I, 60. Things are a little bit different with Jacobi. Although here too we do not know in detail how far Schelling was acquainted directly with Jacobi's texts, there is no doubt that he *was* familiar with his intellectual position. On the development of Schelling's philosophy, see R. Lauth, *Die Entstehung der Schellingschen Identitätsphilosophie in Auseinandersetzung mit Fichtes Wissenschaftslehre (1795–1801)* (Freiburg: Alber, 1975).

42 This is a sketchy presentation of Jacobi's strange but influential argument. An extended discussion of it and its background assumptions can be found in Horstmann, *Die Grenzen der Vernunft*, ch. 2.

43 For a discussion of Kant's theory of scientific explanation which deals with the question of validity see T. E. Wartenberg, "Order through Reason. Kant's Transcendental Justification of Science," *Kant-Studien*, 70 (1979), 409–24, and "Reason and the Practice of Science," in P. Guyer, ed., *The Cambridge Companion to Kant* (Cambridge: Cambridge University Press, 1992), 228–48.

44 This conception is outlined most clearly at the end of the essay *Of the I*. It is here, too, that Schelling emphasizes the importance of Kant's theory of the teleological judgment to his systematic ambitions. For more details see the very well informed discussion by B. Sandkaulen-Bock in *Ausgang vom Unbedingten. Über den Anfang in der Philosophie Schellings* (Göttingen: Vandenhoeck & Ruprecht, 1990).

45 Schelling, *Friedrich Wilhelm Joseph von Schellings sämmtliche Werke*, ed. K. F. A. Schelling (Stuttgart: Cotta, 1856ff.), I, 365. The numbers refer to volume and page of this edition. Translations are my own.

46 Schelling, *Werke*, I, 366.

47 Schelling, *Werke*, I, 366.

48 Schelling, *Werke*, I, 386.

49 Düsing, *Schellings und Hegels erste absolute Metaphysik*, gives a very good introductory account of the systematic details which led Schelling to his new approach.

50 This is shown very convincingly in a recent book by S. Peetz, *Die Freiheit im Wissen. Eine Untersuchung zu Schellings Konzept der Rationalität* (Frankfurt am Main: Klostermann, 1995). See too A. Bowie, in ch. 12 of this volume.

51 I am indebted to Ulrich Schlösser for discussions of the Fichte section of this chapter.

7

CHARLES LARMORE

Hölderlin and Novalis

I Introduction

In Jena in May 1795, Hölderlin and Novalis were introduced to one another in Fichte's presence by their mutual friend, Immanuel Niethammer. How unfortunate that we do not know the details of their conversation![1] For Hölderlin and Novalis were not simply on their way to becoming the two most important poets of Early Romanticism in Germany. They were already philosophers of great accomplishment. At this time, Hölderlin had developed a powerful critique of Fichte's philosophy, and in the following months Novalis would begin to do the same. Moreover, their thought moved in similar directions. Both charged Fichte with wrongly supposing that consciousness enjoys an immediate acquaintance with its own nature. Our subjectivity, they argued, has its basis in a dimension of "Being," which eludes not only introspection but philosophical analysis as well. By "Being" they understood different things. But they agreed in opposing one of the leading assumptions of Fichte's and later Hegel's idealism, namely, that reality is transparent to reason. For both of them, philosophy runs up against limits that poetry alone can point beyond.

Hölderlin's and Novalis's thought remains provocative today for several reasons. They grappled with the difficulties involved in conceiving the self's relation to itself as a form of knowledge. They showed how subjectivity could be denied the status of a self-evident first principle without being dismissed as an illusion, in contrast to recent theories of the "death of the subject." Most engagingly of all, they each worked out a conception of life that would reflect our nature as subjects who must live at a remove from the ground of our being. In fact, we can best understand the thought of Hölderlin and Novalis by focusing on these conceptions. First, however, we need to look at the two ethical ideals that set the terms of German discussion in the 1790s – Kant's ideal of freedom and Schiller's ideal of unity.

II Background: Kant and Schiller

Kant's ethics turns on a dualism between duty and inclination. Moral require-ments are binding upon us unconditionally, whatever the interests which nature and experience have given us. Because conscience apprises us of these categori-cal duties, we must be able to stand back from our "empirical character" and find in this very freedom sufficient reason to act in accord with duty. In fact freedom consists, positively speaking, in giving ourselves impartial rules defining the proper pursuit of our inclinations. The principles of duty are laws which, as rational beings, we impose upon ourselves. Morality is the basis of our sense of freedom.

For Kant, the desires which spring from nature and society can offer no moral guidance. On the contrary, they constitute a threat to our moral being. Leading us easily astray, they stand in need of regulation by morality. Kant went so far as to remark that inclinations are "always burdensome to a rational being, and though he cannot put them aside, they nevertheless elicit from him the wish to be free of them" (*KpV*, Ak 5:118). So extreme a statement could not be his last word, since in the absence of desire morality would have nothing left to govern. But it expresses in a pointed way Kant's opposition between duty and inclina-tion. Desires need to be ruled by moral principle; they can never themselves produce genuine moral commitment. Thus, Kant dismissed out of hand earlier attempts to found morality upon sympathy. A benevolent action arising out of fellow-feeling can have "no true moral value." Indeed, imagining a person without any feeling of sympathy for others, yet disposed to do what is right out of a sense of duty, Kant declared that he would display "beyond compare the highest form of character" (*G*, Ak 4:398).

At his most rigoristic, Kant held therefore not only that our sense of duty has a source independent of inclination, and not only that the inclination to act in accord with duty, having no moral value itself, adds none to the resulting act. He also maintained that the moral worth of an action is more evident, the greater the contrary inclinations the agent must overcome. For then the "sublimity" of morality's demands shows forth more clearly (*G*, Ak 4:425). It is against this view that Schiller protested in his essay of 1793, *Über Anmut und Würde*. "In Kant's moral philosophy," he wrote, "the idea of duty is presented with a harsh-ness that frightens away all grace and that could easily tempt a weak mind to seek moral perfection on the path of a dark and monkish asceticism" (*AW, SW* V, 465).

Schiller believed that Kant's rigorism was understandable, given the need to challenge the dominant view of the time that morality merely serves the agent's happiness. Our sense of duty, he agreed, cannot be based in feelings and desires. Right action springs from the freedom by which we give ourselves a rule of action founded in the impartiality of reason. Yet Schiller also argued that Kant was misled into denying inclinations any positive role in the moral life. Virtue does not pit duty against inclination; on the contrary, it involves taking pleasure in doing duty for duty's sake. A harmony between duty and inclination represents the higher moral ideal because it is what the person struggling with contrary desires would prefer to display. How sincere could such a person's allegiance to morality be, if instead he relished the opposition of desire?

Thus, an element of grace (*Anmut*), wrote Schiller, always inheres in the actions of the truly virtuous person. The tact or ease with which he does the right thing involves a congruence between inclination and duty. Virtuous action is an expression of freedom since it arises from a sense of duty, but it is also an expression of feeling to the extent that the agent cares about those whom he respects. Grace is never deliberate, for feelings do not lie under the control of the will: "one should never look as though he knew about his grace" (*AW, SW* V, 450). As a result, true virtue must be understood as a synthesis of freedom and feeling, reason and sensibility. It is moral beauty, the harmony displayed by the "beautiful soul" (*schöne Seele*). Kant had succumbed to the sort of mistake to which philosophers are chronically driven:

> The things which one must necessarily distinguish when philosophizing are not therefore in reality always separate . . . Human nature is in reality more of a connected whole than philosophers, who are good only at distinguishing, can make it out to be.
>
> (*AW, SW* V, 448, 467)

In place of Kant's dualisms, Schiller extolled the wholeness of the human person, in which reason no longer dominates sensibility, but joins with it.

Yet Schiller could not fully espouse this ideal. His notion of the beautiful soul was inherently unstable because of the Kantian elements it preserved. Kant himself tried to minimize their differences in replying to Schiller's critique (*R*; Ak. 6:23). Conceding that moral action need not be devoid of feeling, he insisted only that grace can play no role in determining the nature of duty, a principle, he observed, which Schiller endorsed. Was Kant's earlier praise of the triumph of duty over inclination as "the highest form of character" therefore just an exaggeration? In fact, his reply shows that rigorism represented the natural tendency of his thought. If duty is determined by reason alone, and reason is the expression of our freedom, how can the moral ideal involve anything more than what we can set out freely to achieve? How can it also include feelings harmonious with duty? Must we not strive as moral beings to live beyond feelings or at least (though this seems contradictory) to shape our feelings to accord with duty?

These conclusions can be avoided, I believe, if we do not suppose at the outset that reason in its moral employment is self-legislating, but regard it instead as responsive to a pre-existing order of reasons.[2] Then there will be no unbridge-able gulf between reason and sensibility. But Schiller was too much of a Kantian to contemplate surrendering the equation of morality with freedom. Thus, at one point in his discussion of grace, he took to calling moral beauty a "duty of appearances" (AW, SW V, 445–6), as though feeling too could be harnessed to the sphere of freedom. In the second part of his essay, devoted to dignity (Würde), he took a different, but equally symptomatic, path: instead of distorting the ideal of grace, he focused on a different ideal, more in keeping with his Kantian allegiances. Beauty of character is unattainable, he observed, because we are by nature divided beings, divided by our will. Even when our inclinations point in the direction of duty, it remains for us to decide whether to follow them or not. The will must be the ruler of our being.

Thus Schiller turned, like Kant before him, to describing the moral life in terms of the ideal of sublimity, in which the will shows itself superior to every given desire. Kant had defined the sublime as the experience of the disproportion between an idea of reason and something in the world we imagine in vain to embody it; as a result, he had seen a special kinship between the sublime and morality, in which reason must "exert its dominance over sensibility" (KU, Ak 5:269). Because Schiller agreed in viewing morality as an expression of our freedom, his thinking too moved inevitably toward this conception of human dignity. Not wishing to disown the ideal of moral beauty, he declared that human perfection entails the combination of grace and dignity (AW, SW V, 481).[3] But that seems an impossible undertaking. Schiller was caught between two contrary ideals.

The sublime expresses the transcendence of freedom, the ability to move beyond all that experience has made of us. Beauty, by contrast, is an ideal of unity, in which our noblest humanity feels at home in the world of experience. The sublime no less than the beautiful, freedom no less than unity, maintained their dual hold over the theoretical imagination of German philosophy in this period. The two aspirations pull in opposite directions, and yet Schiller was not the only one to seek some way of doing justice to them both. That was Hölderlin's ambition too.

III Hölderlin: being and subjectivity

In Hölderlin's preface to the fragment of *Hyperion* published in Schiller's review *Thalia* in 1794, the relation between unity and freedom appears as the theme of his novel. "Man," he wrote,

> would like to be *in* everything and *above* everything, and the motto in Loyola's epitaph:
>
> *non coerceri maximo, contineri tamen a minimo*

serves to designate the all-desiring, all-subjugating dangerous side of man as well as the highest and most beautiful condition he can achieve. (*SA* III, 163)[4]

It might seem that we must choose whether to feel at home in the world around us or to exercise the freedom of standing back and shaping our life ourselves. Yet this passage portrays our ultimate aspiration as wanting to be *both* in and above everything, combining the beautiful and the sublime. Like Schiller, Hölderlin believed that moral freedom, if pursued to the exclusion of a sense of unity with the world, leads to fanaticism. His way of marrying these two ideals was more successful, however, largely because he devised a dynamic conception of the human condition in which they figure as distinct moments.

For Hölderlin, reflection forms the essential obstacle to integrating unity and freedom, for it entails a division between the I and its object, even when the object happens to be itself. Yet he also believed that reflection depends on the presupposition of an underlying unity. The *Thalia* fragment begins by stating that human life unfolds as a movement from a condition of utter simplicity, where our needs coincide with our powers in virtue of our natural endowment alone, toward a condition of complete development, where we achieve a unity with the world through needs and powers we elaborate ourselves. This movement Hölderlin termed man's "eccentric path" (*exzentrische Bahn*). As reflective beings, we move irretrievably beyond an unthinking unity with the world, which continues nonetheless to be the center of our existence. It shapes the sort of relation to the world that, at our best, we go on to pursue, when we aim to be not just above the world, but at one with it as well.

Hölderlin began to work out his conception philosophically shortly after graduating from the Tübinger Stift (where he had been a fellow-student with Hegel and Schelling). Having found a position as preceptor in the vicinity of Jena, he was able to attend Fichte's lectures at the university in 1794–5. Jena was then at the forefront of German philosophy, and not just because of Fichte's presence. His predecessor in the chair of philosophy, Karl Leonhard Reinhold, had introduced the program for post-Kantian philosophy that Fichte was continuing. Moreover, some members of Reinhold's audience had already discovered important reasons to reject this program. Thus, when Fichte arrived in Jena in the spring of 1794, his thinking seemed to many there somewhat *passé*. Laying out this context will be helpful in understanding the most significant philosophical piece Hölderlin wrote, published only in 1961 and usually called *Judgment and Being* (*Urteil und Sein*).[5]

Reinhold had argued that Kant's philosophy could overcome the many difficulties stemming from its dualism of reason and sensibility, if it were recast as a system based upon a single ultimate principle, from which its various theses could be justified and given their proper meaning. The central idea of "representation" (*Vorstellung*) seemed ideal for this purpose, and Reinhold had formulated his fundamental principle thus: "In consciousness a representation is distinguished from what is represented and from what does the representing and is set in relation to them both."[6] Yet skepticism soon arose among Reinhold's auditors (among them Niethammer) about whether any principle could do what Reinhold wanted, namely, justify as well as explain our knowledge of the world as a whole. Influenced by Jacobi's view that reason can only justify one thing relative to another, they argued that no first principle can serve as a foundation (*Grundsatz*) for knowledge. Any principle substantial enough to explain the cardinal features of the mind's relation to the world cannot be self-evident; its justification along with an understanding of its terms can come about only piecemeal and provisionally, as we see how well it organizes the other things we believe to be true. Far from being able to form a finished system, philosophy is therefore fated to be an unending enterprise. The mind's fundamental relation to the world becomes clearer only bit by bit, as inquiry progresses. As editor of the *Philosophisches Journal*, Niethammer made this "anti-foundationalist" critique available to others outside the Reinhold circle.[7]

Fichte pursued a different line of criticism. Persuaded of the need to build upon a supreme principle, he believed that Reinhold had misidentified its nature. Not representation but subjectivity should be the key notion. After all, representation in Reinhold's principle is defined in terms of two activities (distinguishing and relating) whose source can only be the subject itself. Thus, Fichte embarked in his *Science of Knowledge* (*Wissenschaftslehre*) upon a systematic philosophy of the absolute ego, according to which all knowledge is grounded upon the I and its relation to itself. To the Reinhold circle attending his lectures in 1794, however, Fichte's new approach appeared only to perpetuate a mistake they had overcome. When Hölderlin arrived in Jena, he became acquainted with their objections, particularly through Niethammer, an earlier graduate of the Tübinger Stift, a remote relative of his, and the man he called a year later his "philosophical mentor."[8] Niethammer's influence is visible in *Urteil und Sein*, though filtered through a more radical critique of philosophy which was Hölderlin's own.

This text, composed in April 1795, was written on both sides of a detached flyleaf, the one side devoted to judgment, the other to being. Hölderlin's main thesis is that, contrary to Fichte, subjectivity cannot function as the first principle of philosophy, for it cannot be understood in its own terms. The I is essentially an I capable of judging and hence always defined in relation to an object of judgment distinct from it. All judgment (*Urteil*), he remarks in a bit of false etymology, turns on a primordial division (*Ur-Teilung*) between subject and object. This fact alone would show that the I cannot serve as a foundation of knowledge in the way that the absolute ego, supposedly definable in advance of any cognitive relation to the world, was meant to do.[9]

But the argument of *Urteil und Sein* goes further. The distinction between subject and object inherent in all judgment entails that self-consciousness, though involving the idea that subject and object are the same, cannot be explained by appeal to the nature of the I alone. We cannot understand a mental state as our own without judging it to be ours, but in doing so we must distinguish ourselves as the object of judgment from ourselves as judging. "How can I say 'I,'" Hölderlin asked, "without being conscious of myself? But how is self-consciousness possible? Because I oppose myself to myself, separate myself from myself, and yet despite this separation and in being opposed to myself know myself to be the same." Self-consciousness certainly assumes that we are one and the same as that of which we are conscious. But, Hölderlin pointed out, this sense of oneness cannot be explicated in terms of the I alone, since self-consciousness, to the extent that it is an act of the I, entails an inescapable distinction between subject and object.

Some have objected that this argument misses the originality of Fichte's philosophy.[10] Fichte had insisted, against the tradition from Descartes to Kant and Reinhold, that self-awareness is not identical to self-reflection; to make any judgment about our mental state, we must already have an immediate, non-reflective acquaintance with ourselves.[11] Did not Hölderlin overlook this innovation, in supposing that the I, and so the I's relation to itself, must be understood in terms of judgment? Not at all. On the contrary, this objection misses the crux of Hölderlin's argument. He agreed, as shown by the passage just quoted, that I have a way of recognizing myself as myself despite the self-division created by making myself the object of my judgment. His point was that this self-recognition cannot be explained in terms of the nature of the I alone. To be an I consists in being able to say "I," yet in saying "I" I am reflecting, taking up the position of a knowing subject and so contrasting myself with some object.

To grasp subject and object as one in self-consciousness, Hölderlin argued, we must draw upon a sense of their unity antecedent to the standpoint of the judging I. Moreover, this unity or "absolute Being" must underlie the distinction between subject and object inherent in every sort of cognitive attitude – not only in self-consciousness, but also in our relation as knowers to the world. For any sense we have of being one with ourselves, arising as it does from some basis other than the I itself, must by the same token embody a sense of being one with everything else. Subjectivity arises as a disruption of this unity and remains at bottom incomprehensible without it.

How, according to Hölderlin, is Being itself to be understood? Formally, it can be assumed to unite subject and object to such an extent that "no division can be made [between them] without violating the essence of that which is supposedly being separated." This criterion suffices to demarcate Being from the lesser sort of unity (Hölderlin called it *Identität*) that the I by itself can guarantee in self-consciousness, since it is the essence of the knowing subject to be distinct from its object, even in self-consciousness, where "the I is possible only through such a separation of the I from the I." But we learn little thereby about the inner constitution of Being or about the process by which the subject emerges from it. Precisely the unknowability of Being, however, is what Hölderlin wanted to establish. Being cannot be an object of knowledge, since it would then have to be distinct from the knowing subject, instead of embracing subject and object in a prior unity. Being can only be a presupposition that we adopt to make sense of the possibility of reflection. In Hölderlin's eyes, it functions as a ground, not as a principle.[12] We cannot begin with an understanding of Being and deduce the characteristic features of our relation to the world. Such was Hölderlin's version of the critique of philosophizing from first principles that the Reinhold circle had directed against Fichte. He also had his own way of endorsing Niethammer's conception of philosophy as an unending enterprise. It will become visible as we look further at Hölderlin's complex theory of the self and the ideal of life he drew from it.

IV Hölderlin: unity and freedom

For Hölderlin, self-awareness involves two distinct components. On the one hand, I stand back from myself since, as subject, I must distinguish myself from the object of my attention. On the other, I understand myself as being one and the same with my object. These two dimensions give rise, in fact, to the two principal, though opposing, ideals of human life described in the *Thalia* fragment. The subject's distinguishing itself from all that is its object provides the basis of freedom, the ideal of being "above" everything. The subject's sense of being one and the same with itself harbors the intimation of an even greater unity, giving rise to the ideal of being "in" everything. One of Hölderlin's most innovative ideas was that the self, far from ideally enjoying an identity with itself, is essentially pulled in contrary directions. As the *Thalia* fragment shows, he was in possession of this insight before coming to Jena. Working through Fichte's philosophy allowed him to give a deeper philosophical articulation to his belief in life's essential "dissonances."

The very structure of our conscious life, therefore, gives rise to our "eccentric path," in which our assertion of freedom disrupts a prior unity with the world, while remaining rooted in it. To the extent that we heed both dimensions of our nature, we will seek a relation to the world that places a recognition of our freedom within the framework of a more encompassing unity. Yet because Being can never be an object of knowledge in its own right, but can only be elicited as the presupposition behind our capacity for knowledge, we can never perfectly achieve this goal. Or at least we can never do so in the terms which philosophy allows. "The unity of subject and object," Hölderlin wrote several months after *Judgment and Being*, "is possible by means of theory only through infinite approximation (*eine unendliche Annäherung*)."[13]

Hölderlin's points of agreement with Niethammer form part, of course, of an analysis of self-consciousness and a speculative understanding of Being entirely his own. His philosophical thinking went far beyond the more down-to-earth views of the man he considered his mentor. In originality and power, it also outstripped anything his Tübingen classmates, Schelling and Hegel, were able to muster at the time[14] and called into question assumptions that Hegel at least would never consider abandoning. Hölderlin saw in the limits of philosophy reason to believe that poetry fares better in expressing the full reality of the human condition. The superiority of poetry was one of his deepest convictions, growing out of his philosophical reflection and inspiring his work as a poet. Its rationale will become clear as we pursue further his account of the self's inner division and of the possibility of reconciling the ideals of unity and freedom.

Here our guide must be Hölderlin's novel *Hyperion*, a half-poetic, half-philosophical exploration of these themes. Begun in 1792 in Tübingen, *Hyperion* went through a number of versions, until it was published in two volumes in 1797/9. In the Preface to the penultimate version (December 1795), Hölderlin observed that:

> We all travel an eccentric path . . . We have been dislocated from nature, and what appears to have once been *one* is now at odds with itself . . . Often it is as though the world were *everything* and we *nothing*, but often too it is as though we were *everything* and the world *nothing*. Hyperion too was divided between these two extremes. (*SA* III, 236)

Hyperion feels the contrary tendencies of the self so intensely that they take an all-or-nothing form. His story consists in learning to integrate them into a coherent life.

The published version of *Hyperion* is a novel in letter form, but it departs significantly from its eighteenth-century models. All of the events Hyperion, a modern Greek, recounts in these letters to Bellarmin – the instruction he receives from Adamas about the glories of ancient Greece, his love for Diotima, his insurrectional campaign with Alabanda against Turkish rule, the death of Diotima – have taken place before he writes his first letter. Far from expressing his momentary moods in an unfolding drama, Hyperion's letters reflect upon a set of experiences already behind him. They show him working through his past, learning to make sense of the setbacks he encountered, so that his development takes place, not just in the course of his experience, but also through reflection: the Hyperion who writes the last letter is no longer the same as the one who wrote the first. Reflection grows inescapably out of our more immediate experience as the need to put it into intelligible form. By thus building the idea of man's "eccentric path" into the very structure of the novel, Hölderlin achieved a rare synthesis of form and content, since it is with that idea that Hyperion must come to terms.

In his first letters, Hyperion could not be farther from this goal. He regards reflection as a curse, cutting him off from the unthinking oneness with the world which he believes he once enjoyed, particularly in Diotima's company, and which he longs to regain. "Blessed self-oblivion" amidst the beauty of nature is his highest joy. But "a moment of reflection" hurls him down. His existence fractured into opposing extremes, Hyperion exclaims, "Man is a god when he dreams, a beggar when he reflects!" (*SA* III, 9). Reflection destroys all unity with the world because it seems itself to involve a "tremendous striving to be the whole." Yet for all the feeling of homelessness it produces, Hyperion cannot wish it away, for reflection is the sign of his freedom; it shows that he "was not born for the whip and the yoke" (*SA* III, 18). Thus he bounces back and forth between the desire to be "in" and the desire to be "above" everything.

Hyperion moves beyond this divided outlook through recounting his past to Bellarmin. As he comes to take stock of his past experience, his very conception of what it is to reflect changes as well. Adamas's nostalgia for the past, he realizes, could never be his. Instead of following his teacher into the Asian hinterland in search of a people still having the ancient virtues, he has to deal with the world of the present. Alabanda represented one possibility, the struggle for social justice. But he was a moral fanatic, sacrificing every human sentiment to the demands of principle. Early on, Hyperion saw the flaw in a man whose revolt against Turkish rule would later end in a bloodbath. "It has always made the state a hell," he remarked, "that man has wanted to make it his heaven" (*SA* III, 31). The portrait of Alabanda owes a lot to Schiller's critique of Kantian rigorism, and it may have been modelled on Fichte himself, since Alabanda appears only in the versions of the novel written after Hölderlin came to Jena.

In Diotima Hyperion discovered the other extreme, an unreflective being at home in the world instead of the world-alienation he found in Alabanda. Hers was the beauty of nature rather than of art, for at first she is depicted as naïvely lacking any awareness of the beauty Hyperion worshipped in her. And when she later belied this stereotype of the unreflective woman, it was to tell him that he was born for higher things than her, namely, for poetry (*SA* III, 87, 149). Only afterwards, however, does Hyperion grasp the significance of her statement, when he has begun to reflect more deeply upon his past.

Adamas, Alabanda, and Diotima represent, in effect, three different ways of giving life unity – through nostalgia, moral sublimity, and natural beauty. Though identifying with each of these ideals in turn, Hyperion soon discovered something wanting; none of them could stand up to reflection. Whence his initial feeling that oneness and reflection must always be opposed. But in the course of his letters to Bellarmin, Hyperion begins to discern a different meaning in his past. Rather than forming a string of defeats, these experiences of unity disrupted by reflection illustrate the very rhythm of human existence. "If the life of the world consists in the alternation between opening and closing, in going forth and in returning, why is it not even so with the heart of man?" (*SA* III, 38; also 47). The "hidden order" that Hyperion now sees in his life exemplifies the relation between Being and reflection laid out in *Judgment and Being*. Though neither nostalgia for an idealized past, nor devotion to duty, nor natural beauty give perfect expression to Being, they all involve the desire to recapture some kind of unity in life. Nor could Hyperion discover the inadequacy of their claims to completeness, did he not draw upon the inkling of a more encompassing unity. Reflection and unity do not therefore simply stand at odds, as he first believed. Their tension forms a pattern. Our lives move continually back and forth between the effort to achieve some order in our experience and the realization that the order achieved is imperfect, and both these forms of reflective activity draw on the sense of a pre-reflective unity of mind and world which reflection can only approximate. There will never be a moment of completion, only an unending quest fueled by intimations. Hyperion's very name, meaning the one who "goes beyond," symbolizes this insight. And so the last words in the novel are his promise, "More soon" (*Nächstens mehr*).

By virtue of grasping the true character of life's "eccentric path," Hyperion can now take to heart the intellectual understanding of art that he formulated even before writing to Bellarmin. Once, in conversation with Diotima, he had announced that the essence of beauty in art is "the One differentiated in itself" (*das Eine in sich selber unterschiedne*). This definition is very different from the notion of beauty as a selfless unity with nature that figures (later) in his first letters to his friend. But only now can he appreciate its import. At their best, works of art impress upon us through their own example the way all thought draws upon the oneness of Being while also distinguishing itself from its object. Philosophy can approach this fundamental unity only from the outside, by arguing that it is a presupposition we must make to give an adequate account of our experience, for Being is unknowable. Left to itself, philosophy can at best be, as Hyperion says, "the blind demand for an unending progress in the unification and differentiation of some subject matter." Only poetry, "the beginning and the end" of philosophy (*SA* III, 83, 81), can give us a sense of the connection between Being and thought from within. Later Hegel declared that art is "a thing of the past," everything important in the human condition now being expressible in conceptual form. Hölderlin would have disagreed, and not out of mere nostalgia (as Hegel liked to say in dismissing his romantic contemporaries), but as a result of philosophical argument.

After his year in Jena, Hölderlin increasingly turned his energies from philosophy to poetry. He gave up earlier plans of pursuing a teaching position in philosophy; he never completed the essays promised to Niethammer for the *Philosophisches Journal*. Like Hyperion, he recognized that his true calling lay in poetry. The great visionary poems he went on to write build on the scheme already presented in *Judgment and Being* and *Hyperion*. They evoke with religious awe the ultimate, "holy" ground in which mind and world are at one, yet they do so at a remove, by intimation rather than by direct description. Strain as it may against the division between subject and object, poetry remains an act of reflection. The poet must step back from whatever inkling he has of the unity of Being, in order to put it into words. For Hölderlin, the moments of vision are therefore never in the present. They are always past or future, remembered or anticipated, as in the elegy "Bread and Wine" (1800–1). Poetry must guard against the twin follies of trying to take the Holy by storm, as though to describe its innermost nature, and of being instead so fascinated by its opacity as to remain dumbstruck. The proper attitude, for the poet as for all humanity, is gratitude, the celebration of our dependence on a ground that thought can never make transparent to itself.[15]

It would be misleading to describe "the One differentiated in itself" as an ideal of wholeness. Certainly Schiller's notion of grace could be characterized thus, for it refers to the congruence of reason and sensibility, duty and feeling. But Hölderlin's ideal has a more complex structure. Rather than glorifying wholeness, it embraces the inescapable tension between unity and reflection as the expression of thought's rootedness in the opacity of Being. To be sure, Hölderlin sought the resolution of life's dissonances. Yet for him the contrary tendencies of the self are not reconciled by our coming to be at one with ourselves, but by understanding how they work together to form our nature, which is never to coincide with the ground of our being. The end of *Hyperion* compares this reconciliation to love because lovers, however closely conjoined, never lose their separateness (*SA* III, 160).

German romantic thought is often said to be a longing for wholeness and organic unity, a nostalgic flight from modern man's alienation from the world.[16] Yet Hölderlin offers a notable exception to this *idée reçue*. His notion of absolute Being certainly qualifies as an organic whole, but the theme of all his thought is that our aim cannot be to merge with Being. I turn now to the other great philosopher-poet of German romanticism, Novalis (born Friedrich von Hardenberg), whose path crossed Hölderlin's in Jena in 1795. He too challenged the goals of rational transparency and wholeness.

V Novalis: reflection and poetic suggestion

Novalis studied philosophy in Jena with Reinhold in 1790–2, and was well acquainted with various members of his circle, particularly Niethammer. From late 1795 to the fall of 1796, he composed the critical notes on Fichte's philosophy, never published in his lifetime, which have come to be known as his *Fichte Studies*. They show Novalis arguing, for reasons similar to Hölderlin's, that the I cannot provide the basis for the first principle of philosophy as Fichte had imagined. There is no evidence, beyond the report of their meeting, to indicate any mutual influence. But their common debt to Niethammer helps to explain the similarities in their thought.

Novalis believed that on one important point Fichte was right. To him, as to many of his contemporaries, it seemed a genuine insight to claim that the I must have a more immediate form of acquaintance with itself than reflection, with its inevitable distinction between subject and object. But Fichte erred, he objected, in supposing that the I's immediate relation to itself can be explained in terms of the nature of the I itself as a conscious subject. Fichte had invoked the idea of "intellectual intuition" to designate the I's immediate self-awareness. But for Novalis this notion was a composite, a "unifying third," combining the two distinct elements of reflection and feeling.[17] To the extent that intellectual intuition means an act of knowledge, the I's relation to itself is still understood in terms of self-reflection, for there is no knowledge apart from reflection. If instead it is meant to be an acquaintance that the I has with itself prior to all reflection, then it can be only a feeling, passively registering an I whose being is simply given. The fundamental nature of this I, as well as the means by which it can come to reflect upon itself, cannot be explained. Therefore, Novalis concluded, the I cannot serve as the first principle of philosophy.

"Philosophy always has need of *something given* . . . The limits of feeling are the limits of philosophy."[18] This statement shows the influence of Jacobi's general anti-foundationalist argument, which Novalis probably learned to appreciate through his friend Niethammer. All justification being of one proposition relative to another, Jacobi held that philosophy must take its bearings from the mere feeling or unreasoned belief that certain things exist. Novalis had this lesson in mind when working out his critique of Fichte. He also observed that his own argument cannot but proceed from the standpoint of reflection. The concept of "feeling" is deployed in the attempt to reflect upon the limitations of reflection (to reverse, as he liked to say, the "*ordo inversus*" by which our self-awareness seems so immediate as to suggest that it exhausts the I's very existence). Fichte inaugurated the critique of reflection, but his reliance upon the hybrid notion of intellectual intuition shows that he did not go far enough. Novalis sought to do better, but he acknowledged that philosophy can peer beyond the limits of reflection solely in terms available to reflection itself. Thus, to say that the I's pre-reflective acquaintance with itself can only be by way of feeling indicates that the I's existence must count as *given* to the conscious I, instead of consisting in the I's self-awareness (as Fichte believed). And the I's givenness to reflection allows us to conclude that its nature must be a kind of "primordial activity" (*Urhandlung*), since we can infer that feeling, as something passive, must be the effect of something active.[19] But beyond this, he insisted, nothing more can be established.

Novalis's methodological scruples had important consequences. Like Hölderlin, he too talked of reflection being rooted in Being (*das Sein*),[20] and regarded the nature of Being as opaque to philosophical clarification. This was their common ground. Yet Novalis did not mean by such statements what Hölderlin meant in *Judgment and Being*. Being for Hölderlin is the inner unity of mind and world. For Novalis it is always the Being of the I, which he understood as antecedent to the I's self-awareness, but not as underlying all distinction between the I and the world. Philosophizing from the standpoint of reflection, he saw no reason to generalize the pre-reflective Being of the I beyond the I itself. This philosophical divergence entailed differences in their conception of art, as we see if we look at Novalis's collection of aphorisms (*Vermischte Bemerkungen*) which Friedrich Schlegel edited and published in 1798 as *Pollen (Blüthenstaub)*.[21]

The first aphorism, building upon his studies of Fichte, provides the key to understanding the rest: "We seek everywhere the Unconditioned (*das Unbedingte*) and always find only things." The proposition turns on a pun, "*das Unbedingte*" meaning "the unconditioned," but suggesting the idea of what is not a thing (*Ding*). The things of experience are always conditioned: their qualities, behavior, and very existence, depend on their relations to other similarly finite things. By the Unconditioned (or the Absolute) Novalis meant the ultimate reality on which depend the various things we distinguish in experience. In the mid-1790s there were two main candidates for the role of the Absolute: the pantheistic God of Spinoza's *Ethics* and the I of the *Science of Knowledge*. Fichte believed that the I must be the Absolute, since it alone can be the object of a philosophical first principle, serving to justify our knowledge of the world. As we have seen, Novalis followed Niethammer in holding that no first principle is possible in philosophy and argued in particular that the I cannot fill this role, since it lacks the self-transparency which Fichte supposed it possessed.

Yet Novalis never concluded that the very idea of the Absolute is incoherent. On the contrary, the first aphorism in *Pollen* implies that though knowledge of the Absolute lies forever beyond our grasp, we are impelled to seek it all the same. Reason naturally tries to trace things back to their ultimate source in the Unconditioned. The rub is that all we ever come thereby to understand are conditioned things. Nor, as the *Fichte Studies* make clear, did he reject Fichte's view that the Absolute is the I. We can surmise, he believed, that underlying the stand-point of reflection and the knowledge of conditioned things it affords must be the primordial, pre-reflective activity of the I. It is the inner nature of the absolute ego that remains unknowable.

However, we can approach it indirectly. In the *Fichte Studies*, Novalis had written, echoing Niethammer:

> What do I do when I philosophize? I reflect upon some ground . . . All philosophy must therefore end with an absolute ground. But if this is not given to us . . . phi-losophy must be an unending activity.[22]

This idea of "approximation" reappeared in *Pollen*, as in the remark that thought directed toward the Unconditioned is "never nearer than when it seems farthest away" (*VB* 98; *B* 99). The moment of felt distance carries a recognition of the very essence of our goal, which is to always elude us. This unknowability of the Unconditioned is something that philosophy can only *state* as a fact. Yet poetry (*Dichtung*), by which Novalis meant imaginative art in general, can do more.[23] Instead of commenting upon this fact from the outside, poetry is able to *show* the elusiveness of the Absolute. Like Hölderlin, Novalis found in poetry a deeper expressive capacity than philosophy can muster. But again, for him the Absolute that poetry can evoke is not Being as such. It is the Being of the I, its primordial activity from which reflection and knowledge derive. Poetry's aim and method are correspondingly different. "The path of mystery leads inward," he announced (*VB* 17; *B* 16) (*Nach Innen geht der geheimnisvolle Weg*).

The poet's task must be to bring his own thinking into proximity with its ulti-mate ground, to "take hold of his transcendental self, to be at the same time the I of his I" (*VB* 28; *B* 28). Of course, the poet too can only approach this goal, but he does so, not by straining to describe that ground, but by deploying the special resource of poetic speech, which is to suggest more than it explicitly says. In Novalis's view, the ability to use language so as to intimate more than can be ren-dered by paraphrase, to express more than can be made precise, displays the I's primordial activity in its difference from the determinate mode of thinking it takes on in reflection. Poetry is obviously not the I's *Urhandlung* in the pure state, for then it would be unintelligible. Nothing can be suggested except on the basis of something definitely asserted, something "conditioned." But poetry uses the things of our world, even the most common, to evoke a sense of the Absolute. This was for Novalis the essence of romanticism: "To the extent that I give to the lowly a high meaning, to the ordinary a mysterious air, and to the well-known the dignity of the unknown, I am romanticizing it."[24]

The poet thus focuses on some determinate idea at the same time as he moves beyond it, and though the direction of his movement is indicated by his point of departure, there is no way to nail down precisely the point toward which he is heading.[25] Novalis used his account of poetic activity to develop a theory of interpretation. "Only then do I show that I have understood a writer," he remarked, "when I can act in his spirit, when I can, without diminishing his individuality, translate him and alter him in manifold ways" (*VB* 29). To interpret a work of art faithfully is not to determine what it really means. It is to run through some of the things it can be said to mean, since its very intention is to outstrip any particular content it might be assigned. Novalis was one of the first to declare that interpretation is inherently unending, never definitive. "A poem must be quite *inexhaustible*, like a human being."[26] His point was not that what precisely the poem says always eludes us. It was that what it says is such as to exclude the possibility of any adequate interpretation. Because the poem asserts something specific only to transcend its assertion in the direction of an "elsewhere" that is nowhere in particular, its hallmark is "irony" (*VB* 36; *B* 29). Here he referred to Friedrich Schlegel by name, and Schlegel indeed worked out in detail Novalis's aesthetics of irony and infinite interpretation.

VI Schlegel and irony

Novalis entitled the short, numbered texts he intended for publication "remarks" or "aphorisms." Schlegel called his own three collections "fragments," and the title was significant. To the extent that art becomes aware of its nature as art, as he believed it had increasingly done since the Middle Ages, it must recognize that it is necessarily a fragment. Everything it appears to mean can be but part of the indefinitely more that it suggests. "Many works of the ancients have become fragments," he wrote in the *Athenaeum Fragments* (1798), "many works of the moderns are fragments from inception" (§15). His own *Fragments* were meant to illustrate this truth, no less by the abruptness of their form than by their content. As a literary genre, the "fragment" differs importantly from the classical maxim or epigram. They aimed to be complete in themselves, to give full if concise expression to some idea. The fragment, by contrast, is meant to be incomplete, to express the essentially incompletable.

Just as his "fragments" differ from classical maxims, so irony for Schlegel departs from its classical models. Socratic irony consisted in feigning ignorance while possessing knowledge. Quintilian defined irony as the trope in which a speaker substitutes for the proper expression of his thought an expression whose literal meaning is the opposite.[27] In both cases, irony is assumed to involve having some fully determinate thought that one chooses not to express directly. Schlegel's irony is of a very different sort. It involves using some particular set of words to suggest the Absolute; what is not directly, but only indirectly communicated is therefore not some fully determinate thought, but rather something essentially indeterminate. Later, Hegel dismissed Schlegelian irony as mere frivolity, the act of a mind that never means what it seems to mean. But this charge turns on a misconception. Irony, Schegel remarked, is in "the most holy earnest."[28] It does not signal a lack of commitment, for one cannot suggest the infinite except from some particular point of view, employing some determinate form of speech. Thus he observed:

> There are men whose whole activity consists in always saying No. It would be no little thing always to be able to say No correctly, but whoever can do nothing else can certainly not do it correctly.[29]

The ironical mind is not uncommitted, but rather divided, and divided, not between one opinion and its contrary, but between the view it affirms and the realization that no position it adopts can express fully its nature as the activity that gives rise to thought and commitment. Clearly, wholeness was no more Novalis's or Schlegel's ideal than Hölderlin's. Or at least it did not begin to exert a hold over Novalis's thought until later when, as in his essay *Christianity or Europe* (1799), he sang the praise of homogeneous societies. It is essential, however, to notice the important difference in the ways Hölderlin and Novalis refused to make oneness their highest value. For all his insistence on our need to stand at a distance from the unity of Being, Hölderlin incorporated into his ideal a retrospective element – namely, gratitude for the pre-reflective unity of mind and world which makes thought possible. By contrast, Novalis's ideal (and Schlegel's) is resolutely forward-looking. Romantic poetry, Schlegel wrote, is "a *progressive* universal poetry." (*Athenaeum Fragments* §97). The way we are to regard ourselves as never at one with the ground of our being is by gesturing beyond wherever we happen to be. Thankfulness has no part to play.

This difference turns on how they understood the Absolute with which poetry, more than philosophy, puts us in touch. Novalis and Schlegel conceived it in terms of subjectivity. Novalis rejected, of course, the self-transparency of the I that lay at the basis of Fichte's philosophy. But the sort of Being which he and Schlegel after him postulated as the pre-reflective ground of thought is the fundamental activity (the *Urhandlung*) of the I. Hölderlin, however, appealed to an Absolute that precedes any sense of subjectivity. His critique of Fichte cut deeper than theirs: not only is self-consciousness inexplicable in terms of the I's nature itself, but the ground of Being on which it rests cannot be subjective in character, since the very notion of a subject implies a contrast with some object of thought. Being involves a unity of mind and world on which subjectivity depends, and to which it remains indebted.

Novalis and Schlegel embraced a form of the Kantian sublime. They glorified the freedom of the I and its ability to transcend every "finite determination," every particular point of view, on which it may fix. Hölderlin, by contrast, subordinated the sublime to a conception of beauty. He believed that we must acknowledge our debt to a fundamental affinity of mind and world, even if we can glimpse their unity only from the decentered perspective of memory or anticipation, which is the mark of our freedom.

In their different ways, Hölderlin and Novalis both called into question some of the deepest assumptions about reflection and subjectivity shaping not just Fichte's and later Hegel's idealism, but much of the philosophical tradition. Great poets that they were, they were also philosophers of considerable talent, who speak to contemporary concerns. I want to point out in conclusion, however, one central assumption they did not challenge. No more than Fichte did they doubt that the I is at bottom a knowing or judging subject, for they all three (despite the potential in Fichte's own description of the I as an activity of self-positing) understood its relation to itself as primarily one of self-acquaintance. Thus, in arguing against Fichte that self-acquaintance cannot be explained in terms of the conscious subject, which must always be distinct from its object, Hölderlin and Novalis sought its basis elsewhere than in any relation the subject bears to itself, namely, in "Being." But suppose that in the first instance we are not so much knowers as beings committed to rules of thought and action and only thereby capable of knowledge, even of ourselves. Suppose therefore that our fundamental relation to ourselves consists in holding ourselves responsible to reasons. Then we can regard the immediate acquaintance we have with ourselves as rooted, not in "Being," but in our nature as normative beings. It would be worth exploring how much of Hölderlin's and Novalis's speculations about Being could survive this shift in perspective.

NOTES

1 See Manfred Frank, *"Unendliche Annäherung"*. *Die Anfänge der philosophischen Frühromantik* (Frankfurt: Suhrkamp, 1997), 571.

2 See Charles Larmore, "L'autonomie de la morale," *Philosophiques*, 24 (1997), 313–28.

3 So, too, in his essay *Über das Erhabene*, Schiller wrote that beauty and sublimity need to come together so that man will form a "complete whole" (*SW* V, 807).

4 Loyola's motto is "Not to be confined by the largest, but to be contained in the smallest, is divinity." References to 'SA' are to Hölderlin, *Sämtliche Werke, Grosser Stuttgarter Ausgabe*, 15 vols., ed. Friedrich Beissner (Stuttgart: Cotta, 1943–85).

5 Hölderlin, *SA* IV, 216–17. Dieter Henrich's magisterial study of this text, *Der Grund im Bewußtsein. Untersuchungen zu Hölderlins Denken (1794–1795)* (Stuttgart: Klett-Cotta, 1992) is indispensable.

6 See George di Giovanni, "From Jacobi's *Philosophical Novel* to Fichte's Idealism: Some Comments on the 1798–99 'Atheism Dispute,'" *Journal of the History of Philosophy*, 26 (1989), 75–100. See too the discussion of Reinhold in Franks, ch. 5 in this volume.

7 For an analysis of the views of this Reinhold circle, see Henrich, *Der Grund im Bewußtsein*, 113–26, and Manfred Frank's pathbreaking book, *"Unendliche Annäherung,"* part II.

8 See Hölderlin's letter to Niethammer of 24 February 1796.

9 Earlier in the year, Hölderlin had already made this anti-Fichte point in a letter to Hegel (still in Tübingen) of 26 January 1795.

10 See, for example, Jürgen Stolzenberg, "Selbstbewußtsein. Ein Problem der Philosophie nach Kant. Reinhold-Hölderlin-Fichte," *Le premier romantisme allemand*, *Revue internationale de Philosophie*, 3 (1996), 461–82.

11 The point is made *en passant* in Fichte's *Grundlage der gesamten Wissenschaftslehre* (1794) (Fichte, *Werke*, ed. I. H. Fichte [Berlin: de Gruyter, 1991], p. 97), and then at length in his *Versuch einer neuen Darstellung der Wissenschaftslehre* (1797) (*Werke I*, 521–34).

12 See the discussion in Henrich, *Der Grund im Bewußtsein*, ch. VIII (92–113). In the Preface to the penultimate version of *Hyperion*, Hölderlin writes of our having an "inkling" (*Ahnung*) of Being (*SA* III, 236). The similarities between this philosophy of Being and Heidegger's are striking, particularly in light of Heidegger's neglect of Hölderlin's philosophical work in favor of the poetry to which he attached such exceptional importance (*Erläuterungen zu Hölderlins Dichtung*, Frankfurt: Klostermann, 1951).

13 Hölderlin to Schiller, 4 September 1795.

14 He paid Schelling's precocious work, *Vom Ich als Prinzip der Philosophie* (1795), the mixed compliment of telling him, "You have gotten just as far as Fichte."

15 See the poem *Dichterberuf* (1801), lines 55–8: "Doch es zwinget/Nimmer die weite Gewalt den Himmel./Noch ist's auch gut zu weise zu sein. Ihn kennt/Der Dank." For more on vision and gratitude in Hölderlin, see my book *The Romantic Legacy* (New York: Columbia University Press, 1996), 25–8, as well as Henrich, *Der Grund im Bewußtsein*, 614–22.

16 A recent and sophisticated defense of this view is Jean-Marie Schaeffer, *L'art de l'âge moderne* (Paris: Gallimard, 1992), especially 19, 88–9.

17 Novalis, "Fichte-Studien" I.16 in *Schriften*, 5 vols., ed. R. Samuel, H. J. Mähl, and G. Schulz (Stuttgart: Kohlhammer, 1960ff.), II, 114. For his analysis of the I in terms of feeling, see "Fichte-Studien" I.15–22, 32–43 (*Schriften* II, 113–20, 126–33). Novalis's philosophy and his differences with Hölderlin are helpfully discussed in Frank, "*Unendliche Annäherung*" (chs. 32 and 33) and Christian Iber, *Subjektivität, Vernunft und ihre Kritik* (Frankfurt: Suhrkamp, 1999), chs. V and VI.

18 Novalis, "Fichte-Studien" I.15 (*Schriften* II, 113).

19 "Fichte-Studien" I.15 (*Schriften* II, 113f.). See also "Fichte-Studien" I.17 (*Schriften* II, 115).

20 See for example "Fichte-Studien" I.3 (*Schriften* II, 107).

21 References are given in the text to the numbered aphorisms, "*VB*" signifying the *Vermischte Bemerkungen* and "*B*" *Blüthenstaub*. An English translation of *Blüthenstaub*, with helpful notes, appears in F. C. Beiser, ed., *The Early Political Writings of the German Romantics* (Cambridge: Cambridge University Press, 1996), 9–31.

22 Novalis, "Fichte-Studien" V.566 (*Schriften* II, 269).

23 See *VB* 6/*B* 6: "We will never completely understand (*begreifen*) ourselves, but we will and can do a lot better than to understand ourselves."

24 Novalis, *Schriften* II, 545 ("*Vorarbeiten zu verschiedenen Fragmentsammlungen. 1798*" §105). Cf. D. Sturma, ch. 11 in this volume.

25 Cf. *VB* 65/*B* 66: "All the circumstances of our life are materials out of which we can

make what we want . . . Every acquaintance, every incident can be for the person of real intelligence the first member of an infinite series, the beginning of an infinite novel."

26 Novalis, "Fragmente und Studien 1799–1800" §603 (*Schriften* III, 664).

27 Quintilian, *Institutio oratoria* IX.2.

28 F. Schlegel, "Über Goethes Meister" (1798), in *Schriften zur Literatur* (Munich: Hanser, 1970), 266.

29 F. Schlegel, *Athenäumsfragmente* §71. Cf. also §53: "It is equally fatal for the mind to have a system as not to have one. So the mind has to resolve to do both," as well as the similar thought in Novalis, "Fichte-Studien" VI.648 (*Schriften* II, 288–9).

8

TERRY PINKARD

Hegel's *Phenomenology* and *Logic*: an overview

The path to the *Phenomenology*

Hegel always described the 1807 *Phenomenology of Spirit*, his first major published book, as his "voyage of discovery."[1] In that work, he brought to completion in a highly original way a whole series of youthful reflections on various topics, and he came to terms with some issues that had long vexed him. However, he came to display a great ambivalence about the book, never lecturing on it while in Berlin and in 1825 even disavowing it as the proper "introduction" to his system of philosophy, but then later signing a contract in 1831 (the year he died) to publish a revised edition of it. He did not have the same qualms about his *Logic* (published originally between 1812 and 1816). Although he undertook some revisions of parts of the book later in his career, he always saw it more or less as the fundamental keystone of his system. Curiously, though, late in his career, his *Logic* became less and less popular with the students as their interest in his youthful *Phenomenology* began to grow. After his death, the *Phenomenology* rapidly eclipsed the *Logic* as the central Hegelian text.

When Hegel came to the university town of Jena in 1801, he was an unknown figure, having previously published only an anonymous translation of and commentary on a French-language political pamphlet that outlined the abuses of the German-speaking Bernese oligarchy against the French-speaking people of the area. He had quite unsuccessfully attempted to make a career as an independent writer speaking about issues concerning modern society and religion in the light of the upheaval of the French Revolution and debating whether Christianity was a religion adequate to the demands of freedom in modern societies. Until that time, he had supported himself (barely) on the meager stipend he obtained from being a *Hofmeister*, a home-tutor for wealthy families. His first such position was in Berne, but when his closest friend from his seminary days, Friedrich Hölderlin, found him a position in Frankfurt (where Hölderlin was himself a home-tutor), Hegel eagerly accepted the offer. On his arrival in Frankfurt and reunion with his old friend, Hegel at first continued to write copiously on the same kinds of topics concerning religion and modernity. However, his constant and animated contact with Hölderlin was to change not only his philosophical outlook, it was to lead Hegel to change entirely his plan for his life.

Hölderlin, who was perhaps almost as gifted philosophically as he was poetically, had studied with Fichte in Jena during the highly intellectually explosive years of the 1790s. While in Jena, Hölderlin belonged to a group of thinkers allied with Immanuel Niethammer (another Swabian graduate of the Tübingen Seminary) who were quietly criticizing the Fichtean system and calling for a "return to Kant" – not in any orthodox sense of reviving a Kantianism of the letter, but rather in the sense of using Kant himself to get beyond the limitations of the Kantianism of the letter.[2] Probably in 1795, Hölderlin himself broke with Fichtean lines of thought. In *Judgment and Being*, a manuscript that only came to light in the 1960s, he outlined what he took to be the central deficit of Fichte's attempt to "purify" Kantianism.[3] It is a virtual certainty that he discussed the contents of that piece in some depth with Hegel.

Fichte in effect had drawn the conclusion from Kant that all our epistemic and moral claims were in principle revisable, except for that claim itself, that "I" could in principle revise everything.[4] In Fichte's terminology, the pure I therefore had to "posit," elect for itself, what was to count as authoritatively normative for itself, and, so Fichte argued, also had to posit a "Not-I," that is, posit the normative necessity for there being norms that the I itself did not posit. Much of Fichte's early, influential thought turned on the way in which he attempted to respond to what he saw as that basic contradiction involved in the idealist position.

Hölderlin concluded that Fichte's dilemma had to do with the overly subjective way in which Fichte had posed the problem. For Fichte, we begin with a picture of a subject, an I, which is evaluating the experiences it has before it and which is electing to judge them in light of some norms and not others; the issue for such a picture is, of course, how we can possibly vouchsafe the norms that we are electing, and, for Fichte, the answer had to do with the conditions for the possibility of self-consciousness, of the pure I's relating itself to itself and constituting itself in this self-bootstrapping act of self-relation. What Fichte failed to understand, Hölderlin argued, was that prior to this act of "positing," there must be a deeper, more primordial unity – a kind of "orientation" that precedes all our orientations – that determines for us what kind of normative orientation we are to take. Otherwise, Fichte would be claiming, as it were, that we had to deliberate on the principles of deliberation in general before we could deliberate at all. In a reference both to Spinoza and to the kind of terminology at work among the young intellectuals in Jena, Hölderlin describes this unity as "Being" (*Sein*) and claims that it must therefore be prior to any "judgment" made about it. Making a play on the German term for judgment (*Urteil*), Hölderlin went on to argue that all judgments are in fact primordial divisions (*Ur-Teilung*) of some deeper unity.

To understand Hölderlin's admittedly very abstract and obscure point, it is necessary to put it in its post-Kantian context. Both Kant and Fichte showed that we are committed to a view of knowledge as inherently mediated. To make a judgment, as Kant said, was to follow a rule; those rules are required that are the necessary conditions for there to be a unity of self-consciousness at all, for the I to be able to identify itself as the *same* "subject" of *different* experiences. To make a judgment correctly, to "get it right," we had to follow the rules that would hold for all such agents, would hold, in Kant's words, for a "universal self-consciousness."[5] Since there was no consciousness at all of any unsynthesized intuitions, there was nothing to constrain our judgmental activities except the rules that "we" – that "universal self-consciousness" of which Kant spoke – spontaneously generate. Hölderlin's point was simply that all the mediated knowledge, all the judgments we make, presuppose something that cannot itself be judgmentally articulated, namely, an original unity of thought and being.

Hölderlin's reflections on the subjectivistic shortcomings of Fichte's (and by extension, Kant's) own starting points had nothing less than an explosive effect on Hegel. In his youth, Hegel had convinced himself that the truly esoteric elements of Kantian and post-Kantian philosophy were not nearly as important as what he took to describing as the "completion" of the Kantian philosophy through an "application" of it to the revolutionary state of affairs existing in Europe at that time. Under Hölderlin's inspiration, he now understood that the tasks he had undertaken in trying to play the role of a "popular philosopher" had simply begged the real questions. When his father died in 1799, Hegel finally had to face up to reality and to decide on a career for himself. Shaken by the new ideas he had acquired from Hölderlin and by Hölderlin's own growing disenchantment with his situation in the Frankfurt area, Hegel decided to use his small inheritance to make his way into the literary excitements of Jena, where his other good friend from the Tübingen Seminary, F. W. J. Schelling, had become the youthful rising star of post-Kantian German philosophy. His sojourn at Jena was to prove decisive for him; in his stay there from 1801 to 1807, he underwent a dramatic, almost unparalleled intellectual development and became the philosopher he was to be.

The *Phenomenology of Spirit*

Hegel's path to an adequate formulation of his own views was not an easy one. Arriving in Jena, he managed to join the faculty there as an unpaid lecturer and worked with Schelling on a philosophical journal mostly dedicated to explicating and propagating the Schellingian philosophy as a development "beyond"

Fichte's own philosophy. After Schelling left Jena in 1803 in the wake of an amorous scandal, Hegel was left to fend for himself. His development in Jena was in large part a heroic attempt (while under extreme financial pressure and suffering from bouts of deep depression) to mesh his earlier interests in the possibilities of modern life, and his increasingly broad historical and intellectual knowledge, with the influences of his two more successful friends, Hölderlin and Schelling. After producing a great number of published articles and unpublished book-length works, Hegel was finally able to bring his efforts to fruition with his epochal *Phenomenology of Spirit*, published in 1807.

In that work, he transformed Hölderlin's original insight in two significant ways. The original, primordial unity of thought and being was reconceptualized by Hegel as an *intersubjective* unity constituted by patterns of mutual *recognition*, from which other conclusions could indeed be derived. However, Hegel also believed he had to motivate such a change in direction in idealist thought by showing that this conception itself had historically come to be *required* of us, that it was not simply one philosophical option among many.[6]

In Frankfurt, Hegel had come to share with Hölderlin a belief that their modern revolutionary times in fact required something like a "new sensibility," which they called a "new mythology of reason."[7] That required, Hegel concluded, that we work out the fundamental issues of post-Kantian, modern philosophy in a language at once both rigorous and "new," that is, in a language that demands of the reader that he actively participate in thinking through the issues involved, that he not simply be allowed to slip into his old, "received" ways of thought. It also meant that any serious attempt at fashioning that new sensibility had to take on directly the key problems being raised against it, particularly those coming from the influential F. H. Jacobi, to the effect that the Enlightenment appeal to *reason* itself was mistaken, was an act of willful assertion that inevitably led to skepticism of the worst sort – or, to use the term Jacobi himself coined for this purpose, to nihilism itself.

Jacobi had argued that the only alternative was simply to accept the necessity of there being some kind of immediate, non-inferential knowledge of things that underlies all our mediated knowledge, and he called this (in his rather idiosyncratic interpretation of David Hume) "sense-certainty," a matter of pure "faith" that things existed independently of our consciousness of them. If knowledge of physical objects was a matter of such "faith," then, so Jacobi argued, there could not be any objections in principle to relying on "faith" to vouchsafe also our claims about God.

Hegel took on Jacobi's claim at the very outset of his book.[8] Hegel's general point was that there was no possible direct awareness of any kind of "object" that on its own would fix and secure the normative commitments of the judgments we made about it. Even the simplest act of awareness of "sense-certainty" already implicates much more than Jacobi's claim that we are simply aware that individual things "exist," since any attempt at articulating *judgmentally* such putative items of "sense-certainty" necessarily requires that we characterize them as more complex unities of *individual*-things-possessing-*general*-properties of which we are "perceptually" aware.[9] That "perceptual" awareness in turn can itself be judgmentally articulated only against a background understanding of laws and forces which themselves are not objects of direct perceptual awareness but are posited by the faculty of "understanding." However, in judgmentally articulating the structure of these laws and forces, the "understanding" itself generates a set of contradictory, antinomial results that it on its own terms cannot accept.[10] What is revealed by this series of reflections on the way in which "objects" of putative direct awareness might fix the norms by which we judge them is that there *can be no* such intelligible form of direct awareness of things, neither sensory nor intellectual. Instead, we are always aware of things *as* such-and-such, and in making judgments about them, we are actively *taking* things to be this way or that, not simply reporting on things that directly confront us without any form of mediation. As Hegel puts it, our *consciousness* of objects involves our *self*-consciousness of *taking* them to be in a certain way.

If, though, it is our *taking* things to be a certain way that is at issue, then the question is raised as to how we are to deal with these seemingly contradictory views at the heart of our consciousness of the world. Since they cannot be resolved at the level of our direct awareness (either sensuous or "intellectual") of objects, they must be resolved in terms of what kinds of *purposes* we assume ourselves to be accomplishing in making such judgments.[11]

This led Hegel to his most radical reformulation of Kantian philosophy. Kant had said that in making judgments, we follow the "rule" spontaneously prescribed for us by the concepts produced by our own intellects (the "understanding"), and Kant had argued that the necessary, pure "rules" or "concepts of the understanding" were generated by the requirements of ascribing experiences to a "universal self-consciousness." Hegel raised the question as to who or what could have the *authority* to determine what counted as the rules of such a shared, "universal self-consciousness." At first, it might look as if it were "life" itself that did this, that what counts as a necessary rule for us is determined by what ends or goals "life" itself imposes on us (in particular, those of organic sustenance and reproduction). However, as a self-conscious agent aware of himself as taking things as such-and-such, the agent can never simply conceive of himself as a natural being doing only what he is naturally inclined to do. Rather, he is pursuing the fulfillment of his desires in terms of his own, "spontaneous" ranking of them. He possesses, that is, a "negative" relation to those desires and thus never simply "is" what he naturally is but "is what he is" only in terms of this potentially negative self-relation to himself: his implicit *project* for his life, not "life" itself, determines the norms by which he ranks his desires.[12] All that only brings to the forefront of reflection the question of how and on what basis an agent could legitimate those norms or reassure himself of their legitimacy. On the one hand, so it would seem, the norms can be legitimated only by appeal to what is necessary for the *particular* agent to achieve his own aims; on the other hand, the agent can legitimate *his* aims only by showing that it is what *other* agents would do if they were "getting it right." The agent thus comes to demand of others that they recognize *his own way* of formulating those norms, that they confer an entitlement on those norms as being those that a "universal self-consciousness" would necessarily employ. However, without any other mediating influences being present, all such claims to "universal self-consciousness" must necessarily be only the *particular* claims of individual agents that their own way of following out their particular projects for life is the "right" way, that their *individual* grasp of the norms is identical to what "all" agents – what a "universal self-consciousness" – would rightfully grasp.

In the wake of such confrontations between individual agents, a life-and-death struggle for recognition ensues. One agent, placing his own life-project above even the value of life itself, manages to subdue and dominate the other agent, who out of fear of his own life acquiesces and accepts the first agent's particular point of view as authoritative for him, as determining what counts as the correct norms for making theoretical, practical, or aesthetic judgments. The former becomes the master (*Herr*), and the acquiescing agent becomes his vassal (*Knecht*).[13]

The vassal subordinates himself to the master in working on things and on his own subjective life not in light of his own personal projects but only in terms of what is required in general by the master's projects. In the process, however, the vassal acquires a bit of independence from nature and the master, which leads him to reflect on his status. What had seemed correct to him, as the set of norms valid for "all agents," gradually comes to seem to him to be the result of merely contingent passions, luck, and uses of personal power. As that realization sets in, the vassal's normative allegiance to those principles is undermined, however powerless he may actually be to effect any change in the social arrangements. Likewise, the master comes to see that the recognition he receives from the vassal is not true recognition but only compelled acceptance; that realization on his part undermines his own normative allegiance to those principles.

The dialectic of master and vassal is paradigmatic for Hegel's procedure in the *Phenomenology*, and it sets up the possible resolution of itself, namely, through agents exercising a *mutual* imposition of norms on each other. That is, instead of the relations of recognition being one-sided, with one agent imposing the fundamental norms on the other by virtue of the other "letting" those norms be imposed on him, each can reciprocally impose the norms on the other in a spontaneous, self-bootstrapping way. That sense of *mutual* recognition, however, must be historically constructed and achieved, since there is no sensory or intellectual awareness of any kind of "object" that can fix those norms for us. The kind of *self-relation* that agents entertain to themselves – that they are never immediately what they naturally are but always have a potential gap between their norms and their natural status as sensing, desiring beings – means that they can experience a profound alienation from themselves and their surroundings; and as their forms of self-relation are undermined by their own reflections on them, they create a history for themselves, a sense that what is possible and required of them is never a matter of purely abstract reflection but always a reflection in light of a determination of what has happened in their past. In the rest of the *Phenomenology*, Hegel gave an unprecedented argument about what the history of European humanity had made both possible and necessary for itself, and how a historical achievement of a form of mutual recognition had come to be required for us "moderns."

With the collapse of the slave-owning societies of antiquity, "stoical" or "skeptical" stances to our basic norms seemed to be required; only the affirmation of our own freedom, our "negative" stances to all norms, seemed to make agents at home with themselves.[14] However, the kind of skepticism to which that line of development led was in fact self-defeating, and the failures of stoicism and skepticism to shore up an affirmation of unconditioned human independence and freedom culminated in the kind of despair experienced in the ancient world as the old gods and ways of life died out. Despairing of themselves as capable of discovering on their own how to "get it right," European humanity had made itself ready for an account of those norms as coming to them from outside themselves via a revelation from the "unchangeable" source of truth. This amounted to a mutual subjection to a metaphysically conceived "master," mediated by the all-too-human priests of the medieval church. That reign of universal servitude expressed as devotion and formation of ourselves for a "higher" truth, however, put European humanity in the position of formulating a view of the true norms as those formulated by a completely "objective" point of view, which gradually came to be identified with reason itself as the moderns came to believe that they could in fact comprehend the ways of God.

Galileo's and Bacon's new science reassured the early moderns of the power of thought, and the norms of "universal self-consciousness" came to be identified with those imposed by the requirements purely of reason itself.[15] The application of reason to human affairs, though, proved less successful, since putting traditional norms under the microscope of rational criticism only served to dissolve not only them but also their early modern successors. Neither a Faustian pursuit of knowledge in the service of the satisfaction of desire, nor an appeal to the laws of the heart as decisively establishing norms that reason cannot, nor a neo-stoic conception of virtue that identified true self-interest with the greatest altruism, could sustain itself; each spawned its own set of contradictions when examined entirely according to its own terms.[16] The collective failures of those attempts led to the Rousseauian (and Herderian) conception of there necessarily being a fixed, "authentic" self behind our various plans, projects, and desires that itself somehow set and fixed our norms; that authentic self, however, itself unraveled under closer reflection on itself; the "authentic" agent revealed himself not to be the fixed, independent part of the otherwise chaotic modern social world but to be himself as open to as many different interpretations as were his overt actions or expressions.[17]

What was required of modern Europeans, therefore, was a conception of reason as itself being constituted in the give and take of social practice, as consisting in a practice of mutual recognition, conferral of entitlements, and undertaking of commitments. Kant's own formulation of this conception as a "kingdom of ends," of persons mutually and autonomously legislating for each other, captured the sense that what counts as rational is what is capable of formulation in terms of the principles legislated by such an autonomous community. This development had, however, two seemingly explosive consequences: first, what counted as an unconditional reason seemed relative to what counted as a worthy way of life (the "kingdom of ends"); and second, Kant's own formulations did not seem to offer any guidance as to how to move to any set of determinate principles to guide us. This precipitated the modern crisis of reason and Jacobi's charges of impending "nihilism."[18]

For the claims of reason to be vindicated, therefore, it had to be shown that the way of life embodied in the modern appeal to reason had to be capable of generating a determinate orientation for us, *and* to be itself required by the determinate ways in which the past ways of life of European humanity had undermined themselves in a way that required the modern appeal to reason.

This led Hegel to supplement his long chapter on "Reason" with an even longer chapter on the history of spirit (mind, "*Geist*") itself, which began with an account of the ancient Greek paradigm of a spontaneous "ethical harmony."[19] The Greeks, in acting solely on the norms demanded by their social roles, could be confident that their actions would be nonetheless harmonious and that the social whole that emerged and sustained them was itself a thing of beauty. Sophocles' tragedy *Antigone*, however, expressed the deep contradictions always potentially at work in Greek life in their starkest form. Antigone, in doing what was strictly *required* of her as the female defender of the divine law of the household, and Creon, in doing what was strictly required of him as the male defender of the civic order, bring about a mutual destruction instead of a beautiful whole. The tragedy, as a clash of "right with right," only exposed to the Greeks the deep contradictions at work in their way of life, and provoked them into becoming more reflective and "philosophical," which in turn made it impossible to sustain the kind of immediate faith necessary for that kind of "ethical harmony" to continue.

The attempts by the successors to the doomed Greek ethical harmony to fashion a worthy way of life for themselves could, in the absence of such harmony, only result in an extended period of European self-alienation. Hegel's discussion of the logic of that line of development traced the path from the alienated, "formal" unity of the Roman empire, bound by no common ends and held together only by the force of the legions, to the failures of early modern aristocratic ideals of life and politics to sustain conviction in light of the growing merger of bourgeois and aristocratic ideals, and the way in which the crisis brought on by the collapse of the aristocratic ethic led to the oddly sectarian and inconclusive skirmishes between the coexisting movements of skeptical modern Enlightenment and modern emotionalist religions.[20]

Out of those failures emerged the completely fragmented social "whole" of modernity, which because it embodied completely contradictory ideals within itself was seemingly incapable of providing any real guidance for people. Out of this fragmented social life, the modern, despairing experience of "groundlessness" nonetheless gradually took shape as a project of "self-grounding," of working out our rational commitments from within a conception of free, self-determining "subjectivity." This Rousseauian ideal was given political expression in *the* epochal modern event of the French Revolution.[21] However, the Revolution took place in a social order that had completely dissolved, that had no institutional or practice-oriented supports to flesh out what was required of the demands of "absolute freedom" in whose name it was made. Lacking such a shared set of determinate norms, no group in the Revolution could establish itself as being anything more than just another particular point of view, just another "faction." With nothing more to guide it than the highly abstract utilitarian notions bequeathed to it by the Enlightenment, "absolute freedom" violently obliterated the distinction between individuals in the name of an abstract whole – the "Nation" and the "Revolution" – and the Terror replaced the cries for freedom, with the sanitized and routinized executions by guillotine serving to protect the "whole" from those who supposedly threatened it.

The revolutionary destruction of the old order, however, made it possible for the kind of Kantian re-conception of modern self-consciousness to be seen for what it was, the great, penultimate expression of the decisive modernist rupture itself, a conception of spontaneity and autonomy expressing the commitment to a "moral worldview," the ideal of a way of life that recognizes the dignity of all, in which each autonomously wills as a member of the "kingdom of ends." Willing as a member of the "kingdom of ends" required, so Kant argued, that we do duty for duty's sake, since to be truly autonomous, we had not only to determine our ends and maxims ourselves, we also had to motivate ourselves purely by the apprehension of their intrinsic rationality. However, since both Kant and Fichte recognized that to act without *personal* aims is not to be an agent at all, they were both led to dissemble about the necessity of acting only for duty's sake, and they imported additional motivation for their overly rigorous conception of moral duty in the form of various postulates about rewards for virtue in the next life.[22]

The early romantics picked up on the rigorism of the "moral worldview," arguing that it was precisely the failure to acknowledge the uniqueness of the individual and his more intuitive, even emotional connection with the greater scheme of things that underlay the rigoristic deficiencies found in the "moral worldview." The romantics therefore rejected the notion of obedience to the moral *law* and substituted for it the idea of being "true to oneself." The "authentic" romantic thus became, in Hegel's famous characterization, a "beautiful soul," at one with itself and in its pure inwardness unsullied by the fragmentation of the modern world.[23]

Such "beautiful souls" fear action since it threatens their undefiled inward unity by exposing it to the necessarily fragmented interpretations of the social world. They thus split into two camps: there are those who refuse to act out of fear of tarnishing their inward unity and become instead judgmental moralists, holding fast to the rigor of the moral demands as they see it; and there are those who, aware of the necessity of action, adopt an ironical stance towards their actions and towards other agents, acting but always holding that their inward unity is never captured in their particular actions. The emphasis on the "authenticity" and "uniqueness" of each agent, however, implied a frenzy of accusations and counter-accusations of hypocrisy, of each accusing the other of only pretending to be acting out of respect for the demands of morality and actually seeking to impose their own particular views on others. The fact that each accuses the other of doing only what he himself is doing makes it more or less explicit to the agents taken up in these flurries of moralistic and ironic accusation that each is after all only a particular point of view; in acknowledging that, each comes to understand that it is impossible to prise apart the demands of personal interest (and the aims, projects, and evaluations bound up with being an individual agent) and the demands of morality; that "getting it right" means acting according to norms that all agents can share, but that there is nothing fixed and immovable either "outside" or "inside" the agents – either in the moral law or the authentic self – that would definitively anchor those norms; and that only the very modern acknowledgment of our mutual dependencies for our own mindedness puts us in a position rationally to evaluate what really would count as right in this fragmented modern world. That in turn makes it clear that the only way to reconcile ourselves to this fragmented, modern world, to see it as both necessary and *right*, is to accept a certain form of *Christian* reconciliation, an acknowledgment that we are all "sinners," all in need of mutual forgiveness for our own particular lapses, our substitution of our own personal interests for what is universally required of us.

Just as the chapter on "Reason" culminates in a recognition that since the only unconditional reasons were those that were essential components of a worthy way of life, an account of "reason" required a separate account of whether and why the modern way of life was itself necessary and "worthy"; in turn, that account, in culminating in the recognition that modern life required a kind of Christian reconciliation, itself therefore required a separate account on whether and why Christianity had necessarily come to be *the* fully modern religion of both "humanity" and "freedom." Thus, Hegel concluded his book with another long chapter on "Religion."

In Hegel's understanding, religious practice is inherently a collective reflection on what ultimately matters to us, on what humanity's highest interests are, a characteristic it also shares with art and philosophy. As such, religious practice also progresses historically; what is religiously required of a form of mind cannot be determined apart from the historical experience of the way of life in question.

In Hegel's reconstruction, religious practice emerges in its earliest forms as "nature religions" in which the divine is interpreted as an abstract natural "whole" that does not necessarily concern itself with humanity in particular; such "nature religions" culminate in Egyptian religious practices, which, having reached the end of their development, set the stage for their own overcoming in Greek religion, in which the gods took on the form of idealized human beauty.[24] Out of the practices of the individualized and alienated self-reflection of the Roman period that followed the dissolution of Greek beauty and harmony – in which the alienation experienced by the members of the empire gave rise to a new form of subjective interiority that had itself emerged in the Greek experience of becoming "philosophical" – Christianity appeared as the "revelation" in the teachings of Jesus of Nazareth that God was mind, *Geist*, that His nature was fully manifest to us, and that the concerns of divinity and humanity were in harmony with each other – that the divine had in fact become human, had appeared as one concrete individual.[25] The divine, Hegel argued, had been made manifest as rational self-conscious *Geist* itself, and in Christian religion, we acknowledge that as what we worship – not ourselves, but the "divine principle" in ourselves. Christianity, as a religion of humanity in general and not of a particular nation, and as a religion of interiority and freedom, not of authoritarian obedience, was the ground in which modern life took root and flourished and could become reconciled with itself.

It was clear that Hegel was thinking of reformed Protestant Christianity in making that claim, but even such modern Protestantism is not capable of formulating that truth about itself. It could at best express it through its practices of devotion, its rites, and its symbols. For the formulation of the *significance* of Protestant Christianity for modern life, we require "philosophy," the kind of "absolute knowing" that consists in the conceptual articulation and explanation of our own historicized self-understanding as being itself the necessary and correct result of humanity's own history.[26] Modern life is the culmination of the dialectic of mastery and servitude, in which the one-sidedness of the imposition of norms is overcome through a mutual and reciprocal binding of ourselves to norms. The modern faith in reason, so Hegel thought, can only redeem itself and renew itself to the extent that it understands, however symbolically and obliquely, the way in which what counts as rational for us cannot be "given" to us outside of our own practices, but must appear within a determinate type of mutual dependency and an understanding of the contingency and the fallibility of all human projects as a ground for the perpetual practice of forgiveness when we in fact do not "get it right" or when we allow contingent interests and power to shape and distort those projects. The historical project, of comprehending how what had happened and why it had happened had also determined what was now both possible and required of us, completes itself in the philosophical self-knowing that is "our" self-knowledge in the final chapter of the *Phenomenology of Spirit*, Hegel's own self-described "voyage of discovery."

The *Science of Logic*

In the fall of 1831, probably before he began work on a new edition of the *Phenomenology of Spirit*, Hegel scribbled down on a sheet of paper a cursory remark that his Jena *Phenomenology* was written when "the abstract absolute dominated at the time." In the *Logic*, Hegel turned once again to elaborate and develop the central insight he had gained from Hölderlin, developing in a different format that key idea and taking it in a very different direction from anything Hölderlin would have intended. For Hölderlin, the presupposition underlying all our thought was the notion that we were primordially in contact with things, that our judgmental activities of *assertion* presupposed a prior conception of *truth* as a kind of primordial unity of thought and being. Indeed, the fundamental oppositions of conscious life – of subject and object, self and other – are themselves only diremptions necessarily introduced into consciousness by our necessarily having to make judgments that "get it right."[27] "Truth" or "Being" for Hölderlin was thus a "primitive," undefinable conception (although for him it could not function as a "logical primitive" in the sense of an axiom from which other truths could be derived).

Hegel took his *Phenomenology* to have shown that this prior unity that precedes all our more reflective and self-conscious orientations was itself already intersubjectively constituted, that we do not begin reflection as individual agents imprisoned in our private experiences, unable, in Hegel's sarcastic phrase, to get behind the "curtain of appearance." Instead, the primitive notion of "truth" at work in Hölderlin's conception itself presupposes a common world and a community of agents. We begin our thoughts as *participants within* a way of life, having a conception of ourselves as one point of view among many; and the normative structure of this intersubjective unity is constituted by the conferrings of entitlements and undertaking of commitments in patterns of mutual recognition and the ways in which some types of commitments effectively undo the possibility of holding on to others.

Taking that phenomenological conception of agency as his starting point, Hegel concluded that the primary act of judgment involved in trying to articulate that primordial sense of the unity of thought and being (which, following Hölderlin, he expressed in the first category of the *Logic* simply as "Being" itself) itself generated paradoxes about itself, most notably the self-defeating assertion that being and nothing were identical.[28] With that fabled paradox, Hegel intended to draw out how the primitive, undefinable notion of "truth" itself *on its own* generates a more skeptical, "negative" relation of our thinking, our judgmental activity toward itself; how our primitive conception of truth itself already includes within itself the seeds of skepticism about itself.

Very generally, Hegel thought that the development of his *Logic* out of that primordial contradiction only showed that the reassurance that we necessarily seek – that our judgments and the world *really are* not irrevocably divorced from each other – can itself only appear at the *end* of the logical development, that the reassurance comes in articulating the whole "space of reasons," the "Idea," in which our judgmental activity necessarily moves. Almost paradoxically, only at the very beginning and the very end of the *Logic* do we get "truth" in the sense of that primitive conception of a unity of thought and being; but whereas at the beginning of the *Logic* the unity disrupts itself and leads to progressively more paradoxes, at the end it gathers itself up into the "absolute Idea," the sense of the normative whole of the "space of reasons" that always presupposes that conception of truth in order to be able to articulate itself. What drives us to complete that "whole," to develop the "space of reasons" within the terms it sets for itself, are therefore the paradoxes that such partial and abstract attempts at "getting it right" generate prior to their inclusion and resolution within that whole.

Hegel's technical term for that process of resolution was "*Aufhebung*," since in German it nicely carried the disparate meanings of "canceling," "raising," and "preserving." The term seemed ideal since its own vagaries highlighted the way in which our commitments to certain basic kinds of judgments carry with them commitments to other kinds of judgments that at least at first seem to be incompatible with each other (the "canceling" aspect), but which when viewed from the standpoint of the totality of the "space of reasons" are understood to have their own legitimate place within our overall scheme of activities (the "raising" part), and whose tensions are therefore never fully abolished but always remain with us (the "preserving" part).

Hegel divided his *Logic* into what he called three "books": Being, Essence, and Concept, with the principle behind each division having to do with the different "logics" – the normative structure of our entitlements, commitments, and the paradoxes they generate – at work in the fundamentally different kinds of judgments necessary to establish a whole of the "space of reasons." The three "books" concern themselves respectively with the norms for judgments about finite entities that come to be and pass away, judgments about the relation between appearance and reality, and self-reflexive judgments about the ultimate normative structure of our judgmental activities themselves.

In the "Doctrine of Being," an entity (or a judgment) is said in Hegel's terminology to be "finite" when it is not self-contained, when its conditions for existence (or, in the case of judgments, its truth) lie outside of itself. The commitments undertaken within a realm of such finitude further commit us to three basic types of judgments: those relating to the qualitative aspects of things that come to be and pass away, those relating to the quantitative aspects of such finite things, and the judgments of "measure" having to do with the ways in which some judgments combine qualitative and quantitative aspects (as when, for example, we say that the village has grown larger and become a city). Each of these types of judgment commits us to a conception of the "infinite" as the "whole" that legitimates and orients our judgmental activities in that sphere. Indeed, part of the reason why Hegel thought it was so necessary to develop his new "logic" had to do with the way in which he thought traditional, "Aristotelian" logic was incapable of understanding the "infinite" except as either an odd metaphysical "object" of some sort lying at the end of a series (an "infinitesimal") or as an unending series of finite judgments; the differential and integral calculus, he argued, gave us a perfectly adequate way to articulate the conceptual "ideality" of the infinite without our having to resort to either Kant's doctrine of pure intuition of space and time or to romantic doctrines of an apprehension of the infinite in some kind of non-articulable emotional contact with it.[29]

Those kinds of finite judgments, however, eventually commit us to a skepticism as to whether "Being" as a whole really is the way we say it is when we make such judgments about it, and in responding to those doubts, we are required to make judgments that are not themselves about the coming-to-be and passing-away of finite entities but about the relation between that transitory world and our own judgmental activities. The "Doctrine of Essence" concerns itself with those judgments, with the way in which skeptical assertions about the possible gaps between what "seems to be" and what "really is the case" themselves seem to require us to have a conception of a "whole" in which there is already a grasp "in thought" of two different and potentially opposed elements, the *appearance* and *that which is appearing*; and argues that without such a grasp of that "whole" in thought, the kinds of ordinary skeptical judgments we do in fact make (such as when we doubt whether something really is the way it looks) are unintelligible. Built into the very structure of self-conscious judgment itself, Hegel seemed to be arguing, is the necessity of skepticism as well as the necessity of the dissolution of the ultimacy of those skeptical doubts themselves.

The various paradoxes that arise in the "Doctrine of Essence" have to do with the problems in the ways in which we *reflectively* make and then throw into doubt the relations between various appearances and what we take them to be appearances *of*. (What underlies and explains an appearance is called its "essence," in Hegel's technical terminology.) Ultimately, such judgments about the links between "appearance" and "what appears" themselves presume an orienting conception of the world as *one* substance that necessarily manifests itself to judging agents in certain typical ways according to "causal relationships" among the various "accidents" of the "essential" substance. Although that might at first have seemed to vindicate Jacobi's charge that any reliance on reason and logic inevitably led to a Spinozistic conception of substance, any such monistic, substantialist conception, Hegel argued, could not be the last word: the Spinozistic conception generates a whole new set of "reflective" paradoxes about causality itself, that require for their resolution a conception of the "whole" as a self-sufficient system of interactive, reciprocal causation among individual substances – in short, a unity of Spinoza's and Kant's conceptions of the necessary structure of the appearing world.

However, what neither the "Doctrine of Being" nor the "Doctrine of Essence" can explain is the normative structure of the judging activity itself; the norms governing our judging activities are not *themselves* established by the natural world that comes to be and passes away, and the distinction itself between appearance and reality is already a judgmental distinction that "we" have imported into our experience and which cannot itself explain what legitimates the structure of those judgments in the first place. In reflecting on the way in which we locate ourselves in the natural world as parts of the interconnected causal chain, we are implicitly making self-reflexive judgments about the ultimate structure and legitimacy of judgmental activity itself, the normative structure of which constitutes the "Doctrine of the Concept," which cannot itself be given a naturalistic explanation.

As Kant had shown, the structure of our experience of a world as coming to be and passing away and as appearing to us in ways that are not necessarily identical to what the world is "in itself" is necessarily a unified experience of particular things as embodying general features, experiences of "this-suches" as having their place in an ideally conceived "whole." To make judgments about things in that world is thus necessarily to articulate our encounters with those "this-such" complexes against the complex background of the kinds of things at stake in "Being" and "Essence." Following up that Kantian insight, Hegel concluded that the structure of "the concept," as the structure of the unity of experience itself, is therefore the structure of self-consciousness itself and that a non-natural conception of our thought also does not implicate any kind of dualism or reduction of all the world to a metaphysically idealist monism.

In treating the traditional logic of syllogisms, Hegel was therefore not content simply to provide a list of the basic classifications of terms, judgments, and syllogisms, as he charged traditional logic with having done. Instead, he endeavored to demonstrate the necessity of employing certain types of terms and certain types of judgments by showing that our comprehension of the norms at work in our use of terms to pick out individual, particular, and universal items within our experience itself already presupposed that we knew how to use those types of terms in certain types of judgments, and that in turn the use of those judgments already presupposed their use in certain types of syllogistic inference.

Most strikingly, Hegel argued that a theory of the inferential structure of syllogisms could not be self-contained and determined purely formally; *material* notions about what counts, for example, as logical and "pure" must be imported from outside the formal structures themselves. These additional considerations arise from our implicit comprehension of what we are trying to accomplish in making such inferences, in what the mind's basic *interests* are in sorting out things in the world the way we do.

Such interests require, Hegel argued, that we understand the world as having a rational structure to it that is independent of ourselves, an "objectivity" (*Objektivität*) that is divided into the "Ideas" of mechanical, chemical, and teleological systems – roughly: into systems in which the elements are identifiable independently of the laws governing the system (such as gravitational systems); systems in which each of the elements has an "affinity" for combining with other elements (as in chemical affinities); and systems in which the elements are what they are only in terms of their functioning as organs of a "whole" (as is the case with all living things). Such "systems" do not characterize individual types of judgments so much as they characterize various patterns of explanatory inference; and they go beyond our ordinary experiential encounters with the world of finite, transitory entities – they are "Ideas" of the whole.

That this characterization of the "objective" systems of the world is required of us, however, can be itself demonstrated only by an appeal to the more "subjective" notions of the "true" and the "good." The idea of the "true," of our getting our judgments about the world "right," is bound up with our idea of the "good," of what basic interests guide our formulation and testing of such judgments, of what we are trying to accomplish in making such judgments. What is ultimately, however, "good," as the *Phenomenology* had also shown, is that we exercise our own free judgmental powers so that we do "get it right," that we learn to discipline our judgmental activities ourselves according to principles that we alone can impose on ourselves since the world cannot impose those principles on us. What thus counts as rational in this constantly self-correcting, self-evaluating structure is only that which can survive reason's (the "Idea's") own ongoing internal critique of itself.

All judgmental activity thus takes place within the whole of the "space of reasons" – the "absolute Idea," as Hegel calls it. The "absolute Idea" is the general comprehension of the "space of reasons" as articulating the original unity of thought and being – of truth itself – that is active in *Geist*, and the comprehension of the necessity of the original, "abstract" unity's rupturing itself and producing the kind of "negativity" at work in the *Logic*. As developed in this way, the "space of reasons" offers the reassurance that outside of itself there is nothing of *normative* significance, and that it has generated itself in a way that preserves the original, abstract, and primitive conception of "truth" as the unity of thought and being, while at the same time offering an understanding of how such a primitive conception of truth includes and generates its own negativity and skepticism within itself.[30] The "absolute Idea" is thus the normative, self-correcting structure of a rational form of *modern* "social space," and forms the "pure normative structure" of the patterns of reciprocal recognition that make up modern mind, *Geist*.

NOTES

1 Günther Nicolin, ed., *Hegel in Berichten seiner Zeitgenossen* (Hamburg: Felix Meiner Verlag, 1970), no. 107, p. 76. The very translation of the term, *Geist*, in Hegel is contested; the first translator, J. B. Baillie, translated Hegel's book as *Phenomenology of Mind*, whereas A. V. Miller later translated it as *Phenomenology of Spirit*.

2 This connection is brought out in Manfred Frank, *"Unendliche Annäherung." Die Anfänge der philosophischen Frühromantik* (Frankfurt am Main: Suhrkamp, 1997).

3 Friedrich Hölderlin, "Sein Urteil Möglichkeit," in Friedrich Hölderlin, *Sämtliche Werke (Frankfurter Ausgabe)*, vol. XVII, ed. D. E. Sattler, Michael Franz, and Hans Gerhard Steimer (Basel: Roter Stern, 1991), 147–56.

4 See Robert Pippin, *Hegel's Idealism: The Satisfactions of Self-Consciousness* (Cambridge: Cambridge University Press, 1989), and "Fichte's alleged one-sided, subjective, psychological idealism," forthcoming in Günther Zöller, ed., *The Cambridge Companion to Fichte*.

5 In §16 of the 1787 (B) "Transcendental Deduction," Kant says: "As *my* representations

(even if I am not conscious of them as such) they must conform to the condition under which alone they *can* stand together in *one universal self-consciousness*, because otherwise they would not all without exception belong to me. From this original combination many consequences follow." (Italicized phrase supplied by me.) Immanuel Kant, *Critique of Pure Reason*, trans. N. K. Smith (London: Macmillan and Co., 1964).

6 For a discussion of Hegel's philosophical development during this period (and the influence of both Fichte and Kant), see Terry Pinkard, *Hegel: A Biography* (Cambridge: Cambridge University Press, 2000).

7 See "Das älteste Systemprogramm des deutschen Idealismus," in G. W. F. Hegel, *Werke in zwanzig Bänden*, ed. Eva Moldenhauer and Karl Markus Michel (Frankfurt am Main: Suhrkamp, 1971), I, 234–6. (I hesitate to list Hegel as the author, since it seems to me that there is much more evidence that Hölderlin is in fact the author of the piece.) See D. Sturma, ch. 11 in this volume.

8 See *Phenomenology*, (A): I.

9 See *Phenomenology*, (A): II.

10 See *Phenomenology*, (A): III.

11 See *Phenomenology*, (B).

12 On this notion of the agent's "negative self-relation," see the clear and insightful discussion by Robert Pippin, "Naturalness and Mindedness: Hegel's Compatibilism," *European Journal of Philosophy*, 7 (1999), 194–212.

13 See *Phenomenology*, (B): A.

14 See *Phenomenology*, (B): B.

15 See *Phenomenology*, (AA): V: A.

16 See *Phenomenology*, (AA): B: (a), (b), and (c).

17 See *Phenomenology*, (AA): C: (a).

18 See *Phenomenology*, (AA): C: (b) and (c).

19 See *Phenomenology*, (BB): VI: A: (a), (b).

20 See *Phenomenology*, (BB): A: (c); and B: (I) and (II).

21 See *Phenomenology*, (BB): B: III.

22 See *Phenomenology*, (BB): C: (a) and (b).

23 See *Phenomenology*, (BB): C: (c). On the notion of the "beautiful soul" in general, see Robert E. Norton, *The Beautiful Soul: Aesthetic Morality in the Eighteenth Century* (Ithaca: Cornell University Press, 1995).

24 See *Phenomenology*, (CC): VII: A and B.

25 See *Phenomenology*, (CC): VII: C.

26 See *Phenomenology*, (DD): VIII.

27 See Dieter Henrich, *Der Grund im Bewußtsein: Untersuchungen zu Hölderlins Denken (1794–1795)* (Stuttgart: Klett-Cotta, 1992) for the most thorough account of Hölderlin's philosophical activity.

28 As Hegel put it, "[N]ow insofar as the sentence: being and nothing are the same, expresses the identity of these determinations, but in fact equally contains them both as distinguished, the proposition itself contradicts itself and dissolves itself." G. W. F. Hegel, *Science of Logic*, trans. A. V. Miller (London: George Allen & Unwin, 1969), 90; *Wissenschaft der Logik*, in *Werke*, V, 93.

29 Michael Friedman in his *Kant and the Exact Sciences* (Cambridge, MA: Harvard University Press, 1992) argues that Kant's own move to "pure intuitions" can only be understood in terms of the failure of classical logic to provide an understanding of

infinity. One can generate an adequate conception of infinity only by making use of quantifiers and nested quantifiers, a technique not available to classical logic. On Friedman's account, Kant concluded that since our idea of infinity could not be generated by the "monadic" classical logic, it could not therefore be a (monadic) logical concept and must be therefore a "pure intuition." It was crucial to Hegel to reject Kant's move to the necessity of pure intuitions, and hence Hegel's appeal in the *Science of Logic* to the calculus as an example of a correct concept of infinity only expressed his belief that in fact the mathematicians (particularly Lagrange) had already constructed an iterative procedure that gave us a purely conceptual, non-intuitional comprehension of infinity. The formulas of the calculus do not bring us face to face, as it were, with an infinite object; they rather give us a conceptual – that is, *ideal* – grasp of infinity. Lagrange, so Hegel seemed to argue, had implicitly refuted Kant.

30 This is the key to understanding Hegel's otherwise obscure phraseology about the Idea's going "outside" of itself and then "returning" into itself, something that requires more explication than I have the space here to give it. Nonetheless, the basic conception is the following. There is no normative force to things that is not conferred by the "space of reasons," but one of reason's requirements is, for example, in empirical knowledge for the judging agent to "let" his judgments be determined by the objects of perception, as when an agent learns to "let" the empirical object *lead him* to making a certain claim about itself. It is only in reflection that we – as both locating ourselves and being located by others within the space of reasons – articulate how the normative force of the object's claims on us rests on our own activities, not on any "givenness" from the object.

9

ROBERT PIPPIN

Hegel's practical philosophy: the realization of freedom

I

In Hegel's *Encyclopedia* system, what we would nowadays call his practical philosophy is called the "philosophy of spirit." By practical philosophy, we usually mean a philosophical account of the possibility of the distinct sorts of events for which we may appropriately demand reasons or justifications from subjects whom we take to be responsible for such events occurring, or we mean an account of *actions*, and an assessment of what rightly count as such reasons or justifications.[1] The central problem in other words is the status of the condition usually taken as necessary for such a delimitation of a class of events as actions: *freedom*. What is it, is it possible, how important is it?

Such a philosophy of spirit has a specific place in Hegel's systematic enterprise. That system is divided into what looks like the basic or foundational enterprise,[2] a "Science of Logic," or his own version of a theory of concepts and the possibility of conceptual content (an account of all possible account-giving, as it were); and then into a "Philosophy of Nature" and a "Philosophy of Spirit"; or it relies on some argument about why the very possibility of an objective judgment requires just *such* delimited contents, that a successful account must be an account *either* of nature *or* of spirit.[3] (For all their differences, there is a parallel here with Kant's architectonic and the relation between the first *Critique* and the *Metaphysical Foundations of Natural Science* on the one hand, and the *Metaphysics of Morals*, on the other.) Hegel also divides up the domains of nature and spirit in the same way as Kant, as between the realm of necessity and the realm of freedom, or between events for which causes can be sought (which stand under laws, which laws, together with empirical initial conditions, determine a unique future) and actions for which reasons may be demanded (which are enacted because of "conceptions of law").[4] But Hegel's account of the necessity for such a separate realm does not rely on any Kantian claims about the mere phenomenality of nature, the unknowability of things in themselves, and so the permissibility of the practically required assumption that we are uncaused causes, or radically free and spontaneous. Hegel leaves no doubt that he considers a philosophy which leaves the status of our fundamental claim to respect as rational and thereby free agents "unknowable" unworthy of the name philosophy, and deserving rather to be considered a mere "faith," or a species of religion.[5]

Finally, various themes in the philosophy of spirit are divided up into philosophies of subjective, objective, and absolute spirit. These correspond roughly to accounts of the possibility of different forms of determinate mindedness:[6] in relation to nature and the objective world; in relation to each other (or the achievement of successful forms of *like*-mindedness); and in relation to what Hegel calls the Absolute, or comprehensive and finally "unconditioned" forms of self-consciousness (religion, art, philosophy). He admits that these separations are somewhat artificial,[7] that their interrelation is much more complex than such divisions will show. (In *The Philosophy of Right*, he even claims that it is only with the account of sociality in the philosophy of objective spirit that the account of mindedness and action is informed enough to begin to look like a theory of human being.[8])

This is all clear enough on the surface, but Hegel's own account of the possibility of freedom (his case for the distinction between nature (*Natur*) and spirit (*Geist*)), as well as his account of the objective norms of practical rationality (his theory of "objective" spirit), have always been extremely controversial. My hope in the following is that a comprehensive perspective on Hegel's practical philosophy, especially on its more speculative ambitions, might put those controversies in a different light, and might suggest that what Hegel tried to do does not so much answer such criticisms as make clear that the charges are irrelevant, that they presuppose inaccurate characterizations of his project.

II

I begin with the notorious objections. Although Hegel regularly characterizes his practical philosophy (indeed, his philosophy as a whole) as a "philosophy of freedom,"[9] and although he frequently makes it crystal clear that he considers himself a resolute defender of modernity, his practical philosophy has nevertheless been shadowed by two disturbing accusations of illiberal, even reactionary, elements. The first is the charge of "anti-individualism," as if Hegel was insufficiently attentive to the modern claims of individual natural right and indeed supposedly believed that individuals themselves are best understood as mere properties, or as contingent, secondary, ultimately unimportant manifestations of what is truly real, which is a supra-individual "ethical substance."[10] According to this charge, Hegel was an "organicist" about politics, someone who believed that the individual parts of this ethical organism have no more claim to individual standing and intelligibility than a severed hand, a kidney or a lung might have. Each could only be what it *truly* is within some self-sustaining and supra-individual whole.

The second accusation is the suspicion of some sort of unusual historical positivism, a sanctification of what happens as decreed by a divine providence. "What is actual," so goes perhaps the most famous and most quoted of Hegel's phrases, "is rational," and "what is rational is actual."[11] That is, the events of world history must be understood to be moments of a coherent, intelligible, even rationally necessary development, and the story of this development is the story of "World Spirit" (that supra-individual "ethical substance" again, now writ very large) gradually coming to complete self-consciousness about itself. This is the process that supposedly underlies and is responsible for the major historical changes in philosophical, political, religious, and aesthetic history.

These charges are not without apparent textual foundation. Hegel does sometimes call individuals "accidents" of an "ethical substance,"[12] and does write that, with the successful establishing of such an ethical substance, "the self-will of the individual and his own conscience in its attempt to exist for itself and in opposition to ethical substantiality, have disappeared."[13] And there would appear to be the same basis for the second charge, that Hegel is committed to a wildly implausible historical theodicy. In the "Introduction" to *The Philosophy of World History*, he explicitly calls his investigation a "theodicy, a justification of the ways of God,"[14] and he calls the history of the world "a rational process, the rational and necessary evolution of the world spirit."[15] In the "Addition" (or "*Zusatz*") to paragraph 377 in the *Encyclopedia* account of "Subjective Spirit," Hegel firmly rejects accounts of history which reduce it to ". . . a play of meaningless activity and contingent happenings," and insists by contrast that history is ruled by "divine providence."[16]

Yet these quotations, and many others like them, only make clear the challenges to be faced in any interpretation of Hegel. They appeal to notions like "ethical substantiality" that have little historical precedence and clearly depend on a Hegelian (and so markedly revisionist) notion of "substance."[17] And he appears to deny not the claims of individuality as such, but only an extreme notion of a stubborn self-subsistence or "self-will" (*Eigenwilligkeit*) and therewith dangerously dogmatic appeals to private conscience. Moreover, while Hegel appeals often to a notion of divinity, this appeal must also be made consistent with the many passages where he appears to claim a divinization or becoming divine of human being itself,[18] and so relies on no traditional notion of a separate, benevolent deity. Finally, such accusations must somehow be made consistent with passages like the following (from paragraph 482 of the *Encyclopedia*).

> . . . the Greeks and the Romans, Plato and Aristotle, even the Stoics did not have the idea of an actually free will. On the contrary, they thought that only through birth (by being, say, an Athenian or Spartan citizen) or by strength of character, or

education, or by philosophy (the wise man is free even if a slave and in chains), that a person is really free. This idea came into the world through Christianity. According to Christianity, *the individual as such has an infinite value* as the object and aim of the love of God, destined as Spirit to have an absolute relation to God, to have this divine Spirit dwell within him, so that persons as such are destined, or have as their vocation, the highest freedom [my emphasis].[19]

III

The challenge to be faced is then first of all interpretive, not primarily apologetic. It is profoundly unclear what Hegel could have meant in the passages cited in the objections, given what else he had to say and how inconsistent the rest of his writings are with the meaning ascribed to him in the objections. As suggested, such interpretive challenges can be met only by attempting some comprehensive overview of Hegel's practical philosophy, some attempt to understand the sort of questions these claims are supposed to answer.

There is one issue in particular that ought to guide any such reconstruction. It becomes apparent as soon as one tries to take seriously Hegel's qualification at the end of the Addition to paragraph 2 in the "Introduction" of the *PR*, where he explicitly warns that a "familiarity with the nature of scientific procedure in philosophy, as expounded in philosophical logic, is here presupposed." Such a presupposition is clearly everywhere relevant in the first paragraph of the *PR*, where Hegel proclaims that "[t]he subject matter of the philosophical science of right is the Idea of right – the concept of right and its actualization" (p. 25). He goes on in the Remark to stress that "philosophy has to do with ideas" not "mere concepts," and the issue that separates such treatments is "actuality" (included as a moment in any account of the former, but not the latter, where the question of existence is treated as external, a matter of contingency). And he makes clear that introducing the issue of "actuality" into philosophy is not merely a question about whether a concept does or does not happen to have instances corresponding to it in the real world. If that were true it might sound as if Hegel were qualifying his practical philosophy either by restricting philosophy to an analysis or perhaps rational reconstruction of already existing political and social structures[20] (which is itself a prominent interpretation of the "historical positivist" charge against Hegel) or by immediately restricting any consideration of what ought to be to what is practically possible at a historical time, what is "realistic."[21]

But the relation between "concept" and "actuality" is described in much less familiar and much more speculative terms, terms that recall his caution about scientific or "logical" presuppositions in paragraph 2. For we are told that we must consider the actuality of any concept (where actuality is already distinguished somehow from the mere "existence" (*Dasein*) of instances) only in so far as the concept *"gives itself* actuality."[22] This unusual relation between concept and actuality is said not to be "just a harmony, but a complete inter-penetration (*vollkommene Durchdringung*)."[23] Since "the idea of right is freedom," we thus must somehow understand both the concept of such freedom and its "realization" and final actuality, and we must thereby understand how such a concept *"gives itself"* this actuality. (This language is also quite prominent in the "Introduction" to the *Lectures on the Philosophy of World History*, in statements such as "[T]he universal property of spirit is that it actualizes those determinants which it possesses in itself."[24])

Understanding such claims is clearly indispensable in any consideration of the accusations noted above, and to any overall assessment of Hegel, for the claim to actuality is at the heart of both problems. The much-criticized idea that freedom is only "realized" in some shared ethical life (*Sittlichkeit*), that one cannot be free alone, but only as a participant in actual social institutions, especially that an individual can only "really" be free in the state, and the claim that philosophy is not about ideals which we must try to approximate, but that it can only retrospectively comprehend the rationality of the "actual," both depend on how we understand such claims about the status of actuality and how we come to terms with the initially opaque claim that the concept of right, freedom, "gives itself" its own actuality.[25]

IV

One has to start at a fairly high altitude to be able to work one's way to the distinctive claims of Hegel's practical philosophy. The basic speculative claim – about a concept securing or "giving itself" its own "actuality" – is not, however, given the idealist context in which it is made, as foreign as it might at first sound. It immediately recalls the attempts by Kant, first to defend a unique claim to synthetic a priori knowledge without the rationalist assumption about a necessary identity between the order of thought and the order of being, and second, to argue that there was a practical notion, the "exposition" of which already demonstrated its practical validity, that it was "in actuality" binding, what Kant called the "fact of reason."

As for the former, Kant's most "speculative" formulation of the "highest principle of synthetic judgments" already has a Hegelian, concept-giving-itself-content ring to it: "[T]he conditions for the possibility of experience in general [by which Kant means the subjective conditions, the conditions that must be met for a subject to have a coherent, unified experience, accompanied by a continuous 'I think'] are likewise conditions of the possibility of the objects of experience."[26] (The Hegelian notion thus might be thought of as a speculative translation for what Kant called the "constitutive" role of some concepts.) This affinity is even more apparent in Kant's claim:

> But the peculiar thing about transcendental philosophy is this: that in addition to the rule (or rather the general condition for rules), which is given in the pure concept of the understanding, it can at the same time indicate a priori the case to which the rule ought to be applied.[27]

In the practical philosophy, the actuality issue is the question of whether pure reason (or the acknowledgment of pure practical reason's supreme law) actually "can be practical," can actually determine the will. This is supposed to be shown "through a fact wherein pure reason shows itself actually [*in der Tat*] to be practical."[28] This appears to be a claim to some sort of practical undeniability, something Kant thinks can itself be established by appeal to "sound common sense,"[29] but which essentially involves appeal to the very possibility of conceiving of a principle of action devoid of empirical interest and formulated with perfect rational universality. The very entertaining of such a possibility, Kant claims, establishes its *practical* reality. Speaking from the practical or first-person point of view, the very possibility of my awareness of the dictates of a purely conceived practical reason establishes *from that perspective* that I cannot deny that I am subject to such a law and thereby establishes that I can act accordingly. This does not establish that "in reality" I can actually be such a cause (reason is powerless to answer such questions), just that I cannot but so conceive myself, else I try to do something like establish "with reason that there is no reason." Accordingly the very "exposition" of the notion establishes its reality,[30] and, in his most speculative formulation, the actuality of the moral law cannot be established either philosophically or empirically, but it "is firmly established of itself [. . . *steht denoch für sich selbst fest*]."[31] He might as well have said that the "concept gives itself its own actuality."

Hegel, in other words, is also trying to provide an account of philosophical knowledge, independent of experience, not reliant on traditional, epistemologically suspect rationalist assumptions, but which might claim more than "knowledge of the concept" alone, which could claim an a priori knowledge of *content*; or which could determine, independent of experience, that the concept must have such a content. This all involves both a theory of the possibility of content in general – how concepts in their judgmental use and claims to normative authority might successfully pick out and correctly reidentify an aspect of reality – as well as an a priori justification of the validity of certain, universal, non-empirical judgmental claims, claims that all possible content in experience must conform to certain conditions. As in Kant, so in Hegel, the focus is on the possibility of judgmental content, and the claim (greatly expanded and modified in Hegel) is that a case can be made for the sort of content certain judgments *must* have, that they *do* have such a content, and that such a case does not depend on any claim about the deliverances of our sensory contact with the world, or about what we happen to desire.[32] Given a pure concept of the understanding (e.g., causality) we can determine a priori the experiential content ("for us") of such a concept (necessary succession according to a rule) and determine that there could be no content of (our) experience not subject to such a rule (the argument of the Deduction and the Principles). Or we could claim that, given a certain concept – the single, universally applicable, practical law of reason – we can, in this case by appeal to the "fact" of reason itself, or by appeal to something like its practical undeniability, establish its "actuality" or validity, that all rational beings are in fact (as Kant says, *in der Tat*) obligated, bound by, such an imperative.

Both aspects of Kant's case are of course as controversial as anything in Hegel, and, while Kant tries hard to assimilate the theoretical and practical issues within one problematic (he calls the practical problem also a problem of "the synthetic a priori"), that single problematic has not been easy for commentators to make out. But, in these very general terms, Kant and Hegel can be said to share a commitment to a decisive shift in answering the philosophical question about the nature of the link between mind and world, or between reason and sensible interests. A great deal in Hegel's project, and especially a proper understanding of the speculative language (idea, concept, actuality, etc.) in which his practical philosophy is stated, depends on understanding that for Kant and for Hegel after him, the issue of objectivity, or the problem of actual content, has ceased to be an issue about the correct (clear and distinct) grasping or having of an idea or representation, and has become, most broadly, a problem of *legality*, of our being bound by a rule of some sort that prohibits us from judging otherwise. The problem of objectivity has thus shifted from what the world or ideas or meanings, somehow, as some sort of facticity, won't let us say veridically about what there is, to the problem of the source of this internal *normative* constraint, our subjection to a rule about what we ought to judge and ought not to judge.[33] In the same sense, nothing about our matter-of-fact attachments, interests, and desires can be said to count as in themselves responsible for, or even on their own as being reasons for, an action occurring. If they do so count, it can be only that a subject has taken them to count thus, and this again cannot be a manifestation of nature without the problem recurring.[34]

Thus the common bond between the idealisms of Kant and Hegel, for all their immense differences, involves their common commitment to a controversial answer to questions like these: that the source of a basic normative constraint in any judging must somehow at some level lie "in us," either in the nature of the understanding and reason in Kant, or even as results of our own "self-limiting" activity, our legislating, "positing," and self-constraining, as in the direction taken by Fichte and followed by Hegel.[35]

Now Hegel makes this point about a priori knowledge in a number of unusual ways in his speculative philosophy. He sometimes refers to objective a priori judgments as "self-determining," as if any thinker's attempt to represent an object can be said to "set its own rules," and this not merely formally, but with the power non-empirically to determine the content of thought. This contentful judging, which is nevertheless free from empirical determination, is sometimes called an "infinite" judgment (at least because it cannot be said to be determined "finitely" or empirically); it is also called (especially when Hegel discusses the determination not to account for all events by appeal to the norms relevant to the explanation of nature, but to introduce the notions of Spirit) "a free judgment."[36]

This large project, or some version of it (the version just given is controversial) is what must be kept in mind in approaching Hegel's practical philosophy. The two decisive turning points in that philosophy involve (i) the status of the general notion of spirit itself (what sort of "content" the notion could be said to have, why we should believe that there is any such putative content or what sort of "validity" the notion has, why it could not be explicable "naturally," and so forth),[37] and then (ii) the case Hegel makes for what he calls the "objective" realization of any such spiritual being, the "rational system of the will" known as the *Philosophy of Right*. In the broadest possible terms, appreciating this approach means that, first, when we start looking for the kind of case that would justify the delimitation of a range of some events as *actions* – that is, try to justify "the objective validity" of the notion, spirit, or establish that freedom is possible – or, second, when we attempt to demonstrate that persons *are* subject to the specific requirements of "right," and that the notion must finally have a determinate sort of content to function as such a norm (ethical life, or *Sittlichkeit*) – we will not be searching about in the metaphysical or empirical world for the existent truth-makers of such claims. We will instead be looking for the source of what can only be a self-legislated and self-imposed normative constraint. In Kant's case we would be trying to establish a "transcendental" version of this subjective necessity, appealing to some undeniable feature of any possible experience, or we would be appealing to that rather mysterious "fact of reason," or some practically undeniable claim of our own reason on us. Part of the story of the relation between Kant and Hegel comes down to Hegel's deep suspicions of the Kantian strategies just sketched and his decision, again under the influence of Fichte, to take these general claims about self-legislation and self-imposition much more seriously and then to try to work out some theory of the true normative status of such self-legislation. Whereas Kant held out some hope for a "deductive" demonstration of a notion's or a norm's "actuality," or objectivity or bindingness, Hegel's procedures in all his books and lectures are *developmental, not deductive.*[38] The proof procedure shifts from attention to conceptually necessary conditions and logical presuppositions to demonstrations of the partiality of some prior attempt at self-imposed normative authority (and in his *Phenomenology*, accounts of the experience of such partiality and the "lived" implications of such partiality), and the subsequent developments and reformulations necessary to overcome such partiality. Sometimes these developments are highly idealized, to the point of artificiality; sometimes, as we shall see, they offer a historical reconstruction of actual developments as a way of making this point about partiality and development.

Looking at the Hegelian project this way, of course, leads us to a decisive and somewhat unstable turning point in European or what we now call "Continental" philosophy. At this point Kant's great inventions, like his notion of transcendental subjectivity, or of only "practical reality," and his attempt to reconceive a purely rational philosophy in the face of the collapsing authority of traditional rationalism and the unsatisfying modesty of modern empiricism, are being reconceived in developmental terms, and that means also socially and historically. In this way his self-legislating moral subject is reconceived as much more than a practically necessary idea and is instead animated with a historical life. Thus begins the debate about what philosophy (or normativity) really is if such a move can be made, and how it is different (if it is) from a sociology or anthropology of knowledge (from just what we as a matter of fact have taken to be normatively binding), or even from a historical materialism or a contingent form of life, or the way we simply go on, and so forth. Kant's transcendental deduction and claims about the fact of reason may be obscure or even failures, but it is clear enough what he was trying to do and, given his assumptions, why he had to try. Can a "developmental" account establish that such self-imposed rules and constraints could not conflict with "actuality," because they can be said to constitute the possibility of such actuality, to "give themselves" such actuality? Could a narrative of what we had bound ourselves to and altered end up telling us what "actual" normative commitments we now have? How would one go about showing this?[39]

V

The question at hand turns on the consequences of reading Hegel's practical philosophy in the light of this sort of systematic ambition, one wherein the Kantian notion of self-legislation is at the center of everything. The first consequence involves the right way to characterize spirit and its "independence" from nature. In what does the insufficiency of appeals to nature in our explanations and justifications consist, and how might understanding that insufficiency help us understand how spirit "gives itself" its own actuality, in something like the sense suggested above?

Hegel attempts several different sorts of accounts to explain this insufficiency. In his *Phenomenology of Spirit*, he tries to show what the satisfaction of natural desire looks like; how it would be experienced, once experienced in a conflict with other like desire-satisfiers; or how such an imagined "struggle to the death" would only be resolved "naturally" by the death of one of the parties and so with the preservation of a natural or animal satisfaction, or by the experience, given such a conflict, of a new sort of desire, a "desire for the other's desire," or a claim of *entitlement* against such a challenge and so a demand for "*recognition*" of such entitlement. The emergence of this experience is what cannot be understood as, again, the manifestation of natural dispositions because *we* must institute what will count as the fulfillment of such a demand. Nothing in nature will so count unless we determine it should. (And so the centrality of self-legislation re-emerges.) There is no particular reason to count some natural fact, like superior courage and strength, as a warrant for such entitlement, unless there *are* *reasons* to take account of such properties in this normative way. And, Hegel tries then to show, the offering and accepting of reasons requires eventually a mutuality, some claim to genuine authority and so universal acceptability, something not possible in the original Master–Slave relation or its later manifestations. (The paradox Hegel describes has become a well-known element of his philosophy: the Master is recognized by one whom he does not recognize and so is at an "impasse," cannot "legislate" the norm that secures his claim to entitlement, and undermines his own mastery just by being such a master.) In later manifestations of this attempt, which Hegel imagines as an attempt to legislate collectively a normative structure that would successfully realize both an individual's particularity in his or her desires and contingent life history, as well as, universally, a like entitlement for all to such satisfaction, similar sorts of "one-sided" tensions or unresolvable conflicts are presented in a developmental form, in an attempt to demonstrate greater and greater success in so doing.

In the *Encyclopedia* context, Hegel also claims that at some stage of complexity, human beings cease to be able to understand themselves, coordinate their activities and account for themselves to each other, by exclusively invoking the explanatory categories of nature (at first, as a hierarchical, teleologically coherent nature; later, as matter, located in space and time and subject to causal law; in both cases as an appeal to a kind of fate or unfreedom or necessity), and must instead explain and hold themselves to account by eventual appeal to practical reasons, justifications, and responsibility inappropriate in the context of nature.

That is, in this *Encyclopedia* context also, this limitation is fundamentally practical and historical, and the thesis is that that sort of claim is philosophically sufficient to answer the questions posed above. At a certain level of organic, and especially social, complexity the invocation of nature as a reason or warrant ceases to be "appropriate" or becomes *practically* impossible for any subject. (It is thus telling that in *Die Wissenschaft der Logik*, Hegel describes the application of causality to organic and mental life as "inappropriate," *unstatthaft.*[40]) And so, as Hegel notes in the last paragraph of the *Encyclopedia*, it is " . . . the self-knowing reason which divides *itself* into nature and spirit," and so, described this way, " . . . as the self-division of the Idea into both appearances." The question must then concern not our grasp of some real ontological divide, but the reasons for our *instituting* or *constructing* such a normative distinction in our dealings with each other. This means that spirit is a self-imposed norm, a self-legislated realm that we institute and sustain, that exists only by being instituted and sustained.

It is in this sense that the story of the development of subjective, objective, and absolute spirit would be understood as a collective historical achievement, a growing capacity by human beings to understand what is required by collective self-determination (or a decreasing dependence on nature and appeals to nature), to understand better that *that* is what they are doing, and so to expand what can be coherently and collectively regulated and directed by appeal to reasons, justifications, and norms. Spirit, understood this way (that is, by taking full account of Hegel's anti-dualism and his insistence that development is a self-determining development), is thus not the emergence of a non-natural substance, but reflects only the growing capacity of still naturally situated beings in achieving more and more successfully a form of normative and genuinely autonomous like-mindedness. (The greater realization of freedom is then some sort of better, practically realized, embodied understanding of what our responsiveness to and initiation of practical reasons requires, a claim to superiority justified by the practical failure of more restricted appeals.) Understanding Hegel this way both captures best what Hegel actually says about the emergence of Spirit, and does justice to his claim that the development of Spirit reflects the greater and greater realization of freedom, which, as noted, amounts to something like a better responsiveness to, determination by, reason.

Several passages make it very clear that spirit itself for Hegel represents a distinct kind of historical, social achievement, the actual *establishment* rather than mere organic *emergence* of freedom.[41] I quote at length from the most decisive of such passages.

> Within our consciousness, the position is a wholly familiar one, and if we consider spirit from it, if we raise the general question of what spirit is, it becomes apparent from its position between the two extremes that the question implies the further question of where it comes from and whither it tends. Spirit has its beginnings in nature in general . . . The extreme to which spirit tends is its freedom, its infinity, its being in and for itself. These are the two aspects but if we ask what Spirit is, the

immediate answer is that it is this motion, this process of proceeding from, of freeing itself from, nature; this is the being, the substance of spirit itself.[42]

Hegel later in this passage invokes the paradoxical expression that spirit is a "product of itself" and that "its actuality consists in the fact that it has made itself what it is."[43] Hegel is well aware that this is quite a different, non-standard way of putting the issue and the nature/spirit duality:

> Spirit is usually spoken of as subject, as doing something, and apart from what it does, as this motion, this process, as still something particular, its activity being more or less contingent . . .

And Hegel's contrary view is now clearly stated:

> . . . it is of the very nature of spirit to be this absolute liveliness [*Lebendigkeit*], this process, to proceed forth from naturality [*Natürlichkeit*], immediacy, to sublate, to quit its naturality, and to come to itself, and *to free itself*, it being itself only as it comes to itself as such a product of itself; *its actuality being merely that it has made itself into what it is.*[44]

And again, as above, finally: " . . . it is *only* as a result of itself that it is spirit."[45]

VI

These passages and the direction of this approach raise numerous questions. But it should at least be somewhat clearer what Hegel meant by claiming that the concept of right could be said to "give itself" its own "actuality." The "constructivist" or self-legislating formulations cited above suggest just that. Under the assumption that forms of natural self-understanding become practically inappropriate for the coordination and intelligibility of complex conduct, subjects must begin to institute and in various ways hold themselves to normative constraints and ideals. It is by being instituted and held to that they function as norms at all, are actual. Their normative authority is not an expression of nature, but they function as independent forms of self-regulation.[46] However paradoxical it may sound, such notions thus "give themselves" their own actuality; they constitute the normative domain they regulate. There isn't such a domain which we discover and try to do justice to, any more than there are ideal game rules which we discover and try to approximate. The concept gives itself, over time, as a result of a kind of self-education, its own actuality.[47] How this is attempted and what counts as success (actualization) and what as failure is the subject of Hegel's books and lectures.

This is in fact the kind of paradox that Hegel flirts with in all those unusual formulations: "Spirit is a product of itself"; "Spirit is its own result"; "[I]ts actuality is only that it has made itself what it is"; "[S]pirit is only what it knows itself to be," and so forth. In fact, yet again, this sort of paradoxical formulation is not that far from Kant's foundational move in this whole enterprise, the fateful passage in the *Groundwork* where he declares:

> The will is not merely subject to the law but is subject to the law in such a way that it must be regarded also as legislating for itself and only on this account as being subject to the law (of which it can regard itself as the author).[48]

This is of course the Kantian analogue to the idea that a concept can give itself its own actuality. But in Kant's case the paradox is even deeper. The idea of a subject, prior to there being a binding law, authoring one and then subjecting itself to it is extremely hard to imagine. It always seems that such a subject could not be imagined doing so unless he were already subject to some sort of law, a law that decreed he ought so to subject himself, making the paradox of this notion of "self-subjection" all the clearer. The lines from this original problem – the logic of moral self-relation, let us say – to the projects of Fichte and Hegel are complex and knotty, if also tightly binding and indispensable. But it should be clear that Hegel is somewhat better off at the outset since he does not believe there is a single form for such a law, and does not try to establish, by an analysis or deduction from the concept of rational being, that we must subject ourselves to just such a law. His developmental approach, or retrospective reconstruction of what we hold each other to, and how we alter such norms, will raise the question noted above (normativity versus mere historicity), but it makes much clearer than in Kant how we could be said to become, collectively and over time, the "authors" of the ties that bind.

However, again, the basic assumption about alternatives is the same in both Kant and Hegel, and testifies to the essential modernity of both figures. *Nature is morally disenchanted*; it doesn't *mean* anything of relevance to our self-directing lives that we have the wants and desires and passions and limitations that we do.[49] We alone can be responsible for the norms that direct our lives, and so the determination either to constrain or to elect to satisfy those urges. But, contrary to Kant's hopes, the *very idea of rationally directing our lives in this autonomous way* will not therewith tell us what to do or allow us to understand *why* we would be so bound to such an ideal. If, more than anything else, we need to know what it would be to be rationally self-directing and in what sense we would subject ourselves to this norm, rather than merely recognizing it for what it is, such deductive procedures do not promise much success.

VII

Confining ourselves to practical norms, then, in what sense can a norm be said to be "actual," not merely possible? That is, under what conditions can a determinate, action-guiding principle be said to provide a subject with a reason to act? (Such an answer of course would not involve any claim that in such a situation the subject simply would act. People often have very good reasons to do things and yet do not act, or act contrary to their own, actual reasons.) That a course of action would satisfy an interest, or an element of some prior "motivational set," might obviously provide such a reason, but that approach, for the Kantian tradition, simply pushes the important questions back a few steps. Such a set of interests and desires could not be appealed to in this sense if such a set seemed to me the product of manipulation, coercion, restricted information, or even mere chance. Both Hegel and Kant insist on a capacity for some separation and evaluation of what I happen to want and desire, for the reason at issue truly to function as a practical reason for *me* to do something.

As is well known, Kant concentrates on an unconditionally binding norm, the very acknowledgment of which gives a subject a reason to act, does determine the will, is actually (*in der Tat*) practical. But he also realizes that such an answer is incomplete since such a subject is not an addressee of such a law as a purely rational being. If the law is to provide *me* with an obligation to act, proper account must be taken of the "me" in question, since my sensible interests, desires for happiness, contingent commitments and ideals are not somehow external to or just attached to some rational core. They *are* "me." Taking these into account in providing a fuller case for such actuality leads Kant into some turgid waters. Although he appeals to the fact of reason in general to prove that pure reason is practical (that we cannot practically deny its normative authority), he then goes on to talk also about an "incentive" we must have, as the sensible creatures we also are, to act as we ought. Part of the "acknowledgment of the moral law" being actual, really providing me with a reason, involves a complex experience of sensible pain at the restrictions on the satisfaction of my self-love, as well as a great feeling of self-respect just in being able to feel and transcend such pain. Moreover that sensible satisfaction and the incentive it (respect) provides, while never itself a chief reason to act in a morally appropriate way (as if in order to have such an experience), is nevertheless not treated as marginal by Kant, but as indispensable to the answer to the Hegelian question we are posing (what makes the norm "actual"). And he does not stop there. Acknowledgment of the law provides me with a reason, creates a rational incentive, only in so far as I also can envisage the ultimate achievement of much more than moral righteousness alone – the achievement of the "highest good," the achievement of happiness in proportion to moral worth. For *this* to be an element of the law's actuality, I must then also assume various "Postulates of Practical Reason," especially that there is a benevolent, just God and an immortal soul. And even this is hardly the end of the story, since the real actuality of the law also requires a complex theory of character, education, the achievement of a civic commonwealth, and an effective, rational religion.

The exact status of all these considerations, given what appears to be Kant's strict criteria of moral worth, was quite puzzling and frustrating to his successors, especially to Schiller and Hegel, and one can see Hegel's account of actuality as his own response to that puzzlement. On the one hand, all such considerations in Kant appear only to be "helping" elements, useful and motivationally helpful toward my being able to do the right thing when called on, helpful in altering my experience of self-love in a way that reduces its *prima facie* motivational power, and not as integral parts of a moral life itself. Yet, in spite of this, Kant also goes to great length to insist that all such elements are necessary for the moral law to provide creatures like us with a full reason to act.[50]

One can understand Hegel's approach in the *Philosophie des Rechts* as an attempt at a solution to this problem. His substitute, that is, for all these motivational, helping considerations is a more Aristotelian consideration of the original, indispensable role of the ethical community in the formation and very being of individuals. For all the reasons we have discussed, in Hegel as in Kant, I am subject only to laws that I in some sense author and subject myself to. But the legislation of such a law does not consist in some paradoxical single moment of election, whereby a noumenal individual elects as a supreme governing principle, either obedience to the moral law as a life policy, or the priority of self-love and its satisfactions. The formation of and self-subjection to such normative constraints is gradual, collective, and actually historical.[51] Moreover the considerations relevant to the "actuality" of such subjection are not secondary and mere matters of motivational assistance. The claims of reason can only be "actual" in a common ethical life, not only because Hegel thinks of the principles themselves as self-legislating and absolutely constituting the normative domain, but because it is only if the formative institutions of that society are themselves rational that I, as their product, can actually experience the claims of others as reasons for me to act or forbear from acting. This involves a specific case for the rationality of the modern family (where individual partners choose each other on the basis of love, and where the end of familial nurturing is the eventual independence of the children and departure from the private world for the public domain), of the modern institution of private property, and of a representative state; and it involves the right acknowledgment, as reflected in the social institutions themselves (like law), of moral notions of individual responsibility and abstract right notions of entitlement. It also involves a defensible historical narrative accounting properly for the role that appeals to freedom have begun to play in modernity. That is a tall order. But since we do not face normative claims as singular, unattached, noumenal beings, capable of acting as uncaused causes, but as subjects located in historical time (as modern subjects) in various non-detachable social and ethical relations to others, such an approach to the problem of the realization of the supreme modern norm, freedom, is, for all its difficulties, I would suggest, much to be preferred.

NOTES

1 The most distinctive feature of Hegel's account of this issue is that he does not treat the boundary between natural events and spiritual activities as a hard and fast either/or. This can lead to some unusual discussions. See for example, his account of boredom in *Hegel's Philosophy of Mind*, trans. William Wallace and A. V. Miller (*PM* hereafter) (Oxford: Oxford University Press, 1971), 69.

2 This is difficult to state precisely. It would appear to mean: that account which is presupposed by any other but which does not itself presuppose any other. But that would not be correct, since Hegel insists that the right image for his system is a circle, not this sort of edifice. But for present purposes, wherein we only need stress the greater importance of the *Logic*, such a summation is relatively harmless.

3 It could of course, as in the case of *The Science of Logic*, also be an account of the very possibility of account-giving.

4 "Everything in nature works according to laws. Only a rational being has the capacity of acting according to the *conception* of laws (i.e., according to principles)." *Foundations of the Metaphysics of Morals*, trans. Lewis White Beck (*F* hereafter) (New York: Macmillan, 1990), 29 (Ak 4:412). See also *Critique of Practical Reason*, trans. Lewis White Beck (*CprR* hereafter) (Indianapolis: Bobbs-Merrill, 1956), 17–18 (Ak 5:19–20).

5 Cf. *Faith and Knowledge*, trans. Walter Cerf and H. S. Harris (Albany: State University of New York Press, 1977), 96. For more on the relation between Kant and Hegel on the "limitation of knowledge" theme, see my article, "Idealism and Agency in Kant and Hegel," *Journal of Philosophy*, 88 (1991), 532–41.

6 As far as I know, Hegel does not use the rough German equivalents for these Wittgensteinian terms ("*gesinnt*," or "*gleichgesinnt*" perhaps). But since his account of spirit is not an account of what he calls a "soul thing" (*Seelending*), or of mental content, ideas, or subjective forms, another term is needed that will not immediately suggest subjective states of mind, states of consciousness, or the grasping of a content. In Hegel's account, understanding such a content *is* being minded in a way, and that means something like having the capacity to wield a notion appropriately. Cf. my Introduction to *Idealism as Modernism: Hegelian Variations* (*IM* hereafter) (Cambridge: Cambridge University Press, 1997), 1–25.

7 Cf. what Hegel says about the "external" forms of transition in the *Encyclopedia* presentation, *PM*, no. 575.

8 Cf. the remark to §190 in *Elements of the Philosophy of Right*, trans. H. B. Nisbet (*PR* hereafter) (Cambridge: Cambridge University Press, 1991).

9 Cf *Hegel's Logic, Being Part One of the Encyclopedia of the Philosophical Sciences*, trans. William Wallace (*EL* hereafter) (Oxford: Clarendon Press, 1982), §23, and the Remark to §24, p. 39: ". . . freedom means that the other thing with which you deal is a second self – so that you never leave your own ground but *give the law to yourself*." (My emphasis; this characterization of thinking as self-legislation will be central to the general characterization of normativity given later in this chapter.)

10 An excellent statement of this kind of criticism can be found in Michael Theunissen,

"Die verdrängte Intersubjektivität in Hegels Philosophie des Rechts," in D. Henrich and R.-P. Horstmann, eds., *Hegels Philosophie des Rechts* (Stuttgart: Klett-Cotta, 1982). I dispute Theunissen's characterization of the Berlin Hegel in "What is the Question for which Hegel's Theory of Recognition is the Answer?," forthcoming in *The European Journal of Philosophy*.

11 *PR*, p. 20.

12 *PR*, §145Z.

13 *PR*, §152.

14 G. W. F. Hegel, *Lectures on the Philosophy of World History: Introduction*, trans. H.B. Nisbet (*LPW*, hereafter) (Cambridge: Cambridge University Press, 1975), 42.

15 *LPW* 29.

16 G. W. F. Hegel, *Hegels Philosophie des subjektiven Geistes / Hegel's Philosophy of Subjective Spirit*, 3 vols., trans. and ed. M. Petry (*PSS* hereafter) (Dordrecht: Riedel, 1978), §377, *Zusatz*, p. 9.

17 Cf. the well-known claim: "That the true is actual only as system, or that Substance is essentially Subject, is expressed in the representation of the Absolute as Spirit – the most sublime Notion and the one which belongs to the modern age and its religion." *Hegel's Phenomenology of Spirit*, trans. A. V. Miller (*PhS* hereafter) (Oxford: Oxford University Press, 1977), 14. For more on this claim about "the Absolute" see my article, "You Can't Get There from Here: Transition Problems in Hegel's *Phenomenology of Spirit*," in F. Beiser, ed., *The Cambridge Companion to Hegel* (Cambridge: Cambridge University Press, 1993), 58–63. Also see this passage from the Introduction to the world history lectures: "The substance of spirit is freedom. From this we can infer that its end in the historical process is the freedom of the subject to follow its own conscience and morality, and to pursue and implement its own universal ends; it also implies that the subject has infinite value and that it must become conscious of its supremacy. The end of the world spirit is *realized* in substance through the freedom of each individual" (*LPW* 55).

18 Here is one of the boldest: ". . . it is of the essence of spirit to be free, and so to be free for itself, not to remain within the immediacy of what is natural. On account of the position from which we are assessing what we call human spirit, we have spirit within a relationship as the middle between two extremes: nature and God; the one being for man, the point of departure, the other being the ultimate end, the absolute goal" (*PSS* 7).

19 See again the passage cited in note 17 above. In the *PR*, at §260, Hegel summarizes more concisely than anywhere else the importance of both the "subjective" and "objective" sides of the realization of freedom. "The principle of modern states has enormous strength and depth because it allows the principle of subjectivity to attain fulfillment in the self-sufficient extreme of personal particularity, while at the same time bringing it back to substantial unity, and so preserving this unity in the principle of subjectivity itself" (*PR* 282). Hegel then contrasts this accomplishment with antiquity, wherein "particularity had not yet been released and set at liberty and brought back to universality." And he concludes that "only when both moments [the objective universal and individual subjectivity] are present in full measure can the state be regarded as articulated and truly organized" (*PR* 283).

20 This option is for all intents and purposes rejected by Hegel in the Remark to *PR* §2, where he states explicitly that the existing form of right, what people at a time actually think right is (what is called their "representation" or *Vorstellung*), need have

nothing to do with a concept's "true" actuality. He uses the Roman legal understanding of slavery as a case in point, where what was taken to be consistent with right is not, "actually" (26). In the Berlin (1830) version of the *Encyclopedia Logic*, in §6, Hegel patiently and in great detail explains that of course he did not mean by the famous phrase from the *PR* Preface to forestall criticism of existing regimes (" . . . for who is not acute enough to see a great deal in his own surroundings which is really far from being as it ought to be?" *EL* 10). His point, he stresses, was to criticize a certain notion of practical rationality, what we would today call a defense of "external reasons," and to defend a version of "internalism," the claim that, "[i]f there are reasons for action, it must be that people sometimes act for these reasons, and if they do, their reasons must figure in some correct explanation of their actions." Bernard Williams, "Internal and External Reasons," in *Moral Luck* (Cambridge: Cambridge University Press, 1981), 102. For more on the relevance of this distinction to Hegel's account of actuality, see my "Hegel's Ethical Rationalism," *IM* 417–50.

21 He rejects this possible interpretation in the Remark to §3, denying that any "systematic" understanding of right has anything to do with "a positive code of laws such as is required by an actual state" (*PR* 28–9).

22 *PR* 25.

23 *PR* 26.

24 *LPW* 57.

25 It is also obvious that, whatever Hegel's actual position, what he was *taken to mean* by some descendants influenced world history like almost no other philosophy. The idea of providing for a person's "real" or "objective" freedom opened the door that led eventually to "People's Democratic Republics" and other Orwellian claimants to such a title of reality. This legacy has long distorted discussions of Hegel and indeed distorted a proper appreciation of the whole Continental tradition in normative theory, the Rousseau–Kant–Fichte–Hegel tradition.

26 Kant, *The Critique of Pure Reason*, trans. Norman Kemp Smith (New York: St. Martin's Press, 1929), A158/B197.

27 *CPuR* B175/A135.

28 *CprR* 43 (Ak 5:42).

29 *CprR* 108–9 (Ak 5:105–6).

30 *CprR* 47 (Ak 5:46).

31 *CprR* 48 (Ak 5:47).

32 Since concepts are understood functionally, demonstrating what content judgments must have could be expressed by a demonstration of what one must be able to do with a concept, how one can and cannot wield it in judgments. That is what the notion of content has become, after Kant's attack on rationalism and empiricism. The origin of this approach is Kant's functional account of concepts as rules, or "predicates of possible judgments." See the account in my *Kant's Theory of Form: An Essay on the Critique of Pure Reason* (New Haven: Yale University Press, 1982), ch. four, 88–123.

33 See my *Kant's Theory of Form*, ch. six, "The Transcendental Deduction," 151–87, and ch. two, "Kantian and Hegelian Idealism," in my *Hegel's Idealism: The Satisfactions of Self-Consciousness* (Cambridge: Cambridge University Press, 1989), 16–41.

34 For a brief sketch of the significance of such a claim about the reflexive character of experience, see my "Apperception and the Difference Between Kantian and Hegelian Idealism," in G. Funke and T. Seebohm, eds., *Proceedings of the Sixth International Kant Congress* (Washington, DC: University Press of America, 1988), 535–50.

35 The crucial turning point in the idealist tradition is Fichte, a figure also essential for understanding how normative issues in theoretical and practical philosophy began to be assimilated. See my article, "Fichte's alleged one-sided, subjective, psychological idealism," forthcoming in Günter Zöller, ed., *The Cambridge Companion to Fichte*.

36 *PSS*, §388.

37 Cf. my "Naturalness and Mindedness: Hegel's Compatibilism," *The European Journal of Philosophy*, 7 (1999), 194–212.

38 Even though Kant titled the section in which he introduces the Fact of Reason "Of the Deduction of the Principles of Pure Practical Reason," he quickly admits that such a deduction of the moral principle would be "vainly sought"; *CprR* 48 (Ak 5:47). So, despite the title, it is not quite right to call Kant's justifying procedure in the second *Critique* "deductive." If anything the appeal to the fact of reason is closer to the metaphysical "expositions" in the Transcendental Aesthetic, or an exposition that is thereby a validation.

39 For more on the controversies and the role of the "actualization" claim in the details of Hegel's social and political philosophy, see my "Hegel's Political Argument and the Problem of *Verwirklichung*," *Political Theory* (1981), 509–32, and "The Rose and the Owl: Some Remarks on the Theory–Practice Problem in Hegel," *Independent Journal of Philosophy* (1979), 7–16.

40 Hegel, *Science of Logic*, trans. A. V. Miller (London: George Allen & Unwin, 1969), 562.

41 On the idea of the sociality of reason itself, see Terry Pinkard's valuable discussion in *Hegel's Phenomenology: The Sociality of Reason* (Cambridge: Cambridge University Press, 1994).

42 *PSS* 6–7.

43 *PSS* 6–7.

44 *PSS* 6–7.

45 *PSS* 6–7.

46 On spirit as a "negation" of nature and on the role of reason in establishing such a negation, see my "Naturalness and Mindedness: Hegel's Compatibilism." The interpretive direction suggested here, "left Hegelian" as it is, might look like a familiar, and ever more popular, one in Anglophone interpretations – a pragmatism, perhaps a radical pragmatism. (See Richard Rorty's comments on "Naturalness and Mindedness," published in this same volume.) There is, however, something non-negotiable, let's say, in Hegel's account that makes such interpretations incomplete. Said summarily, the status of freedom in Hegel is "absolute"; its historical character is only a matter of its "realization."

47 The *Phenomenology* is supposed to be the story of this self-education and so a "ladder to the Absolute." The claim is that the collective social and intellectual experiences of European civilizations, especially their experience of profound cultural and political breakdowns, can be understood as a form of progressive self-education about what it is to be a human being. We are, in other words, learning that we are free and what it means to be free (what the political, aesthetic, and religious implications are of this gradual self-education), and in such a self-consciousness we are just thereby becoming the free subjects we are "implicitly," or "*an sich*."

48 *F* 48 (Ak 4:431).

49 This does not of course mean that the status of nature is irrelevant to what Kant calls our "moral destiny." The issue is how to think comprehensively about the relation

between such a destiny and nature, and Kant's struggles with that issue are apparent in everything from the doctrine of the highest good to the *Critique of Judgment*.

50 The strongest claim of all: "Since, now, the furthering of the highest good . . . is an a priori necessary object of our will and is inseparably related to the moral law, the impossibility of the highest good must prove the falsity of the moral law also. If, therefore, the highest good is impossible according to practical rules, then the moral law which commands that it be furthered must be fantastic, directed to empty imaginary ends, and consequently inherently false" (*CprR* 118; Ak, 5:114). In section V thereafter, Kant goes on to insist on the necessity of the postulation of a just God and the immortality of the soul, again as necessary conditions for the practical reality of the moral law. *CprR* 128ff. (Ak, 5:124ff.)

51 The best example of how this is supposed to work is ch. six of the *Phenomenology*, on "spirit." This is an account of the way in which agents attempt to stand behind, "take" responsibility for, their deeds, an issue that involves at its center the status of the kind of reasons that can be offered when challenged, from the dispute between Antigone and Creon, with a very close, barely "separated" relation between subjects and communal (divided, self-contradictory) ethical life, to a claim for radical independence in figures like Diderot's Rameau's Nephew and the stance of romantic irony.

10

GÜNTER ZÖLLER

German realism: the self-limitation of idealist thinking in Fichte, Schelling, and Schopenhauer

I Idealism and realism

Richard Kroner's monumental study of German Idealism, *From Kant to Hegel*,[1] portrays that philosophical movement as a teleological process brought under way by Kant, originally advanced, in different ways, by Fichte and Schelling, and culminating in the universal synthesis of all prior views and standpoints that is Hegel's system.[2] This linear, progressivist, and finalist perspective is informed by Hegel's self-understanding of his place at the end of the history of philosophy and owes much to Hegel's own work in writing the history of philosophy in general and the history of modern philosophy in particular. But it has not remained the only, or even the dominant, reading of German Idealism. Over the past few decades a number of philosophers and scholars have argued for the superior role of Schelling in the later development of German Idealism and sought to show that it was with Schelling and not Hegel that the movement reached its deepest and most far-reaching insights.[3] Similarly, there has been a reassessment of the place that Fichte occupies through his later works in the history of German Idealism.[4] Finally, even Schopenhauer, once excluded from the German idealist canon, has been incorporated into a more comprehensively conceived genealogy of classical German philosophy between Kant and Hegel.[5]

These revisions in the understanding of German Idealism are backed by some remarkable historical facts. In addition to the early works of Fichte and Schelling that served Hegel as the stepping stones in the ascent to the summit of his own system, there exist entire bodies of work by Fichte as well as Schelling that were either not at all known or not very influential during the lifetimes of their authors, but that have undergone a considerable posthumous reception based on the editions of Fichte's and Schelling's collected works which were undertaken first in the mid-nineteenth century and again in the second half of the twentieth century.[6] In the light of those later, mostly posthumous, works, even the earlier works of Fichte and Schelling take on a different appearance, one that points in the direction not of their appropriation through Hegel but of their continuation in Fichte's and Schelling's own later works.

In the case of Schopenhauer, the historical facts that establish his deeper affinities to the German idealists are his first-hand familiarity with the thinking of the late Fichte, whose lectures he attended at the university of Berlin in 1812–13, and his intimate knowledge of Schelling's late work on human freedom from 1809. Moreover, Schopenhauer's almost total lack of influence during his own lifetime, and the fact that his influence was posthumous, during the second half of the nineteenth century, should not detract from the circumstance that the formation and publication of his complete philosophical system, as contained in the first edition of his main work, *The World as Will and Representation*, was concluded by the end of 1818 – which makes him, and not Hegel, the author of the first completely executed post-Kantian philosophical system.

The collective effect of these revised readings of Fichte, Schelling, and Schopenhauer is that of a counter-image to the Hegelian picture of German Idealism. Where Hegel insists on the rationality of the actual, the all-pervasive power of reason, the exhaustive subsumption of the contingent under the universal, the absolutely certain knowledge that the absolute is mind or spirit, and the ultimate reconciliation of all contrast and strife, Fichte, Schelling, and Schopenhauer can be seen as stressing the limits of such an idealist picture of the world, according to which everywhere in nature and history reason is always dealing only with itself. In entertaining the thought that there is more to reality than reason, that there is more to the absolute than the mind's speculative self-knowledge, that strife and struggle provide powerful, perhaps lasting, resistance to all efforts at reconciliation and completion, these philosophers uncover and address aspects and dimensions of self and world that elude the powers of reason.

In placing reason in relation to a space on which it borders but that it cannot enter, Fichte, Schelling, and Schopenhauer, each in their own way, continue the Kantian project of articulating the grounds and bounds of reason. Like Kant, they seek to strike a balance between the idealist recognition that the natural and social worlds reflect reason's demands and interests and the realist insight that the world is more than the work of reason. In continuing and strengthening the realist counterweight of Kantian idealism, these philosophers also, in effect, address some of the criticisms that had been directed against the one-sidedness of Kantian and post-Kantian idealism by Johann Georg Hamann, Johann Gottfried Herder, and Friedrich Heinrich Jacobi, who had insisted that reason is neither self-sufficient nor productive of all reality.

The realist self-supplementation of German Idealism in Fichte, Schelling, and Schopenhauer renders obsolete the recent fashionable attempts to identify alleged shortcomings of Kantian and post-Kantian idealism and to offer a ludic, "post-modern" replacement for the entire project of philosophical modernism. A radical critique of German Idealism is already to be found at the very core of that movement itself, and deserves to be counted as one of its greatest accomplishments. Moreover, the seriousness and perseverance with which Fichte, Schelling, and Schopenhauer undertook the idealist self-critique contrasts remarkably with the strategies of piecemeal adoption and selective recycling practiced by some of their self-appointed heirs in the late twentieth century.

Fichte, Schelling, and Schopenhauer each modify the idealist outlook they inherited from Kant by systematically reevaluating the status of nature, body, will, and affective experience, all of which receive recognition as primary factors in human reality and in reality *tout court*. To be sure, this reevaluation of reality does not amount to an outright cancellation of the idealist insistence on the constitutive role of reason. Rather, Kantian and post-Kantian idealism undergoes an emendation: the apparent self-sufficiency of reason is complemented, in fact completed, by being traced back to a dimension of ultimate origin or being that is beyond reason but without which there would be no reason.

This concerted effort at a realist supplementation of idealism on the part of Fichte, Schelling, and Schopenhauer amounts to a radical critique of the system of absolute, purely rational idealism as developed by Hegel. To be sure, Hegel is often not the explicit target of these ideal-realist developments, and in some cases the critique even preceded the actual development or publication of Hegel's views. Yet Fichte, Schelling, and Schopenhauer provide the basic arsenal for the subsequent attacks on Hegelian idealism to be found in such diverse thinkers as Kierkegaard, Feuerbach, and Marx.

This chapter will discuss the elements and dimensions of realism in the works of Fichte, Schelling, and Schopenhauer. In each case the focus will be on the relation between the real and the ideal, the rational and the irrational, the cognitive and the conative in the individual philosopher. A brief conclusion relates the findings to subsequent developments in nineteenth- and twentieth-century philosophy.

II Fichte

At first blush, Fichte might seem the least likely candidate for a realist restriction of post-Kantian idealism. After all, the standard picture of Fichte as a subjective idealist portrays him as eliminating Kantian things in themselves and enthroning the absolute I as the principle and ground of everything. Nevertheless, there are clear limits to Fichte's idealism regarding subjectivity and its correlate, objectivity. For one, the subject that is placed at the center of Fichte's philosophy is the finite subject, or, to risk an empirical-anthropological specification, the human being. The absolute I underlying finite subjectivity (or human existence) is an I only in the attenuated sense of being the absolute condition or form of the finite I. Accordingly, the insistence on self-constitution or "genesis" (Fichte's term) is matched, or rather balanced, by an equal insistence on "facticity" (again Fichte's term) in the workings of the subject.[7]

Moreover, in his philosophical work Fichte seems to have come to distinguish ever more clearly between the absolute itself as such and the I as the latter's appearance, thereby suggesting a grounding of the subject and the latter's world of objects in some more fundamental reality. To be sure, this increasing dissociation of the I from the absolute does not amount to a return to Kantian things in themselves. But it points to Fichte's recognition that the I is not the master in its own house – a recognition that may well have been present from early on but that received greater articulation as the years went by.

Absolute I and finite I

The basic concern of Fichte's philosophy with finite reason is captured in his own characterization of the core of his philosophical project, the *Wissenschaftslehre*, as providing a "pragmatic history of the human mind."[8] The central feature of the human mind is the I (*Ich*) or reason as such. Following Kant's distinction between theoretical (or cognitive) and practical (or conative) reason, Fichte contrasts the "theoretical" or "intelligent I" and the "practical I."[9] The two I's are to be taken not as separate entities but as distinct, though intimately related, moments or aspects of the one, unitary structure of rational mind. The "absolute I" that informs the operations of both the theoretical and the practical I has a twofold role in the mind's history, as told by Fichte's philosophy. It marks the elusive, almost mythical point of origin that precedes the I's self-differentiation as theoretical and practical I – an origin in which the I is everything and everything is I; and it figures as the equally elusive, ideal goal of a complete reconstruction of the I's original position, in which all subsequent differentiations vanish again. Real mental life takes place in between these infinitely remote points of origin and termination.[10]

In the case of the theoretical I, the mind's finitude manifests itself as the fact that the I refers cognitively to something other than itself, viz., some object or, more abstractly put, the Not-I (*Nicht-Ich*). To be sure, the Not-I is not given as a ready-made external reality or object to be taken in by the I. Rather, the I itself introduces the Not-I – "posits" it, as Fichte puts it in a terminology that combines logical and ontological concepts. More specifically, the I's positing of the Not-I is a reflection of the limits of the I's activity of self-positing.

The I finds that its own, spontaneous activity is held in check in a way that resists further scrutiny. As Fichte puts it in a terminology derived from physics, the I's outgoing, "centrifugal" activity hits upon something that makes it turn back onto itself or become "centripetal."[11] In response to the check (*Anstoß*)[12] on its original activity, the I posits the Not-I in general along with the entire realm of objects as the latter's specifications. While the rules for the positing of the Not-I and the objects originate in the I itself, the very fact that the rules come into play is due to the check that the I undergoes in its basic self-experience as limited or finite. The idealist production of representations and their objects is set in motion by the encounter with a reality that eludes derivation from and through the I.

The realism that *grounds* Fichte's transcendental idealist theory of representation and, more generally, his transcendental idealist theory of consciousness and objects of all kinds is not to be confused with Kant's "empirical realism," which is *grounded* in transcendental idealism. The realism in question does not concern the relative, subject-relative reality of experience and its objects, that is, the appearances, but absolute reality, independent of the subject and its positings. Yet Fichte's realism is not "transcendent" or "dogmatic"[13] – it does not illicitly transcend the bounds of human cognition. Rather, any thought of a reality limiting the I's activity is developed from within the I, based on its self-experience as radically limited or finite. Fichte himself calls his idealism a limited, or more precisely a self-limited, and hence "critical," idealism. He says it is a "real-idealism" as much as an "ideal-realism,"[14] thereby indicating that none of its constituent parts can be reduced to the other one.

But for Fichte, the I is not only a theoretical I, an I that represents the Not-I. It is also a practical I, an I involved in doing. As practical, the I finds its doing held in check by an affective encounter of resistance in the form of "feeling" (*Gefühl*),[15] or, as Kant would put it, "sensation" (*Empfindung*). As counterpart to the check on the theoretical I, feeling is the practical presence of the Not-I in and to the I.

The point of the I's specifically practical activity is a self-initiated change of feelings, in which one feeling is substituted for another one. More specifically, the practical I seeks to minimize the Not-I (under the latter's practical guise as feeling) by increasingly replacing the I's theoretical determination through the Not-I with the Not-I's practical determination through the I. The objects of cognition are to be the results of prior volition and action; what seems given from the cognitive perspective of the theoretical I is to be the result of some willing and doing on the part of the practical I. To be sure, the complete practical determination of the Not-I through the I, and hence the abolition of the difference between the two in favor of an all-encompassing I, is an ideal, an unreachable but also unavoidable goal that orients the I's pursuits. The practical I remains forever striving.[16]

None of the cognitive or volitional activities of the I will ever enable it to shake off its theoretical and practical limitations under the double guise of check and feeling. The very occurrence of consciousness or self-consciousness on the part of the I presupposes the continued presence of a reality that is not of the I's own making. There would not be a conscious and self-conscious subject without a sphere of objects to be known or acted upon by that subject. And while it may be the case that any such objects are already the products of the I's theoretical or practical activity, the very presence of such a sphere for activity and production is not due to the I. On the contrary, in an important sense the I is due to it.

The I and the absolute

The dependence of the I on something other than itself becomes an ever more prominent concern in Fichte's further work on the *Wissenschaftslehre*. Throughout, Fichte seeks to combine two equally important insights: that everything that is to have reality for the I – as the latter's object of cognition or as its object of volition – must be thought or made ("posited") by the I; and that there are constraints on the I's positing that point to a reality outside of and prior to the I itself. It is no surprise, then, that it proves exceedingly difficult for Fichte to give a specific account of the absolute as the reality that is originally independent of the I. For everything that is thought by the I is already affected by the I's own forms of thinking and thereby rendered finite, not to say human.

Not surprisingly, Fichte's initial attempts to think the unthinkable or the absolute as such occur in the context of the philosophy of religion and in the popular language of religion itself. Drawing on Kant's moral theology, in which faith in God is based on moral certainty, Fichte identifies God and the moral world order outright.[17] To be sure, the latter is to be understood not as an already established, fixed reality but as an emerging and self-ordering whole. It is an ordering order and not an ordered order. Accordingly, God or the absolute is conceived as nothing outside or beyond this moral order of the world. The notion of God as a personal otherworldly being is merely a popular, essentially symbolic way of representing the philosophical conception of the absolute as the world's ideal order under the moral law. Typically, in his own popular works, Fichte represents the divine as "holy" or "infinite will," thereby drawing on the I's basic feature as practical or conative reason.[18]

Yet even in Fichte's speculative conception of God, which does away with all anthropomorphic representations of the divine, the reality of the absolute remains tied to the I, more specifically to the I's moral certainty. Belief or faith in God is simply a reflection of belief in one's moral vocation. Moreover, the absolute remains essentially related to the I in a further, more radical sense. For it is only from the perspective of a finite rational being confronting other such beings (human individuals) that the idea of God or the moral order as the guarantor of the coordination among the individual human beings arises. God and human being, or the absolute and the I, are reciprocal terms. One does not come into play without the other – at least not for the I.

Fichte's continued thinking about the human subject in relation to absolute reality led him to regard the I as the appearance (*Erscheinung*) of the absolute. The I is now regarded not as the ultimate ground but as the mode or form (*Ichform*) for the appearance of the absolute, which does not appear itself and as such. Accordingly, at the center of Fichte's later thinking about the absolute ground of all knowledge, theoretical or practical, stands the relation in which knowledge *qua* absolute knowledge stands to its ground in absolute being, or in short, in the absolute.[19]

Fichte conceives of the basic relation between knowledge and the absolute as "image" (*Bild*).[20] The discrepancy between image and reality here serves to convey the inferiority of knowledge with respect to absolute being. But the conception of knowledge as image also indicates the formative (*bildende*) power of knowledge, its ability to produce images. To be sure, it is not being as such that is rendered in the image-creating activity of knowledge. What is imaged in the image (or shaped in the shaping, as one could say based on Fichte's plastic understanding of "image" as the result of some *Bilden*) is nothing that has any being outside and independent of the image. Things may seem different if the I is not yet sufficiently enlightened about itself – it may appear as though there were something that subsequently and additionally came to be known (or imaged). But actually there is nothing that has any being of its own outside absolute being and its appearance, that is, knowledge.

Fichte examines the relation between the I and the absolute in two directions: as ascent from the I (or, as he now often puts it, knowledge) to its absolute ground or ground in the absolute, and as descent from the absolute to its manifestation as I or knowledge. With respect to the former direction, he stresses the need for the self-cancellation and self-annihilation of thinking in the face of the unthinkable absolute.[21] In order to think to the unthinkable, thinking has to unthink itself.

As regards the latter direction, he insists on the presence of the absolute *in* the I. It is the absolute itself that manifests itself under the form of the thinking and willing I. Accordingly, formulations such as "I think" and "I will," previously used by Fichte to stress the absolute spontaneity and autonomy of the I, are reexamined and rephrased in light of the insight that the I as such is not the ground of all thinking and willing, but only the basic mode or form under which thinking and willing take place. Instead of "I think" Fichte employs the gnomic phrase "knowledge thinks" (*das Wissen denkt*).[22] And he suggests the analogous locution "the will wills" when stating " . . . I deny you entirely this, that *you* will."[23]

Yet the secret agency of the absolute in and as the thinking and willing I mitigates against any dissociation of the absolute from the I – or of the I from the absolute. Fichte's idealism remains a real-idealism: the I, along with the world that it thinks and wills, points to an absolute reality without which no such thinking and willing would take place. Conversely, Fichte's realism remains an ideal-realism: any thought of the ultimate reality behind the I is still the I's thought.

III Schelling

The relation between freedom and facticity, on the one hand, and system or total-ity, on the other hand, also lies at the center of Schelling's philosophical work, whose development reaches from his early years in close association with Fichte's philosophy of the I, then through increasingly independent and novel work on the relation between nature and the absolute, and finally to his later thought on the role of history and religion in the self-realization of the absolute.

Throughout his development Schelling considers it philosophy's task to start with the absolute. This marks a departure from the oblique, epistemological rather than metaphysical approach introduced by Kant and still very much carried forward by Fichte. For Kant and Fichte, the absolute can come into view only from the perspective of the finite, human mind. Moreover, both Kant and Fichte insist on the essential limitations of the human mind in grasping the absolute, which can only be approximated by cognition and has to be rendered in images.

Schelling's much more straightforward approach to the absolute seems influ-enced by Spinoza's metaphysics, which underwent a considerable revival in late eighteenth-century Germany. Spinoza's metaphysics takes its beginning from the concept of the absolute or God and, most importantly, from the reality of that concept, in order to proceed to God's two attributes (mind and matter) and their infinitely many modifications, which make up the human and natural world. For Spinoza, God is not a personal being distinct from the rest of reality, but in fact identical with reality or "nature." Schelling shares this pantheistic conception of God, but he does not follow Spinoza's determinism and naturalism, according to which there is no freedom anywhere and everything is governed by nature's laws. Rather, he seeks to combine a Spinozistic metaphysics of the absolute with a Kantian and Fichtean insistence on the unconditional reality of freedom, with respect to both the human will and God himself.

Given its pantheistic conception, and its procedure of beginning with the absolute, the chief concerns of Schelling's philosophy are always the relation between the finite and the infinite and the relation between mind or spirit, includ-ing the human mind, and nature. The earlier Schelling stresses the continuity, and even the ultimate identity, between nature and mind as well as between the infinite and the finite. By contrast, in the later Schelling there are to be found striking distinctions and dissociations between the divine and the human as well as between the divine and the natural. Throughout Schelling's thinking, though, there is a systematic concern with a reality outside of and prior to any thinking and willing, human or divine.

Nature and the absolute

In his early publications Schelling appears as a close associate and follower of Fichte's. Yet viewed in light of the direction away from Fichte that his work was soon to take, one may detect in Schelling, even from the beginning, a certain distance from Fichte. Thus, when discussing in one of his first works "the I as the principle of philosophy,"[24] Schelling, unlike Fichte, is not referring to the transcendental structure, or any moment thereof, underlying all (human) consciousness of self and world. Rather, for Schelling, "the I" is the undifferentiated, absolutely unconditional being behind everything – the divine point of origin for every thing and person. Schelling gives a metaphysically realist reading to Fichte's (and Kant's) transcendental I.

Moreover, the realist conception of the absolute leads Schelling to a fundamental reassessment of dogmatism in philosophy.[25] Kant and Fichte had rejected as uncritical the alleged acquaintance of the dogmatist with things as they are in themselves, independent of the shaping influence of the human forms of knowing. By contrast, for Schelling dogmatism and criticism, or realism and idealism, constitute genuine, alternative philosophical standpoints. To be sure, neither dogmatism nor criticism is capable of grasping the ultimate, sole object of all philosophizing, the absolute, through theoretical cognition or knowledge. For both kinds of philosophy the absolute can be approached only practically or through human conduct – as an infinite assimilation of all Not-I to the I in (transcendental) idealism, and as an equally unending, gradual immersion of the I into the absolute in (transcendental) realism.

The complementary, rather than exclusionary, relation between criticism and dogmatism in the philosophy of the absolute becomes fully apparent in Schelling's project of a "philosophy of nature" (Naturphilosophie).[26] Conceived as the systematic counterweight to Kantian-Fichtean transcendental philosophy and its idealist derivation of nature from the mind, the philosophy of nature takes the realist approach of deducing mind from nature. The concept of nature operative here is that of organic, organized, and self-organizing nature. Accordingly, the occurrence of conscious mental life is not to be understood as the advent of a new being but as the emergence of mind from its unconscious, "sleeping" state in nature. Schelling also refers to the common nature of the I and nature as "mind" or "spirit" (Geist).[27]

In a further step Schelling sought to undergird the relation of equivalence between nature (or the real) and mind (or the ideal) with an account of their common origin in an undifferentiated ultimate reality, that is, the absolute as the point of indifference between the ideal and the real. In Schelling's philosophy of absolute identity (*Identitätsphilosophie*)[28] the real and the ideal appear as diverging series of the absolute's self-differentiation. The differences between nature and mind can be seen as quantitative differences in the allocation of the real and the ideal factor in a given entity. The development from the real to the ideal, or from nature to mind, as grasped by the latter, is actually the absolute's process of first differentiating the finite from its own infinity and then reintegrating the two in the development of mind or spirit.

The nature of the absolute

The philosophy of identity, which grounds the idealism of transcendental philosophy and the realism of the philosophy of nature in an indifferentism of absolute identity, did not remain Schelling's last word on the relation between the ideal and the real. In particular, he felt the need to supplement the minimal notion of the absolute as completely devoid of any differentiation with an account of how to conceive of any egress from such an absolute. How could there be anything besides the absolute itself? Schelling's answer involved a reconceptualization of the absolute that located the ground for division and diremption in the internally complex nature of the absolute itself. In the process, the absolute, for Schelling, came to take on, in addition to the mark of reason, the contrary feature of the chaotic and irrational.

Schelling first localized the "darker" side of the absolute in his *Philosophical Inquiries into the Nature of Human Freedom*.[29] Understanding freedom in human beings as the ability to choose between good and evil gives rise to the question of how evil willing can occur in a world of divine and hence perfect origin. While maintaining that any actual evil willing is always the doing, and hence the responsibility, of the human individual, Schelling points to a basis for the possibility of such failure in the complex nature of the divine itself. More specifically, he distinguishes, first generally and then specifically with respect to God, between the "ground" (*Grund*) or "nature" (*Natur*) of a being and the latter's "existence" (*Existenz*).[30] God's ground is a dark yearning or will that is as yet unenlightened by the intellect, but which longs for such enlightenment and illumination. The process of God's original realization consists in the self-induced and self-executed transmutation of the dark, unarticulated original unity into the distinct, articulated "image" (*Ein-Bildung*) or "eidos" (*Idea*) of God.[31] Schelling conceives of the original divine process as the subjugation of nature and will in God.

The duality of (blind) nature and (enlightened) existence is not limited to God's original self-constitution. It is said to permeate all of creation, which thus repeats on a finite scale the divine process of self-realization from will to reason. In finite individuals the dark, blind will manifests itself as particular will that stands in opposition to the enlightened or universal will. The freedom unique to human beings is based on the essential severance of the particular from the universal will. Evil is the state of perversion in which the particular will triumphs over the universal will. But human beings do not only participate in God's nature as dark will; they also share in the liberating, universalizing force of the divine light. Hence a return to the good, which is equally an act of freedom and requires a supreme effort of the will on the part of human beings, is always possible – and even forms part of the overall scheme of history as God's revelation or realization over time.

The distinction between God's ground or nature (being) and God himself (existence), together with the associated view of history as God's self-actualization, supplement Schelling's own earlier pantheistic conception of the absolute, which now refers primarily to the ground in God, with the theistic notion of God's personal, even historical being – a "becoming God" (*werdender Gott*). In Schelling's later work it is not only God's own inner nature as dark, chaotic will that marks the underlying irrational character of reality. The presence of the personal God in the history of the world suspends the rational, predictable order of the world. Accordingly, Schelling distinguishes between two kinds of philosophy: "negative" or "purely rational philosophy" (*negative, rein rationale Philosophie*), which can grasp only what is rational about the real, and "positive philosophy" (*positive Philosophie*), which is a higher empiricism based on (supersensory) data inaccessible to reason as such.

In a larger sense, "positive philosophy" is the philosophy of religion, or the philosophical consideration of all forms of religion; in a narrower sense, "positive philosophy" is the philosophy based on the Christian religion. Schelling also distinguishes two basic forms of religion, natural and supranatural religion, and correlates them with the two basic forms of positive philosophy or philosophy of religion: "philosophy of mythology" (*Philosophie der Mythologie*) and "philosophy of revelation" (*Philosophie der Offenbarung*), respectively.

Schelling never gave his "positive philosophy" a definitive form. It has survived in lecture manuscripts and transcripts.[32] Its significance in the present context lies not so much in its many doctrinal details as in its basic stand toward the powers that reason, and specifically philosophy, has for grasping reality. Building on the scholastic distinction between "what something is" (*was*) and "that it is" (*daß*),[33] Schelling insists that reason can only construct possibilities and that reality alone can provide us, by means of experience, with the fact that a thing exists. For the late Schelling, being – that is true, real being – transcends reason.

IV Schopenhauer

The conviction that reality exceeds the domain of reason also stands at the center of Schopenhauer's philosophical system, in which the fundamental irrational reality is the will (*Wille*) as the true Kantian thing in itself. Yet what might seem a dubious relapse into pre-critical metaphysical claims about the absolute nature of things is actually a radical extension of the transcendental stand, according to which the reality of experience and its objects is essentially informed by the basic human ways of experiencing the world. Schopenhauer widens the experiential basis of philosophy by including, in addition to the cognitive sphere, the affective and emotional dimension of human existence, subsumed under the term "will."

In Schopenhauer the will is no longer reason rendered practical but a force in the self, or a part of the self, that is originally independent of the self's rational faculties and is even to be considered its true core. Moreover, Schopenhauer transposes the irrational basis of character from the self as will to the world as experienced by the self. Arguing on the basis of the affective self-experience of human beings, he concludes that striving and the associated unceasing ebb and flow of satisfaction and dissatisfaction (pleasure and pain) are the hallmark of all reality. A less narrowly psychological term for the striving nature of both self and world might be "drive."

Schopenhauer goes on to supplement his account of the self and the world as will with a story of a cosmic struggle between the will and the intellect. Originally one of the will's own creatures, the human intellect can emancipate itself either temporarily (in the experience of great art) or entirely (in religious ascesis) from the tyranny of the will. Yet ultimately it is the will itself, through its increasingly intellectual manifestations, that comes to recognize itself for what it is (sheer irrational striving), and then (ideally or tendentially) to turn against itself or "negate itself." Schopenhauer summarizes this overall development of the world, from blind will through knowing will to will-less intellect, with the "one thought" that the world is the self-knowledge of the will.[34] The idealist process of revelation has turned into one of disillusionment and self-rejection.

Reason, ground, and will

Before turning to the dark and hitherto hidden underside of the world – its nature as will – Schopenhauer develops at great length an essentially Kantian, transcendental idealist picture of the "world as representation" (*Welt als Vorstellung*).[35] Schopenhauer follows Kant by claiming that the world of experience is dependent on the universal cognitive functions of the human mind. The fundamental law governing the cognitive relation between the human subject *qua* knower and the world as represented is the principle of sufficient reason (*Satz vom zureichenden Grund*), according to which nothing ensues without a sufficient reason or ground (Latin *ratio*, German *Grund*).[36] This principle governs the relation of ground and consequent (*ratio* and *rationatum*) between representations (or represented objects) of all kinds. Schopenhauer distinguishes four basic forms (or a "fourfold root," as he puts it) of the principle of sufficient reason, each with its own object domain and each based on a different capacity of the human cognitive faculty.

First there is the principle of the sufficient reason of *becoming*, or the causal principle in the traditional sense, that governs physical objects in relation to the *understanding*. Next comes the principle of the sufficient reason of *being*, governing mathematical objects in relation to *pure intuition*; followed by the principle of the sufficient reason of *knowing*, concerning logical objects, or logical relations between objects, based on *reason*. Finally, there is the principle of the sufficient reason of *doing* or *acting*, which holds between psychological objects or affective mental states and their outward manifestations, based on *inner sense* or *empirical self-consciousness*. In each case, the principle specifies the connections (real, mathematical, logical, and psychological, respectively) between representations or represented objects as so many instances of the principle's general point that nothing is without a ground or reason.

On Schopenhauer's idealist account, the principle of sufficient reason as the universal law governing all representations and their objects is issued by the subject *qua* intellect. The subject in its capacity as intellect brings everything else under the rule of the principle, thus establishing a universal order among representations (and their objects) according to the schema of ground and consequent. Yet the intellect itself is not subject to the principle. As the transcendental form of everything represented, the subject *qua* intellect is the ungrounded conveyor of all grounding relations. For Schopenhauer, the fundamental relation between the subject *qua* intellect and the sum-total of its objects ("world as representation") is not a one-sided relation between the grounding and the grounded, but a reciprocal relation or correlation: no subject without object and vice versa.[37]

Similarly, the will as the reality behind or beneath the "world as representation" is not to be regarded as the ground or, even more specifically, the cause of the higher, representational world. It is precisely the mark of the will in the self and, by extension, of the will in the world that it is itself groundless and does not in turn function as the ground of anything else. There is no reason or ground to the being of the will, nor to any of its manifestations. Rationality or groundedness occurs only in the "world as representation," dependent on the intellect. To be sure, ultimately it is the will itself (as the sole source of reality) that manifests itself in and as the intellect in thinking beings. But the relation between the will as such and the sufficiently grounded objects of the intellect is only indirect; never is there a direct, lawfully governed grounding of a given representation or object in the will as such.

Schopenhauer terms the ungrounded as well as ungrounding manifestations of the will its "objectity" (*Objektität*)[38] and likens them to Platonic forms as the transcendental images that underlie but do not cause the world of appearances. Moreover, the proper cognitive subject for the grasp of such supraindividual, ideal objects is not the individuated subject operating through the principle of sufficient reason but the detached, depersonalized, "pure subject of cognition" (*reines Subjekt der Erkenntnis*), which may result from extraordinary aesthetic experience involving a complete identification with an ideal object.[39] Curiously, then, it is not only the will itself that eludes the scope of the principle of sufficient reason. The pure intellect also exceeds the limits of rationality or groundedness. Moreover, in its deindividualized, generic form, the intellect also lies outside the domain of the will, from which, nonetheless, it ultimately stems. The end point of the will's process of self-knowledge and the ensuing self-negation is a will-less and wordless intellect in which all reality has been negated – by itself.

The identity of body and will

In strict correlation to the overall distinction between the world as will and the world as representation, Schopenhauer contrasts the "subject of knowing" – the transcendental condition of all cognitive reference to the world – with the "subject of willing," which functions as the transcendental condition of all affective world-relations.[40] Accordingly, he attributes to the self a dual perspective on itself – one cognitive, the other conative.[41]

In the cognitive self-relation, the self *qua* subject of cognition stands in an immediate cognitive relation to itself. Schopenhauer maintains that the self's cognitive relations to other objects (objects other than itself) are based on, and mediated by, an immediate cognitive self-relation. He construes the cognitive self-relation as a relation between the subject of cognition, on the one hand, and the subject of willing, which is here taken as an object of cognition, on the other hand. Furthermore, the relation is not one between separately existing entities but a relation of identity: the subject of knowing is the same being as its immediate cognitive object, namely, the subject of willing. Most importantly, though, the identity between the two subjects is also immediately grasped by the self whose subjects they are. The self possesses immediate certainty about the identity of the two subjects with each other and with itself.

Schopenhauer admits his own – and everyone else's – inability to explain the identity, and the immediate knowledge of the identity, of the self amidst its differentiation into intellect and will. He even terms the identity of the subject of cognition and the subject of volition the "miracle *par excellence*," and refers to it as the "world knot" (*Weltknoten*)[42] – a hint that the identity of intellect and will in the self has its cosmic counterpart in the identity of intellect and will with respect to the world at large. The distinctions are the result of self-differentiation and refer back to some originary sameness.

In addition to an immediate cognitive self-relation, Schopenhauer countenances the self's affective or conative relation to itself, in which the self as subject of willing affectively experiences its own material reality as "animated body" (*organischer Leib*).[43] This relation, too, involves an identity. Besides the identity between the knower and the known, there is to be found in the self the identity between the willing (the act of willing) and the willed (the willed action). On Schopenhauer's construal an act of willing does not cause, and hence remotely activate, a bodily event (such as the lifting of an arm). Rather, the bodily action *is* the act of willing in its outward manifestation. The two are identical and to be distinguished only in their modes of manifestation, one being mental, the other physical. According to Schopenhauer, the (human) will is always already *embodied* will.

Like the identity of knower and known in the cognitive self, the identity of the willing and the willed in the conative self can be seen to have cosmic repercussions in the context of Schopenhauer's extended anthropo-cosmic analogy. The identity of human will and human body translates into the identity of the will and the world. The world *is* manifest will. This formula even covers the "world as representation," which is an indirect manifestation of the will, by way of the will manifesting itself as intellect and the world appearing under the intellect's principle of sufficient reason. To negate the will is to negate the world and vice versa. All that would remain after such self-abolition of reality is, with the famous last word of the first edition of *The World as Will and Representation*, "nothing" (*nichts*).

V Existence preceding essence

The common thread that weaves through the thinking about the relation between reality and reason in Fichte, Schelling, and Schopenhauer is the sense of a gap between the rational and the real. The real is no longer congruent with the rational but is something that, originally or ultimately, exceeds the grasp of reason. The common term used to designate the alternative, praeter-rational nature of reality is that of "the will," and more specifically of the "freedom of the will" – its freedom from rational necessitation. By dissociating the will from reason, including the latter's practical, volition-forming and action-inducing employment, the three philosophers point to a force which shapes human reality, and reality in general, but which does not belong to an order that is pre-given, and hence is able to guide the will. The will's willing is strictly self-grounded, which suggests to each of the three philosophers, albeit in different ways, a radical self-determination and self-sufficiency of the will.

At the human level, the emancipation of the will from reason or the intellect is disclosed most clearly in the view that in its most inner core, as will, the human being is free from all natural determination. Building on the Kantian distinction between a human being's overt, manifest or "empirical character" and the underlying, non-empirical or "intelligible character," each of the three philosophers maintains that we each are free in determining who we are and what "intelligible character" we adopt.[44] For Fichte, Schelling, and Schopenhauer, the intelligible character determines the actions of a human being without being determined in turn by anything but the individual's spontaneous election of who to be. In one sense, then, we are the creatures of our character (or will); but in another sense our character is our own creation. We make ourselves, and we can undo and remake ourselves – albeit not at an empirical level but in non-empirical, transcendental self-genesis. It is this notion that our human *existence* (that we are) precedes our yet to be given – self-given – *essence* (who we are) that became the anti-essentialist, praeter-rational, voluntarist legacy of German Idealism to concrete, "existential" thinking, from Kierkegaard (a one-time student of the late Schelling), through Nietzsche (Schopenhauer's heir), to Heidegger (who owes more to Fichte and Schelling than he lets on).

NOTES

1 *Von Kant bis Hegel*, 2nd edn. (Tübingen: Mohr, 1961).

2 Throughout this chapter abbreviated references to editions and primary works are as follows: Fichte *SW: Johann Gottlieb Fichte's sämmtliche Werke*, ed. Immanuel Hermann Fichte, 8 vols. (Berlin: Veit & Co., 1845/6; reprinted as *Fichtes Werke*, 11 vols. (Berlin: de Gruyter, 1971), vols. 1–8); Fichte, *WL* 1804: Johann Gottlieb Fichte, *Die Wissenschaftslehre. Zweiter Vortrag im Jahre 1804 vom 16. April bis 8. Juni*, ed. Reinhard Lauth and Joachim Widmann (Hamburg: Meiner, 1975); Fichte, *TL: Über das Verhältniss der Logik zur Philosophie oder transscendentale Logik*, ed. Reinhard Lauth and Peter K. Schneider, with the collaboration of Kurt Hiller (Hamburg: Meiner, 1982); Schelling, *SW: Friedrich Wilhelm Joseph von Schellings sämmtliche Werke*, ed. Karl Friedrich August Schelling, 14 vols. (Stuttgart and Augsburg: Cotta, 1856–61); Schopenhauer, *SW*: Arthur Schopenhauer, *Sämtliche Werke*, ed. Arthur Hübscher, 7 vols., 4th edn. (Mannheim: Brockhaus, 1988). Since the latter edition begins a new pagination for each work by Schopenhauer contained in a given volume, it will sometimes be necessary to specify the work in question, which will be done by parenthetically adding the work's English title. Unfortunately only a small number of the works considered in this chapter are currently available in English translations. Wherever possible, the German citations are followed, after a slash, by English

references, using the following abbreviations: Fichte, *SK*: Fichte, *Science of Knowledge with the First and Second Introductions*, trans. Peter Heath and John Lachs (Cambridge: Cambridge University Press, 1982); Fichte, *VM*: Johann Gottlieb Fichte, *The Vocation of Man*, trans. Peter Preuss (Indianapolis: Hackett, 1987); Fichte, *IW*: J. G. Fichte, *Introductions to the Wissenschaftslehre and Other Writings* (1797–1800), ed. and trans. Daniel Breazeale (Indianapolis: Hackett, 1994); Schelling, *UHK*: F. W. J. Schelling, *The Unconditional in Human Knowledge: Four Early Essays, 1794–1796*, trans. and commentary by Fritz Marti (Lewisburg: Bucknell University Press, 1980); Schelling, *PI*: F. W. J. Schelling, *Philosophical Inquiries into the Nature of Human Freedom*, trans. James Gutmann (La Salle, IL: Open Court, 1989); Schopenhauer, *FR*: Arthur Schopenhauer, *On the Fourfold Root of the Principle of Sufficient Reason*, trans. Eric F. Payne (La Salle, IL: Open Court, 1989); Schopenhauer, *WW*: Arthur Schopenhauer, *The World as Will and Representation*, trans. Eric F. Payne, 2 vols. (New York: Dover, 1974); Schopenhauer, *PE*: Arthur Schopenhauer, *Prize Essay on the Freedom of the Will*, trans. Eric F. Payne and ed. Günter Zöller (Cambridge: Cambridge University Press, 1999).

3 See Horst Fuhrmans, *Schellings letzte Philosophie. Die negative und positive Philosophie im Einsatz des Spätidealismus* (Berlin: Junker & Dünnhaupt, 1940); Walter Schulz, *Die Vollendung des deutschen Idealismus in der Spätphilosophie Schellings*, 2nd edn. (Pfullingen: Neske, 1975); Martin Heidegger, *Schellings Abhandlung über das Wesen der menschlichen Freiheit*, ed. H. Feick (Tübingen: Niemeyer, 1971); Thomas Buchheim, *Eins von Allem. Die Selbstbescheidung des Idealismus in Schellings Spätphilosophie* (Hamburg: Meiner, 1992). In the past years there has been a deluge of primary and secondary publications on the later Schelling.

4 See Wolfgang Janke, *Fichte. Sein und Reflexion – Grundlagen der kritischen Vernunft* (Berlin/New York: de Gruyter, 1970); Reinhard Lauth, *Die Entstehung von Schellings Identitätsphilosophie in der Auseinandersetzung mit Fichtes Wissenschaftslehre (1795–1801)* (Munich and Freiburg: Alber, 1975); Ludwig Siep, *Hegels Fichtekritik und die Wissenschaftslehre von 1804* (Munich and Freiburg: Alber, 1970); Peter Baumanns, *J. G. Fichte. Kritische Gesamtdarstellung seiner Philosophie* (Freiburg and Munich: Alber, 1990); Johannes Brachtendorf, *Fichtes Lehre vom Sein. Eine kritische Darstellung der Wissenschaftslehren von 1794, 1798/99 und 1812* (Paderborn: Schöningh, 1995).

5 See Rudolf Malter, *Arthur Schopenhauer. Transzendentalphilosophie und Metaphysik des Willens* (Stuttgart-Bad Canstatt: Frommann-Holzboog, 1991); Günter Zöller, "Schopenhauer and the Problem of Metaphysics: Critical Reflections on Rudolf Malter's Interpretation," *Man and World*, 28 (1995), 1–10.

6 In addition to the 19th-century editions of Fichte and Schelling detailed in note 2, there is: *Johann Gottlieb Fichte's nachgelassene Schriften*, ed. Immanuel Hermann Fichte, 3 vols. (Bonn: Adolph-Marcus 1834/5; reprinted as *Fichtes Werke*, 11 vols. [Berlin: de Gruyter, 1971], vols. 9–11). The 20th-century editions are: *J. G. Fichte-Gesamtausgabe der Bayerischen Akademie der Wissenschaften*, ed. Reinhard Lauth and Hans Gliwitzky (Stuttgart-Bad Cannstatt: Frommann-Holzboog, 1962ff.) and Friedrich Wilhelm Joseph Schelling, *Historisch-kritische Ausgabe*, ed. Wilhelm G. Jacobs, Hermann Krings and Hermann Zeltner (Stuttgart-Bad Cannstatt: Frommann-Holzboog, 1976ff.).

7 On Fichte's theory of finite subjectivity, see Günter Zöller, *Fichte's Transcendental Philosophy. The Original Duplicity of Intelligence and Will* (Cambridge: Cambridge University Press, 1998).

8 Fichte, *SW* I, 222. The term "Wissenschaftslehre" (literally "Doctrine of Knowledge") is Fichte's technical term for scientific philosophy in the Kantian spirit. Fichte gave some twenty different presentations of the *Wissenschaftslehre*. The first (and only) detailed version published by Fichte himself is that of 1794–5 (Fichte, *SW* I, 86–328).

9 See Fichte, *SW* I, 271/ Fichte, *SK* 239.

10 On the distinction between absolute I and individual I in Fichte, see Günter Zöller, "Die Individualität des Ich in Fichtes zweiter Jenaer Wissenschaftslehre (1796–99)," *Revue Internationale de Philosophie*, 206 (1998), 641–63.

11 See Fichte, *SW* I, 273ff./ Fichte, *SK* 240ff.

12 See Fichte, *SW* I, 210ff./ Fichte, *SK* 189ff.

13 Fichte, *SW* I, 155/ Fichte, *SK* 147.

14 Fichte, *SW* I, 281/ Fichte, *SK* 246–7.

15 See Fichte, *SW* I, 289ff./ Fichte, *SK* 254ff.

16 See Fichte, *SW* I, 261ff./ Fichte, *SK* 230ff.

17 See Fichte, *SW* V, 177–89/ Fichte, *IW* 142–54. On Fichte's conception of faith in relation to Kant, see Günter Zöller, "'Das Element aller Gewissheit': Jacobi, Kant und Fichte über den Glauben," *Fichte-Studien*, 14 (1998), 21–41.

18 See Fichte, *SW* II, 297ff./ Fichte, *VM* 106ff.

19 A major document of this phase of Fichte's thinking is Fichte, *WL* 1804. For a further discussion of Fichte's later philosophy see Günter Zöller, "Denken und Wollen beim späten Fichte," *Fichte-Studien*, 17 (forthcoming), and "Einheit und Differenz von Fichtes Theorie des Wollens," *Philosophisches Jahrbuch*, 106 (1999), 430–40.

20 See, for example, Fichte, *WL* 1804, 66ff.

21 See Fichte, *WL* 1804, 111ff.

22 Fichte, *TL* 17, 19, 27, 34, 124.

23 Fichte, *TL* 225.

24 See Schelling, *SW* I, 149–244/ Schelling, *UHK* 63–128.

25 See Schelling, *SW* I, 281–342/ Schelling, *UHK* 156–96.

26 Schelling's scattered writings on the philosophy of nature are to be found in Schelling *SW* III, IV, V, and VII.

27 Schelling, *SW* II, 38.

28 See Schelling, *SW* IV, 105–212.

29 Schelling, *SW* VII, 333–416/ Schelling, *PI*.

30 See Schelling, *SW* VII, 357ff./ Schelling, *PI* 31ff.

31 See Schelling, *SW* VII, 362ff./ Schelling, *PI* 37ff.

32 See, for example, Schelling, *SW* XIII, 1–174. An important supplement to the previously known texts from Schelling's later years is the recently discovered original, Munich version of the "philosophy of revelation": Friedrich Wilhelm Joseph Schelling, *Urfassung der Philosophie der Offenbarung*, ed. Walter E. Ehrhardt, 2 vols. (Hamburg: Meiner, 1992).

33 Schelling, *SW* XIII, 57–8.

34 See Schopenhauer, *SW* II, vii, 303, 320, 337, 483/ Schopenhauer, *WW* I, xii, 257, 272, 286, 408.

35 See Schopenhauer, *SW* II, 1–109/Schopenhauer, *WW* I, 1–91.

36 See Schopenhauer, *SW* I, 150–60 (*On the Fourfold Root of the Principle of Sufficient Reason*)/ Schopenhauer, *FR* 221–36.

37 See Schopenhauer, *SW* I, 27, 141f. (*On the Fourfold Root of the Principle of Sufficient Reason*)/ Schopenhauer, *FR* 42f., 208f.

38 Schopenhauer, *SW* II, 129/ Schopenhauer, *WW* I, 108.

39 See Schopenhauer, *SW* II, 207ff./ Schopenhauer *WW* I, 195ff.
40 See Schopenhauer, *SW* I, 140ff. (*On the Fourfold Root of the Principle of Sufficient Reason*)/ Schopenhauer, *FR* 207ff.
41 On Schopenhauer's theory of the self, see Günter Zöller, "Schopenhauer on the Self," in Christopher Janaway, ed., *The Cambridge Companion to Schopenhauer* (Cambridge: Cambridge University Press, 1999), 18–43.
42 See Schopenhauer, *SW* I, 143 (*On the Fourfold Root of the Principle of Sufficient Reason*)/ Schopenhauer, *FR* 211.
43 See Schopenhauer *SW* II, 119, III, 280/ Schopenhauer *WW* I, 100, *WW* II, 248.
44 See Fichte, *SW* IV, 132ff.; Schelling, *SW* VII, 384ff./ Schelling, *PI* 61ff.; Schopenhauer, *SW* IV, 94–8 (*Prize Essay on the Freedom of the Will*)/ Schopenhauer, *PE* 85–8.

11

DIETER STURMA

Politics and the New Mythology: the turn to Late Romanticism

Introduction

In its philosophical and political aspects the romantic movement is firmly linked to German Idealism. Like idealism, the philosophy of the romantics counts terms such as "organism," "individuality," and "imagination" as part of its systematic basis and distances itself from terms such as "mechanism," "division," and "atomism." Even though German Idealism and the early romantic movement are characterized by a decidedly critical reaction to the Enlightenment, they agree with several of its key political convictions.

The turn of the century represents a break in romantic philosophy. The end of collaboration on the journal *Athenaeum* by Novalis and the brothers Friedrich and August Wilhelm Schlegel marks the transition to the later romantic period. The Berlin circle (1810–15) and the Vienna circle that formed around Joseph Görres after 1820 are important stages of this later period. Even though Fichte and Schelling still pursued ambitious speculative projects, the main figures of Late Romanticism lost interest in philosophical projects. Instead, the examination of the history of Christian and German culture, speculation on nature, projects in aesthetics, and, above all, a new formulation of concepts of the state and politics moved into the center of attention.

The French Revolution brought about a special interconnection between philosophy, literature, and politics at the close of the eighteenth century. This combination of events opened up theoretical, practical, and aesthetic perspectives that inspired the political thought of the romantics. The spokespersons of the romantic movement repeatedly pointed out the exceptional nature of this combination. In his *Athenaeum Fragments*[1] Friedrich Schlegel names the French Revolution, Fichte's *Science of Knowledge*, and Goethe's *Wilhelm Meister* as the most important influences of his age, and he treats them as major revolutions in world history. The young Jacobins of the Tübinger Stift and the romantics of the Jena circle felt that the French Revolution and the new developments in philosophy and literature were beginning to form the outlines of a special unity of reason, imagination, and politics – a unity that was taking on the shape of a concrete utopia. The French Revolution was perceived as the sure sign of a cultural development that could be regarded as a major stage of progress in the consciousness of freedom. The romantics saw history as moving from a period of local achievements to a cosmopolitan era. Local achievements were exemplified by classical antiquity, medieval Christianity, and Renaissance humanism, whereas the cosmopolitan era was characterized by the introduction of human rights in Rousseau's philosophy and in the constitution of the French Revolution. The transition to this new period was given a mythological interpretation by the romantics. Because of later events in France, however, disillusionment set in during the second half of the nineties, and only the mythology remained. The politics of the late romantics lost its revolutionary thrust, and under the influence of the political restoration it developed yet another cultural mythology. The language of political Late Romanticism was dominated once again by the terms of the old powers of church and monarchy.

Predecessors of the New Mythology and political romanticism

Jean-Jacques Rousseau had a crucial influence on all philosophical and literary movements at the end of the eighteenth century. The romantics in particular were supplied by Rousseau with nearly all of their motifs for the criticism of the Enlightenment. Above all, his later works – which center on a complex understanding of nature and the terms imagination, emotion, and authenticity – left traces in the thought of Herder, Hölderlin, Novalis, Friedrich Schlegel, and the philosophers of German Idealism. Because of his influence on the politics of his time, Rousseau also stands for the combination of revolutionary politics and philosophy. When the revolutionary impetus in the romantic doctrines lessened, Rousseau's influence also declined.

Even though the romantic movement opposed many Enlightenment doctrines, Kant's ethics and aesthetics were a crucial influence on it. In these areas he was seen as the legitimate heir of Rousseau. His uncompromising interpretation of autonomy and moral consciousness made a lasting impression on the young idealists and romantics. They adopted the Kantian term "productive imagination," which is of crucial importance for the systematic background of philosophical romanticism.

Herder, whose philosophy is influenced equally by Rousseau and Kant, combined ideas from the Enlightenment and its critics in a way that proved influential for German romanticism. In spite of his strong humanistic leanings he rejected the revolutionary tendencies among the early idealists and romantics. Herder presented a series of works on mythology. His early work, *On the Modern Use of Mythology* (1767), is mainly concerned with the rehabilitation of Nordic mythology and its disassociation from classical mythologies.[2] For the program of constructing a New Mythology in early German Idealism and philosophical romanticism, his work *Iduna, or the Apple of Rejuvenation* (1796)[3] is significant. In this work he shows the constitutive cultural function of mythology. Herder's reflections center on the poetical imagination that shapes human culture. Because of productive imagination, human experience is not merely the representation of a world with which it is confronted, but a process of expression and *Bildung*.

In its emphasis on both aesthetics and the criticism of the Enlightenment, Schiller's work *On the Aesthetic Education of Humanity in a Series of Letters* (1795)[4] supplies an important basis for romantic politics. Schiller's vision of society begins with a radical rejection of the one-sidedness of modern society, which leads either to a society of savages or a society of barbarians. One can be in opposition to oneself in two ways: one becomes a savage when feelings reign over principles, and one becomes a barbarian when principles destroy feelings. The savage despises art and accepts nature as absolute ruler. The barbarian dishonors nature and is willing to be a "slave of his slave." Schiller sees the solution to this problem in moral and aesthetic education. One should make nature a friend and exert control only over its arbitrariness. Under the condition of a moral and aesthetic education it becomes possible to transform the state of need (*Notstaat*) into a state of freedom. Schiller's opposition of the *Notstaat* and the state of freedom reflects the alternatives of Hobbes's and Rousseau's social contracts. Following Rousseau, Schiller argues for the idea of a new community that overcomes the egoists' *Notstaat*.

The treatises on perpetual peace

In the nineties the influences of Rousseau, Kant, Herder, Schiller, and Fichte were developed further into an independent system by several young philosophers and writers. The discussion of Kant's work *On Perpetual Peace* was an important stage in this development. In the second half of the nineties the treatises on perpetual peace document a transition from an era of programs in revolutionary politics, philosophy, and literature to a period dominated by a withdrawal from support of the French Revolution. This transition led into the phase of Late Romanticism. The first group that modified and even radicalized Kant's program in a positive reception of the events of the French Revolution included Fichte, [5] Friedrich Schlegel,[6] and Görres.[7] Herder took a middle position in his thoughts on perpetual peace in the *Letters on the Advancement of Humanity*.[8] A decided departure from the revolutionary programs of Early Romanticism and early German Idealism can be observed especially in Novalis[9] and Friedrich Gentz.[10]

Kant wrote his work *On Perpetual Peace: A Philosophical Proposal* in 1795. It advocates the idea of universal civil rights by extending the republican constitutions of national states to a law of nations that is founded on a confederacy of free states. The goal to be striven for is a league of nations, not one state that incorporates all nations. Kant expected this construction to be the realization of man's morality within a culture developing under ideal political conditions. In the appendix of his work, Kant[11] analyzes the precarious relationship of politics and morals. The conflict between ethics and politics reveals itself in the tension between demands such as "be wise as the serpent," on the one hand, and "be honest as the dove," on the other hand. As an alternative to such extreme positions, Kant strives for a legal restriction of unbridled self-interest and competitiveness. Even though Kant does not ascribe a privileged role to philosophy in political decision-making processes, philosophy is of decisive significance as the guardian of moral principles of justice. Despite restraints on the role that philosophy can play in the social sphere, Kant regards the advice of philosophers as indispensable. Although he concedes pragmatic or practical points in the realization of politics, he is not willing to allow any question about the supremacy of ethics over politics.[12] Because the moral principle of humanity cannot be eliminated, there is no fundamental disagreement between ethics and politics. Conflict arises only from the selfish tendencies of people who mistake self-interest for reason. Unlike Plato, Kant supports a philosophical restraint on the giving of political advice. In political decision-making processes the philosopher cannot claim the status of an expert. His responsibility is to give voice to practical reason in political practice. Kant aims for a political moralism that maintains a priority of morality over politics. Despite its very restrained style, Kant's *Perpetual Peace* carries several implications for the relationship between individual and community that were not unnoticed by its readers. It provoked an enormous echo, which triggered a discussion that overlapped with the interpretation of the events of the French Revolution and finally led to the transition from the revolutionary phase of political romanticism to the period of the restoration.

Fichte responded positively to Kant in a review in 1796.[13] In his general criticism of Kant the ethical and political interpretation of the French Revolution plays an important role. In his work *Contribution to the Correction of Public Judgment of the French Revolution* (1793) Fichte pointed out that the question of right should not be judged by history.[14] An assessment of French events thus needs to take account of the problem of social justice. Fichte was willing to carry Kant's idea of a republic further in the direction of a politics of autonomy: "Every man is naturally free and nobody but he himself is entitled to make him follow a law."[15] According to Fichte, the proper social conditions for the construction of an ideal national and international republic do not obtain yet. Political oppression and social injustice still shape the various modes of social life. Under conditions such as these, an appeal to the moral law is insufficient, for "the law is only formal, in that everybody is to restrict their freedom, but not material, in how far this should be done." Fichte did not see any reason for skepticism concerning the development of human culture. On the contrary, he thought a glimpse into the workshops of our culture gives sufficient reason for optimism. In this context Fichte was thinking especially of the revolutions of France and North America.

In the same year that Fichte's review was published, Friedrich Schlegel's *Essay on the Concept of Republicanism Occasioned by the Kantian tract "Perpetual Peace"* appeared. Schlegel was openly critical of liberalism. To him, the state is the primary end of a human community. Therefore the mechanistic isolation of the individual is to be avoided in political theory. Schlegel rejected the idea that the political value of a republican state is determined solely by an "extensive quantum." According to him, a republic cannot be realized without an "intensive quantum" of experienced community, liberty, and equality. Morality is the indispensable condition for the realization of a perfect state. Accordingly, Schlegel could not accept Kant's separation of ethics and politics. To his mind such a view was nothing but "political trickery." In this context Schlegel saw the role of political education to be of paramount importance. The concept of perpetual peace remains empty unless it is founded on the laws of political history and the principles of political education. The distinctions between ethics and politics that determine Kant's *Perpetual Peace* throughout need to be disposed of as inappropriate. Schlegel's essay already contains several motifs and definitions that lead away from Kant's political liberalism as well as from the political projects of early German Idealism and Early Romanticism.

In 1795 Joseph Görres's essay *Universal Peace, an Ideal* was published. It introduced the concept of the French Revolution as a landmark in the cultural history of human rights. This interpretation in terms of the philosophy of history came hand in hand with a clear cosmopolitanism. Because humanity has already achieved such remarkable progress and managed to breathe life into the machinery of contemporary states, the move to a situation of true cosmopolitanism should not prove difficult. Görres also takes a critical stance regarding mechanistic concepts of the state. His critique of mechanism, however, is not restricted to the relationship between the individual and the community, but is expanded to embrace the community of nations. According to Görres, the Jacobins did not win human rights only for their nation alone. The significance of the French Revolution lies in its having realized the idea of human rights for everyone.[16] Görres did not hold on for long to his emphatic praise of the epoch-making significance of the French Revolution, but, under the impact of Napoleon's rise turned away from being an adherent of it. In this way, Görres is a typical example of the change from Early to Late Romanticism.

The New Mythology

The intellectual efforts of Early Romanticism center on the program of a New Mythology, a mythology that can do for modernity what traditional mythology did for ancient cultures. Apart from its religious and cultural associations the term "mythology" in romanticism denotes a practical overcoming of the narrow boundaries of discursive knowledge. Mythological reconstructions are by no means restricted to the present or the past. What is gained in and from history is supposed to shape the culture of the future. A characteristic of the early romantics and idealists is the appropriation of models from antiquity. This can be seen clearly in Hölderlin and Schlegel. The mythological understanding of history found a further development in Novalis's essay *Christianity or Europe*, which marks the transition to the neo-conservative period of Late Romanticism. The program of the New Mythology is expressed concisely in the so-called *Oldest Systematic Programme of German Idealism* (1796/7), in which poetry is declared to be the teacher of mankind and a "mythology of reason" is proclaimed as the new religion. Other key stages in the development of the New Mythology are Friedrich Schlegel's *Discourse on Mythology* and Schelling's program for a mythological view of nature.

The concept of the New Mythology is determined primarily by a combination of the ideas of the French Revolution and classical German philosophy. Even in his later years, when he had long since become disillusioned, Hegel still enthusiastically pointed to the connection between the French Revolution and idealist philosophy. It had been a wonderful sunrise and a sublime movement, with an enthusiasm that prevailed as if a true reconciliation of the divine and the world had just now come into being.[17] In the philosophy of Kant, Fichte, and Schelling the Revolution found its conceptual expression. Thus the French and German people together formed this great epoch in their own ways.[18]

This combination of the French Revolution and idealist philosophy found its most impressive reflection in the *Systematic Programme*, a document whose author is still unknown. It is certain that Hölderlin, Schelling, and Hegel took part in its writing. The program begins with a combination of the theories of Spinozistic monism and monistic idealism, theories that reject metaphysical presuppositions of a God-given order. The complete idealist system does not leave an ultimate distinction between theoretical and practical philosophy. The world is understood as constituted by a free and self-conscious moral being. This world is the only conceivable *creatio ex nihilo*. Therefore, all of metaphysics is subsumed under ethics. This tendency can be observed already in Kant, but he follows it through only half-heartedly. A free and self-conscious being does not have to search for immortality and absolute reality in a transcendent realm. Morality has its justification in itself and does not require any reinforcement or reward. The moral world is not opposed to an independent world. Rather, nature itself makes a moral world possible. But nature defined in such a way cannot be understood by means of mechanistic natural sciences proceeding from experiment to experiment. Only a "speculative physics" that contains the basic concepts of teleology and of organism can approach nature in an appropriate, non-reductionist fashion.

The concepts of teleology and organism determine the *Systematic Programme*'s critical attitude toward state and society. Present and past models of society are criticized because the state controls persons like a machine. A state like this needs to be replaced by a community in which every person contributes freedom as a constitutive element. In their vision of the state as an organism in which each individual's freedom converges in the freedom of all, the authors of the *Systematic Programme* are influenced by Shaftesbury and Rousseau. From the perspective of an organic state, perpetual peace is a derivative concept, just as constitution, government, and legislation are derivative. The fields of theoretical and practical philosophy achieve unity in the idea of beauty. The idea of beauty has a role like Plato's idea of justice, which organizes the ideal state. In the concept of beauty, truth and benevolence are unified, so that an aesthetic judgment is the highest act of reason. This interdependence binds philosophy to poetry. The moral unity of law and ends is elevated to the higher dignity of a cultural utopia. Philosophy and poetry can unfold their cultural impact only in the framework of a New Mythology that possesses the unifying force of a folk-religion without losing the dignity of reason. The New Mythology is a mythology of reason that combines the monotheism of reason with the polytheism of imagination. Following Rousseau and Herder, the authors of the *Systematic Programme* hope for the overcoming of social divisions, a process that has already been begun by the Enlightenment:

> Until we make ideas aesthetic, i.e., mythological, they will have no interest for the people. Conversely, until mythology is rational, the philosopher must be ashamed of it. Hence the enlightened and unenlightened must shake hands in the end: mythology must become philosophical in order to make people rational, and philosophy must become mythological in order to make philosophers sensuous.[19]

The New Mythology does not strive for a return to outdated social conditions. In this respect it follows the concepts of Rousseau's social contract and Schiller's aesthetic state. At the height of the French Revolution, Rousseau's students summarized this program in front of the national convention in the following way: Nothing is to be left untried in order to fulfill nature's wishes, to reach the destination of humanity, and to fulfill the promises of philosophy so as to relieve providence from the long reign of vice and tyranny.

In his *Discourse on Mythology* Schlegel followed the general perspectives of the New Mythology. Although there is no evidence that he had knowledge of the *Systematic Programme*, some of his phrasing seems to refer directly to it. However, Schlegel's concept of universal poetry contains noticeably different accents. Universal poetry is envisioned as a project for poeticizing life and society, and it is to operate from the innermost depth of the spirit by means of a symbolic language. The phrase "operating from the inside" summarizes his theory of the expressiveness of the life form (*Lebensform*) of humanity. The romantics adopted this theory from Herder. According to this thesis, the life form of humanity finds expression in its own characteristic language. The New Mythology has to be formed out of the deepest depths of the spirit; it has to be the most artistic of all artworks. The new expression of the life form of humanity in the shape of the New Mythology is to counteract the fragmentation of the social world, which reaches even into poetry. For Schlegel, the cultural project of the New Mythology is future-oriented, not the reiteration of an old superstition. The New Mythology aims to regain a "center of life" that lies not in the past but in the future. In its approach the New Mythology is not reactionary. It is a program in the literal sense. The mythologies of antiquity may have fulfilled the same function in the past, but for the demands of a new age they can be used only indirectly. Their ethical and aesthetic ideas can support the process of being educated in a New Mythology. The New Mythology, however, represents not a repetition of history, but a coming age.

Schlegel acknowledged the crucial contributions that philosophical idealism makes to universal poetry. Idealism in theoretical and practical philosophy is just as much a manifestation of the new historical age as are its political revolutions. Like the *Systematic Programme*, Schlegel's *Discourse on Mythology* includes nature in its reflections and emphasizes the idea of a speculative physics. From the perspective of the philosophy of nature, in which he was strongly influenced by Schelling, Schlegel viewed the situation of physics positively. According to him, physics is learning to decipher the secrets of nature from the paradoxes of dynamics. What is still lacking is a "mythological view of nature." He sees this view as the great turning point in the philosophy of nature of his age. Like the *Systematic Programme*, Schlegel's epistemological and ontological program is modeled on Spinoza. It adopts Spinoza's monistic integration of the imagination. Its basis is fundamentally independent of the individual subject. At the same time it involves a capacity that enables humanity to realize the finite elements within infinity. The New Mythology's objectivity derives from human culture, which is not simply arbitrary or conventional but reflects human nature:

> Mythology is such an artwork of nature. In its texture the highest is formed truly, everything is in connection and transformation, formed and transformed, and this forming and transforming is precisely its characteristic procedure, its inner life, its method, if I may say so.[20]

The true culture of human life can dispose over quasi-divine power. But man first must become conscious of this power.

A new accent in the philosophical program of the New Mythology is set by Novalis. As a contribution to the problem of the relationship of the conditioned and the unconditioned, he develops the term "romanticizing."

> The world must be romanticized. Then one will again find the original sense. Romanticizing is nothing more than a qualitative involution. In this operation the lower self is identified with a better self. In this manner we are a qualitative series of powers. This operation is still completely unknown. When I give the common-place a higher meaning, the customary a mysterious appearance, the known the dignity of the unknown, the finite the illusion of the infinite, I romanticize it. The operation is the converse for the higher, unknown, mystical and infinite; through this connection it becomes logarithimized. It receives a customary expression. Romantic philosophy. *Lingua romana*. Reciprocal elevation and debasement.[21]

Novalis's definition of romanticizing is an outcome of Kant's Copernican Revolution and Fichte's *Science of Knowledge*. The subject's activities, and in particular its productive imagination, express the whole of the subject's infinity, which encompasses both itself and the seemingly independent world.[22] In the light of these theories, the imagination's role cannot be reduced to a merely aesthetic function. Rather, it fulfills functions in the philosophy of language, epistemology, and cultural philosophy. In a refinement of the originally Kantian idea that imagination is both productive and receptive, the imagination is conceived here as a constitutive element of the productive acquisition of the world. The imagination constructs and reconstrues, imagines and finds.[23]

In addition to the systematic significance of the term New Mythology, its interconnections with the sphere of art are obvious. Caspar David Friedrich's paintings are characteristic examples of the romantic interpretation of human transience within nature. They often present human beings turned toward a seemingly limitless landscape in which symbols of transience are depicted. For Hölderlin and Novalis, the systematic goals of the New Mythology are connected with poetic means of expression. Hölderlin in particular remains closely connected to the images of Greek mythology. In the poem "Bread and Wine" he speaks of the "poet in a needy time" who has to fulfill a cultural mission within "great nature." The poem constructs a narrative that combines a person's stages of life and humanity's development from antiquity to Christianity. In his novel *Heinrich von Ofterdingen* Novalis composes an independent form of mythology that centers on the mysterious ideal of the blue flower.[24] Both Hölderlin and Novalis seek correspondences with Greek and medieval mythologies. Their program is to gain territory for a New Mythology of the future by expanding the perspectives of imagination into the past.

Throughout his philosophical development, Schelling was concerned with the philosophy of mythology. One of his first works was *On Myths, Historical Sayings and the Philosophy of the Ancient World*, and in the last stages of his work he conceived a philosophy of mythology. It is certain that he contributed to the *Systematic Programme*.[25] For Schelling, the purpose of mythology is to express the universal presence of infinity.[26] The distinctive feature of his New Mythology is its close connection to a systematic philosophy of nature. Even after 1800, at the end of his work on the philosophy of identity and at the beginning of his later philosophy, he often spoke of wanting to express "all philosophy of nature in symbols of mythology."[27] According to Schelling, seeing nature in terms of mythology is the first step toward the creation of a true mythology, a mythology relevant to modernity.

In the context of the New Mythology, art represents a special dimension of objectivity. The object of art is not raw nature, but something organic. A general system of symbols is the organizing principle of art and imbues its object with a soul. Schelling gives certain poorly crafted statues in the Arabian deserts as examples of failed art. Of these it is said that they will cost the souls of their creators on judgment day. True art is nothing but "the repetition of the first symbolism of god in nature."[28] Objects of art exist and have a meaning, just like the objects of nature. Their shapes have the same timeless reality as the shapes of plants and people. Therefore, the symbolism that expresses itself in mythology comes from nature and returns to it. Mythological creations can be developed only in relation to nature. Like all the other conceptions of the New Mythology, Schelling's approach has high expectations for a radical cultural transformation of society. Even though the theoretical framework has changed noticeably, the expectations are the same as in the *Systematic Programme*. The New Mythology points to a higher state of culture in which individuals and humanity as a whole become one again. The decline of public freedom in the slavery of private life is lamented. According to Schelling, the deterioration of public life into the "indifferent sphere" of "the individuality and dullness of private life"[29] can be replaced only by the totality of a nation that acts like an organism or a person. The nation stands for the political unity of a people, and it alone makes true public life possible. The objectivity of science, art, and religion is dependent on this unity. Schelling's philosophical interest in an independent foundation in "being" itself is also a revealing sign of his move to Late Romanticism. The ideal foundation in being replaces the constitutive role of imagination, which had dominated the system of philosophical romanticism for close to a decade.

Basic outlines of the New Mythology

Mythologies are shared representations of a community or society. They are expressed in the determining factors of human culture: language, religion, art, politics. They are the immediate expression of the lived and experienced reality of a culture. Regardless of their varying mythic, polytheistic, or theistic manifestations, they are similar in that they provide historical meaning and give value to human life. In this notion the romantic concept of the New Mythology has stood the test of time and philosophical romanticism remains part of the general language of modern culture. Its roots are in early theories that followed Rousseau and strongly criticized the Enlightenment's one-sidedness, and it led to a development that resulted in the Frankfurt school's criticism of instrumental reason. The Frankfurt school (especially Adorno) also rehabilitated the constitutive role that the New Mythology assigns to art – a trait that gets lost in Late Romanticism.

Unfortunately, philosophical romanticism and German Idealism leave unclear the means by which a new "center of life" can be regained after the destruction of traditional value systems. The days when art in general and poetry in particular are entrusted with the role of being the teacher of humanity ended with the last decade of the eighteenth century. That period was succeeded by an era of neo-conservative political visions. Whereas the early form of New Mythology is conceived as a mythology of reason that aims not at irrationality but at the elevation of reason to a higher stage, Late Romanticism opposes reason. Irrationality in its different manifestations is a common symptom of Late Romanticism.

With the transition to Late Romanticism ethics also experienced a substantial shift. The New Mythology had been dominated by an ethical program according to which free beings carry the spiritual world within themselves and do not need to search for God and immortality outside of themselves. After 1800 there was a widespread phenomenon of ethical projects that rest on particularistic concepts of a people or a nation.

Mythology and new conservatism

Even where they pursue purely systematic or aesthetic aims, the innovations of early German Idealism and Early Romanticism always contain a series of political implications. The relation between philosophical and political romanticism was not stable, however, and new accents in one field necessarily caused changes in the other. Events in France during the last decade of the eighteenth century in particular functioned as a catalyst. Novalis brought about the first major change in the relation between political and philosophical romanticism in 1798. His work *Faith and Love, or the King and the Queen* expressly champions monarchy as the ideal state, adequately represented by the royal couple. Likewise, the essay *Christianity or Europe* is in its main parts an apology for Christian culture. It is to awaken Europe and perform a peace-making role on a global scale. Schelling reacted to this new goal with biting scorn in his *The Epicurean Confession of Heinz Widerporst*.[30]

The new conservatism of Late Romanticism relies in part on models of thought from Early Romanticism and early German Idealism. Nonetheless, its political reactionism was not inevitable. It developed out of the New Mythology for contingent reasons. The neo-conservative position of political romanticism has its main representatives in Friedrich Schlegel, Joseph Görres, Franz von Baader, and Adam Müller. The relationship between individual and community lies at the center of the romantic movement in general and political romanticism in particular. Both German Idealism and political romanticism at all stages rejected an understanding of community according to which a culture is the mere sum of its individuals. The principle of the unity of individual and community was developed already in the *Systematic Programme*. Novalis retained this core idea of the New Mythology. His *Faith and Love* stresses the individual's experience of community. Similar passages can be found in *Christianity or Europe* and in the work of Görres and Friedrich Schlegel. The romantics were convinced that man cannot exist outside community: "To become and remain human, man needs the state. Without a state, man is a savage. All culture results from the relationship between man and state."[31] Political conceptions of the unity of individual and community can also be found in the thought of Adam Müller and Friedrich Gentz. This conception intends a strong integration of persons into the community. In addition, the state itself is understood as a person. Friedrich Schlegel stresses that every state is an individual existing with its own specific character, and that it governs itself according to specific laws, customs, and practices.

Late Romanticism defines the relation between person and community in a way that differs from the program of early German Idealism and the early romantics. This turn becomes apparent in the rejection of the cosmopolitanism that was at the core of the ideology of the young Jacobins. To the extent that the specific character of a cultural community is emphasized, the concept of cosmopolitanism recedes. The relationship between person and community is no longer seen as symmetrical but as derivative. When Schelling said that a state is perfect when "every member in being a means for the whole is an end to itself,"[32] he had in mind Rousseau as well as the natural concept of an organism. In Late Romanticism there is a strong tendency to set aside the aesthetic individualism and cosmopolitanism of early German Idealism and Early Romanticism for an emphasis on the constitutive functions of a cultural community. Nonetheless, the relation of political romanticism and the New Mythology is more complicated than some of the political credos of some conservative romantics may suggest. The community in which Late Romanticism in particular sets its hopes is not something that already exists or has existed in the past but something that still needs to be created.[33]

Novalis saw the cultural function of poetry as analogous to religion. He, too, holds the established discursive means of knowledge to be unsuitable[34] for assuring epistemic, ethical, and aesthetic transcendence: "We seek everywhere the unconditioned, and always find only the conditioned."[35] Although Novalis demanded that personal and cultural life should be determined by art, his attempt to create by means of poetry a new unity of nature, religion, and history introduced a neo-conservative conception of political romanticism. Novalis accused the politics of his time of being half-hearted and remaining in a condition of "half-state–half-nature." The perfect state is the poetic state, which removes the opposition between the arbitrariness of nature and the compulsion of art. Such a state acts as an autonomous entity, a *macroanthropos*, and has to be visible as such for everyone. Therefore, he complained that contemporary states were not visible enough.[36] In *Faith and Love* Novalis pointed to the monarchy as the appropriate realization of a poetic state: "The king is the pure life principle of the state, just like the sun in the planetary system."[37] Novalis's support of the monarchy, however, was not unconditional. Following Early Romanticism's criticism of the state, he was strongly critical of Frederick the Great's "Prussian state machinery." He viewed the French Revolution as a passing phase in human history, and in contrast to Burke and his conservative followers, he saw the demise of the feudal state as justified. Novalis's interest in the monarchy lay in the role he assigned to the royal couple as moral models. Novalis presented a poetic outline of the history of Europe from the perspective of an ideal model of the Christian Middle Ages. This outline is determined by the conviction that the Enlightenment cannot do justice to our emotional and religious needs. Although Novalis regarded the Christian Middle Ages as a cultural ideal, he did not expect a simple return to a society under the leadership of Catholicism. His expectations were directed toward a future Christianity that is socially alive and culturally effective. In this context he envisioned a visible church which transcends national boundaries. Novalis transformed the secular New Mythology of Early Romanticism and early German Idealism into a concrete cultural ideal. The holy period of perpetual peace is to have the New Jerusalem as the world's capital.[38]

The ethical and cultural enthusiasm of the early stages of philosophical romanticism and German Idealism vanishes after 1800 and is replaced by a program of moral and religious education. This program is clearly visible in Friedrich Schlegel's *Philosophical Lectures* (1804/6), which support an education in public morality that is to be implemented by the state. Politics should perform educational tasks for cultural reasons. The church serves as a model for this politics. In *The Signature of the Age* (1820/3), Schlegel emphasized this connection. The nature of a healthy state is characterized by an inner peace that can be guaranteed only by the church. He regarded the old German Christian empire before the nation's religious division as the greatest and organically richest political system that had ever existed.[39]

The political idealization of the Christian Middle Ages can also be found in Adam Müller's *Elements of Political Theory* (1809) – the paradigm for the political theory of Late Romanticism. Like Friedrich Schlegel and Franz von Baader (a central figure in the Munich circle), Adam Müller was convinced that the state is an organism that can exist only on the foundation of religion. He revered the past as God-given and condemned all interventions against traditional political structures as the destruction of an organic process. This neo-conservative reinterpretation of the concept of organism is characteristic of Late Romanticism. The values and ideals of political romanticism in its late stages were conceived from a highly traditional perspective. It should not be overlooked, however, that this retrospective view was still directed forward. This direction marks the difference between new conservatism and merely reactionary politics. Where the politics of Late Romanticism follows revisionary goals it can be described as a revolutionary conservatism.

The results of philosophical romanticism

Philosophical romanticism is an attempt to mold reality through the medium of philosophy and art. Its creative formation of reality fulfills a unifying function that transcends the apparent contradictions of the so-called real world. Romanticism can also take on the form of a cultural and political theory. The methodological approach of political romanticism is either revisionary or revolutionary. Both revision and revolution can proceed in an egalitarian and modernist or a traditional and pre-modernist fashion. Accordingly, among the romantics there were supporters both of the republic and of the monarchy. Romantic pre-modernism should not be mistaken for reactionary politics in every case, because its political strategies often aim at an innovative cultural project.

Philosophical romanticism's methodological approach is holistic and is therefore committed to criticism of the Enlightenment. It strives for a unification of practical and theoretical philosophy. In this context the central systematic term is that of the imagination. Philosophical romanticism refers to an all-encompassing cosmos in order to explain the complicated relations that obtain between person and community as well as between nature and culture. Therefore philosophical romanticism has to be both individualistic and universalistic. It approaches the difficult task of connecting these opposites with a monistic holism that contains individualistic sub-differentiations. Because of these complicated interconnections every individual expresses and signifies the whole.

In epistemology, philosophical romanticism proposes a conception that integrates internalism and externalism. Its internalism results from the systematic implications of the terms imagination and expression. Its externalism follows from the great importance ascribed to a holistic concept of nature. An important epistemological contribution of its version of internalism lies in its rejection of any form of simplistic representationalism. The overemphasis on internalism found in subjective idealism is avoided by the romantic use of the concept of nature as a corrective.

The concept of nature is central to the romantic contextualization of reason. This role becomes very apparent within the framework of Schelling's naturalistic history of self-consciousness. The contextualization of reason also extends to the political philosophy of romanticism. It is a basic conviction of political romanticism that abstract reason, reason conceived outside the social sphere, remains empty and therefore without any reference to real people. Because the content and the options for a personal life-plan depend on the cultural conditions of one's social sphere, reason has to be positioned within a community. Only there can it develop its reflective, evaluative, and normative powers. Here philosophical romanticism draws heavily on Rousseau, Herder, Schiller, and Wilhelm von Humboldt, who made an effort to balance the concepts of individuality and community. It subscribes to a concept of humanism that integrates reason and emotions, universality and individuality, and cosmopolitanism and nationalism. The expansion of individual self-determination to political and cultural self-determination, combined with the ethical and cultural revision of given social realities, is also an important part of this humanism, which grows weaker in Late Romanticism but does not vanish altogether. Characteristic of romanticism's cosmopolitan humanism is the criticism of both irrationality and abstract reason, and of relativism and abstract universalism. In Late Romanticism, the concept of community becomes more and more narrow. After cosmopolitan beginnings it is now restricted to the limits of nations. In this conservative outlook communitarians draw on several developments of Late Romanticism.[40] A further similarity is a fundamental revision of the essentially liberal trend in modern ethics and politics. Above all, communitarians discard the liberal separation of individual self-determination and cultural self-determination. They are convinced that a person's self-determination over time can be founded only in strong ties to a communal ethics, and that no society can remain intact over longer periods if its values are not literally kept alive by its members.

Epilogue: the completion of German Idealism in Schelling's late philosophy

Schelling's late philosophy is the only major philosophical development[41] to come out of romanticism after 1800. In the course of his philosophy, Schelling constructs a complicated model of the relation between nature and culture. He ascribes a high importance to the concept of mythology within his philosophical system. The individual's role is determined by its place in history and its relation to an all-encompassing nature. The fundamental role of mythology is explained in far-reaching interpretations of the past, present, and future place of humanity within nature. Schelling sees the first step toward a true mythology in the rebirth of a symbolic view of nature.

According to Schelling, the transition from transcendental philosophy to a philosophy of nature is not made by merely positing something externally opposed to self-consciousness. It is the general mistake of idealism – including Hegel's objective idealism – that it is not interested in the specific nature of that to which self-conscious reflection refers. Schelling objects to Fichte that the mere fact that an outside world exists for me does not mean that it exists only for me or only through me. According to Schelling, the immanence of subjectivity that appears impenetrable to Fichte rests on a fallacy. Idealism by no means excludes naturalistic realism.[42] Schelling obtains a crucial stimulus for his revision of idealism from Kant's third *Critique*. Kant speaks cautiously of a justified expectation that we may ascribe teleological structures to nature in general. According to Schelling we have to go further: nature cannot accidentally coincide with human principles of knowledge. Rather, knowledge about nature becomes possible only *because* it is an organism and functions according to the same basic principles as we do. Nature is understood as an organic whole of mind and matter that unfolds in complicated stages. Schelling assumes that understanding nature in this way prevents the opposition between mechanism and organism that caused so many problems for the idealistic post-Kantians, because on his view the inner structure of reality is determined by a principle that constitutes both organic and inorganic nature. Given the structural parallel between nature and mind, the dualism of what is given and what is produced can be overcome. This unity allows us to understand the position of subjectivity in nature as the beginning of a series of extensions of self-consciousness into nature. According to Schelling's naturalistic history of self-consciousness, subjectivity is not only grounded in nature but is also its expression. He describes this connection throughout his philosophy with the Platonic metaphor of a connecting tie or bond (*Band*). Because of the "secret tie" that holds opposites together, nature can be understood as visible mind and mind as invisible nature.

Schelling's *Treatise on Human Freedom* (1809)[43] breaks with philosophical idealism and takes on a direction that avoids the extremes of an abstract conception of human freedom on the one hand, and a dissolution of freedom in cultural or naturalistic reductionism on the other hand. In contrast to theories of liberty that orient themselves on formal or negative definitions, Schelling searches for a realistic and viable concept of liberty, which for him must value a capacity for both good and evil. Schelling defines evil as the manifestation of the selfhood (*Selbstheit*) of human existence, a process whereby an individual person's freedom acquires an ontological status. Schelling speaks of selfhood as a will that recognizes itself in complete freedom, one that is not merely a tool of a universal will operating in nature but is something that is above and apart from all nature. With this voluntaristic thesis Schelling leaves behind the theoretical framework of philosophical romanticism and the mainstream of German Idealism. The discovery of the groundlessness of human freedom leads Schelling to a dramatic turn in the theory of the self and subjectivity: he rejects the notion that the self is the key to self-understanding. In self-consciousness an individual person gets caught up in egocentric circles that are mistakenly regarded as expressions of one's true self. Schelling's philosophy rejects egocentric arrogance and demands a step outside oneself. What is remarkable in Schelling's expositions on the contextuality and irreducibility of human subjectivity is the boldness with which he takes on two extreme positions at the same time. Because of the deeply rooted contextuality of life, individuals can never control the conditions of existence, but their freedom drives human beings to try to do so over and over again. According to Schelling, subjectivity can find itself only in what is not itself. The tragedy of subjectivity lies in the fact that it has to lose its individuality in order to find itself.

The basic problem of Schelling's philosophy, the relation between the conditioned and the absolute, remains virulent in his late works: the absolute can be transformed into the conditioned without reason, but the conditioned cannot know the absolute. However, this does not lead to a resigned return to a simple dualism. Reason does not posit something totally opposite to it; instead, it sets its own "absolute" – something that was originally defined as an independent cause (for instance, in traditional rational theology). Kant had shown the limits of reason, but Schelling shows that reason has to limit itself. It cannot accept a limitation entirely from the outside if it is to retain the ability to complete its own potential for reflection and reasoning. The setting of a foundation outside of itself as an absolute foundation is a sign of its own perfection. Thus, the limit of reason lies neither in any deficiency nor in any imperfection of reason. As reason it can have a foundation only in something that is in one sense outside of itself. Schelling developed his theory of self-limitation within a conception of negative and positive philosophy that he saw as a conclusive reply to Hegel. He accused Hegel of not having recognized the fundamental difference between necessities of reason and necessities of existence. Negative philosophy, which includes

Hegel's logic, is concerned merely with forms and structures of existence. However, the fact *that* something exists cannot be explained in this way. In reflections on the groundlessness of reason, the traces of subjectivity become unrecognizable. This sets Schelling apart from Hegel, who held on to the *form* of subjectivity in every aspect of his work. In the end, the unsolvable mystery is human existence itself:

> Far from making the world, man, and his actions comprehensible, he is himself what is most incomprehensible, and this continually drives me to the opinion of the unhappiness of all being, a conviction which has been voiced in so many pained expressions in past and present. It is precisely man who drives me to the last despairing question: Why is there anything at all? Why is there not nothing?[44]

Schelling has come a long way – from a mythology of reason and the conception of an absolutely free and self-conscious being created from nothing, to an acknowledgment of the mystery of all being. This acknowledgment became inescapable for him in the end because the concept of nothingness, which early idealism had transformed too quickly into a concept of something produced by subjectivity, became the center of his philosophy. In this end point, Late Romanticism culminates in Schelling's anticipation of existentialism and other later non-idealist movements in philosophy.

NOTES

1 The *Athenaeums Fragmente* first appeared in the *Athenaeum. Eine Zeitschrift von August Wilhelm Schlegel und Friedrich Schlegel*, vol. 1, Zweites Stück in June 1798 (reprinted Darmstadt: Wissenschaftliche Buchgesellschaft, 1983).
2 Johann Gottfried Herder, *Sämmtliche Werke*, ed. Bernhard Suphan, I (Berlin: Wiedmann, 1877–1913), 426–49. See Manfred Frank, *Der kommende Gott. Vorlesungen über die Neue Mythologie* (Frankfurt: Suhrkamp, 1982), 123–51.
3 Herder, *Sämmtliche Werke*, XVIII, 483–502.
4 See Friedrich Schiller, *Werke*, Nationalausgabe, ed. Benno von Wiese, XX (Weimar: Böhlau, 1962), 309–412.
5 "Zum ewigen Frieden. Ein philosophischer Entwurf von Immanuel Kant," (1795) in *Kant's gesammelte Schriften*, ed. Königlich Preußische Akademie der Wissenschaften, VIII (Berlin: W. de Gruyter, 1912), 341–86.
6 "Versuch über den Begriff des Republikanismus. Veranlaßt durch die Kantische Schrift zum ewigen Frieden" (1795) in *Kritische Friedrich-Schlegel-Ausgabe*, ed. Ernst Behler, VII (Paderborn: Schöningh, 1968), 11–25.
7 "Der allgemeine Frieden, ein Ideal" (1795) in Joseph Görres, *Gesammelte Schriften*, ed. Wilhelm Schellberg and Adolf Dyroff, I (Cologne: Gilde, 1928), 11–68.
8 "Zum ewigen Frieden. Eine Irokesische Anstalt/Sieben Gesinnungen der großen Friedensfrau [118./119. Brief zu Beförderung der Humanität]," (1797) in Herder, *Sämmtliche Werke*, XVIII, 267–74.
9 "Die Christenheit oder Europa" (1799) in Novalis, *Werke*, ed. Hans-Joachim Mähl, II (Munich/Vienna: Hanser, 1978), 731–50.

10 "Über den ewigen Frieden" (1800) in Friedrich Gentz, *Gesammelte Schriften*, ed. Günther Kronenbitte, V (Hildesheim: Olms, 1999), 603–82.

11 See Kant's "Über die Mißhelligkeit zwischen der Moral und der Politik in Absicht auf den ewigen Frieden," in *Kant's gesämmelte Schriften* VIII, 1.

12 See Kant, "Zum ewigen Frieden," in *Kant's gesämmelte Schriften* VIII, 380.

13 See Johann Gottlieb Fichte, *J. G. Fichte-Gesamtausgabe der Bayerischen Akademie der Wissenschaften*, ed. Reinhard Lauth, Hans Jacob and Hans Gliwitzky, III (Stuttgart-Bad Cannstatt: Frommann-Holzboog, 1966), 217–28.

14 See Fichte, *Gesamtausgabe* I, 193–404.

15 See Fichte, *Gesamtausgabe*, I, 384.

16 See Görres, "Der allgemeine Frieden, ein Ideal," *Gesammelte Schriften* I, 23.

17 See Georg Wilhelm Friedrich Hegel, *Werke in zwanzig Bänden*, ed. Eva Moldenhauer and Karl Marcus Michel, XII (Frankfurt am Main: Suhrkamp, 1971), 314.

18 See Hegel, *Werke in zwanzig Bänden*, ed. Eva Moldenhauer and Karl Marcus Michel, XX (Frankfurt am Main: Suhrkamp, 1971), 314.

19 See Christoph Jamme and Helmut Schneider, eds., *Mythologie der Vernunft. Hegels 'ältestes Systemprogramm' des deutschen Idealismus* (Frankfurt: Suhrkamp, 1984). An English translation of the "Oldest Systematic Programme," along with works by Novalis and Schlegel, appears in Frederick Beiser, ed., *The Early Political Writings of the German Romantics* (Cambridge: Cambridge University Press, 1996). Translations in this chapter are by the editor, with page references also given to Beiser where relevant.

20 *Kritische Friedrich-Schlegel-Ausgabe*, ed. Ernst Behler, II (Paderborn: Schöningh, 1967), 318.

21 See Novalis, *Werke*, II, 334; Beiser, *Early Political Writings*, 85.

22 This idea finds its exemplary form in Schelling's philosophy of nature, which is determined by the identity in essence of spirit and nature; see below.

23 See Charles Larmore, *The Romantic Legacy* (New York: Columbia University Press, 1996), 11–30.

24 See Novalis, *Werke*, I, 237–413.

25 A note in the *System des transzendentalen Idealismus* seems to refer to the new mythology of the *Systematic Programme*. See *Friedrich Wilhelm Joseph von Schellings sämmtliche Werke*, ed. Karl Friedrich August Schelling, III (Stuttgart and Augsburg: Cotta, 1856–61), 629.

26 See Schelling, *Sämmtliche Werke*, V, 413.

27 Schelling, *Sämmtliche Werke*, V, 446.

28 Schelling, *Sämmtliche Werke*, VI, 571.

29 Schelling, *Sämmtliche Werke*, VI, 572.

30 See F. W. J. Schelling, *Briefe und Dokumente*, ed. Horst Fuhrmans, II (Bonn: Bouvier, 1973), 205–14.

31 See Novalis, *Werke*, II, 548.

32 Schelling, *Sämmtliche Werke*, V, 232.

33 See Larmore, *Romantic Legacy*, 61.

34 See "Fragmente und Studien I" (1799/1800) in Novalis, *Werke*, II, 767: "Perhaps the highest task of logic is to destroy the principle of contradiction."

35 See "Blüthenstaub/Vermischte Bemerkungen" (1797/8) in Novalis, *Werke*, II, 227/226; Beiser, *Early Political Writings*, 9.

36 See "Glauben und Liebe" (1798) in Novalis, *Werke*, II, 295; Beiser, *Early Political Writings*, 40.

37 See Novalis, *Werke*, II, 293; Beiser, *Early Political Writings*, 39.

38 See Novalis, *Werke*, II, 750.

39 See *Kritische Friedrich-Schlegel-Ausgabe*, ed. Ernst Behler, VII (Paderborn: Schöningh, 1966), 552.

40 See Charles Larmore, *Patterns of Moral Complexity* (Cambridge: Cambridge University Press, 1987).

41 Walter Schulz takes Schelling's late philosophy to be the completion of German Idealism. See Walter Schulz, *Die Vollendung des Deutschen Idealismus in der Spätphilosophie Schellings*, 2nd edn. (Pfullingen: Neske, 1975).

42 See Dieter Sturma, "The Nature of Subjectivity. Schelling's Philosophy of Nature and the Mystery of Its Origins," in Sally Sedgwick, ed., *The Idea of a System of Transcendental Idealism in Kant, Fichte, Schelling and Hegel* (Cambridge: Cambridge University Press, 2000).

43 See Otfried Höffe and Annemarie Pieper, eds., F. W. J. *Schelling: Über das Wesen der menschlichen Freiheit* (Berlin: Akademie, 1995).

44 Schelling, *Sämmtliche Werke*, XIII, 7.

12

ANDREW BOWIE

German Idealism and the arts

I Truth, art, and philosophy

The complexity of the relationship between German Idealism and the arts becomes apparent if one considers the following contentions from two of its most famous texts. Hegel announced in his *Lectures on Aesthetics*, given in the 1820s, that "[t]he *science* of art is . . . in our time much more necessary than at times in which art for itself as art provided complete satisfaction."[1] In his 1800 *System of Transcendental Idealism* Schelling claimed, in contrast, that art is "the only true and eternal organ and document of philosophy, which always and continuously documents what philosophy cannot represent externally."[2] Some of the most important debates in modern philosophy, whose significance extends not only beyond their initial appearance in German Idealism but also beyond the narrowly conceived sphere of aesthetics, took place in the space between these positions.[3] Why, then, did these opposed positions develop, and why do the reasons for their development make this such a vital issue in modern philosophy? Hans-Georg Gadamer offers a framework for responding to these questions when he claims, in relation to Kant and his successors:

> Only when philosophy and metaphysics got into crisis in relation to the cognitive claims of the sciences did they discover again their proximity to poetry which they had denied since Plato . . . Since then it makes sense to acknowledge the autonomous claim to truth of literature, but this takes place at the price of an unexplained relationship to the truth of scientific knowledge.[4]

The relationship in German Idealism between the "claim to truth" of literature (and other art) and scientific truth is, then, an indicator of fundamental questions in modernity. However, interpreting this relationship is anything but straightforward.

The contours of the topic of German Idealism and the arts are, for example, often outlined in a story like the following, which illustrates one common way of elaborating Gadamer's framework. Toward the end of the eighteenth century criticisms of the "dogmatic" Enlightenment belief in an inbuilt rational structure of the world on the part of David Hume, J. G. Herder, the Kant of the *Critique of Pure Reason*, and others combine with Alexander Baumgarten's revaluation of sensuous perception in his *Aesthetica* (1750, 1758) and Kant's attempt to complete his critical philosophy by reflections on art in the *Critique of Judgment* (1790) to suggest the need for new ways of mapping the relationship between subjectivity and the world of objects. The aim is to take account of the active role of the mind in the genesis of knowledge and in ethical self-legislation, and this gives a new significance to aesthetic production and experience. In the wake of his reading of Kant's and Fichte's accounts of the ineliminable philosophical role for human freedom, Friedrich Schiller appeals in his *Letters on the Aesthetic Education of Man* (1795) to sensuous ways of communicating the idea of freedom to the broader public through works of art, thus making explicit the sociopolitical dimension of the new subject of aesthetics. Schiller's ideas are taken up both in aspects of Early Romanticism and in the "Oldest System Programme of German Idealism" (probably written by either Hegel or Schelling in 1796). This text talks of "the highest act of reason, which embraces all Ideas" as "an aesthetic act" because it synthesizes understanding and reason, and links the sensuous objective material of the work to the super-sensuous "idea" of freedom – something which cannot itself appear but is symbolized by the work and can thus be communicated within society. Schelling develops related notions in the *System of Transcendental Idealism* and in aspects of his *Philosophy of Art* (1802–3) before ceasing to regard art as fundamental to his philosophical project. After his early enthusiasm for the idea of an aesthetic reconciliation of divisions between subjectivity and objects in the world, Hegel too becomes more circumspect about the philosophical significance of art in his *Aesthetics*. During the decline of German Idealism after the death of Hegel, idealist aesthetics is overtaken by positions, like those of Schopenhauer and Nietzsche, which, although influenced by idealism, reject central tenets of idealist thought.

This story is not necessarily historically or philosophically misleading, but it does little to convey the enduring significance of the issues involved. The problem is that the story presupposes the nature of the divide that it should itself be used to interrogate, by assuming that there is something called philosophy that rediscovers its relationship to something called art. Given that the crucial aspect of the story itself is, as Gadamer indicates, the *relationship* between competing claims to truth, one cannot presuppose that the nature of the division between philosophy and art can be truly defined by philosophy. The core issue of the philosophy of the period of German Idealism is whether foundations can be established that will replace the metaphysics discredited by Kant, and this means that the relationship of philosophical accounts of truth to the truth of both science and art is itself also being renegotiated. It is, moreover, no coincidence that the very concept of "art" in one of its most widely used modern senses is also largely a product of this period, resulting from the liberation of at least some forms of creative production from employment in the service of theology and from predominantly instrumental social functions. This liberation is expressed in terms of the imagination's ability to transcend the existing rules of the particular medium and thus produce artifacts that can be understood and appreciated only by going beyond such rules. Instead of being conceived of principally in terms of mimesis, representation, or entertainment, art begins to be conceived of in terms of its ability to reveal the world in ways that may not be possible without art.

Such new conceptions of art are vitally connected to the simultaneous emergence of the idea, in the work of Hamann, Herder, Humboldt, and Schleiermacher, that language itself is, as Charles Taylor has put it, "constitutive" or "expressive" of the world's intelligibility, rather than solely a re-presentation of what is already there.[5] In consequence, art's very status as art has to do with processes of secularization which, while undermining the idea of the divine origin of language and making possible new conceptions of language, also lead philosophers like Kant to their questioning of the "dogmatic" Enlightenment idea that science and philosophy can be known to represent the truth of a "ready-made world." By merely presupposing an answer to what philosophy is in relation to art, one cannot, then, come to terms with the import of the early Schelling's idea (which he developed while in contact with the early romantic thinkers Friedrich Schlegel and Novalis in Jena) that art does something *philosophically* essential that philosophy itself cannot do. Schelling's idea may be hyperbolic, but a crucial change in the reception and production of art toward the end of the eighteenth century and in the early decades of the nineteenth century can help to explain why it touched on something significant.

II Music and "feeling"

During this period music without words changed for many thinkers in Europe from being a subordinate form of art to being the highest form of art. This change was accompanied by the composition, by Haydn, Mozart, Beethoven, and Schubert, of arguably the greatest music ever written.[6] Both phenomena have to do precisely with the reasons for the widespread questioning, in philosophy and elsewhere, of the idea of thought as exclusively a representation of what is already there in the world. Wordless music is most resistant to being understood in representational terms, and this is why the new ways of understanding music can be seen as an indication of a broader conceptual transformation. Friedrich Schlegel, the most original thinker in Early Romanticism, whose influence on Hegel has still to be adequately evaluated,[7] encapsulated what is involved in this shift when he argued against Enlightenment views of music in 1798: "One has tried for so long to apply mathematics to music and painting; now try it the other way round."[8] Elsewhere he claims that, given the failure of language to comprehend "feeling," which is the "root of all consciousness," "communication and representation must be added to; and this happens through *music* which is, though, here to be regarded less as a representational art than as philosophical language, and really lies higher than mere art."[9] Schlegel's preparedness to invert the received wisdom with regard to art and philosophy illustrates why it is inappropriate to see the topic of German Idealism and the arts just from the side of philosophy. But how is one to understand his remarks?[10] Answering this question takes one to the heart of a major concern of German Idealism. The crucial term here is "feeling." What, then, is meant by the term?

A central aim of German Idealism is the overcoming of the Kantian division between appearances and things in themselves, and of other related divisions, like those between necessity and freedom, receptivity and spontaneity, on the grounds that such divisions threaten to render the intelligibility of experience incomprehensible. In the *Critique of Pure Reason* Kant argues that all experiences depended on an I that was "able to accompany" them. However, he left in the dark the nature of the philosopher's access to this I, which links moments of receptivity and spontaneity in the same consciousness across time. In one of the fundamental texts in the genesis of German Idealism, *On the Doctrine of Spinoza* (1789 edition), F. H. Jacobi sums up the crucial problem in his claim that "[w]e only have a feeling, even of our own existence, not a concept."[11] Concepts are rules for identifying objects and are applied under the conditions of space and time to this or that object at this or that moment. There can, though, be no rule for identifying oneself in this manner, not least because the continuity of the self is essential to the rule-based cognition of objects in the first place. This continuity seems therefore to entail an "immediate" awareness that is not reducible to fallible rule-governed knowledge communicable in general terms. In the light of his familiarity with such ideas Schleiermacher was later to characterize feeling, which he uses interchangeably with the term "immediate self-consciousness," in terms of the idea that "as thinkers we are only in the single act [of thought]; but as beings we are the unity of all single acts and moments."[12] You may know what I know, because knowledge relies on the application of shareable rules, but you cannot have access to my "feeling" as such, which transcends any particular cognition (including, of course, my own). The idea therefore emerges that any attempt to communicate the self's feeling that makes its experience coherent must employ non-conceptual means. Significantly, Kant himself had already moved in the direction of such ideas in the *Critique of Judgment*.

Kant here directs his attention to a domain of judgment that had been ignored in the first two Critiques, namely judgments based on discriminations by the subject between the pleasurable and the non-pleasurable.[13] There is a feeling (in the more everyday sense – though this too involves the aspect of immediacy) of pleasure in aesthetic perception that derives, he maintains, from a sense of a coherence in nature that cannot be known, insofar as knowledge can result only from the application to a particular intuition of a general concept in a "determining judgment." Judgment works "according to the principle of the aptness of nature to our capacity for cognition,"[14] but we do not know how far this aptness extends because it can be confirmed only in the ongoing contingent process of scientific investigation. This process does, though, rely on the ability actively to generate new general concepts from particulars in "reflective judgment," and this resembles the structure of aesthetic pleasure, which derives from the free play of the same cognitive powers that are required for generating new concepts. The philosophical significance of the aesthetic for Kant lies in the counter-factual possibility of *universal* assent in judgments of taste, which underlies the assertion that something is beautiful, rather than merely pleasing to me. The possibility of consensus in relation to feeling points, Kant claims, to "what can be regarded as the supersensuous substrate of mankind,"[15] where nature and freedom would be linked.

It is here that Kant comes closer to the sense of "feeling" outlined above, at the same time as pointing to the ways in which German Idealism would attempt, especially in relation to art, to give philosophical access to the "supersensuous substrate." The possibility of consensus invoked by Kant hints at a unity in the "subjective purposiveness of nature for the power of judgment,"[16] which would link nature in itself to the activity of our thinking. Perhaps most importantly – and this is too rarely noticed – Kant also goes so far as to maintain that a "common sense," of the kind "required for the universal communicability of a feeling," is "the necessary condition of the universal communicability of our cognition."[17] He even uses a musical analogy to argue this, talking of the "tuning/attunement" (*Stimmung*) of the cognitive powers, which is differently "proportioned," depending on the object in question, and which "can only be determined by feeling (not by concepts)."[18] Schlegel's remark about inverting the priority of music and mathematics can therefore be seen as following from arguments like Kant's: if scientific cognition relies on mathematical concepts, and concepts can only be communicated if one postulates a shared intelligibility of the world that is prior to conceptual thinking, then what is expressed by non-conceptual music is fundamental to the possibility of philosophy.[19] It is not hard to argue, therefore, that the seemingly irrational romantic insistence on the centrality of art – particularly wordless music – for philosophy can actually draw significant support from Kant. If the results of our cognitive abilities can be communicated only on the basis of the postulated "common sense" also required for the possibility of agreements in judgments of beauty, then the most fundamental relationship of the subject to the world is at the level of immediate "feeling," rather than of what "mediated" concepts may tell us about knowledge of the world of appearance. In the light of arguments like this it is not surprising that art plays such an important role in the philosophy of the period.

III Immediacy and mediation

German idealist and early romantic conceptions of art and philosophy can be somewhat crudely divided by their responses to the non-conceptual "immediacy" inherent in the notion of feeling.[20] As we shall see, this is essentially a division over the limits and nature of conceptual thinking. The tension between feeling and concepts is played out in terms of attempts to overcome the Cartesian split between the subjective world of thinking and the objective world.

The basic question entailed in the notion of immediacy is revealed by Jacobi in the letters on Spinoza. Jacobi interprets Spinoza's thesis that "all determination is negation" as meaning that each element of knowledge gains its identity only in relation to other elements of knowledge. Furthermore, each thing is what it is by its not being the other things which "condition" it. In consequence one is inevitably left by any determinate claim to knowledge with what Jacobi terms chains of ("mediated") "conditioned conditions," thus with regresses of conditions which seem to preclude any access to the "unconditioned" that would stop the regress. Observable nature is available to us only in this conditioned manner, which means that any sense of the "unconditioned" must take us beyond sensuously available nature to what is "supersensuous." This is what makes Jacobi privilege theology over philosophy in his account of why the world is intelligible.[21] Kant had explained our ability to know in terms of the spontaneity of the understanding, which was itself not necessitated in the way that the causally linked world of intuitions given in receptivity is necessitated. Consequently the understanding is itself in one sense "unconditioned": as the ground of the intelligibility of receptivity it cannot itself be subject to the conditions of receptivity. Kant postulated a faculty of "productive imagination" which, via the capacity of "schematism," renders empirical input that is never in fact identical into identifiable forms. The imagination thus seems to take an unconditional place in philosophy's attempt to explain the world's intelligibility.

This is why Fichte has no hesitation in giving the "productive" aspect of thought the central role in his 1794 *Science of Knowledge* (*Wissenschaftslehre*), thereby opening up the path for many subsequent arguments about the centrality of art for philosophy. The question that concerns Fichte is how to conceive of the relationship between the conditioned world of nature and the unconditioned intellect and will, without falling back into a dualism that would make the intelligibility of the appearing world incomprehensible. Any attempt to explain the intellect is essentially an attempt to "mediate" it by relating it to something else. However, this seems necessarily to lead into another regress of mediated relations, in which the supposedly self-determining intellect would actually be grounded in something else, when what is required is a way of understanding that is *not* dependent on something else. If self-consciousness is taken to be wholly immediate, then it is unclear how we could have any access to it, given that such access requires a – mediated – relationship between what is seeking such access and what is being investigated. Fichte's response to this problem is to introduce the grounding notion of "intellectual intuition" – by which he means one's ability actively to reflect upon one's own thinking – as the only case of an immediate identity between subject and object which does not depend on any further condition.[22] As Manfred Frank has pointed out, though, the very notion of intellectual intuition involves a reflexive duality; this is why the romantics replace it with the irreflexive notion of "feeling" and reject its role as the ultimate foundation of philosophy. Fichte's crucial argument is that a wholly objective, deterministic world could not give rise to self-determining subjectivity which can itself give rise to effects in the objective world. He therefore assumes a necessary priority of the I if the limitation by the Not-I (the appearing world) required for there to be an intelligible world is to be *apprehended* as a limitation at all. This position evidently gives total idealist priority to "mind" and will over nature. However, Fichte was aware that in his terms philosophy cannot *explain* the – free – activity upon which it relies for its very existence. How does one conceptually objectify freedom without its ceasing to be itself by becoming a conditioned object? There is, then, a necessary philosophical opacity in the attempt to give an account of the I that would definitively ground our knowledge.

IV Schelling: art and the unconscious

It is in relation to this stage of Fichte's idealist account of the I that Schelling tries, in the *System of Transcendental Idealism*, to combine some of Fichte's arguments both with aspects of the Spinozism that forms the basis of his own *Naturphilosophie*, and with early romantic contentions about art's relationship to philosophy.[23] Schelling sees his task as the demonstration that freedom can in fact be rendered objective, namely by the work of art. This would demonstrate that the moving principles of objective nature and of subjective mind are ultimately identical, so that the Kantian division between nature and freedom is overcome and humankind is reintegrated into a teleologically conceived nature. In his *Naturphilosophie* of the later 1790s Schelling had understood nature in terms of the Spinozist division between *natura naturans* and *natura naturata*, regarding the former as the non-appearing "productive" ground of the latter, the world of appearing transient "products." In Fichte a similar structure pertained with regard to the I, in the form of the relationship between the grounding productive I of intellectual intuition and the empirical I of particular thoughts. Schelling wishes in the *System of Transcendental Idealism* to demonstrate that "the same activity which is productive *with consciousness* in free activity is productive in the production of the world *without consciousness*," thus combining Fichte and Spinozism.[24] What is required to show this is an activity which is "at the same time *conscious and unconscious*," and Schelling begins by postulating that "that simultaneously conscious and unconscious activity will be shown within the subjective, *within consciousness itself*," namely in "aesthetic activity." In explanation he terms the "objective world" of nature "only the primordial, still unconscious poetry of the mind," and he claims that the "*philosophy of art*" is required to unify the unconscious and conscious aspects of the world.[25] It does so by showing the relationship between how aesthetic production makes "the unconscious" manifest in external "products" (works of art as empirical objects in the world which are, *qua* art, more than merely conditioned objects), and how "philosophical production" is internally productive in intellectual intuition.[26] The result will be that "aesthetic intuition is only intellectual intuition that has become objective."[27] Art renders objective what philosophy can only present subjectively, which is how the *System of Transcendental Idealism* aims to circumvent the inability of Fichte's philosophy to explain freedom.

Schelling expresses the central idea which informs the *System of Transcendental Idealism* in a chiasmus:

> [N]ature begins unconsciously and ends consciously [that is, with the self-determining I], the production is not purposive, but the product is. In the activity which we are talking about here the I must begin with consciousness (subjectively) and end in the unconscious or *objectively*; the I is conscious according to the production, unconscious with regard to the product.[28]

His conception is derived from Kant's account of genius, "the innate aptitude [*ingenium*] *through which* nature gives the rule to art."[29] For Kant fully conscious artistic production would have to take place wholly in terms of rules, but he insists that art cannot come about in this manner because it must always establish new rules if it is to go beyond mere craft. For Schelling nature is itself precisely "unconscious productivity," so that when artists consciously decide to produce a work they must also rely on the unconscious aspect of productivity. The fact that the interplay between conscious and unconscious produces something intelligible which cannot be reduced to a law-bound explanation is, then, the basis of Schelling's claim that the aesthetic tells us more about reality (the "absolute") than could ever be scientifically or philosophically explained. Whereas law-bound explanations only add to the chain of conditions, making science an endless task, the inexhaustibility of the meaning of the artwork is experienced directly in the fact that it is "capable of an endless interpretation."[30] A piece of music, for example, is in one sense a physical object which can be quantified in terms of pitches and durations and explained in terms of physical laws whose status changes as more of the interconnections of the physical world are discovered, but none of those explanations can make it into a piece of music. This status is of a completely different order from the physical facts and depends upon the freedom of listeners to hear significances that are not inferable from the physical facts or even from the intentions of the composer.

The conclusion of the *System of Transcendental Idealism*, that art is "the only true and eternal organ and document of philosophy, which always and continuously documents what philosophy cannot represent externally,"[31] faces the objection that there is no transhistorical, cross-cultural agreement either about what art is, or about which works are works of art. This objection, though, takes us to the heart of the idealist/romantic divide, and at this stage Schelling is more on the romantic side. The very fact that there is no universal consensus about art can itself be understood as resulting from art's resistance to conceptual determination: if there were a concept of art, a rule for identifying something as art, art in these terms would arguably be abolished, because it would have the same status as any object classifiable by a concept. This is one way of interpreting a consequence of Hegel's position described below. For Schelling, however, instead of being a reason to reject art on the grounds of the disputed status of any particular work, art's resistance to conceptual classification can be seen as what makes art significant in challenging our established conceptions and opening up new possibilities of grasping and articulating the world and ourselves.

In contemporary philosophy questions raised by such considerations still occur in theories of metaphor. Donald Davidson, for example, sees the significance of the resistance of metaphors to paraphrase and literalization in terms of how they "make us notice" things, which Heidegger termed their capacity for "world-disclosure." Whereas literal meaning depends on semantic rules, metaphors would no longer be living metaphors if they were wholly rule-dependent. In the terms of the *System of Transcendental Idealism*, words are on the one hand "products," results of "unconscious productivity" that are manifest as real objects, and on the other hand, they can only *be* words if they involve "conscious productivity" that endows them with meaning. In remarks of the kind that had a substantial influence on Coleridge's version of romanticism, Schelling claims that nature is "a poem which lies locked away in secret miraculous writing," so that "through the sensuous world [of nature] meaning only shows as it does through words."[32] On this view, the literal meanings of words are the result of making language into an objectified "product," and metaphors make apparent the resistance of language to wholesale literalization. To the artist, nature is "only the ideal world appearing under continual limitations";[33] in order to get beyond the limitations of the sensuous world, which are what give rise to science and philosophy's endless task, the artist has to reveal the unlimited in a limited product, and this connects metaphor's resistance to literalization with the work of art's manifestation of productivity.

The *System of Transcendental Idealism* concludes with the call for a "return of science [meaning both philosophy and the natural sciences] to poetry," which would take place via a "new mythology that is not the invention of a single poet but of a new race (*Geschlecht*) which, as it were, only imagines One poet."[34] This call was influential, but Schelling leaves it open how such a mythology could emerge and in what it would actually consist. Related ideas would later inform Nietzsche's *Birth of Tragedy*, which, in the positivist and materialist climate of the early 1870s, claimed that the realization will eventually dawn that science is only another form of art, an imposition of order, of the kind characteristic of mythology, on what is in itself merely contingent. The potentially worrying implications of such ideas in the light of subsequent misuses of mythology in modernity should not conceal the fact that both Nietzsche and Schelling were justifiably concerned with the question of "nihilism." Jacobi had claimed that nihilism was the result of the reduction by modern science of the meanings of the world to what can be understood in terms of the principle of sufficient reason, a reduction that appears today in the many forms of scientism. Given that the most catastrophic aspects of modernity often result from the combination of perverted mythology with the technological results of modern science, even questionable attempts to rethink the relationship of science to the rest of human culture can offer more potential for philosophical insight than philosophical positions that subordinate all thinking to the perspective of the sciences. What, then, does reflection on art in subsequent German Idealism have to offer in this respect?

V Idealism and romanticism: Hegel and the end of art

Schelling himself did not sustain the priority given to art in his early work. In the *Philosophy of Art* of 1802–3 philosophy is already given equal status with art. The theme of language and art continues, though, to play an informative role. Schelling claims that "[v]ery few people reflect upon the fact that even the language in which they express themselves is the most complete work of art,"[35] and the implications of this remark can reveal the basic idea of his whole text. Language, Schelling explains, is "the direct expression of an ideal – of knowledge, thought, feeling, will, etc. – in something real, and, as such, a work of art."[36] Art and philosophy offer different ways of "constructing" the same "absolute identity," where "beauty is the indifference of freedom and necessity seen in something real," namely the work *qua* material object, and truth is the same "indifference" expressed in an "ideal" system of thought.[37] The principle of his philosophy of identity is contained in Schelling's description of *all* intelligible reality as a "primary speaking": it is both knowable via "ideal" concepts and manifested as "real" matter, in the same way as "ideal" meaning relates to "real" words. The *Philosophy of Art* establishes an ascending hierarchy of arts in terms of the relative roles of the ideal and the real, the infinite and the finite, within each art, beginning with music, which is most dependent upon time, and therefore most finite, and going on via the visual arts to literature. The highest form of art is, as it would be for Hegel, drama. In an anticipation of Wagner, Schelling concludes with reflections on the "most complete combination of all arts . . . which was the drama of antiquity," and he wonders if opera, which is at present merely a "caricature" of ancient drama, may become able to lead back to "ancient drama combined with music and song."[38]

The romantic implication of the *System of Transcendental Idealism* (about which Schelling himself is not always clear) was that its essential insight cannot be realized by itself as a philosophical text, but can only be communicated in the work of art. The *Philosophy of Art*'s systematization of the arts tends, on the other hand, to suggest in idealist fashion that the truth of art is realized in philosophy's account of the nature of the differing kinds of art. In the *Philosophy of Art* the tension between idealist and romantic conceptions becomes evident in the following problem. If language is indeed a "work of art," philosophy's own dependence on language *qua* combination of ideal and real means that philosophy cannot simply be the "ideal" construction of the absolute, as opposed to art's symbolic construction of the absolute in the "real." For philosophy to achieve its aim in these terms would require the establishment of a "general philosophical language," something which Hamann and other critics of the Enlightenment had claimed was impossible. According to Hamann's critique of Kant in 1784, which helps to inaugurate the essential claims of modern hermeneutics, our understanding always relies on our having acquired a particular natural language, so our grasp of the philosophical language must always depend on natural language, thus undermining its totalizing "philosophical" claims.[39] The question of the relationship between universalizing philosophical claims and the particularizing effects of language has recurred ever since in modern philosophy, appearing for example in the contrast between the desire of Russell and other early analytical philosophers for a logically purified language, and Heidegger's and Gadamer's views of language and world-disclosure or the later Wittgenstein's conception of language games and forms of life. The aim of the strong foundational idealist project exemplified by Hegel can be seen in this perspective as the elimination of the contingent particularity inherent in natural language as part of an attempt to arrive at a philosophical account of the absolute, and this is one way of understanding why Hegel announces the "end of art" in his *Aesthetics*.

The difficulties in interpreting Hegel's famous announcement cited at the beginning of this chapter lie not least in establishing at what level his remarks are to be understood.[40] If they are an observation about the growing dominance by the natural sciences of the direction of the modern world, Hegel's claims can hardly be gainsaid. The idea that art could play the role that Greek tragedy may for a time have played for the polis was resuscitated by Wagner and the early Nietzsche in the light of Schelling and other romantic thinkers, but as a claim about the relative importance of science and art in determining the direction of the modern world it is evidently absurd. However, it is clear that Hegel is concerned not just with the sciences, but also with *philosophy*'s account of the place of the sciences in the whole development of modernity. Hegel knows that the sciences alone, like other rationalizing aspects of the modern world, such as the division of labor, lead to a growing disintegration of the forms of traditional society. Philosophy's task is therefore to reveal how the ensuing divisions, manifest in the capitalist economy, modern individualism, and the destruction by science of mythical accounts of nature, are rationally necessary, and to help, where needed, to establish new forms of unification in modernity. It is here that an essential divide between idealism and romanticism is located.

In 1796 Novalis had already asked what would be the case if an "absolute ground" were unattainable, and he claimed that "the drive to philosophy would [then] be an endless activity," so that "[t]he absolute which is given to us can only be known negatively by our acting and finding that what we are seeking is not attained by any action."[41] The romantic conviction that the result of philosophy is a "longing for the infinite" as a regulative idea, rather than an articulation of an absolute ground, resembles the claim, taken up in the *System of Transcendental Idealism*, that art is a better way of approaching the absolute than philosophy. In failing to exhaust the artwork's meaning we feel the apparently finite object's "infinite" status by realizing that it is not reducible to concepts. An illuminating mediating figure here is K. W. F. Solger (1780–1819), for whom Hegel expresses great admiration in the *Aesthetics* and in a long review. Solger argues that art is the means of presenting the timeless, universal "idea" of things. His conviction that art necessarily relies upon the negativity inherent in the transience of all particular things brings him in one respect close to Hegel. Hegel also says that the particulars of the empirical world are inherently "negative," because what they are at a particular moment is dependent on time and on their relations in cognition to other particulars. For Solger the limitations of the particular become manifest in the contrast between the universal idea, which makes an artifact into art by revealing a truth not manifest in the chaotic manifold of the empirical world, and the contingent particulars that are required to make a work of art. This contrast also gives transient access to a universality beyond the limitations of the particulars by making them significant as parts of a whole whose meaning transcends them even as it also destroys them. However – and here Solger's divergence from Hegel and proximity to the romantics becomes apparent – the universality of the idea is itself sacrificed by its having to appear in time via the material of the work. This unavoidable duality of creation and destruction, infinity and finitude, is the basis of Solger's notion of "irony," which is derived from Friedrich Schlegel. The source of Solger's divergence from Hegel is most apparent in his view, taking up the doctrine of the resistance of being to conceptuality suggested by the romantics,[42] that everything in the world has a "wholly necessary being which exists completely for itself," and therefore cannot be definitively mediated.[43] Hegel's idealist alternative is precisely that this conception of being must itself be mediated by its relation to thought, and this is part of what leads to the arguments of his *Aesthetics*.

In certain respects Hegel is very close to the early romantic pattern of thought because he also sees the feeling of a need for the absolute as the result of a constant failure. His difference from the romantics lies in his conviction that this failure can ultimately be transcended by philosophy. The danger of conceptual thinking for Jacobi and the romantics lay in its potential for nihilism (see also below). If the value of each aspect of the world comes about only because of its mediated relations to other aspects of the world, then the threat of nihilistic regress can be overcome only by some form of meaningful immediacy that resists conceptual articulation[44] or by a final gathering together of all mediations. The first conception is the source of the close link between theology and aesthetics at this time, both of which can be regarded as relying, as Schleiermacher's work in particular suggests, on the immediacy of "feeling." For Schleiermacher, feeling expresses the irreducibility of each individual's relationship to the world, something they can never make fully transparent, even to themselves. Each mediated moment of our experience that we can objectify by reflecting on it in relation to other moments depends on a more fundamental "complete [hence immediate] taking up of the whole of existence in a moment,"[45] something which Schleiermacher believes is made accessible in aesthetic experience but is therefore resistant to final articulation in philosophy. Hegel, on the other hand, is famously scornful of any kind of "immediacy," be it in "intellectual intuition" or feeling, and he remarks, for example, that the "feeling of dependence" that was the basis of Schleiermacher's religion meant that a dog would be the best Christian. Hegel's philosophy relies on the power of totalizing conceptual mediation finally to transcend itself, so that the negative dependence on other things of all particulars leads ultimately to their integration as parts of a conceptually articulable positive totality. Hegel's absolute is, in Dieter Henrich's phrase, "the finite to the extent to which the finite is nothing at all but negative relation to itself."[46] By taking nihilism to its conclusion Hegel thinks it will be overcome. Another way of seeing this, as Frank has suggested, is to regard Hegel's system as "ironic" in the romantic sense – until it reaches its conclusion, when the irony is itself destroyed.

The crucial aspect of this conception in relation to aesthetics lies in the fact that, for philosophy to attain its highest insights, the world of the "finite determinations" of the understanding has to be more radically overcome than it is in the still particular work of art. This point is evident in the following contention from Hegel's *Logic*:

> If . . . the Idea should not have the value of truth because it is *transcendent* in relation to appearances, because no object in the sensuous world that corresponds to it can be given, this is a peculiar misunderstanding via which the Idea is not granted objective validity because it lacks that which constitutes appearance, the *untrue being* of the objective world.[47]

Art can consequently be only the "sensuous *appearing* of the Idea" because of its dependence on this "untrue being."[48] The philosophical dignity of each form of art is therefore a function of the degree to which it negates the dependence of Spirit (*Geist*) on the material world, so that architecture, for example, is a lower form of art than music. The basic conception is already implied by Hegel's inversion of Kant's placing of natural beauty before the beauty of art: "[N]atural beauty appears only as a reflex of beauty which belongs to Spirit."[49] The priority for Hegel, as for Fichte, is therefore on the intelligibility that is the product of Spirit.

Hegel's account of the three stages of the history of art adds a thoroughgoing historical dimension to reflection on art that is largely lacking (apart from Schlegel) in the thinkers discussed so far. The account mirrors the essential moves elsewhere in Hegel's system, from the indeterminate immediacy of being to the mediating universals required for the apprehension of the truth of the object. The history of art has three stages. "Symbolic" art is exemplified by the Sphinx, the "symbol of the symbolic itself."[50] Spirit here attempts to emerge from the animal realm into the human, but does not fully succeed, because the animal body remains as the contingency preventing its proper material realization. "Classical" art unites "meaning and corporeality": "only the externality of man is capable of revealing the spiritual in a sensuous manner," which Hegel thinks it does in classical Greek sculpture.[51] "Romantic" art, which is initially understood as Christianity, no longer attaches essential significance to the transience of the body, so "we get as the final point of the romantic per se the randomness of the external and the internal and a falling apart of these two sides, via which art negates itself [*sich aufhebt*] and shows the necessity for consciousness to appropriate higher forms for the grasping of truth than art is able to offer."[52] This leads to the contention that religion and philosophy are superior articulations of Spirit because they are progressively less tied to the particular. The arts themselves are then further divided, as they were in Schelling, into an ascending hierarchy. For Hegel this begins with architecture, followed by sculpture; these (which themselves take symbolic, classical and romantic forms) are followed by the "romantic" arts of painting, music, and literature. The highest art is drama, perhaps surprisingly in the form of comedy, because comedy allows Spirit to enjoy the dissolution of all particular human purposes and, in doing so, points beyond the particularity of art altogether. As an account of the development of the history of art, Hegel's analysis of the relationship between material and Spirit offers a wealth of insights, and subsequent developments in the history of art toward abstraction and the attacks on the autonomy of art in the modernist avant-garde make great sense in this scheme.

Once again, however, it is important to establish at which level the contentions about art are to be understood. The power of Hegel's wider argument is evident in his assertion that progress in the modern world relies upon overcoming the particularity characteristic of the aesthetic:

> The constitution of reflection of our contemporary life makes it necessary, both in relation to the will and in relation to judgment, to establish general view-points and accordingly to regulate the particular, so that general forms, laws, duties, rights, maxims are valid as the bases of determination and are the principle rulers.[53]

This privileging of the universal over the particular is clearly vital in many respects as the means of combating particularist irrationalism in modernity. At the same time, the proximity of Hegel's remarks to Max Weber's account of the rationalization which empties the modern world of the meanings that sustained traditional societies suggests a more problematic dimension, one which is apparent in Hegel's further contention that "[t]he *science* of art is thus in our time much more necessary than in times in which art for itself as art provided complete satisfaction."[54] What, though, if philosophy itself cannot provide complete satisfaction?

The essential metaphysical point of Hegel's philosophy lies in its demonstration that the apparent limits of subjective thought are precisely what compel subjectivity to transcend itself. The subject then articulates its founding role at the *end* of the system, having understood its feeling of limitation at the beginning to be the apparently "immediate" ground of its ultimately unlimited nature that is revealed in the process of mediation. For the later Heidegger, who takes the implications of this issue to their most revealing extreme, the dominance of subjectivity in modern philosophy here exemplified by Hegel leads to the claim that philosophy and the natural sciences are actually part of the *same* attempt of subjectivity to ground its own operations. The idea, characteristic of contemporary cognitive science, that consciousness can be explained in the same terms as the rest of nature is, in Heidegger's terms, *itself* the product of the subject's growing control of nature which characterizes modernity. The ultimate result, though, is that "[t]he development of the sciences is at the same time their separation from philosophy and the establishment of their independence. This process belongs to the end/completion (*Vollendung*) of philosophy."[55] For Heidegger, it is not, as Hegel claims, that art is overtaken by philosophy as that which both explains the necessity of the divisions characteristic of modernity and creates a new explanatory totality. Instead, philosophy itself comes to an end because its universalizing tasks, based on the capacity of thought for abstraction, are better dealt with by the sciences. Furthermore, art in the form of the "essential" poets points, Heidegger suggests, to the need for a new kind of "thinking" that no longer imposes its frameworks on being but rather listens to the "words of being." A related view of the role of subjectivity in Hegel occurs in Adorno, who claims that Hegel "hypostasizes the structuring of all being by subjectivity as the absolute. He regards the non-identical solely as a fetter on subjectivity, instead of determining the experience of non-identity as the telos of the aesthetic subject, as its emancipation."[56] Adorno's "non-identical" plays a similar role to immediate being in the romantics and Solger: in both cases the resistance of the particular to subsumption into classifying thought is the source of attention to art as the locus of insights which philosophy and science cannot provide.

The decisive issue behind the divergence between Hegel's idealism, and the romantic conception echoed in differing ways in Heidegger and Adorno, is nihilism. Whereas Hegel sees mediation as the path to absolute knowledge in the manner we have observed, the same totalizing relational manner of thinking is regarded by Adorno (and in some respects Heidegger) as forming an essential link in modernity between the constitution of metaphysical systems like Hegel's and of the natural sciences via the principle of determination as negation, the idea of language as a system of differences without positive terms, and the capitalist economy of exchange values which only have value in relation to each other. The "nihilistic" consequence of these kinds of system arises from the sense that nothing is therefore of value in itself, because the modern world imposes arbitrary forms of identity on the particularity of things (and people), which repress the ways in which they can resist such identification.[57] Although this wholesale identification of relational systems, be it in terms of Heidegger's "Western metaphysics" or Adorno's "context of delusion," is highly debatable, the implied questioning of the limits of rule-determined conceptual thinking cannot simply be dismissed.

Consider the sociology of art, which is one form that Hegel's "science of art" can be seen as taking in the twentieth century, not least via the influence of Hegel's thought. The aim of a sociological approach can be to explain a form of art in terms of the social and historical determinants that lead, for example, to the masterpieces of Viennese classicism. The danger is that what the works are understood as conveying will result in a circular manner from assumptions about what such determinants are. As Adorno realized, such "Hegelian" analyses are indeed a vital part of a philosophical response to art; the alternative is a dangerous blindness to the realities of the modern sociopolitical world which affect the most apparently immanent aspects of works of art. At the same time, the analyses can fail to come to terms with what the work itself may tell us about history in a way that nothing else can. Furthermore, the work's resistance to being subsumed into an explanatory paradigm such as "history" or "society" can be regarded as the source of its continued survival as a means of making new sense or challenging expectations in different historical and social contexts.

The result of these differing approaches is an uneasy tension whose source can be located in the tension we have observed between mediation and immediacy. This tension, between the demand to explain art as one further aspect of modernity, and the sense that such explanation can too easily obscure what only art is able to disclose, is the legacy of German idealist and romantic reflections on art and philosophy. The legacy is evidently not restricted to the sphere of art, which, as we have seen, cannot anyway be delimited in a stable manner. Contemporary philosophy keeps running up against the tension between the idea that its task is to explain language as the condition of the possibility of the means by which we increasingly control the natural world, and the idea that language's constitutive and world-disclosing role will always subvert the fulfillment of this task in the name of a particularity that ultimately cannot be explained. In this way German idealist questions about art remain questions about the future direction of philosophy.

NOTES

1 G. W. F. Hegel, *Ästhetik* (Berlin and Weimar: Aufbau, 1965), I, 21.
2 K. F. A. Schelling, ed., *Friedrich Wilhelm Joseph von Schellings sämmtliche Werke*, 14 vols. (Stuttgart and Augsburg: Cotta, 1856–61), I/3, 627.
3 Andrew Bowie, "German Philosophy Today: Between Idealism, Romanticism and Pragmatism," in Anthony O'Hear, ed., *German Philosophy Since Kant*, Royal Institute of Philosophy Lectures (Cambridge: Cambridge University Press, 1999).
4 Hans-Georg Gadamer, *Ästhetik und Poetik I. Kunst als Aussage* (Tübingen: J. C. B. Mohr, 1993).
5 See Charles Taylor, *Hegel* (Cambridge: Cambridge University Press, 1975), ch. 1.
6 See Andrew Bowie, *Aesthetics and Subjectivity. From Kant to Nietzsche* (Manchester: Manchester University Press, 1993, rev. edn. 2000); Carl Dahlhaus, *The Idea of Absolute Music*, trans. Roger Lustig (Chicago: University of Chicago Press, 1989);

John Neubauer, *The Emancipation of Music from Language. Departure from Mimesis in Eighteenth-Century Aesthetics* (New Haven and London: Yale University Press, 1986).

7 It is likely that Hegel heard Schlegel's lectures in 1801, not least because certain key "Hegelian" ideas are present in those lectures.

8 Friedrich Schlegel, *Kritische Schriften und Fragmente 1–6* (Paderborn: Schöningh, 1988), V, 41.

9 Friedrich Schlegel, *Philosophische Vorlesungen* (Munich/Paderborn/Vienna: Schöningh, 1964), II, 57.

10 I have dealt with this issue in relation to music in more detail in "Music and the Rise of Aesthetics," in Jim Samson, ed., *The Cambridge History of Nineteenth Century Music* (Cambridge: Cambridge University Press, forthcoming).

11 Friedrich Heinrich Jacobi, *Über die Lehre des Spinoza in Briefen an den Herrn Moses Mendelssohn* (Breslau: Loewe, 1789), 420.

12 Friedrich Schleiermacher, *Friedrich Schleiermachers Dialektik*, ed. R. Odebrecht (Leipzig: Hinrichs, 1942), 274–5.

13 See Anthony J. Cascardi, *Consequences of Enlightenment* (Cambridge: Cambridge University Press, 1999); Paul Guyer, *Kant and the Claims of Taste*, 2nd edn. (Cambridge: Cambridge University Press, 1997).

14 Immanuel Kant, *Kritik der Urteilskraft* (Frankfurt am Main: Suhrkamp, 1977), Bxlii, Axxxix.

15 Kant, *KU*, B237, A234.

16 Kant, *KU*, B237, A234.

17 Kant, *KU*, B66; see Wolfgang Welsch, *Vernunft. Die zeitgenössische Vernunftkritik und das Konzept der transversalen Vernunft* (Frankfurt am Main: Suhrkamp, 1996), 490–5.

18 Kant, *KU*, B66.

19 In the *Anthropology from a Pragmatic Point of View* Kant suggests that the difference in a child before and after it learns to refer to itself as "I" is that "Previously it just *felt* itself, now it *thinks* itself." Immanuel Kant, *Anthropologie in pragmatischer Hinsicht* (Stuttgart: Reclam, 1983), 37.

20 See Manfred Frank, *Einführung in die frühromantische Ästhetik* (Frankfurt am Main: Suhrkamp, 1989), and *"Unendliche Annäherung". Die Anfänge der philosophischen frühromantik* (Frankfurt am Main: Suhrkamp, 1997).

21 See Andrew Bowie, *From Romanticism to Critical Theory: The Philosophy of German Literary Theory* (London: Routledge, 1997).

22 See Günter Zöller, *Fichte's Transcendental Philosophy. The Original Duplicity of Intelligence and Will* (Cambridge: Cambridge University Press, 1998), 36. Fichte soon realized that this structure still leaves one with the problem of how such a relationship can establish the identity between the I as subject and the I as object, unless it is presupposed.

23 On Schelling see Bowie, *Schelling and Modern European Philosophy*; Dieter Jähnig, *Schelling. Die Kunst in der Philosophie*, 2 vols. (Pfullingen: Neske, 1966); Dale Snow, *Schelling and the End of Idealism* (Albany: State University of New York Press, 1996).

24 Schelling, *SW* I/3, 348.

25 Schelling, *SW* I/3, 349.

26 Schelling, *SW* I/3, 351.

27 Schelling, *SW* I/3, 627.

28 Schelling, *SW* I/3, 613.
29 Kant, *KU*, B181, A178–9.
30 Schelling, *SW* I/3, 620.
31 Schelling, *SW* I/3, 627.
32 Schelling, *SW* I/3, 628.
33 Schelling, *SW* I/3, 628.
34 Schelling, *SW* I/3, 629. Compare Max Horkheimer and Theodor Adorno's *Dialectic of Enlightenment* (New York: Herder and Herder, 1972).
35 Schelling, *SW* I/5, 186.
36 Schelling, *SW* I/5, 310.
37 Schelling, *SW* I/5, 383.
38 Schelling, *SW* I/5, 736.
39 See Bowie, *Aesthetics and Subjectivity*, ch. 6; cf. Dahlstrom, ch. 4 of this volume.
40 On Hegel see Bowie, *Aesthetics and Subjectivity*, ch. 5; Stephen Bungay, *Beauty and Truth: A Study of Hegel's Aesthetics* (Oxford: Clarendon Press, 1984); Cascardi, *Consequences of Enlightenment*, ch. 3.
41 Novalis, *Band* 2. *Das philosophisch-theoretische Werk*, ed. Hans-Joachim Mähl (Munich and Vienna: Hanser, 1978), 181.
42 See Frank, *Einführung in die frühromantische Ästhetik*.
43 K. W. F. Solger, *Nachgelassene Schriften und Briefwechsel* (Heidelberg: Schneider, 1973), II, 220; and see K. W. F. Solger, *Erwin. Vier Gespräche über das Schöne und die Kunst* (Munich: Fink, 1971) and *Vorlesungen über Ästhetik* (Karben: Wald, 1996).
44 As we saw in Solger, this immediacy may be only transient: the work of art appears, but is not art if it is seen *merely* as an appearing object.
45 Schleiermacher, *Dialektik*, 122.
46 Dieter Henrich, *Selbstverhältnisse: Gedanken und Auslegungen zu den Grundlagen der klassischen deutschen Philosophie* (Stuttgart: Reclam, 1982), 160.
47 G. W. F. Hegel, *Werke*, ed. Eva Moldenhauer and Karl Marcus Michel, 20 vols. (Frankfurt am Main: Suhrkamp, 1969–71), VI, *Wissenschaft der Logik II*, 463.
48 Hegel, *Ästhetik*, I, 117.
49 Hegel, *Ästhetik*, I, 14.
50 Hegel, *Ästhetik*, I, 352.
51 Hegel, *Ästhetik*, I, 418, 419.
52 Hegel, *Ästhetik*, I, 509.
53 Hegel, *Ästhetik*, I, 21.
54 Hegel, *Ästhetik*, I, 21.
55 Martin Heidegger, *Zur Sache des Denkens* (Tübingen: Niemeyer, 1988), 63.
56 Theodor W. Adorno, *Ästhetische Theorie* (Frankfurt am Main: Suhrkamp, 1973), 119.
57 See Bowie, *From Romanticism to Critical Theory*. This implication was already suggested by Jacobi, who brought the word nihilism into wider currency.

KARL AMERIKS

The legacy of idealism in the philosophy of Feuerbach, Marx, and Kierkegaard

The leading figures of the generation that came to philosophical maturity in the 1840s[1] stressed, from the start, their sharp disagreements with the systematic idealism of their predecessors. As Søren Kierkegaard's pseudonymous author Johannes de Silentio makes clear in *Fear and Trembling*, the one thing that he is *not* writing is "the System,"[2] that is, any version of Hegelian idealism. Ludwig Feuerbach and Karl Marx could have said the same. Their followers, to this day, understandably emphasize those aspects of their heroes' work that take them so far away from German Idealism that they can appear to be an attempt to "leave philosophy"[3] altogether and to replace it with radical critique, revolutionary activism, and rigorous empirical science. In addition, all three thinkers agree on the charge that most of German Idealism, like much of modern philosophy in general, can be dismissed as little more than an alienating effort to carry out theology by other means. Their agreement on this point is all the more remarkable since it arose despite obvious and deep disagreements: Feuerbach and Marx came to bury all religion, whereas Kierkegaard aimed to rejuvenate it by calling for a return to Christian orthodoxy.

This standard self-portrait of the wholesale rejection of German Idealism by its immediate successors stands in need of correction now that we know much more about the genesis of these philosophies than was common knowledge earlier. Hegel's work in particular has come to be understood as a much more liberating influence than his immediate detractors would have us believe.[4] Similarly, Marx's earliest "philosophical and economic manuscripts," which became available only in the 1930s, reveal that even the most "realistic" of thinkers was very concerned with the abstract details of the idealist tradition.[5] Even if the main immediate effect of the philosophies of the 1840s was to reinforce the decline of idealism in general, one of the most remarkable strengths of German Idealism lies in the fact that so many of its ideas remain incorporated in the work of even its most vocal opponents.

I Feuerbach

Within the camp of Hegel's immediate successors, it was Feuerbach who developed the most influential philosophical reaction to idealism. The mainstream of German Idealism had long encouraged a dismantling of the orthodox attachment to a traditional and literal reading of Christian claims. In the vacuum created by Hegel's death this dismantling took on a feverish pace and involved the utilization of three major strategies. One strategy emphasized focusing critically on the *historical* details of religious statements and pointing out significant contradictions between the narratives provided in the Gospels. Another method (introduced by David Friedrich Strauss) involved denying the primary significance of overt literal claims in biblical accounts while suggesting that its narratives could be understood as representing a *covert* and more important "mythic" truth, a truth reflecting the collective aspirations of the early Christian communities. One could appreciate the kerygmatic value of a group committed to a life focused on "salvation stories" even if those stories might not correspond to any natural or supernatural facts.

The third and most radical approach was Feuerbach's. He argued directly that *even in its covert meaning* Christianity is a bundle of contradictions, and the logical conclusion of its unraveling is an exaltation of humanity. This process does not "save" religious consciousness as such but reveals it as ripe for replacement by anthropology and a "philosophy of the future" that inverts rather than appropriates theological doctrines. For a while, all radical thinkers in Germany became Feuerbachians and took his work to signify a dethroning of Hegelianism.[6] Ironically, however, it is precisely on the issue of religion that Feuerbach's philosophical doctrines remain most deeply influenced by Hegel. They can be understood as little more than a filling out of the details of Hegel's scathing account of orthodox Christianity as a form of "unhappy consciousness" in the *Phenomenology of Spirit*.[7]

The enormous dependence of Feuerbach on Hegel was masked for a number of reasons. Hegel was directly familiar with the Atheism Controversy that occurred in Jena when Fichte lost his academic post in Jena in 1799 after brazenly presenting a version of "moral religion" that, unlike Kant's, savaged (as "contradictory") rather than salvaged the postulation of a supernatural personal God and an immortal human soul. What upset the German authorities (Goethe was Fichte's superior) was not the content of Fichte's view but the straightforwardness of his presentation of it. This scandal taught later idealists the importance of cloaking their radical humanistic doctrines in an esoteric form. Hegel's chapter on "unhappy consciousness" is a classic of this genre. In nearly impenetrable passages about the inner conflict of an "unalterable" and a "particular" consciousness, "self-divided" and "gazing" into itself, Hegel pictured orthodox Christianity, especially in its medieval form, as the deepest alienation, as an internalizing of the master–slave relation within one's mind and throughout one's religious activity. In such religion, the individual imagines a perfect "unalterable" mind that reigns over humans in a *transcendent, contingent,* and *asymmetric* way. The underlying point of Hegel's dialectic is that the frustration at the heart of such religious experience, the humiliation of the self as it acknowledges its inferiority in the depths of its feeling, work, and thought (through the ideals of the vows of chastity, poverty, and total obedience), is grounded in a valid implicit thirst for individual satisfaction (reward in heaven). This pent-up demand eventually forces the reversal that occurs with the Reformation and brings about the acknowledgment of the sanctity of secular life. By turning the medieval world on its head and introducing new ideals of fulfillment in marriage, business, and the construction of a free state, heaven is brought down to earth "in the spiritual daylight of the present."[8] The church is demoted from its position as an absolute authority to a merely heuristic role as a factory of dialectical symbols for the appreciation of the world's thoroughgoing rational unity. The "unalterable" and previously hypostatized Divine Spirit becomes the self-realization of the human spirit in the *immanent* sphere of modern social institutions – institutions that provide (and are understood as providing) structures that are in a *necessary* and *symmetric* relation to the satisfaction of finite individuals. The old image of the gracious lowering of God the Father to an Incarnation in individual flesh becomes speculatively reinterpreted as an inverted anticipation of the modern liberation of individual human consciousness as such from its own alienating projections.

The general notion of self-alienation, and of the overcoming of alienation, is at the heart of the whole idealist story of the satisfaction of self-consciousness; its account of religion is merely the most notorious chapter in this story. For the idealists, the self's satisfaction is always a matter of achieving "unity in difference" in the form of a "freedom" that comes from "being at home" with oneself through an other, from experiencing the relation to the other as a way of finding and fulfilling rather than losing oneself. "Alienation" occurs when one still does not recognize that "the other" that is essential to oneself is also dependent on oneself; one treats that which is in part dependent on oneself as if it were independent. In this way people make a fetish of religious, economic, and political institutions, imagining that their structures have an independent authority – until they eventually realize that whatever authority these "universals" have is given to them by the basic needs of real individuals.

All these points are reiterated and their detailed implications made plain in Feuerbach's *The Essence of Christianity.* After having shown, in earlier work, the same recklessness as Fichte by openly declaring the falsity of a fundamental postulate of the old faith – human immortality – Feuerbach also suffered the same fate.[9] He lost his chance for an academic position, and, sensing that there was no more to lose, he chose to write down as directly as he could all the radical ideas he had absorbed from Hegel.

This is not to say that Feuerbach's critique of religion depends entirely on Hegel. Feuerbach's philosophy employs three general and quite distinct epistemological strategies, and only the first overlaps with Hegel's own perspective. Feuerbach's first and best-known strategy is a psychological theory of "projection" that is developed along very simplified Hegelian lines and is offered as a causal account of the *origin* of religious belief. Feuerbach's second strategy involves the radical empiricist (and non-Hegelian) doctrine that the *justification* of statements in general has to derive from sensation. His third strategy involves the even more radical doctrine that the mere *meaning* of any statement transcending human experience has to be totally empty. The second and third doctrines might be intended as attempts to make up for the obvious philosophical insufficiency of the first doctrine. Although the "projection" theory continues to have considerable popular influence (e.g., in contemporary Freudian dismissals of religion), by itself it is little more than a crude version of the "genetic fallacy," a version that does not even bother to offer a genetic story with genuinely scientific credentials. Even if it were true (or it could somehow be shown to be at least likely) that projections like those alleged to occur on Feuerbach's psychological theory have been the causes of all our *actual* attachments to religious belief, it still would not follow that the statements expressed in such beliefs could have absolutely no truth or possible justification.

Feuerbach's radical empiricist doctrines of justification and meaning would "clinch the case" against religion, but they can be of philosophical use here only if they can be given a non-question-begging justification. It is unclear, however, whether doctrines making such strong claims as Feuerbach's can ever be established, and the strategy of relying on them suffers from the oddity of tying oneself down to enormously controversial general philosophical theses in order to challenge a few specific and rather extravagant claims. Hegel himself disparaged this overly ambitious kind of empiricism,[10] as did Marx, and so on this point Feuerbach was left with the company of crude positivists rather than dialecticians. In the end, Feuerbach is probably read most charitably on this issue if he is taken to be offering not a *philosophical refutation* of traditional religious belief but only a *popular diagnosis* of it for those who have already lost conviction. He appears to be presuming that most of his readers are already pre-theoretically inclined to be so suspicious in practice about taking religion literally that *they* are not looking for much more than some kind of natural psychological hypothesis about how the remarkable phenomenon of religious orthodoxy could ever have arisen.

Feuerbach realized that "fall back" positions are possible for defenders of religious claims. Right after using the projection theory to dismiss orthodox religion, Feuerbach discusses what he calls a "milder way," a strategy that retreats to a quasi-Kantian defense of religion. The "milder" or "transcendental" philosopher is described as holding on to a distinction between God "in himself" and "for us." Unlike negative theology, this position is not satisfied with allowing a simple absolute being that is a subject without positive properties. It concedes to common belief the idea that God should be thought of in terms of some predicates, but it also concedes to epistemological developments in modern philosophy that there are deep difficulties in warranting specific predications about God. Thus, it reserves divine properties for an unknowable characterization of God "in himself" as opposed to what he is "for us." At this point Feuerbach introduces his central notion of our "species being": "[I]f my conception is determined by the constitution of my species, the distinction between what an object is in itself, and what it is for me ceases; for this conception is an absolute one."[11]

Feuerbach appears to be presuming that if the "transcendentalist" tries to use the notion of an "in itself" to leave room for statements about God to have predicates that signify anything beyond the ideal properties of humanity as a species, such as perfect human love, power, intelligence, etc., then he must be dismissed for speaking nonsense.[12] There supposedly is not and cannot be anything beyond the "absolute" standard of the natural phenomenon of the human species, and all distinctions between what is "for us" and "in itself" must be understood as mere relative distinctions between how things actually appear to a particular individual and how they could be sensibly manifested to humanity in general. On this view, traditional religious language does not have to be totally discarded, but its talk about divine love and similar properties must be understood as an unhappy hypostatization of what are genuine predicates of humanity's capacities as a species. A proper understanding of our "species being" is thus the solution to unhappy consciousness. The notion of the human species itself is Feuerbach's epistemological, ontological, and ethical *substitute* for the absolute role that was previously played by the notion of God as traditionally understood.

Because Feuerbach realized that his analysis might be taken to be no more than a version of Hegel's own view expressed in clearer terms, he added a critique directed against Hegel, a critique alleging a "contradiction in the speculative [i.e., Hegelian] doctrine of God." Before criticizing Hegel, however, Feuerbach noted that the "speculative doctrine of God" should be understood as more than simply a clumsy modern replacement for Christianity. It can be regarded as the culmination of a long-standing mystical strand within Christianity itself, a strand that treats creation as an act needed for God's own sake. According to this view, "Only in the positing of what is other than himself, of the world, does God posit himself as God. Is God almighty without Creation? No! Omnipotence first realizes, proves itself in creation."[13] In this way some pre-modern Christians can be understood as having already applied to God the general idealist notion that the satisfaction of self-consciousness requires a recognition of one's self by another self. But on Feuerbach's analysis, the "speculative" version of this notion ends in "contradiction": "God has his consciousness in man, and man has his being in God? Man's knowledge of God is *God's* knowledge of himself? What a divorcing and a contradiction! The true statement is this: man's knowledge of 'God' is *man's* knowledge of himself, of his own nature."[14]

It is easy enough to see what Feuerbach takes to be absurd here. He imagines Hegel to be postulating that "speculative religion" culminates in a pairing of divine consciousness and human consciousness: as human selves become aware of the world's perfection, God's self realizes itself precisely through this last perfection, the perfection in human consciousness. Just as lord and bondsman could overcome alienation through a genuinely equal mutual recognition, so religion might seem to require the overcoming of unhappy consciousness by God and humanity achieving a situation of mutual recognition. Feuerbach totally rejects such an idea, however, not merely because it must remain asymmetric in many ways, but more fundamentally because he takes anything posited beyond the human species to be meaningless. Hence there simply is no real "divine consciousness" that can recognize or be recognized.

There is a flaw in Feuerbach's interpretation. Although there is a symbolic sense in which Hegel believed that "God" is fulfilled through human consciousness, this is not to ascribe literal *consciousness* to God or to assume he is a separate being, let alone to say that humans have their fulfillment in their relation to such a consciousness. Consciousness (in the relevant higher "self-conscious" sense) is a term that Hegel, like other idealists from Fichte on, reserved for human beings.[15] It is obvious from his criticism of unhappy consciousness that Hegel would be the last to posit God as a separate transcendent individual. For the prudential reasons discussed earlier, as well as because of an allegiance to the "mystic" strand found within Christianity itself that Feuerbach notes, it is not surprising that Hegel speaks of "God" and of "God's self-realization" in the course of the development of humanity. Hegel can, and does, say similar things about nations and their "spirit" being realized in the course of the development of individual human beings and their institutions. Nonetheless, just as it is absurd to ascribe to Hegel for this reason a belief that there is an individual such as Germany that is itself literally in a *state* of self-consciousness, so too it is absurd to ascribe to him a belief in a literal, psychological "self-consciousness" of a separate divine being.

Although it is important to realize that for Hegel there is not actually a divine "consciousness" that determines human life, it turns out that Feuerbach is still correct in sensing a basic contrast between his own position and Hegel's. The key difference is simply that for Hegel, unlike Feuerbach, the "species being" of humanity, as a mere part of nature, is not itself an absolute ground, an ultimate term; like anything in nature, it must be determined in its essence by the "activity" of the "Notion itself." This claim goes far beyond what Feuerbach would allow, but by itself it is not a "contradictory" or alienating view; it is just another variant of the traditional rationalist view that there is a philosophical and not merely natural necessity that ultimately underlies the pattern of human life. It is also a view that will turn out to have great relevance for the evaluation of Marx as an alternative to Hegel.

II Marx

Marx's immediate reaction to idealism is tied up entirely in his appropriation and radicalization of Feuerbach's approach. His early philosophical development can be divided into three phases: (1) early manuscripts that criticize Hegel and capitalism by extending to the economic sphere Feuerbach's use of Hegel's notion of alienation (1843–4); (2) a transitional phase of manifestoes that emphasize differences with Feuerbach (1845–6); and (3) a final phase summed up in his famous "Preface" outlining the doctrine of historical materialism (1859).

Marx's initial and most direct attacks on idealism occur in his "Critique of Hegel's 'Philosophy of Right.'" This critique is structured by a description of Hegel's philosophy as a form of "mystifying criticism."[16] The term "mystifying" is of course meant negatively, but in using the term "criticism" here Marx means to *praise* Hegel. Marx at first describes his own position as a critical form of "naturalism," rather than either "idealism" (orthodox Hegelianism) or "materialism,"[17] precisely because he wants to emphasize critical elements in Hegel that he believes Feuerbach neglected. "Materialism" at this point is Marx's term not for an ontological position but for what he takes to be Feuerbach's inadequately critical version of *epistemology*. This epistemology places too much emphasis on our passive sensibility (our mere response to the impact of matter) rather than on the three active features of human knowing that Hegel had stressed: (1) a fundamental dependence on stages of sociohistorical development; (2) a need to be developed through actual labor rather than mere thought; and (3) a dialectical pattern of progress that requires conflict and reversal (e.g., in the master/slave relation and what Hegel in general called "determinate negation").[18]

Marx's critique of Hegel as "mystifying" begins with the charge of what he calls the "double error" of idealism, but ultimately he presses three main objections to Hegel's system. One objection says that Hegel's idealism holds that all "is" thought; a second objection upbraids Hegel for holding that all "ends" in thought; and a third and most basic objection contends that Hegel's idealism is committed to the thesis that all "rests" in thought, that is, that forms of consciousness are generally causes of forms of life rather than vice versa.[19] Each of these charges has some source in Hegel's writing, but most of them can be rebutted by a moderately charitable reading of Hegel's intentions. In the end, however, there remains an important and valid point that Marx brings against Hegel's *Philosophy of Right* – although even this point can be argued to rest largely on a difference in praxis. It depends on how some principles should be concretely applied in view of one's interpretation of complex historical facts, rather than on a philosophical difference in ultimate principles concerning a genuine disagreement on "idealism" as such.

Here is one way that Marx expresses the charge that for Hegel all *is* thought: "The whole of the *Encyclopedia* is nothing but the extended being of the philosophical mind, its self-objectification . . . In the *Phenomenology* . . . when Hegel conceives wealth, the power of the state, etc. as entities alienated from the human being, he conceives them only in their thought form."[20] The source of Marx's irritation is understandable. In his *Encyclopedia*, the summation of his philosophy of logic, nature, and spirit, Hegel's idealistic system does place every-thing, even the phenomena of nature, into relation with "philosophical mind"; it never means to discuss nature entirely "on its own." Similarly, the *Phenomenology of Spirit* (or "mind," *Geist*) discusses phenomena such as the state in terms of how they figure in various attitudes of consciousness rather than, for example, as "concrete" historical, political, and military entities. But such an approach is hardly surprising in a book that has "spirit" in its title (and was also originally called "the experience of consciousness"), or in a system that places the structure of nature between abstract concepts and concrete features of mind (i.e., distinctively human activity) in order to map the interrelations of these three domains. Hegel's focus would be absurd *if* he actually thought that any of these phenomena could be discussed *only* in terms of consciousness, as if one could not do "real" history, economics, physics, etc. – but this is surely not his own view at all. (Marx suffered from the disadvantage of not having seen some of Hegel's most concrete works on these subjects, early essays that were not generally available in the 1840s.) Although Hegel calls himself an idealist, this fact – just like Marx's early rejection of what he calls "materialism" – should not be taken as an endorsement of the view that matter does not exist at all or that it cannot ever be studied on its own.[21] The genuine issue between Marx and Hegel's real view has to do not with a dispute about whether material nature exists but rather with the question of *how* philosophy should approach nature, an issue that leads into Marx's two other objections – the charges that in Hegel's system all "ends in" and "rests on" thought.

Like Marx's first objection, the charge that Hegel ends with thought has an understandable source in a fairly innocent feature of the structure of Hegel's work. Since Hegel takes human thought to be the most complicated development in nature, it is no surprise that his *Encyclopedia* comes to it only after discussing the pre-human sphere. It is also true that Hegel ends his discussion of "spirit" as such not with "objective" spirit – the relatively concrete domain of social and economic interactions – but rather with thought in the relatively abstract sense of "absolute spirit," that is, the domains of art, religion, and (at the very end) philosophy. But here again the genuine issue between Marx and Hegel depends entirely on *how* this turn to thought is understood. In one sense Marx also holds that thought, especially philosophical thought, comes at the end, since it is an activity of what he calls (see below) the "superstructure." It arises, if it arises at all, when the "basis" allows for it, and the menial labor of the "day" is done. In his famous remark that "the owl of Minerva spreads its wings only with the falling of the dusk," Hegel reveals a deep agreement with not only this general idea found in Marx's view about the temporal relation of "base" and "super-structure," but also with the much stronger and even more Marxian idea that the very *content* of philosophy is "one's age gathered in thought," that is, a reflection of life's more concrete institutions.[22] Thus Hegel often stresses that the kind of alienated thought that comes at the end of a culture's "golden age" reflects the specific forms of real alienation within that culture. The problems of the Greek institution of slavery, for example, are reflected in Aristotle's philosophical treatment of inequality and in the contours of the doomed "absolute spirit" of the ancient world in general.

Marx goes on to specify his objection to Hegel's system for ending in thought by claiming that Hegel's philosophy "ends" as a "confirmation of illusory being,"[23] and therefore it is itself no more than another reflection in alienated thought of the real alienation of society. This point is significant, but it cannot serve as an objection to Hegel's *general descriptive* thesis that culture "ends" in thought. That thesis by itself does not always imply an unfortunate evaluative claim. Clearly, *if* a culture is *not* alienated, then, given the descriptive thesis, it would also end in thought, and in that case its non-alienated thought would be something to be praised – for both Hegel and Marx. In so far as Marx can have a relevant *objection* to Hegel here, it must have to do with the more specific question of whether our pre-socialist society is so fundamentally alienated that even its most advanced structures (and hence their reflection in thought) *must* be mere "illusory being," that is, a frustration of the true needs of humanity.

Marx discusses these structures in terms of Hegel's list of categories of "objective spirit," or practical life, in the *Philosophy of Right*: private right, morality, the family, civil society, the state.[24] It is hard not to be sympathetic to Marx's critique when one recalls that Hegel defends the modern instantiation of these categories in the form of institutions such as primogeniture, capital punishment, endless warfare, monarchy, and a class-based economic and political structure that on Hegel's own account entails contradictory phenomena such as impoverishing overproduction, a humiliating and ineffective dole system, and a relentlessly exploitative drive to imperialism.[25] No wonder Marx complains, "In Hegel, therefore, the negation of the negation is not the confirmation of true being by the negation of illusory being. It is the confirmation of illusory being."[26] That is, modern civil society, which negates the immediacy of nature while codifying itself in alienating institutions, is not itself "negated," or transcended, in a practical rather than merely speculative way, but is simply reflected and reinforced by the *Philosophy of Right*. Hegel is to be condemned for not working for the destruction of these questionable institutions and for being content with "reconciling" people in the absolute spirit of the age that accompanies them. This complaint has its justification, but it should not be taken to show that Hegel would ever want any objective structure to be "confirmed" in absolute spirit, rather than concretely "negated," *if* he saw that the structure of objective spirit really is thoroughly "illusory" and alienating.

Marx's understandable complaint turns into a misunderstanding in so far as he fails to appreciate this last point and goes on to suggest that all Hegel is *interested* in are satisfactions of mere thought rather than "true" forms of objective being: "[T]he supercession (*Aufhebung*) of objectivity in the form of alienation ... signifies for Hegel also, or primarily, the supercession of *objectivity*, since it is not the determinate character of the object but its *objective* character which is the scandal of alienation for self-consciousness."[27] The mistake here is to suggest that Hegel wants to do away with objectivity altogether, rather than simply to overcome bad forms of objectivity. Aside from strictly polemical intentions, the only source for this influential but implausible reading by Marx must be Hegel's overly colorful way of speaking about *how* his system ends in thought. Hegel does speak about how, in the culmination of absolute spirit – which is the philosophy of his own system – an "end" is reached in which nature's objectivity "as such" is "canceled," and the concept "returns" to itself.[28] But the "canceling" that Hegel has in mind here is nothing more than the formal "negation" that is involved in placing objective structures into explicit and maximally clear thought forms; it has nothing to do with literally destroying objectivity or nature, or pretending that we could ever do without objectivity *altogether*. Presumably, Marx's own ideal society would "end" similarly with some economic-philosophic attempt at a comprehension of its situation, and this would also "transcend" mere objectivity, that is, it would accomplish a stage of reflection that brings us beyond our unreflective practices.

Marx's third objection to Hegel's idealism is similar to Feuerbach's charge of a "contradiction" in the "speculative doctrine of God." Whereas Feuerbach attacks the mere thought of an existent divine consciousness, Marx stresses the problem of what he takes to be its alleged role as an efficient and final cause:

"[T]his movement [the dialectic of human life] . . . is regarded as a *divine process* . . . This process must have a bearer, a subject; but the subject first emerges as a result. This result, the subject knowing itself as absolute self-consciousness, is *therefore God, absolute spirit, the self-knowing and self-manifesting Idea.*"[29] It might seem that this objection, like Feuerbach's, is entirely inappropriate because, as was noted above, Hegel's "owl" represents the view that philosophic thought has its "base" precisely in society, rather than vice versa. In other words, Hegel need not be taken to mean that, even in the higher achievements of spirit, "consciousness determines life," rather than the other way, let alone that the whole process is directed by God as an actual self-consciousness.[30] Nonetheless, there remains a deep disagreement here between Marx and Hegel.

The difference lies in the fact that, even though Hegel does stress many ways in which "life determines consciousness," he also believes (as was noted above in the contrast with Feuerbach's notion of species being) that "life" is not an ultimate term, that there is something that determines it in turn. In Hegel's three-part system, there is an ultimate source for *both* life (nature) and consciousness (spirit), namely the domain of Notions (treated in the *Logic*), which fulfills itself as what Hegel calls the "Idea." This is not a mental entity, but rather the rational realization of the Notion in *actuality* (for Hegel, basic Notions are essentially self-actualizing, very much like the concept of God in traditional ontological arguments). Unfortunately, the term "Idea" often has a psychological connotation in modern thought, and hence Marx understandably, but improperly, presumes that it implies Hegel is taking it to be *literally* a property of God in the traditional sense as a "subject" and "self-conscious" being. Clearly, *if* Marx's objection to Hegel rests simply on this unnecessary presumption, then it can be judged to remain unfair and inadequate.[31] In fact, however, even if this mistaken interpretive presumption is entirely dismissed, there remains, as with Feuerbach, a different and more fundamental objection to Hegel. This objection consists simply in pointing out that "life" may not need anything more ultimate than itself – not even a "Notion." That is, even if Hegel's "Idea" should not be assumed to involve a commitment to a personal God, it does *seem* to signify something quite extraordinary, something that is not mere nature, and something that Hegel's naturalist successors would understandably reject.

Matters are not so simple, however, because Marx is not just any kind of naturalist. It was noted above that Marx accepts and emphasizes Hegel's "critical" perspective. This point can be expanded by showing in some detail (see below) that Marx allows that Hegel's "dialectic" – the intricate pattern of philosophical forms underlying both the *Logic* and *Phenomenology* – is not merely a helpful fiction but is an essential key to uncovering necessities more basic than any structures that can be found by mere empiricism. In this way it turns out that Marx himself, like Hegel, is committed to something that is much more than "mere nature." As with Hegel, this something is not a ghostly guiding "consciousness" – and yet its effects are exactly *as if* there is such a guide. In so far as Marx can be read as accepting this much, it becomes difficult to distinguish his most basic philosophical perspective from Hegel's idealism after all. We have just examined Marx's objections to the view that everything supposedly "is," or "ends," or "rests" in what is only "thought," and this examination has not revealed any *philosophical* points that apply clearly against *Hegel's idealism* as such. If this idealism is not a straw man position, and not the opposite of all realism or materialism, but rather the notion that there are deeply necessary, rational, and (ultimately) extremely progressive ("ideal") structures governing human life and society[32] – then idealism turns out to have a very tenacious legacy. Philosophically speaking, it may be best understood as not the opposite of left wing Hegelianism but rather its underlying and moving "spirit."

Three brief and central texts illustrate this point. The first two are from Marx's transitional period, his remarks against "ideology in general and German ideology in particular," and his "Theses on Feuerbach," and the third is from his mature period, the famous "Preface" to *A Contribution to the Critique of Political Economy.*

In the *German Ideology* Marx moves beyond an appropriation of Feuerbach to a critique of Feuerbach's own critical approach as one "that has never quitted the realm of philosophy."[33] This is a striking claim because Marx's own earlier work, even his notes on alienated labor, were themselves still an instance of Feuerbachian philosophy. It is true that he begins "from a *contemporary* economic fact. The worker becomes poorer the more wealth he produces."[34] Marx does not stay at the economic level, however, but moves from this fact to explain how it displays the structure of human alienation as such. Just as Feuerbach made Hegel's notion of alienation more concrete by adding details to the *Phenomenology*'s critique of orthodox religion, Marx makes the phenomenon of contemporary alienation more concrete by adding philosophical points about the alienation of modern economic life. Feuerbach's key term, "species being," turns out to be central to Marx's analysis, but it is now defined, in more activist terms, as our distinctive capacity for producing "free from physical need."[35] As German Idealism had already stressed, alienation is fundamentally a matter of our treating as independent something that is of our own making. Marx appropriates this point by turning to economics in a Feuerbachian way: in losing control over the concrete *products* of our labor, as well as over the very *activity* and value of our own work and thus, simultaneously, over our relation to *other persons* (class colleagues and class enemies) as well as *ourselves*, we are above all alienated in our species being. We have turned the "freedom" of our own non-necessitated activity into something taken to be necessary.

In his "Theses on Feuerbach" Marx makes his most famous announcement:

"[P]hilosophers have only interpreted the world in different ways, the point is to change it" (final Thesis, XI; cf. Theses II, IV, VIII). Obviously, however, some people have "only changed the world in different ways" as well, so the point now must be to change it in a *correct* way. Hence it is fortunate that Marx did some philosophy on his own before he criticized Feuerbach. Marx can not only charge Feuerbach (and, later, "ideology in general") with not being genuinely active at all; he can also (with the benefit of appreciating Hegel's more critical philosophy) criticize him for not having the right perspective for moving into correct action. Feuerbach's philosophy suffers in general from having a much too passive ("old materialist") epistemology (Theses I and V); hence it carries out its critical reflection (the exposure of religion as alienation) in a much too abstract, non-historical manner (Theses VI and VII); and so, when it moves on even to think about becoming activist, it forgets "that the educator must himself be educated" (Thesis III), and its plans for change remain infected by its armchair, individualist orientation (Theses IX and X). Feuerbach forgets the thoroughly social nature of our "species being" and the fact that it is more than just a manifestation of something we have distinctively in common as a species. Our "free production" is also a function that concerns the species as such, for the concrete capacities of the species as a society are its source and end.

The "Theses on Feuerbach" raises a general issue that Marx confronts most directly in the *German Ideology*. The issue concerns the question of how any philosophical position can be critiqued once philosophy is regarded – as Marx explicitly regards it – as "mere criticism" and "ideology," that is, as a mere reflection of more basic forces.[36] Once this position is taken seriously it would seem that whatever Marx, or anyone else, might have to *say* against a particular view would itself also be subject to the suspicion of being mere ideology. The "educator himself must be educated" – but who, especially in the current alienated world, can point the way to a non-question-begging education? Marx offers an answer: "The premises from which we begin are not arbitrary ones, not dogmas, but real premises."[37] The Archimedian point here is alleged to be "hard" science – the "real" truths of economic analysis as opposed to philosophical speculation. Or so it may seem. Just as Marx is not just any kind of naturalist, he is also not a sheer positivist. He is not naïve enough to assume that the "facts" that reveal the basic structures of concrete alienation, let alone the clues to overcoming it, can be found by just any glance at history: "This method is not devoid of premises . . . On the contrary, our difficulties only begin when we set about the observation and the arrangement – the real depiction of our historical material."[38]

This concession leads to a further problem: where does Marx get his crucial structural clues for properly "arranging" historical material? On this question there is no better guide than his own summary in his "Preface" of 1859:

The general conclusion at which I arrived and which, once reached, continued to serve as the guiding thread of my studies, may be formulated briefly as follows: In the social production which men carry out they enter into definite relations that are indispensable and independent of their will; these relations of production correspond to definite stages of their material powers of production. [1] The totality of these relations of production constitutes the economic structure of society – the real foundation, on which legal and political superstructures arise and to which definite forms of social consciousness correspond. The mode of production determines the [2a] general character of the social, political and spiritual processes of life. It is not the consciousness of men that determines their being but, on the contrary, their social being determines their consciousness. [3] At a certain stage of their development, the material forces of production come in conflict with the existing relations of production, or – what is but a legal expression for the same thing – with the property relations within which they had been at work before. From forms of development of the forces of production these relations turn into fetters. Then occurs a period of social revolution. With the change of the economic foundation the entire immense superstructure is more or less rapidly transformed. [2b] In considering such transformations the distinction should always be made between the material transformation of the economic conditions of production, which can be determined with the precision of natural science, and the legal, political, religious, aesthetic, or philosophical – in short ideological forms in which men become conscious of this conflict and fight it out. [4] Just as our opinion of an individual is not based on what he thinks of himself, so can we not judge of such a period of transformation by its own consciousness; on the contrary, this consciousness must rather be explained from the contradictions of material life, from the existing conflict between the social forces of production and the relations of production. [5] No social order ever disappears before all the productive forces for which there is room in it have developed; and new, higher relations of production never appear before the material conditions of their existence have matured in the womb of the old society. Therefore, mankind always sets for itself only such problems as it can solve; since, on closer examination, it will always be found that the problem itself arises only when the material conditions for its solution already exist or are at least in the process of formation. [6] In broad outline we can designate the Asiatic, the ancient, the feudal, and the modern bourgeois modes of production as progressive epochs in the economic formation of society. [7] The bourgeois relations of production are the last antagonistic form of the social process of production; not in the sense of individual antagonisms, but of conflict arising from conditions surrounding the life of individuals in society. At the same time the productive forces developing in the womb of bourgeois society create the material conditions for the solution of that antagonism. With this social formation, therefore, the prehistory of human society has come to an end.[39]

There are at least seven fundamental philosophical points in this passage that can be understood as a direct "economic" application of Hegel's account of the "pathway of consciousness." Although the enormous practical significance of Marx's revolutionary emphasis on specific economic factors cannot be denied, the structural features of Marx's "historical materialism" clearly reflect Hegel's "idealistic" system in its central doctrine that history has (1) basic levels, (2) limits, (3) dialectical structure, (4) opacity, (5) fullness of development, (6) stages, and (7) finality.

(1) Like Hegel, Marx regards higher conscious achievements, the "superstructure" of art, religion, and philosophy, as based in more concrete social institutions. Unlike Hegel, he is primarily interested in tracing the level of "objective spirit" itself (which is the immediate basis for absolute spirit) to an underlying basis not only in "relations of production" but also in more fundamental "powers of production."[40]

(2) Like Hegel, Marx emphasizes that it is only "the general character" of mental life that can be explained and, in some very rough way, predicted. Details at the level of "material transformation" cannot be mechanically projected on to details at the level of "ideological forms."

(3) Like Hegel, Marx stresses that fundamental transformations involve the dialectic of "determinate negation." Economic developments mirror the "unhappy" pattern of the projection of an infinite God, reigning over all, which involves "forms of development" that "turn into their fetters." Oppressed people lift themselves internally by exalting something external at the cost of themselves, and then they develop under this alienation to a point at which they reverse it externally, having nothing to lose but their own "fetters." What is negated, however, is not the entire content of one's earlier projects but only its alienating form.

(4) Like Hegel (and Kant), Marx stresses that these transformations happen "behind the back of consciousness,"[41] through a cunning of nature and reason. We "cannot judge" an age by its "own consciousness," that is, by the participants who are going through the "contradictions" whose resolution they have yet to appreciate. There is, nonetheless, a necessary external explanation of these contradictions, one that Marx finds in economic relations, while Hegel is concerned with tracing them to even deeper conceptual relations.

(5) Like Hegel, Marx insists that there are no shortcuts in dialectical development; no older order "ever disappears" until all the developments and contradictions of the previous order have been worked through.[42] It is no accident that the *Phenomenology* and world history are both long stories.

(6) Like Hegel, Marx distinguishes four basic periods of history: "Asiatic, ancient, feudal, and modern." These are the very periods that Hegel distinguished in terms of their attitudes to freedom;[43] Marx stresses in more detail how their attitudes are rooted in specific economic structures concerning the possibility of "free production."

(7) Like Hegel, Marx thinks that in his own time we see human development coming to "an end," that is, approaching a culmination that represents a first stage of genuinely rational organization. Of course, unlike Hegel, Marx identifies this stage with the future socialist reorganization of advanced European societies, rather than with the high point of the bourgeois state in the nineteenth century.

In sum, there is no mystery about where Marx looked to find his orientation in "arranging" the facts of history so that he could dissolve "ideology" from a standpoint with "real premises." Even though he hardly justified the (just noted) seven basic features of history by arguments of the kind found in Hegel's *Phenomenology* and *Logic*, the remarkable overlap of his conclusions with Hegel's must be much more than a coincidence. Whether or not Marx himself would be open in principle to an orthodox Hegelian derivation of these features, he and many of his followers certainly seemed to regard them not as mere hypotheses but as an ultimate and unrevisable ground, an expression of necessities that any future science and society would have to accommodate. To this extent, his philosophy can be read as taking over the most fundamental philosophical project of German Idealism: the glorification of human history as having a thoroughly dialectical shape in its development as the complete and immanent fulfillment of self-consciousness.

III Kierkegaard

The standard way of approaching Hegel's legacy is to make a sharp distinction between the left ("old") Hegelian and right ("young") Hegelian schools that emerged soon after his death.[44] The position represented by Kierkegaard requires that a further distinction be made. By arguing that the "essence" of religion is the development of "human morality," and that this eventually leaves modern institutions free from any literal commitment to the supernatural ontological claims of traditional Christianity,[45] Hegel forced a choice between a number of quite different options. Right Hegelians tended to combine relatively conservative social inclinations with a theoretical background in the speculative liberal traditions of enlightened Protestant theology (somewhat like their contemporaneous "Transcendentalist" cousins in early liberated circles in New England).[46] They were eager to protect the status quo by embracing a reading of Christianity that freed it entirely from the threats of modern historical and scientific research. The "conflict between science and theology,"[47] which many intellectuals liked to think was the great crisis of the century, was no problem at all for these Hegelians. If the Christian story is simply a symbol of, and a historical catalyst for, the appreciation of what are essentially speculative and moral doctrines rather than factual claims, then the latest findings of physics, geology, biology, psychology, etc., need not be the slightest embarrassment to Christianity. At the same time, however, left Hegelians, such as Feuerbach, argued that precisely because religion could now be understood (by the most advanced philosophy of the time) as nothing more than a vehicle for human liberation, there was no longer a need for institutions designated specifically as religious. On their reading of the facts, the moral education that traditional religion might at one time have encouraged could now be replaced by explicitly secular organizations.

Kierkegaard presents a third option that goes beyond both these left and right wing Hegelian responses. He agrees with the right wing in praising Christianity, but, more fundamentally, he agrees with the left wing that *if* Christianity plays a merely authoritarian or dispensable educational role, then, as institutional "Christendom," it should be rejected.[48] His most fundamental point, however, is a vigorous denial of the general Hegelian reduction of Christianity to little more than an instrument of rationalistic morality, and in this way he undercuts the basic supposition common to the right and the left wing schools.

Kierkegaard's relation to idealism is not the confrontation of one "system" with another, or the attempted substitution for philosophy of an anthropological science or a program for necessary social liberation. Nonetheless, he borrows more from German Idealism than his relentless campaign against Hegel would lead one to expect. This background is indicated in the title of one of his major works, *Stages on Life's Way*, as well as in the subtitle he chose for his classic *Fear and Trembling: A Dialectical Lyric*.[49] At the center of Kierkegaard's thought is a project that parallels the plot of Hegel's *Phenomenology*, namely, a philosophical outline of the ideal "pathway of consciousness." Whereas Hegel describes four main stages in the social history of "freedom," Kierkegaard focuses on four "stages on life's way" in the development of individual freedom. These stages are deeply Hegelian because they are ordered dialectically in a series of determinate negations, and they exhibit a progression of stages that employs – and then reorders – the key phases of Hegel's "objective" and "absolute" spirit. In place of Hegel's sequence – ethics, aesthetics, religion, philosophy – Kierkegaard uses the ascending order: aesthetics, ethics, philosophical religion, orthodox religion.

The first stage in Kierkegaard's account, the aesthetic, is defined by the attitude of giving primacy to the individual self. This primacy can be exhibited in a fairly crude and immediate life of feeling, but its adult form (see the first set of chapters of *Either/Or*) is a highly reflective set of attitudes, "aesthetic life" in a broadly philosophical sense. Its ultimate focus is not pleasure or beauty as such, but ironic satisfactions of the kind favored by German romanticism: the endless pursuit of "the interesting," as the subject discovers its capacity to reflect and to "see through" all objective structures.[50]

In the second stage, the ethical, the priorities are reversed. Ethical persons are defined by having tamed subjective reflection by objective reason, and by having learned to put others above themselves. This stage can be manifested in merely following the common duties of everyday life (see the second set of chapters of *Either/Or*) and Hegelian *Sittlichkeit*, but it can also take the extreme form of tragic sacrifice in giving one's own life, or that of an individual very close to oneself (as in the example of Brutus, who must authorize his own son's death to preserve the law[51]), so that the "universal," the community as such, can be protected. (Kierkegaard also holds, like Kant, that a full appreciation of the ethical involves a recognition of radical evil.)

The third stage, the religious, brings another dialectical reversal: satisfaction is sought no longer in the "finite" realm, individual or social, but rather in something literally infinite, God. It is possible to present matters as if there are only these basic three stages for Kierkegaard, but he makes such a deep distinction between two types of religious attitudes, "A" and "B," that it is more accurate to speak of four main stages on life's way.

"Religiousness A," which parallels an attitude called "infinite resignation" in *Fear and Trembling*, is taken by Kierkegaard to be the highest stage that can be reached by reason as such. One might think of this stage as exemplified by those who accept the classical arguments for God in rationalist philosophy, but Kierkegaard introduces this attitude in terms of a natural development within any self that seeks a truly deep form of satisfaction, something that the lower stages cannot provide. The aesthetic person is too immature to know the lasting value of commitment to others, while the ethical person remains vulnerable to the pain of sacrifice and to the alienating sense that, in the end, its own satisfaction as an individual is of paltry value. In devoting oneself to something infinite, one finally gains something for oneself beyond the limits of "finite" life, be it aesthetic or ethical. Kierkegaard specifies a threefold advantage gained by the "knight of resignation." Its constant focus on the infinite "beyond" provides it for the first time with a thoroughly deep and personal *unity* as a focus of its intentions; this unity in turn first reveals the "eternal validity" of one's true *self*, the free and unbounded and, in part, essentially rational self that can alone be the source of such a focus; and the object of the focus, a necessarily transcendent item, leaves the self for the first time "*resilient*": nothing that can happen at the finite level can "shake" such a self, since it has "resigned" itself from literally "putting its self into" finite and transient goods.[52]

From our perspective, this kind of resignation might at first appear to parallel what Hegel had in mind – and deplored – in "unhappy consciousness." The remarkable fact is that Kierkegaard seems to be presenting this stage as something that should appear as sane, rather than alienated, and as clearly meeting Hegel's own most important standards. Unlike the lower stages, it is presented as satisfying the individual self as such in both a rational and eternal form. Like the other stages, resignation can be exemplified in a number of ways, but all of these maintain the special virtues of thorough unity, enhanced self-consciousness, and resilience. Kierkegaard introduces it with a story about a poor lad devoted to a princess he could never expect to marry in this life. This story can easily be taken to point to a purer type of fully "infinite" resignation that focuses entirely on God and takes what Kierkegaard calls the "monastic" turn. Perhaps Kierkegaard would allow that somewhere between an ideal princess and a genuinely transcendent and personal God, Hegel's absolute rational system might also serve as an understandable object of something like infinite resignation.[53]

Fully specifying the content of Religiousness A is not Kierkegaard's highest concern because his main point is that this level is still far from genuinely satisfying the self. Like the ethical hero, the knight of resignation remains frustrated in a fundamental way. Each can take pride in its own heroic attitude, and each can savor the value of something enormous – either the finite but quite immense realm of ethics, or the transcendent and literally infinite object of resignation. In either case, however, one's self as a finite and passionate being remains condemned. Precisely in order to be a hero at these stages, one dare not hold on with full force to one's interest in one's ordinary individuality as such.

Hegel has a short-cut solution for this problem that Kierkegaard must have considered. In *Fear and Trembling*, Kierkegaard treats Hegel as the philosopher who makes the ethical "the absolute."[54] This strategy does justice to the fact, noted earlier, that in Hegel's idealism, it is objective spirit, social life in all its concrete dimensions, that appears to be the fundamental area of human fulfillment. Art, religion, and philosophy merely express in their more reflective ways the basic structures that spirit manifests in objective self-satisfaction. Central to this satisfaction is the value that Hegel calls "freedom," the "being at home" with oneself through being related to others in a mutually satisfying manner, and in particular through participating in structures that link individuals and the "universal" (the rational society of the *Philosophy of Right*) in a deeply symmetric, necessary, and immanent way. Hegel equates this kind of "freedom" with the achievement of "infinitude."[55] He is, of course, using neither of these terms in their traditional meaning. By a "free" self he does not mean one with a known power of absolute choice, of uncaused causality, as in the philosophy of Augustine, Kant, or Kierkegaard. "Freedom" for Hegel is rather a state of self-relation, of rational "self-determination" in a formal rather than absolute efficient sense.[56] "Infinity" is another Hegelian term for the same property, since, as he uses the word, an "in-finite" being is one that has no limits in the sense of an external bound but is rationally fulfilled in an endless reflexive and symmetric relation to itself and other selves. It is not literally uncaused, or without end in space or time, but rather "concrete," that is, "substantive" and "subjective" at once. By being a developed individual, at home in a particular rational society, and appreciating this society's place in the rational scheme of reality in general, the Hegelian self is simultaneously finite and "infinite," reconciled and in balance.[57]

Kierkegaard cannot believe that the self (especially any self alive to Western history) can be fully satisfied in such a purported reconciliation. He would say this, no doubt, even if he were made fully aware of all the difficulties in modern society that Marx stresses *and also* believed in all the improvements in society that Marx anticipates. Kierkegaard's ultimate problem with the value of the social domain has nothing to do with the specific structures of Hegelian ethical and political theory; it has to do with his own belief that the individual self as such has a dimension to which no such structure can do full justice – and that it is this dimension alone that properly deserves the term "infinite."[58] Following the German romantics, whom Hegel castigated as hopelessly eccentric,[59] Kierkegaard takes the notion of the infinite in this sense to have a not to be denied vertiginous pull on the self, and to have a meaning that can never be captured by the new definitions Hegel had manufactured (in this way even the aesthetic stage reveals a value that is dialectically satisfied in the final, and only the final, stage of life). Here Kierkegaard lays the groundwork for later existentialism by emphasizing two traditional notions in a way that parallels not Hegel but Schelling (and, earlier, Kant).[60] The two most basic truths in Kierkegaard's philosophy uncannily correspond to precisely the two main departures from early idealism that Schelling came to emphasize in his late work: the "positive," or underivable, facts of our absolute freedom and the existence of God (as an individual) – facts that cannot be equated with either a "reconciled" part or the all-inclusive whole of Hegel's thoroughly rational theoretical system.

It is only in the final stage on life's way, Religiousness B, that the self can face its infinite aspirations in a satisfied way. Unlike the knight of resignation, the Kierkegaardian knight of faith is devoted to both the finite and the infinite. The God it worships is not the abstract "philosopher's God," infinite and aloof, but a being whose Incarnation paradoxically combines infinitude and finitude both in itself and in its promise of satisfaction for the believer. Kierkegaard reads the story of Abraham as an anticipation of this paradox. Abraham does not simply resign himself in obedience; he makes a "double movement," believing that he is serving a transcendent, infinite God, a partner of his own infinite self, and also that this God will allow him, in some way that reason cannot foresee or explain, to retain satisfaction in a finite way, among his people and the generations to come. Abraham's story is used by Kierkegaard to illustrate how each Christian believer must commit to a paradoxical double movement. First, there is the long but "strictly human" step toward appreciating the full force of the ethical as well as the need to respect a value beyond the finite altogether. Secondly, "by virtue of the absurd," there is the return to oneself as forgiven and as anticipating salvation, a satisfaction of one's passion and finitude. This step is not merely free, in an absolute sense, as all the individual stages are; it is the only one that in principle lacks any rational foundation and thus can never be justified to others. This is why Kierkegaard called his work a dialectical *lyric*. The key transition is a "leap of faith," and it cannot be made or grounded by any logic, not even that of speculative idealism. Moreover, as Kierkegaard emphasizes in his even bleaker late work, the *Sickness unto Death*, the failure to take this last step does not leave us "fairly well off," three quarters of the way toward satisfaction. On the contrary, it leaves us in a perpetual disequilibrium between the finite and infinite sides of our own self, in an ever deepening despair, with all the pervasive patterns of deception of self and others that Sartre eventually catalogued in his marvelous Kierkegaardian epitaph to idealism, *Being and Nothingness*.

If, in our own time, most reflective intellectuals are defined, above all else, by a rejection of the traditional philosopher's optimistic attitude toward rationalism (a rejection reinforced by Nietzsche, Heidegger, Sartre, the post-modernists and many others working in Kierkegaard's wake), then – whether or not we can follow Kierkegaard's leap of faith – we are, in our non-rationalism, still much closer to him than to Hegel, or Feuerbach, or Marx. In that case, unless something like "rational faith" (itself a seemingly paradoxical term) can be resurrected with integrity, it can appear that the end of the idealist era brings us back to the fundamental choices presented by Hamann and Jacobi at the birth of German Idealism: the either/or of traditional faith or despair.[61]

NOTES

1 After Hegel died in 1831, important post-Hegelian works appeared as early as the 1830s, notably D. F. Strauss, *Life of Jesus Critically Examined* (1835), trans. G. Eliot (London: Sonnenschein, 1906) and L. Feuerbach, "Towards a Critique of Hegelian Philosophy" (1839), in L. S. Stepelevich, ed., *The Young Hegelians: An Anthology* (Cambridge: Cambridge University Press, 1983), 95–128. But the main works of the period, and my main focus, are: L. Feuerbach, *The Essence of Christianity* (1841), trans. G. Eliot (New York: Harper, 1957), and *Principles of the Philosophy of the Future* (1843), trans. M. Vogel (Indianapolis: Hackett, 1986); K. Marx, "A Contribution to the Critique of Hegel's 'Philosophy of Right'"(1843), in *Karl Marx: Early Writings*, trans. and ed. T. Bottomore (New York: McGraw-Hill, 1964), 195–219, "Economic and Philosophical Manuscripts" (1844), in *Karl Marx: Early Writings*, 61–194, "Theses on Feuerbach" (1845), in *Karl Marx: Selected Writings in Sociology and Social Philosophy*, trans. and ed. T. Bottomore (London: C. A. Watts & Co., 1956), 67–9, and *The German Ideology* (1846), ed. R. Pascal (New York: International Publishers, 1947); S. Kierkegaard, *Fear and Trembling* (1843), trans. H. V. and E. H. Hong (Princeton: Princeton University Press, 1983), and *The Sickness unto Death* (1849), trans. H. V. and E. H. Hong (Princeton: Princeton University Press, 1980).

2 Kierkegaard, *Fear and Trembling*, 8.

3 See Daniel Brudney, *Marx's Attempt to Leave Philosophy* (Cambridge, MA: Harvard University Press, 1998).

4 On Hegel's early manuscripts and concrete political interests, see Jürgen Habermas, *Theory and Practice*, trans. J. Viertel (Boston: Beacon Press, 1974), chs. 3–5; and G. Lukacs, *The Young Hegel*, trans. R. Livingstone (Cambridge, MA: MIT Press, 1975).

5 See Marx, "A Contribution to the Critique of Hegel's 'Philosophy of Right.'"

6 See Robert Nola, "The Young Hegelians, Feuerbach and Marx," in Robert M. Solomon and Kathleen M. Higgins, eds., *The Age of German Idealism* (London: Routledge, 1993), 305.

7 See Hegel, *Phenomenology of Spirit*, trans. A. V. Miller (Oxford: Oxford University Press, 1977), sec. 207–16, and cf. *Hegel's Early Theological Writings*, trans. T. M. Knox (Chicago: University of Chicago Press, 1948).

8 Hegel, *Phenomenology of Spirit*, sec. 177.

9 See Marx Wartofsky, *Feuerbach* (Cambridge: Cambridge University Press, 1977), xviii.

10 See Merold Westphal, *History and Truth in Hegel's Phenomenology*, 3rd edn. (Bloomington: Indiana University Press, 1998), 72–80.

11 Feuerbach, *Essence of Christianity*, 16; cf. Hegel, *Phenomenology of Spirit*, sec. 85.

12 This objection denies Kant's own attempt to provide general meanings for possible predications about God on the basis of a theory of pure categories supplemented by a form of justification that relies on pure moral considerations.

13 Feuerbach, *Essence of Christianity*, 227.

14 Feuerbach, *Essence of Christianity*, 230. I have added the single quotes and emphasis. "Speculation" is a term Hegel used to describe his own philosophy in a positive way.

15 See Fichte, "On the Foundation of our Belief in a Divine Government of the Universe," in Patrick Gardiner, ed., *Nineteenth-Century Philosophy* (New York: Free Press, 1969), 26: "The concept of God as a separate substance is impossible and contradictory." Trans. Paul Edwards, from *Philosophisches Journal*, 8 (1798), ed. F. Niethammer. See above, my Introduction to this volume, at n. 10.

16 *Karl Marx: Early Writings*, 202. Cf. Hegel, *Phenomenology of Spirit*, Introduction.

17 *Karl Marx: Early Writings*, 206.

18 *Karl Marx: Early Writings*, 202–3.

19 *Karl Marx: Early Writings*, 200.

20 *Karl Marx: Early Writings*, 200.

21 This issue has been complicated by old English translations of Hegel that ascribe to him statements such as "the being which the world has is only semblance, not real being," when what Hegel really says is "the world does indeed have being, but only the being of appearance," i.e., appearances are grounded and not themselves self-caused. Original translation from Hegel's "Lesser Logic," *The Logic of Hegel*, trans. W. Wallace (Oxford: Oxford University Press, 1892), §50.

22 *Hegel's Philosophy of Right*, trans. T. M. Knox (Oxford: Oxford University Press, 1952), 13.

23 *Karl Marx: Early Writings*, 211.

24 *Hegel's Philosophy of Right*, §§243–8.

25 See Michael Hardimon, *Hegel's Social Philosophy: The Project of Reconciliation* (Cambridge: Cambridge University Press, 1994).

26 *Karl Marx: Early Writings*, 211.

27 *Karl Marx: Early Writings*, 209.

28 E.g., *Hegel's Philosophy of Mind*, trans. W. Wallace and A. V. Miller (Oxford: Oxford University Press, 1971), §381: "Rather it is nature which is posited by mind."

29 *Karl Marx: Early Writings*, 214. Cf. at n. 14 above.

30 Cf. Marx, *The German Ideology*, 15: "life is not determined by consciousness, but consciousness by life."

31 See e.g., the discussion of Spinoza in *The Logic of Hegel* §50, where Hegel carefully distances himself from a personalist conception of God.

32 For a general discussion of "idealism," see above at n. 7 in my Introduction to this volume.

33 Marx, *The German Ideology*, 4.

34 *Karl Marx: Early Writings*, 122: "It is just the same as in religion. The more of himself that man attributes to God, the less he has left in himself."

35 *Karl Marx: Early Writings*, 128.

36 Marx, *The German Ideology*, 5–6.

37 Marx, *The German Ideology*, 6.

38 Marx, *The German Ideology*, 15.

39 Marx, *A Contribution to the Critique of Political Economy*, trans. N. I. Stone (Chicago: Charles H. Kerr and Co., 1904), 11–12.

40 This point is stressed in G. A. Cohen, *Karl Marx's Theory of History: A Defense* (Princeton: Princeton University Press, 1980).

41 See Hegel, *Phenomenology of Spirit*, sec. 87, on the idea that the dialectic is "not known to the consciousness we are observing."

42 See Hegel, *Phenomenology of Spirit*, sec. 89, on the need to go through "nothing less than the entire system."

43 See the phases distinguished in Hegel, *The Philosophy of History*, trans. J. Sibree (New York: Wiley, 1956).

44 See John Edward Toews, *Hegelianism: The Path Toward Dialectical Humanism, 1805–1841* (Cambridge: Cambridge University Press, 1980).

45 See e.g., *Hegel's Early Theological Writings*, 68: "The aim and essence of all true religion, our religion included, is human morality."

46 I am indebted to a vivid account of these parallels developed in a paper by Nicholas Boyle, "'Art,' Literature, and Theology: Learning from Germany" (forthcoming from University of Notre Dame Press).

47 See e.g., Andrew Dickson White, *A History of the Warfare of Science with Theology in Christendom* (Gloucester, MA: Peter Smith, 1978, repr. of 1st edn., 1896).

48 *Kierkegaard's Attack upon "Christendom," 1854–1855*, trans. W. Lowrie (Princeton: Princeton University Press, 1944).

49 Many of Kierkegaard's other titles are also obviously directed against Hegel's systematic approach, e.g., *Concluding Unscientific Postscript*, and *Philosophical Fragments*. There are also many ironic dimensions to Kierkegaard's pseudonymous approach, and the notion of "lyric," which I cannot due justice to here.

50 See Karsten Harries, *The Meaning of Modern Art: A Philosophical Interpretation* (Evanston: Northwestern University Press, 1968), ch. 5; and cf. Terry Eagleton, *The Ideology of the Aesthetic* (Cambridge, MA: Basil Blackwell, 1990), ch. 7.

51 Kierkegaard, *Fear and Trembling*, 59.

52 Kierkegaard, *Fear and Trembling*, 44.

53 Kierkegaard discusses as one of the first forms of the despair of "infinitude" the "fantastic" attitude in which one identifies with "inhuman knowledge" (*Sickness unto Death*, 31).

54 Kierkegaard, *Fear and Trembling*, 54.

55 See *Hegel's Philosophy of Right*, §§4–24, esp. §13, on thinking rather than mere will as "infinite," and §22: "it is the will whose potentialities have become fully explicit which is truly infinite because its object has become itself."

56 *Hegel's Philosophy of Right*, §23: "only in freedom of this kind is the will by itself without qualification, because then it is related to nothing but itself."

57 See *Hegel's Philosophy of Right*, p. 12: "we recognize reason as the rose of the cross in the present, this is the rational insight that reconciles us to the actual . . . to comprehend, not only to dwell in what is substantive."

58 As Kierkegaard makes clear in *Sickness unto Death*, the infinite dimension is in fact present at all stages of life, and so there is a kind of infinity in the aesthetic and ethical dimensions as well, but it does not have the literal transcendent dimension that is discovered only with resignation.

59 See Otto Pöggeler, *Hegels Kritik der Romantik*, rev. ed. (Munich: Fink, 1998).

60 On Kierkegaard's education and his attendance at Schelling's 1841 Berlin lectures, see James Collins, *The Mind of Kierkegaard* (Chicago: Henry Regnery, 1953); cf. Sturma, ch. 11 above.

61 See above, Beiser, ch. 1; Dahlstrom, ch. 4; and Franks, ch. 5.

BIBLIOGRAPHY

The following bibliography is necessarily selective. It gives priority to books over articles, recent work over earlier, English over other languages, philosophy over other subjects, works that concern themes of the era as a whole over narrower studies, and in particular items directly relevant to the chapters in this volume. It should be taken to be only a starting point for exploring the immense literature on the period. For more specific guides, see the bibliographies in the Cambridge Companions to Kant, Fichte, Hegel, Schopenhauer, Kierkegaard, and Marx. This bibliography is organized first into sections on primary sources (collections, then the four major figures, then other figures) and then corresponding sections on secondary sources.

PRIMARY SOURCES

Collections

Behler, Ernst, ed. *The Philosophy of German Idealism: Fichte, Jacobi, and Schelling.* New York: Continuum, 1987.

Beiser, Frederick C., trans. and ed. *The Early Political Writings of the German Romantics.* Cambridge: Cambridge University Press, 1996.

Chamberlain, Timothy J., ed. *Eighteenth Century German Criticism.* New York: Continuum, 1992.

di Giovanni, George and Harris, Henry S., trans. and eds. *Between Kant and Hegel.* Albany: State University of New York Press, 1985.

Nisbet, H. B., ed. *German Aesthetic and Literary Criticism.* Cambridge: Cambridge University Press, 1985.

Reiss, Hans, ed. *The Political Thought of the German Romantics (1793–1815).* Oxford: Blackwell, 1955.

Schmidt, James, ed. *What is Enlightenment? Eighteenth Century Answers and Twentieth Century Questions.* Berkeley: University of California Press, 1996.

Schulte-Seiss, Jochen, ed. *Theory as Practice: A Critical Anthology of Early German Romantic Writings.* Minneapolis: University of Minnesota Press, 1997.

Simpson, David, ed. *The Origins of Modern Critical Thought: German Aesthetic and Literary Criticism from Lessing to Hegel.* Cambridge: Cambridge University Press, 1988.

Stepelevich, Lawrence S., ed. *The Young Hegelians: An Anthology.* Cambridge: Cambridge University Press, 1983.

Taylor, Ronald, ed. *The Romantic Tradition in Germany: An Anthology with Critical Essays and Commentaries.* London: Methuen, 1970.

Willson, A. Leslie, ed. *German Romantic Criticism.* New York: Continuum, 1982.

Fichte

Fichte, Immanuel Hermann, ed. *Johann Gottlieb Fichte's sämmtliche Werke.* 8 vols. Berlin: Veit & Co., 1845/6. Reprinted as vols. I–VIII, *Fichtes Werke.* 11 vols. Berlin: de Gruyter, 1971.

Johann Gottlieb Fichte's nachgelassene Schriften. 3 vols. Bonn: Adolph-Marcus 1834/5. Reprinted as vols. IX–XI, *Fichtes Werke.* 11 vols. Berlin: de Gruyter, 1971.

Fuchs, Erich, ed. *Züricher Vorlesungen über den Begriff der Wissenschaftslehre, Februar 1974.* Neuried: Ars Una, 1996.

Lauth, Reinhard, Gliwitzky, Hans, and Jacob, Hans, eds. *J. G. Fichte-Gesamtausgabe der Bayerischen Akademie der Wissenschaften.* Stuttgart-Bad Cannstatt: Frommann-Holzboog, 1962ff.

English translations

Botterman, J. and Rash, W., trans. "A Crystal Clear Report to the General Public Concerning the Actual Essence of the Newest Philosophy: An Attempt to Force the Reader to Understand" (1801) in Ernst Behler, ed., *The Philosophy of German Idealism.* New York: Continuum, 1987, 39–115.

Breazeale, Daniel, trans. and ed. *Early Philosophical Writings.* Ithaca: Cornell University Press, 1988.

Foundations of the Transcendental Philosophy (Wissenschaftslehre) Nova Methodo (1796–99). Ithaca: Cornell University Press, 1992.

Introductions to the Wissenschaftslehre and Other Writings (1797–1800). Indianapolis: Hackett, 1994.

Edwards, Paul, trans. "On the Foundation of our Belief in a Divine Government of the Universe" (1798) in Patrick L. Gardiner, ed., *Nineteenth Century Philosophy.* New York: Free Press, 1969, 19–28.

Green, Garrett, trans. *Attempt at a Critique of All Revelation (1792, 1793).* New York: Cambridge University Press, 1978.

Heath, Peter and Lachs, John, trans. *Science of Knowledge with the First and Second Introductions.* Cambridge: Cambridge University Press, 1982.

Jones, R. F. and Turnbull, George Henry, trans. *Addresses to the German Nation,* ed. George Armstrong Kelly. New York: Harper & Row, 1968.

Neuhouser, Frederick and Baur, Michael, trans. and eds. *Foundations of Natural Right.* Cambridge: Cambridge University Press, 2000.

Preuss, Peter, trans. *The Vocation of Man.* Indianapolis: Hackett, 1987.

Hegel

Deutsche Forschungsgemeinschaft in Verbindung mit der Rheinisch-westfälischen Akademie der Wissenschaften, ed. *Gesammelte Werke. Kritische Ausgabe.* 13 vols. to date. Hamburg: Meiner, 1968f.

Henrich, Dieter, ed. *Philosophie des Rechts: Die Vorlesung von 1819/20.* Frankfurt: Suhrkamp, 1983.

Hoffmeister, Johannes, ed. *Dokumente zu Hegels Entwicklung.* Stuttgart: Frommann, 1936.
Briefe von und an Hegel, vol. I. Hamburg: Meiner, 1969.
Ilting, Karl Heinz, ed. *Vorlesungen über Rechtsphilosophie.* 4 vols. Stuttgart: Frommann, 1973–6.
Marheineke, Phillip, *et al.,* eds. *G. W. F. Hegel's Werke.* 18 vols. Berlin: Duncker and Humblot, 1832–45.
Moldenhauer, Eva and Michel, Karl Markus, eds. *Werke in zwanzig Bänden.* 20 vols. Frankfurt am Main: Suhrkamp, 1969–71.

English translations
Brown, Robert, ed. *Lectures on the History of Philosophy.* 3 vols. Berkeley: University of California Press, 1990.
Burbidge, John S., trans. *The Jena System 1804/05: Logic and Metaphysics.* Montreal and Kingston: McGill/Queen's University Press, 1986.
Cerf, Walter and Harris, Henry S., trans. *Difference Between the Systems of Fichte and Schelling.* Albany: State University of New York Press, 1977.
Faith and Knowledge. Albany: State University of New York Press, 1977.
System of Ethical Life and First Philosophy of Spirit. Albany: State University of New York Press, 1979.
Dobbins, John and Fuss, Peter, trans. *Three Essays 1793–1795.* Notre Dame: University of Notre Dame Press, 1984.
Geraets, Théodore F., Harris, Henry S., and Suchting, Wallis Arthur, trans. *The Encyclopedia Logic.* Indianapolis: Hackett, 1991.
Hodgson, Peter and Brown, R. F., trans. *Lectures on the Philosophy of Religion.* 3 vols. Berkeley: University of California Press, 1984–6.
Knox, Thomas Malcolm, trans. *Hegel's Aesthetics.* Oxford: Clarendon Press, 1964.
Miller, Arnold V., trans. *Science of Logic.* London: George Allen & Unwin, 1969.
Philosophy of Nature. Oxford: Oxford University Press, 1970.
The Philosophical Propadeutic, ed. Michael George and Andrew Vincent. Oxford: Blackwell, 1986.
Nisbet, Hugh Barr, trans. *Lectures on the Philosophy of World History: Introduction.* Cambridge: Cambridge University Press, 1975.
Elements of the Philosophy of Right, ed. Allen Wood. Cambridge: Cambridge University Press, 1991.
Petry, Michael John, trans. and ed. *Hegels Philosophie des subjektiven Geistes / Hegel's Philosophy of Subjective Spirit.* 3 vols. Dordrecht: Riedel, 1978.
Wallace, William, trans. *Hegel's Philosophy of Mind.* Oxford: Oxford University Press, 1971.

Kant

Kant's gesammelte Schriften. Ausgabe der königlich preussischen Akademie der Wissenschaften. Berlin: W. de Gruyter, 1900– .
Weischedel, Wilhelm, ed. *Werke in sechs Bänden.* Wiesbaden: Insel Verlag, 1956–62.

English translations
Allison, Henry E., trans. *The Kant–Eberhard Controversy: An English Translation together with Supplementary Materials and a Historical-Analytical Introduction of*

Immanuel Kant's 'On a New Discovery According to Which Any New Critique of Pure Reason Has Been Made Superfluous by an Earlier One.' Baltimore: Johns Hopkins University Press, 1973.

Ameriks, Karl and Naragon, Steven, trans. and eds. *Lectures on Metaphysics.* Cambridge: Cambridge University Press, 1997.

Ellington, James, trans. *Metaphysical Foundations of Natural Science.* Indianapolis: Bobbs-Merrill, 1970.

Förster, Eckart and Rosen, Michael, trans. and eds. *Opus postumum.* Cambridge: Cambridge University Press, 1993.

Gregor, Mary, trans. *Anthropology From a Pragmatic Point of View.* The Hague: Martinus Nijhoff, 1974.

The Conflict of the Faculties. New York: Abaris Books, 1979. (Repr. University of Nebraska Press, 1992.)

Metaphysics of Morals, introduction by Roger Sullivan. Cambridge: Cambridge University Press, 1996.

Practical Philosophy, introduction by Allen Wood. Cambridge: Cambridge University Press, 1996.

Critique of Practical Reason, introduction by Andrews Reath. Cambridge: Cambridge University Press, 1997.

Groundwork of the Metaphysics of Morals, introduction by Christine Korsgaard. Cambridge: Cambridge University Press, 1997.

Guyer, Paul and Wood, Allen, trans. and ed. *Critique of Pure Reason.* Cambridge: Cambridge University Press, 1998.

Hatfield, Gary, trans. and ed. *Immanuel Kant: Prolegomena to Any Future Metaphysics that Will be Able to Come Forward as Science.* Cambridge: Cambridge University Press, 1997.

Heath, Peter and Schneewind, Jerome B., trans. and eds. *Lectures on Ethics.* New York: Cambridge University Press, 1997.

Humphrey, Ted, trans. *What Real Progress Has Metaphysics Made in Germany since the Time of Leibniz and Wolff?* New York: Abaris Books, 1983.

Kemp Smith, Norman, trans. *The Critique of Pure Reason*, 2nd edn. London: Macmillan, 1933.

Pluhar, Werner, trans. *Critique of Judgment, Including the First Introduction.* Indianapolis: Hackett, 1987.

Walford, David, trans. and ed. *Theoretical Philosophy, 1755–1770.* Cambridge: Cambridge University Press, 1992.

Wood, Allen and Clark, Gertrude, trans. *Lectures on Philosophical Theology.* Ithaca: Cornell University Press, 1978.

Wood, Allen and di Giovanni, George, trans. and eds. *Religion and Rational Theology.* Cambridge: Cambridge University Press, 1996.

Religion within the Boundaries of Mere Reason and Other Writings, introduction by Robert M. Adams. Cambridge: Cambridge University Press, 1998.

Young, J. Michael. *Lectures on Logic.* New York: Cambridge University Press, 1992.

Zweig, Arnulf, trans. and ed. *Correspondence.* Cambridge: Cambridge University Press, 1999.

Schelling

Düsing, Klaus. *Schellings und Hegels erste absolute Metaphysik (1801–2)*. Zusammen-fassende Vorlesungsnachschriften von Ignaz Paul Vitalis Troxter. Ed. with commentary by Klaus Düsing. Cologne: Dinter, 1988.

Frank, Manfred and Kurz, Gerhard, eds. *Materialien zu Schellings philosophischen Anfängen*. Frankfurt: Suhrkamp, 1995.

Fuhrmans, Horst, ed. *Briefe und Dokumente*. Bonn: Bouvier, 1973.

Jacobs, Wilhelm G., Krings, Hermann, and Zeltner, Hermann, eds. *Historisch-kritische Ausgabe*. Stuttgart-Bad Cannstatt: Frommann-Holzboog, 1976ff.

Schelling, Karl Friedrich August, ed. *Friedrich Wilhelm Joseph von Schellings sämmtliche Werke*. 14 vols. Stuttgart: Cotta, 1856–61.

Schulz, Walter, ed. *Fichte-Schelling Briefwechsel*. Frankfurt: Suhrkamp, 1968.

Weischedel, Wolfgang, ed. *Streit um die göttlichen Dinge. Die Auseinandersetzung zwischen Jacobi und Schelling*. Darmstadt: Wissenschaftliche Buchgesellschaft, 1967.

English translations

Bowie, Andrew. *On the History of Modern Philosophy*. Cambridge: Cambridge University Press, 1994.

Gutmann, James, trans. *Philosophical Inquiries into the Nature of Human Freedom*. La Salle, IL: Open Court, 1989.

Harris, Errol and Heath, Peter, trans. *Ideas for a Philosophy of Nature*. Cambridge: Cambridge University Press, 1988.

Heath, Peter, trans. *System of Transcendental Idealism (1800)*. Charlottesville, VA: University Press of Virginia, 1978.

Marti, Fritz, trans. and ed. *The Unconditional in Human Knowledge: Four Early Essays, 1794–1796*. Lewisburg: Bucknell University Press, 1980.

Morgan, E. S. and Guterman, Norbert, trans. *On University Studies*. Athens: Ohio University Press, 1966.

Pfau, Thomas, trans. and ed. *Idealism and the Endgame of Theory: Three Essays by F. W. J. Schelling*. Albany: State University of New York Press, 1994.

Stott, Douglas W., trans. *The Philosophy of Art*. Minneapolis: University of Minnesota Press, 1989.

Vater, Michael G., trans. *Bruno, or On the Natural and the Divine Principle of Things*. Albany: State University of New York Press, 1984.

Other primary sources

Engels, Friedrich. *Ludwig Feuerbach and the Outcome of Classical German Philosophy*. New York: International Publishers, 1978.

Feuerbach, Ludwig. *The Essence of Christianity*, trans. George Eliot. New York: Harper, 1957.

Gesammelte Werke. Ed. Werner Schuffenhauer. Berlin: Akademie-Verlag, 1967– .

Principles of the Philosophy of the Future, trans. Manfred Vogel. Indianapolis: Hackett, 1986.

Hamann, Johann Georg. *Hamanns Schriften*, ed. F. Roth. Berlin: Riemer, 1821–5.

Sämtliche Werke. 6 vols., ed. J. Nadler. Vienna: Herder, 1949–57.

Briefwechsel. 6 vols., ed. Walter Ziesemer and Arthur Henkel. Wiesbaden: Insel, 1955–75.

Hamann's Socratic Memorabilia: A Translation and Commentary, trans. James C. O'Flaherty. Baltimore: Johns Hopkins University Press, 1967.

The Tongues of Men: Hegel and Hamann on Religious Language and History, trans. and ed. Stephen Dunning. Missoula: Scholars Press, 1979.

Herder, Johann Gottfried. *Sämtliche Werke*. 32 vols., ed. Bernhard Suphan. Berlin: Wiedman, 1877–1913.

God, Some Conversations, trans. Frederick Burkhardt. Indianapolis: Bobbs-Merrill, 1962.

On the Origin of Language (selections from Jean-Jacques Rousseau and J. G. Herder), trans. and ed. J. H. Moran and A. Goode. New York: Ungar, 1966.

Johann Gottfried Herder: Selected Early Works, 1764–1767: Addresses, Essays, and Drafts; Fragments on Recent German Literature, trans. Ernest Menze and Michael Palma, and ed. Ernest A. Menze and Karl Menges. University Park, PA: Pennsylvania State University Press, 1991.

Against Pure Reason: Writings on Religion, Language, and History, trans. and ed. Marcia Bunge. Minneapolis: Fortress Press, 1993.

Hölderlin, Friedrich. *Hölderlin: Sämtliche Werke, Grosser Stuttgarter Ausgabe*. 15 vols., ed. Friedrich Beissner. Stuttgart: Cotta, 1943–85.

Hyperion: or, The Hermit in Greece, trans. Willard R. Trask. New York: Ungar, 1965.

Essays and Letters on Theory, trans. and ed. Thomas Pfau. Albany: State University of New York Press, 1988.

Humboldt, Wilhelm von. *On Language: On the Diversity of Human Language Construction and its Influence on the Mental Development of the Species*, trans. Peter Heath and with an introduction by Michael Losonsky. Cambridge: Cambridge University Press, 1999.

Jacobi, Friedrich Heinrich. *David Hume über den Glauben oder Idealismus und Realismus*. Breslau: Löwe, 1787. Repr. New York: Garland, 1983.

Werke, ed. Friedrich Köppen and Friedrich von Roth. Leipzig: Gerhard Fleischer, 1812–25. Repr. Darmstadt: Wissenschaftliche Buchgesellschaft, 1968.

Werke, ed. Klaus Hammacher and Walter Jaeschke. Hamburg: Meiner, 1998.

Friedrich Heinrich Jacobi: The Main Philosophical Writings and the Novel Allwill, trans. and ed. George di Giovanni. Montreal: McGill-Queen's University Press, 1994.

Kierkegaard, Søren. *Stages on Life's Way*, trans. Walter Lowrie. Princeton: Princeton University Press, 1940.

Kierkegaard's Attack upon "Christendom," 1854–1855, trans. Walter Lowrie. Princeton: Princeton University Press, 1944.

Philosophical Fragments, trans. David Swenson and Edna H. Hong, and ed. N. Thulstrup. Princeton: Princeton University Press, 1962.

The Point of View for my Work as an Author, trans. Walter Lowrie. New York: Harper & Row, 1962.

Samlede Vaerker. 20 vols., ed. Peter Preisler Rohde. Copenhagen: Gyldendalske Boghandel, 1962–3.

Concluding Unscientific Postscript, trans. David Swenson and Walter Lowrie. Princeton: Princeton University Press, 1974.

The Sickness unto Death, trans. Howard V. and Edna H. Hong. Princeton: Princeton University Press, 1980.

Either/Or. 2 vols., trans. David Swenson and Lillian Marvin Swenson. Princeton: Princeton University Press, 1983.

Fear and Trembling, trans. Howard V. and Edna H. Hong. Princeton: Princeton University Press, 1983.

Maimon, Salomon. *Giv'at ha-Moreh*, trans. and ed. Samuel Hugo Bergman and Nathan Rotenstreich. Jerusalem: Israel Academy of Sciences and Humanities, 1965.

Gesämmelte Werke, ed. Valerio Verra. Hildesheim: Olms, 1970.

Marx, Karl. *A Contribution to the Critique of Political Economy*, trans. N. I. Stone. Chicago: Charles H. Kerr and Co., 1904.

The German Ideology, ed. Roy Pascal. New York: International Publishers, 1947.

Karl Marx, Friedrich Engels: Historisch-Kritisch Gesamtausgabe. Ed. D. Ryazonov and Vladimir Viktorovich Adoratskii. Berlin: Dietz Verlag, 1956– .

Karl Marx: Selected Writings in Sociology and Social Philosophy, trans. and ed. Tom Bottomore. London: C. A. Watts & Co., 1956.

Karl Marx: Early Writings, trans. and ed. Tom Bottomore. New York: McGraw-Hill, 1964.

Mendelssohn, Moses. *Gesammelte Schriften, Jubiläumsausgabe*, ed. A. Altman *et al.* Stuttgart: Holzborg, 1971.

Philosophical Writings. Ed. Daniel O. Dahlstrom. Cambridge: Cambridge University Press, 1997.

Niethammer, Friedrich Immanuel. *Korrespondenz mit dem Klagenfurter Herbert-Kreis*, ed. Wilhelm Baum. Vienna: Turia + Kant, 1995.

Novalis (Friedrich von Hardenberg). *Hymns to the Night and Other Selected Writings*, trans. Charles E. Passage. Indianapolis: Bobbs-Merrill, 1960.

Novalis Schriften, 5 vols., ed. Richard Samuel, Hans Joachim Mähl, and Gerhard Schulz. Stuttgart: Kohlhammer, 1960–88.

Philosophical Writings, trans. and ed. Margaret Mahony Stoljar. Albany: State University of New York Press, 1997.

Reinhold, Karl Leonard. "Briefe über die Kantische Philosophie," *Der Teutsche Merkur*. Weimar: 1786–7.

Versuch einer neuen Theorie des menschlichen Vorstellungsvermögens. Jena: Widtmann and Mauke, 1789.

Briefe über die Kantische Philosophie I–II. Jena: Mauke, 1790–2.

Beyträge zur Berichtigung bisheriger Missverständisse der Philosophen I–II. Jena: Mauke, 1790–4.

Über das Fundament des philosophischen Wissens. Jena: Mauke, 1791. Repr. Hamburg: Meiner, 1978. Partly translated in George di Giovanni and Henry S. Harris, eds., *Between Kant and Hegel*. Albany: State University of New York Press, 1985.

Korrespondenz 1773–1788, ed. Reinhard Lauth, Eberhard Hellar, and Kurt Hiller. Stuttgart-Bad Cannstatt: Frommann-Holzboog, 1983.

Karl Leonhard Reinhold: Eine annotierte Bibliographie, ed. Alexander von Schonborn. Stuttgart: Frommann-Holzboog, 1991.

Schiller, Friedrich. *Sämmtliche Werke*. 5 vols., ed. Gerhard Fricke. Munich: Hanser, 1959.

Werke. Nationalausgabe, 43 vols., ed. Benno von Wiese. Weimar: Böhlau, 1962.

On the Aesthetic Education of Man, trans. Elizabeth Wilkinson and L. A. Willoughby. New York: Oxford University Press, 1982.

Schiller: Essays, trans. and ed. Walter Hinderer and Daniel O. Dahlstrom. New York: Continuum, 1993.

Schlegel, August Wilhelm. *Sämmtliche Werke*. 16 vols., ed. Eduard Böcking. Leipzig: Weidmannsche Verlag, 1846–8.

Schlegel, Friedrich von. *Kritische Friedrich-Schlegel-Ausgabe*. 35 vols., ed. Ernst Behler, Jean Jacques Anstett, and Hans Eichner. Paderborn: Schöningh, 1958– .

Dialogue on Poetry and Literary Aphorisms, trans. Ernst Behler and Roman Stone. University Park: Pennsylvania State University Press, 1968.

Friedrich Schlegel's Lucinde and the Fragments, trans. and ed. Peter Firchow. Minneapolis: University of Minnesota Press, 1991.

Schleiermacher, Friedrich Ernst Daniel. *Friedrich Schleiermachers Sämmtliche Werke*. 32 vols. Berlin: G. Reimer, 1834–64.

Hermeneutik und Kritik, ed. Manfred Frank. Frankfurt: Suhrkamp, 1977.

Friedrich Schleiermachers Ethik 1812/1813, ed. Hans-Joachim Birkner. Hamburg: Meiner, 1990.

On the Highest Good, trans. and annotated H. Victor Froese. Lewiston, ME: Edwin Mellin Press, 1992.

On Religion: Speeches to Its Cultured Despisers, trans. Richard Crouter. Cambridge: Cambridge University Press, 1996.

"Hermeneutics and Criticism" and Other Texts, trans. and ed. Andrew Bowie. Cambridge: Cambridge University Press, 1998.

Schopenhauer, Arthur. *The World as Will and Representation*. 2 vols., trans. Eric F. Payne. New York: Dover, 1974.

Sämtliche Werke. 7 vols., ed. Arthur Hübscher, 4th edn. Mannheim: Brockhaus, 1988.

On the Fourfold Root of the Principle of Sufficient Reason, trans. Eric F. Payne. La Salle, IL: Open Court, 1989.

On the Basis of Morality, trans. Eric T. Payne. Indianapolis: Bobbs-Merill, 1995.

Prize Essay on the Freedom of the Will, trans. Eric F. Payne and ed. Günter Zöller. Cambridge: Cambridge University Press, 1999.

Solger, Karl Wilhelm Ferdinand. *Nachgelassene Schriften und Briefwechsel*, vol. II. Heidelberg: Schneider, 1973.

Erwin. Vier Gespräche über das Schöne und die Kunst. Munich: Fink, 1971.

Vorlesungen über Ästhetik. Darmstadt: Wissenschaftliche Buchgesellschaft, 1973.

Tieck, Ludwig. *Kritische Schriften*. 4 vols. Leipzig: G. Reimer, 1848–52.

Wizenmann, Thomas. *Die Resultate der Jacobischen und Mendelssohnschen Philosophie*. Leipzig: Göschen, 1786. Reprinted Hildesheim: Gerstenberg, 1984.

SECONDARY SOURCES

General works

Aesthetics

Abrams, Meyer H. *Natural Supernaturalism: Tradition and Revolution in Romantic Literature*. New York: W. W. Norton, 1971.

Behler, Ernst. *German Romantic Literary Theory*. Cambridge: Cambridge University Press, 1993.

Blackall, Eric A. *The Novels of the German Romantics*. Ithaca: Cornell University Press, 1983.

Bowie, Andrew. *Aesthetics and Subjectivity: From Kant to Nietzsche*. Manchester: Manchester University Press, 1993 (2nd edn., completely revised, 2000).

From Romanticism to Critical Theory: The Philosophy of German Literary Theory. London: Routledge, 1997.

Dahlhaus, Carl. *The Idea of Absolute Music*, trans. Roger Lustig. Chicago: University of Chicago Press, 1989.

De Man, Paul. *The Rhetoric of Romanticism*. New York: Columbia University Press, 1984.

The Romantic School and Other Essays, ed. Joat Hermond and Robert C. Holub. New York: Continuum, 1985.

Romanticism and Contemporary Criticism: the Gauss Seminar and Other Papers. Baltimore: Johns Hopkins University Press, 1993.

Aesthetic Ideology, ed. Andrzej Warminski. Minneapolis: University of Minnesota Press, 1996.

Eagleton, Terry. *The Ideology of the Aesthetic*. Cambridge, MA: Blackwell, 1990.

Eldridge, Richard, ed. *Beyond Representation: Philosophy and Poetic Imagination*. Cambridge: Cambridge University Press, 1996.

Frank, Manfred. *Der kommende Gott. Vorlesungen über die Neue Mythologie*. Frankfurt: Suhrkamp, 1982.

Einführung in die frühromantische Ästhetik. Frankfurt: Suhrkamp, 1989.

The Subject and the Text: Essays on Literary Theory and Philosophy, trans. Helen Atkins, and ed. Andrew Bowie. Cambridge: Cambridge University Press, 1997.

Gadamer, Hans-Georg. *Literature and Philosophy in Dialogue: Essays in German Literary Theory*, trans. Robert H. Paslick. Albany: State University of New York Press, 1994.

Harries, Karsten. *The Meaning of Modern Art: A Philosophical Interpretation*. Evanston: Northwestern University Press, 1968.

Hohendahl, Peter Uwe, ed. *A History of German Literary Criticism 1730–1980*. Lincoln, NE: University of Nebraska Press, 1980.

Lacoue-Lebarthe, Philippe and Nancy, Jean-Luc. *The Literary Absolute: The Theory of Literature in German Romanticism*, trans. Philip Barnard and Cheryl Lester. Albany: State University of New York Press, 1988.

Larmore, Charles. *The Romantic Legacy*. New York: Columbia University Press, 1996.

Neubauer, John. *The Emancipation of Music from Language. Departure from Mimesis in Eighteenth-Century Aesthetics*. New Haven and London: Yale University Press, 1986.

Norton, Robert E. *The Beautiful Soul: Aesthetic Morality in the Eighteenth Century*. Ithaca: Cornell University Press, 1995.

Rorty, Richard. "Nineteenth-Century Idealism and Twentieth-Century Textualism," *Monist*, 64 (1981), 155–74.

Rosen, Charles. *Romantic Poets, Critics, and Other Madmen*. Cambridge, MA: Harvard University Press, 1988.

Savile, Anthony. *Aesthetic Reconstructions: The Seminal Writings of Lessing, Kant, and Schiller*. Oxford: Blackwell, 1987.

Seyhan, Azade. *Representation and Its Discontents: The Critical Legacy of German Romanticism*. Berkeley: University of California Press, 1992.

Szondi, Peter. *Schriften 1*. Frankfurt: Suhrkamp, 1978.

Till, Nicholas. *Mozart and the Enlightenment: Truth, Virtue, and Beauty in Mozart's Operas*. New York: W.W. Norton, 1993.

Todorov, Tzvetan. *Theories of the Symbol*, trans. Catherine Porter. Ithaca, NY: Cornell University Press, 1982.

Walzel, Oskar Franz. *German Romanticism*, trans. A. E. Lussky. New York: Putnam, 1932.

Wellek, René. *The History of Modern Criticism: 1750–1950*, vol. II: *The Romantic Age*. London: Jonathan Cape, 1955.

Collections

Ameriks, Karl and Sturma, Dieter, eds. *The Modern Subject: Conceptions of the Self in Classical German Philosophy*. Albany: State University of New York Press, 1995.

Baur, Michael and Dahlstrom, Daniel, eds. *The Emergence of German Idealism*. Washington, DC: Catholic University of America Press, 1999.

Critchley, Simon and Dews, Peter, eds. *Deconstructive Subjectivities*. Albany: State University of New York Press, 1996.

Cunningham, Andrew and Jardine, Nicholas, eds. *Romanticism and the Sciences*. Cambridge: Cambridge University Press, 1990.

Jamme, Christoph and Schneider, Helmut, eds. *Mythologie der Vernunft. Hegels 'ältestes Systemprogramm' des deutschen Idealismus*. Frankfurt: Suhrkamp, 1984.

Klemm, David and Zöller, Günter, eds. *Figuring the Self: Subject, Absolute, and Others in Classical German Philosophy*. Albany: State University of New York Press, 1997.

Mell, Donald, Braun, Theodore, and Palmer, Lucia, eds. *Man, God, and Nature in the Enlightenment*. East Lansing, MI: Colleagues Press, 1988.

Sedgwick, Sally, ed. *The Reception of Kant's Critical Philosophy: Fichte, Schelling, and Hegel*. Cambridge: Cambridge University Press, 2000.

Solomon, Robert M. and Higgins, Kathleen M., eds. *The Age of German Idealism*. London: Routledge, 1993.

History

Boyle, Nicholas. *Goethe: The Poet and the Age*, vol. I. Oxford: Oxford University Press, 1992.

Bruford, Walter. *Culture and Society in Classical Weimar*. Cambridge: Cambridge University Press, 1962.

Brunschwig, Henri. *Enlightenment and Romanticism in Eighteenth Century Prussia*, trans. Frank Jellinek. Chicago: University of Chicago Press, 1974.

Haym, Rudolph. *Die romantische Schule*. Berlin: Gaertner, 1870. Repr. Darmstadt: Wissenschaftliche Buchgesellschaft, 1977.

Heine, Heinrich. *Religion and Philosophy in Germany: A Fragment*, trans. John Snodgrass. Albany: State University of New York Press, 1986.

Henrich, Dieter, ed. *Carl Immanuel Diez, Briefwechsel und Kantische Schriften*. Stuttgart: Klett-Cotta, 1997.

Hinske, Norbert. *Der Aufbruch in den Kantianismus: der Frühkantianismus an der Universität Jena von 1785–1800 und seine Vorgeschichte*. Stuttgart: Frommann-Holzboog, 1995.

Hull, Isabel V. *Sexuality, State, and Civil Society in Germany, 1700–1815*. Ithaca: Cornell University Press, 1996.

La Vopa, Anthony. *Grace, Talent, and Merit: Poor Students, Clerical Careers, and Professional Ideology in Eighteenth-century Germany*. Cambridge: Cambridge University Press, 1988.

Stäel, Madame de. *Germany*. 3 vols. London: John Murray, 1813.

Weigl, Eberhard. *Schauplätze der deutschen Aufklärung: Eine Städterundgang*. Hamburg: Rowohlt, 1997.

Ziolkowski, Theodore. *The Institutions of German Romanticism*. Princeton: Princeton University Press, 1990.

Das Wunderjahr in Jena: Geist und Gesellschaft 1794/5. Stuttgart: Klett-Cotta, 1997.

Overviews

Ameriks, Karl. *Kant and the Fate of Autonomy: Problems in the Appropriation of the Critical Philosophy.* Cambridge: Cambridge University Press, 2000.

Beck, Lewis White. *Early German Philosophy: Kant and His Predecessors.* Cambridge, MA: Harvard University Press, 1969.

Beiser, Frederick C. *The Fate of Reason: German Philosophy from Kant to Fichte.* Cambridge, MA: Harvard University Press, 1987.

Berlin, Isaiah. *The Roots of Romanticism*, ed. Henry Hardy. Princeton, NJ: Princeton University Press, 1999.

Bowie, Andrew. "German Philosophy Today: Between Idealism, Romanticism and Pragmatism," in Anthony O'Hear, ed., *German Philosophy Since Kant*, Royal Institute of Philosophy Lectures. Cambridge: Cambridge University Press, 1999.

Coleridge, Samuel Taylor. *Biographia Literaria*, ed. George Watson. London: John Dent, 1975.

Cranston, Maurice. *The Romantic Movement.* Cambridge, MA: Blackwell, 1994.

Fackenheim, Emil. *The God Within: Kant, Schelling, and Historicity.* Toronto: University of Toronto Press, 1996.

Frank, Manfred. *"Unendliche Annäherung." Die Anfänge der philosophischen Frühromantik.* Frankfurt: Suhrkamp, 1997.

Henrich, Dieter. *Selbstverhältnisse: Gedanken und Auslegungen zu den Grundlagen der klassischen deutschen Philosophie.* Stuttgart: Reclam, 1982.

Konstellationen: Probleme und Debatten am Ursprung der idealistischen Philosophie (1789–1795). Stuttgart: Klett-Cotta, 1991.

"The Origins of the Theory of the Subject," in *Philosophical Interventions in the Unfinished Project of the Enlightenment*, ed. Axel Honneth *et al.* Cambridge, MA: MIT Press, 1992.

Horstmann, Rolf-Peter. *Die Grenzen der Vernunft: Eine Untersuchung zu Zielen und Motiven des Deutschen Idealismus.* Frankfurt: Anton Hain, 1991.

Hösle, Vittorio. *Objective Idealism, Ethics, and Politics.* Notre Dame: University of Notre Dame Press, 1998.

Kroner, Richard. *Von Kant bis Hegel.* 2 vols. Tübingen: Mohr, 1921, 1924.

Kuehn, Manfred. *Scottish Common Sense in Germany, 1768–1800.* Kingston and Montreal: McGill-Queen's University Press, 1987.

Lovejoy, Arthur O. *The Reason, the Understanding, and Time.* Baltimore: Johns Hopkins University Press, 1961.

Mandelbaum, Maurice. *History, Man, and Reason: A Study in Nineteenth-Century Thought.* Baltimore: Johns Hopkins University Press, 1971.

Mead, George Herbert. *Movements of Thought in the Nineteenth Century.* Chicago: University of Chicago Press, 1936.

Michelet, Karl Ludwig. *Geschichte der letzten Systeme der Philosophie in Deutschland von Kant bis Hegel.* 2 vols. Berlin, 1837/8.

Pfleiderer, Otto. *The Development of Theology in Germany since Kant*, trans. J. F. Smith. London: Sonnenschein, 1893.

Royce, Josiah. *Lectures on Modern Idealism.* New Haven: Yale University Press, 1919.

Santayana, George. *Egotism in German Philosophy.* New York: Scribner, 1915.

Schacht, Richard. *Hegel and After: Studies in Continental Philosophy Between Kant and Sartre.* Pittsburgh: University of Pittsburgh Press, 1975.

Siep, Ludwig. *Praktische Philosophie im Deutschen Idealismus.* Frankfurt: Suhrkamp, 1992.

Taylor, Charles. *The Sources of the Self: The Making of Modern Identity.* Cambridge, MA: Harvard University Press, 1989.

Timm, Hermann. *Gott und die Freiheit.* Frankfurt am Main: Klostermann, 1974.

Politics

Aris, Reinhold. *History of Political Thought in Germany from 1789 to 1815.* London: Cass, 1936.

Beiser, Frederick, C. *Enlightenment, Revolution, and Romanticism: The Genesis of Modern German Political Thought.* Cambridge, MA: Harvard University Press, 1992.

Dewey, John. *German Politics and Philosophy.* New York: Henry Holt, 1915.

Epstein, Klaus. *The Genesis of German Conservatism.* Princeton: Princeton University Press, 1966.

Habermas, Jürgen. *Theory and Practice,* trans. J. Viertel. Boston: Beacon Press, 1974.

Schmitt, Carl. *Political Romanticism,* trans. Guy Oakes. Cambridge, MA: MIT Press, 1986.

On Fichte

Adamson, Robert. *Fichte.* Edinburgh: Blackwood, 1881.

Baumanns, Peter. *J. G. Fichte. Kritische Gesamtdarstellung seiner Philosophie.* Freiburg and Munich: Alber, 1990.

Brachtendorf, Johannes. *Fichtes Lehre vom Sein. Eine kritische Darstellung der Wissenschaftslehren von 1794, 1798/99 und 1812.* Paderborn: Schöningh, 1995.

Breazeale, Daniel. "Fichte's 'Aenesidemus' Review and the Transformation of German Idealism," *The Review of Metaphysics,* 34 (1980/1), 545–68.

Breazeale, Daniel and Rockmore, Thomas, eds. *Fichte: Historical Contexts/ Contemporary Controversies.* Atlantic Highlands: Humanities Press, 1997.

Guéroult, Martial. *L'évolution et la structure de la doctrine de la science de Fichte.* 2 vols. Paris: Société de l'édition Les Belles Lettres, 1930.

Henrich, Dieter. "Fichte's Original Insight," trans. David Lachterman in *Contemporary German Philosophy,* 1 (1982), 15–52.

Hogrebe, Wolfram, ed. *Fichtes Wissenschaftslehre 1794.* Frankfurt: Suhrkamp, 1995.

Martin, Wayne. *Idealism and Objectivity: Understanding Fichte's Jena Project.* Stanford: Stanford University Press, 1997.

Neuhouser, Frederick. *Fichte's Theory of Subjectivity.* Cambridge: Cambridge University Press, 1990.

Siep, Ludwig. *Hegels Fichtekritik und die Wissenschaftslehre von 1804.* Freiburg/Munich: Alber, 1970.

Stolzenberg, Jürgen. *Fichtes Begriff der intellektuellen Anschauung. Die Entwicklung in den Wissenschaftslehren von 1793/94 bis 1801/1802.* Stuttgart: Klett-Cotta, 1986.

Williams, Robert R. *Recognition: Fichte and Hegel on the Other.* Albany: State University of New York Press, 1992.

Zöller, Günter. *Fichte's Transcendental Philosophy. The Original Duplicity of Intelligence and Will.* Cambridge: Cambridge University Press, 1998.

Zöller, Günter, ed. *The Cambridge Companion to Fichte.* Cambridge: Cambridge University Press, forthcoming.

On Hegel

Avineri, Shlomo. *Hegel's Theory of the Modern State*. Cambridge: Cambridge University Press, 1972.

Beiser, Frederick C., ed. *The Cambridge Companion to Hegel*. Cambridge: Cambridge University Press, 1993.

Cohen, Robert S. and Wartofsky, Marx W., eds. *Hegel and the Sciences*. Dordrecht: Nijhoff, 1983.

Croce, Benedetto. *What is Living and What is Dead in the Philosophy of Hegel*, trans. Douglas Ainslie. New York: Russell & Russell, 1969.

De Vries, Willem. *Hegel's Theory of Mental Activity: An Introduction to Theoretical Spirit*. Ithaca: Cornell University Press, 1988.

D'Hondt, Jacques. *Hegel in his Time*, trans. John Burbidge. Peterborough, Ont.: Broadview Press, 1988.

di Giovanni, George, ed. *Essays on Hegel's Logic*. Albany: State University of New York Press, 1990.

Dickey, Lawrence. *Hegel: Religion, Economics, and the Politics of Spirit, 1770–1807*. Cambridge: Cambridge University Press, 1987.

Dilthey, Wilhelm. *Die Jugendgeschichte Hegels*, in *Gesammelte Schriften*, vol. IV. Stuttgart: Tuebner, 1962–5.

Elder, Crawford. *Appropriating Hegel*. Aberdeen: Aberdeen University Press, 1980.

Findlay, John Niemeyer. *Hegel: A Re-examination*. London: George Allen and Unwin, 1958.

Forster, Michael. *Hegel and Skepticism*. Cambridge, MA: Harvard University Press, 1989.
   Hegel's Idea of a Phenomenology of Spirit. Chicago: University of Chicago Press, 1998.

Fulda, Hans Friedrich. *Das Problem einer Einleitung in Hegels Wissenschaft der Logik*. Frankfurt: Klostermann, 1965.

Gadamer, Hans-Georg, ed. *Hegel's Dialectic: Five Hermeneutical Studies*, trans. Christopher Smith. New Haven: Yale University Press, 1976.

Hardimon, Michael. *Hegel's Social Philosophy: The Project of Reconciliation*. Cambridge: Cambridge University Press, 1994.

Harris, Henry S. *Hegel's Development: Towards the Daylight (1770–1801)*. Oxford: Oxford University Press, 1972.
   Hegel's Development: Night Thoughts (Jena 1801–1806). Oxford: Oxford University Press, 1983.

Houlgate, Stephen, ed. *Hegel and the Philosophy of Nature*. Albany: State University of New York Press, 1998.

Hyppolite, Jean. *Genesis and Structure of the Phenomenology of Spirit*, trans. S. Cherniak and R. Heckmann. Evanston, IL: Northwestern University Press, 1974.

Inwood, Michael. *Hegel*. London: Routledge & Kegan Paul, 1983.

Jaeschke, Walter. *Reason in Religion: the Foundations of Hegel's Philosophy of Religion*, trans. J. Michael Stewart and Peter C. Hodgson. Berkeley: University of California Press, 1990.

Kojève, Alexandre. *Introduction to the Reading of Hegel*, trans. J. H. Nichols. New York: Basic Books, 1960.

Marcuse, Herbert. *Reason and Revolution*. London: Routledge & Kegan Paul, 1941.

Nicolin, Günther, ed. *Hegel in Berichten seiner Zeitgenossen*. Hamburg: Felix Meiner Verlag, 1970.

Norman, Richard. *Hegel's Phenomenology: A Philosophical Introduction.* London: Sussex University Press, 1976.

Pinkard, Terry. *Hegel's Phenomenology: The Sociality of Reason.* Cambridge: Cambridge University Press, 1994.

Hegel: A Biography. Cambridge: Cambridge University Press, 2000.

Pippin, Robert. *Hegel's Idealism: The Satisfactions of Self-Consciousness.* Cambridge: Cambridge University Press, 1989.

Idealism as Modernism: Hegelian Variations. Cambridge: Cambridge University Press, 1997.

Priest, Stephen, ed. *Hegel's Critique of Kant.* Oxford: Oxford University Press, 1987.

Ritter, Joachim. *Hegel and the French Revolution.* Cambridge, MA: MIT Press, 1982.

Rockmore, Tom. *Before and After Hegel: A Historical Introduction to Hegel's Thought.* Berkeley: University of California Press, 1993.

Rosenkranz, Karl. *Georg Wilhelm Friedrich Hegels Leben.* Darmstadt: Wissenschaftliche Buchgesellschaft, 1963.

Shklar, Judith. *Freedom and Independence: A Study of the Political Ideas in Hegel's Phenomenology of Mind.* Cambridge: Cambridge University Press, 1976.

Smith, Steven. *Hegel's Critique of Liberalism: Rights in Context.* Chicago: University of Chicago Press, 1989.

Taylor, Charles. *Hegel.* Cambridge: Cambridge University Press, 1975.

Toews, John Edward. *Hegelianism: The Path Toward Dialectical Humanism, 1805–1841.* Cambridge: Cambridge University Press, 1980.

Westphal, Kenneth. *Hegel's Epistemological Realism: A Study of the Aim and Method of Hegel's Phenomenology of Spirit.* Dordrecht: Kluwer, 1989.

Westphal, Merold. *History and Truth in Hegel's Phenomenology,* 3rd edn. Bloomington: Indiana University Press, 1998.

White, Alan. *Absolute Knowledge: Hegel and the Problem of Metaphysics.* Athens: Ohio University Press, 1983.

Wildt, Andreas. *Autonomie und Anerkennung: Hegels Moralitätskritik im Lichte seiner Fichte Rezeption.* Stuttgart: Klett-Cotta, 1982.

Wood, Allen. *Hegel's Ethical Thought.* Cambridge: Cambridge University Press, 1990.

On Kant

Allison, Henry E. *Kant's Transcendental Idealism.* New Haven: Yale University Press, 1983.

Kant's Theory of Freedom. Cambridge: Cambridge University Press, 1990.

Idealism and Freedom. Cambridge: Cambridge University Press, 1996.

Ameriks, Karl. *Kant's Theory of Mind: An Analysis of the Paralogisms of Pure Reason,* 2nd edn. Oxford: Oxford University Press, 2000.

Arendt, Hannah. *Lectures on Kant's Political Philosophy,* ed. Ronald Beiner. Chicago: University of Chicago Press, 1982.

Beck, Lewis White. *A Commentary on Kant's Critique of Practical Reason.* Chicago: University of Chicago Press, 1960.

Beiner, Ronald and Booth, James, eds. *Kant and Political Philosophy: The Contemporary Legacy.* New Haven: Yale University Press, 1993.

Bennett, Jonathan. *Kant's Dialectic.* Cambridge: Cambridge University Press, 1974.

Bohman, James and Lutz-Bachmann, Matthias, eds. *Perpetual Peace: Essays on Kant's Cosmopolitan Ideal.* Cambridge, MA: MIT Press, 1997.

Cassirer, Ernst. *Kant's Life and Thought*, trans. James Haden. New Haven: Yale University Press, 1981.

Findlay, John Niemeyer. *Kant and the Transcendental Object: A Hermeneutic Study.* Oxford: Clarendon Press, 1981.

Förster, Eckart, ed. *Kant's Transcendental Deductions: The Three Critiques and the Opus Postumum.* Stanford: Stanford University Press, 1989.

Fricke, Christel. *Kants Theorie des reinen Geschmacksurteils.* Berlin: Walter de Gruyter, 1990.

Friedman, Michael. *Kant and the Exact Sciences.* Cambridge, MA: Harvard University Press, 1992.

Gram, Moltke S. *The Transcendental Turn: The Foundations of Kant's Idealism.* Gainesville: The University Press of Florida, 1984.

Guyer, Paul. *Kant and the Claims of Knowledge.* Cambridge: Cambridge University Press, 1987.

Kant and the Experience of Freedom. Cambridge: Cambridge University Press, 1996.

Kant and the Claims of Taste, 2nd edn. Cambridge: Cambridge University Press, 1997.

Guyer, Paul, ed. *The Cambridge Companion to Kant.* Cambridge: Cambridge University Press, 1992.

Hare, John. *The Moral Gap: Kantian Ethics, Human Limits, and God's Assistance.* Oxford: Oxford University Press, 1996.

Henrich, Dieter. "The Proof-Structure of Kant's Transcendental Deduction," *The Review of Metaphysics*, 22 (1969), 640–59.

Aesthetic Judgment and the Moral Image of the World: Studies in Kant. Stanford, CA: Stanford University Press, 1992.

The Unity of Reason: Essays on Kant's Philosophy, ed. Richard Velkley. Cambridge, MA: Harvard University Press, 1994.

Höffe, Otfried. *Immanuel Kant*, trans. Marshall Farrier. Albany: State University of New York Press, 1994.

Kemp, John. *The Philosophy of Kant.* London: Oxford University Press, 1968.

Kemp Smith, Norman. *A Commentary to Kant's Critique of Pure Reason*, 2nd edn. London: Macmillan, 1923.

Korsgaard, Christine. *Creating the Kingdom of Ends.* Cambridge: Cambridge University Press, 1996.

Korsgaard, Christine, *et al. The Sources of Normativity.* Cambridge: Cambridge University Press, 1996.

Kuehn, Manfred. *Kant: A Life.* Cambridge: Cambridge University Press, 2000.

Kulenkampff, Jens. *Kants Logik des ästhetischen Urteils.* Frankfurt am Main: Vittorio Klostermann, 1978.

Loades, Ann L. *Kant and Job's Comforters.* New Castle: Avero, 1985.

Longuenesse, Beatrice. *Kant and the Capacity to Judge.* Princeton: Princeton University Press, 1998.

Meerbote, Ralf, ed. *Kant's Aesthetics.* Atascadero, CA: Ridgeview, 1991.

Munzel, G. Felicitas. *Kant's Conception of Moral Character: the "Critical" Link of Morality, Anthropology, and Reflective Judgment.* Chicago: University of Chicago Press, 1999.

Nell, Onora (O'Neill). *Acting on Principle: An Essay on Kantian Ethics.* New York: Columbia University Press, 1975.

O'Neill, Onora. *Constructions of Reason: Explorations of Kant's Practical Philosophy.* Cambridge: Cambridge University Press, 1989.

Parrini, Paolo, ed. *Kant and Contemporary Epistemology*. Dordrecht: Kluwer, 1991.

Pippin, Robert B. *Kant's Theory of Form: An Essay on the Critique of Pure Reason*. New Haven: Yale University Press, 1982.

Prauss, Gerold. *Erscheinung bei Kant: Ein Problem der Kritik der reinen Vernunft*. Berlin: Walter de Gruyter, 1971.

Kant über Freiheit als Autonomie. Frankfurt am Main: Vittorio Klostermann, 1983.

Prauss, Gerold, ed. *Kant: Zur Deutung seiner Theorie von Erkennen und Handeln*. Cologne: Kiepenheuer & Witsch, 1973.

Rawls, John. "Kantian Constructivism in Moral Theory," *The Journal of Philosophy*, 77 (1980), 515–72.

Reiner, Hans. *Duty and Inclination: The Fundamentals of Morality Discussed and Redefined with Special Regard to Kant and Schiller*, trans. Mark Santos. The Hague: Martinus Nijhoff, 1983.

Rossi, Philip and Wreen, Michael, eds. *Kant's Philosophy of Religion Reconsidered*. Bloomington: Indiana University Press, 1991.

Schott, Robin May, ed. *Feminist Interpretations of Kant*. University Park, PA: University of Pennsylvania Press, 1997.

Schultz, Johann. *Exposition of Kant's Critique of Pure Reason*, trans. and ed. James C. Morrison. Ottawa: University of Ottawa Press, 1995.

Sellars, Wilfrid. *Science and Metaphysics: Variations on Kantian Themes*. London: Routledge & Kegan Paul, 1968.

Shell, Susan Meld. *The Embodiment of Reason*. Chicago: University of Chicago Press, 1996.

Strawson, Peter F. *The Bounds of Sense: An Essay on Kant's Critique of Pure Reason*. London: Methuen, 1966.

Sturma, Dieter. *Kant über Selbstbewusstsein*. Hildesheim: Ohms, 1985.

Van Cleve, James. *Problems from Kant*. Oxford: Oxford University Press, 1999.

van der Linden, Harry. *Kantian Ethics and Socialism*. Indianapolis: Hackett, 1988.

Velkley, Richard L. *Freedom and the Ends of Reason: On the Moral Foundations of Kant's Critical Philosophy*. Chicago: University of Chicago Press, 1989.

Walker, Ralph C. S. *Kant*. Boston: Routledge & Kegan Paul, 1978.

Watkins, Eric, ed. *Kant and the Sciences*. Oxford: Oxford University Press, 2000.

Wood, Allen. *Kant's Moral Religion*. Ithaca: Cornell University Press, 1970.

Kant's Rational Theology. Ithaca: Cornell University Press, 1978.

Kant's Ethical Thought. Cambridge: Cambridge University Press, 1999.

Yovel, Yirmiahu. *Kant and the Philosophy of History*. Princeton, NJ: Princeton University Press, 1980.

Zammito, John. *The Genesis of Kant's 'Critique of Judgment.'* Chicago: University of Chicago Press, 1992.

On Schelling

Bowie, Andrew. *Schelling and Modern European Philosophy*. London: Routledge, 1993.

Franz, Michael. *Schellings Tübinger Platon-Studien*. Göttingen: Vandenhoeck & Ruprecht, 1996.

Jacobs, Wilhelm G. *Zwischen Revolution und Orthodoxie? Schelling und seine Freunde im Stift und an der Universität Tübingen: Texte und Untersuchungen*. Stuttgart: Frommann-Holzboog, 1989.

Jähnig, Dieter. *Schelling. Die Kunst in der Philosophie*. 2 vols. Pfullingen: Neske, 1966.

O'Meara, Thomas. *Romantic Idealism and Roman Catholicism: Schelling and the Theologians*. Notre Dame: University of Notre Dame Press, 1982.

Schulz, Walter. *Die Vollendung des deutschen Idealismus in der Spätphilosophie Schellings*, 2nd edn. Pfullingen: Neske, 1975.

Snow, Dale. *Schelling and the End of Idealism*. Albany: State University of New York Press, 1996.

Tillich, Paul. *The Construction of the History of Religion in Schelling's Positive Philosophy: Its Presuppositions and Principles*, trans. V. Nuovo. Lewisburg, PA: Bucknell University Press, 1974.

White, Alan. *Schelling: Introduction to the System of Freedom*. New Haven and London: Yale University Press, 1983.

On other figures

Adorno, Theodor. *Kierkegaard: Constructions of the Aesthetic*, trans. R. Hullot-Kentor. Minneapolis: University of Minnesota Press, 1989.

Altmann, Alexander. *Moses Mendelssohn*. Alabama: University of Alabama Press, 1973.

Berlin, Isaiah. *Vico and Herder: Two Studies in the History of Ideas*. London: Hogarth, 1976.

The Magus of the North: J. G. Hamann and the Origins of Modern Irrationalism, ed. Henry Hardy. New York: Farrar, Straus & Giroux, 1993.

Berner, Christian. *La Philosophie de Schleiermacher*. Paris: Editions du Cerf, 1995.

Bondeli, Martin. *Das Anfangsproblem bei Karl Leonhard Reinhold. Eine systematische und entwicklungsgeschichtliche Untersuchung zur Philosophie Reinholds in der Zeit von 1789 bis 1803*. Frankfurt: Klostermann, 1995.

Brandt, Richard. *The Philosophy of Schleiermacher: The Development of his Theory of Scientific and Religious Knowledge*. New York: Greenwood Press, 1968.

Breazeale, Daniel. "Between Kant and Fichte: K. L. Reinhold's 'Elementary Philosophy,'" *The Review of Metaphysics*, 35 (1981/82), 785–821.

Breckman, Warren. *Marx, the Young Hegelians, and the Origins of Radical Social Theory: Dethroning the Self*. Cambridge: Cambridge University Press, 1999.

Brudney, Daniel. *Marx's Attempt to Leave Philosophy*. Cambridge, MA: Harvard University Press, 1998.

Carver, Terrell, ed. *The Cambridge Companion to Marx*. Cambridge: Cambridge University Press, 1991.

Clark Jr., Robert Thomas. *Herder, His Life and Thought*. Berkeley: University of California Press, 1955.

Cohen, Gerald A. *Karl Marx's Theory of History: A Defense*. Princeton: Princeton University Press, 1980.

Dickson, Gwen Griffith. *Johann Georg Hamann's Relational Metacriticism*. Berlin: de Gruyter, 1995.

Dilthey, Wilhelm. *Das Leben Schleiermachers*. Berlin and Leipzig: W. de Gruyter, 1922.

German, Terence J. *Hamann on Language and Religion*. Oxford: Oxford University Press, 1981.

Hannay, Alastair and Marino, Gordon, eds. *The Cambridge Companion to Kierkegaard*. Cambridge: Cambridge University Press, 1998.

Haym, Rudolph. *Herder, nach seinem Leben und seinen Werken dargestellt*. 2 vols. Berlin: Gaertner, 1877, 1880, and 1885.

Henrich, Dieter. *Der Grund im Bewusstsein: Untersuchungen zu Hölderlins Denken (1794–1795)*. Stuttgart: Klett-Cotta, 1992.

The Course of Remembrance and Other Essays on Hölderlin, ed. with introduction by Eckart Förster. Stanford: Stanford University Press, 1997.

Horstmann, Rolf-Peter. "Maimon's Criticism of Reinhold's 'Satz des Bewusstseins,'" in Lewis White Beck, ed., *Proceedings of the Third International Kant Congress*. Dordrecht, 1972, 330–8.

Jacquette, Dale, ed. *Schopenhauer, Philosophy, and the Arts*. Cambridge: Cambridge University Press, 1996.

Janaway, Christopher. *Self and World in Schopenhauer's Philosophy*. Oxford: Clarendon Press, 1989.

Janaway, Christopher, ed. *The Cambridge Companion to Schopenhauer*. Cambridge: Cambridge University Press, 1999.

Kirmmse, Bruce H. *Kierkegaard in Golden Age Denmark*. Bloomington: Indiana University Press, 1990.

Kneller, Jane. "Romantic Conceptions of the Self in Hölderlin and Novalis," in David Klemm and Günter Zöller, eds., *Figuring the Self: Subject, Absolute, and Others in Classical German Philosophy*. Albany: State University of New York Press, 1997, 134–48.

Lauth, Reinhard, ed. *Philosophie aus einem Prinzip: Karl Leonhard Reinhold*. Bonn: Bouvier, 1974.

Mackey, Louis. *Kierkegaard: A Kind of Poet*. Philadelphia: University of Pennsylvania Press, 1971.

Molnár, Géza von. *Romantic Vision, Ethical Context: Novalis and Artistic Autonomy*. Minneapolis: University of Minnesota Press, 1987.

Norton, Robert E. *Herder's Aesthetics and the European Enlightenment*. Ithaca: Cornell University Press, 1991.

O'Brien, William Arctander. *Novalis, Signs of Revolution*. Durham: Duke University Press, 1995.

O'Flaherty, James C. *Johann Georg Hamann*. Boston: Twayne, 1979.

Perkins, Robert L., ed. *Kierkegaard's Fear and Trembling: Critical Appraisals*. Birmingham, AL: University of Alabama Press, 1981.

Roche, Mark. *Dynamic Stillness: Philosophical Conceptions of Ruhe in Schiller, Hölderlin, Buchner, and Heine*. Tübingen: Niemeyer, 1987.

Roehr, Sabine. *A Primer on the German Enlightenment with a Translation of Reinhold's Fundamental Concepts and Principles of Ethics*. Columbia: University of Missouri Press, 1995.

Stamm, Marcelo. *Systemkrise: Die Elementarphilosophie in der Debatte (1789–1794)*. Stuttgart: Klett-Cotta, forthcoming.

Stoljar, Margaret. *Athenaeum: A Critical Commentary*. Bern: Herbert Lang, 1973.

Taylor, Charles. "The Importance of Herder," in E. and A. Margalit, eds., *Isaiah Berlin: A Celebration*. Chicago: University of Chicago Press, 1991.

Uerlings, Herbert. *Friedrich von Hardenberg, genannt Novalis: Werk und Forschung*. Stuttgart: Metzler, 1991.

Wartofsky, Marx. *Feuerbach*. Cambridge: Cambridge University Press, 1977.

INDEX